P9-CDL-180

The Legacy of Ricardo

The Legacy of Ricardo

Edited by

GIOVANNI A. CARAVALE

Basil Blackwell

© Giovanni A. Caravale 1985

First published 1985

Basil Blackwell Ltd
108 Cowley Road, Oxford OX4 1JF, UK

Basil Blackwell Inc.
432 Park Avenue South, Suite 1505,
New York, NY 10016, USA

Published with the support of the Consiglio Nazionale delle Ricerche, Rome

British Library Cataloguing in Publication Data
The legacy of Ricardo.
1. Ricardo, David
I. Caravale, Giovanni A.
330.15′3   HB103.R5
ISBN 0-631-13617-7

Library of Congress Cataloging in Publication Data
The Legacy of Ricardo.
Includes index.
1. Ricardo, David, 1772–1823—Addresses, essays,
lectures.   I. Caravale, Giovanni.
HB103.R5L45   1985   330.15′3   84-28332
ISBN 0-631-13617-7

Typeset by Advanced Filmsetters (Glasgow) Ltd
Printed in Great Britain by Bell and Bain Ltd, Glasgow

Contents

v

Preface

Since the appearance of the first volumes of Sraffa's masterly edition of Ricardo's *Works and Correspondence*, the profession has witnessed an impressive acceleration of the flow of literature on Ricardian economics, accompanied by attempts systematically to connect the interpretative positions to the different traditions of economic thought and by a growing concern for problems of methodology. The aim of the seminar held in Perugia in May 1981—at which previous drafts of the papers here collected were first presented—was to try to take bearings on the situation and, in so far as possible, to understand better the reasons for disagreement. In fact, the contributions supplied a comprehensive spectrum of the main interpretative positions on Ricardo ranging from the neoclassical 'New View' to various types of Sraffa-based reconstructions of Ricardo's thought.

In these short introductory notes I shall not attempt to summarize the contents of the individual papers but rather to offer a synthetic and noncritical presentation of the main approaches that come to light, both in the discussion of the basic lines of Ricardo's analysis considered as a whole and in the examination of specific themes in Ricardian theory.

The 'New View' places the main emphasis on the notion of market equilibrium emerging from transactions in both commodities and 'factors'. On this basis the substantial identity is maintained between classical 'natural' and neoclassical long-run 'normal' prices, no separation between theory of output and price determination being admissible. One version of this 'View' focuses on the definition and role of a dynamic reference path conceived as a centre of gravity for market values. Criticism of non-neoclassical interpretations of Ricardo is also supplied from the standpoint of the treatment of 'time' in Ricardian models.

The Sraffa-based reconstructions of Ricardo's theory are instead centred on the notion of natural equilibrium, strictly linked to the idea of an exogenously given real wage. Within this context two approaches may be distinguished. The first tends to identify the core of Ricardo's contribution in the analysis of the profit—wage relation with given input coefficients of labour and means of production: attention is focused on alternative ways of distributing a given product and on the resulting class antagonism between workers and capitalists. On the methodological plane, the level of output is viewed as separate from, and given prior to the determination of, prices. The second approach emphasizes instead the relation between diminishing returns and capital accumulation as the central issue of Ricardo's analysis. This view offers a natural equilibrium interpretation aimed at encompassing problems of value, distribution and growth; contrary to the first Sraffa-based approach, it focuses on the dynamic inverse relation between rate of profit and money wage as determined by the rising price of 'corn'. In sharp contrast with the implication of the first approach, the emerging class antagonism is here identified with the conflict of interest between *rentiers* and capitalists, and the problem of the so-called separation between quantities and prices would seem no longer to represent the dividing line between market and natural equilibrium reconstructions of Ricardo's theory.

Some of the above-mentioned divergences are also apparent in terms of the question regarding Ricardo's 'early theory of profits'—the analysis of the determination and tendency of the rate of profit carried out by Ricardo prior to the *Principles*. On this ground, two clearly opposite readings of Ricardo emerge. The first identifies the rational foundation of the theory in what we have been accustomed to call, with Sraffa, the 'corn model', i.e. the idea of a 'material rate of profit' definable without reference to prices. In substance, this approach tends to emphasize the existence of a continuous line of development between this aspect of Ricardo's thought, the labour theory of value and the analytical structure of Sraffa's standard system. The other interpretation tends rather to emphasize a continuity between the early theory of profits and the analysis developed in the *Principles*, and revolves around the connection between diminishing returns, money wage rate and the rate of profit in the perspective of a general equilibrium type of analysis. The implications of this contrast—a very difficult one to settle on the basis of textual evidence alone—seem to be of two types: on the one hand, the emphasis on a connection between Ricardo and Sraffa in terms of what has been called the 'aggregative' or 'surplus' approach (definition of the rate of profit independently of prices); on the other hand, the too-strict association of the idea of interconnection between variables with the functioning of the market in general equilibrium theory, which tends to underrate the role of the same interconnection in the natural equilibrium interpretations of Ricardo, obviously to be linked with Sraffa's general solution of the system of prices.

In point of fact, the idea of interconnection between variables appears to play such a central role in the debate that one of the most authoritative contributions in the volume, sees it as a major element distinguishing the analytical structure of Ricardo's theory from that of Sraffa (alongside the contrast between a 'dynamic' and a 'static' type of analysis, and the alleged different meaning of prices in the two contexts). The structure of Sraffa's model, according to this view, is characterized by a fully interlinked system of production, whereas nothing of this could be found in Ricardo—an opinion that implicitly challenges both the approach of other papers in the volume and that of recent literature in the field of what may be called the analytical interpretation of the history of economic thought.

The specific issue of the relation between the nature of technological progress and the long-term prospects for employment (Ricardo's 'machinery question') is also discussed in detail with reference to the analytical framework of Ricardo and of subsequent theories. This makes it possible to bring to light the complexity of the question, crucial not only for Ricardo's times.

Ricardo's theory is a focal point of reference, both for the history of economic thought and for economic analysis. The various interpretations thus end up by bearing upon the current debate in economics and may contribute to a clarification of the reasons for disagreement among contemporary economists. In fact, much of the interest of the interpretative debate on Ricardo stems from the circumstance that it may also be seen as representing to some extent a sort of mirror image of the contrast between different paradigms in economics. Considering the substantial analytical difficulties lately encountered by both mainstream and unorthodox theories, perhaps the efforts to reabsorb Ricardo—'father' of such relevant subsequent developments—in one tradition of thought or the other may thus appear as unconscious attempts to recapture one's 'Paradigm Lost'.

G.A.C.

Acknowledgements

The editor and authors are grateful for permission to include the following articles which, as they now stand or in different versions, have been previously published—in particular

Giovanni A. Caravale's paper is a modified and enlarged version of an article which appeared in *Giornale degli Economisti* March–April 1982 (XLI), under the title of 'Note Sulla Teoria Ricardiana Del Valore, Della Distribuzione e Dello Sviluppo'.

Carlo Casarosa's paper is a slightly enlarged version of an article which appeared in M. Baranzini (ed.), *Advances in Economic Theory* (Blackwell, Oxford, 1982; St Martin's Press, New York).

Pierangelo Garegnani's paper appeared in *Cambridge Journal of Economics*, 6(1), 1982.

Samuel Hollander's paper was given as the Harold A. Innis lecture to the Canadian Economics Association, June 1982 and appeared subsequently in the *Canadian Journal of Economics* (4) 1982.

Ferdinando Meacci's paper appeared in *Ricerche Economiche* (1–2), 1983.

Pier Luigi Porta's paper is a modified version of an article which appeared in *Ricerche Economiche* 1982 (3) as 'Recent reinterpretations of the Ricardian System'.

Alessandro Roncaglia's paper appeared in *Journal of Post-Keynesian Economics* 4 (3), 1982.

PART I

A Methodological Overview

1

What Ricardo Said
and What Ricardo Meant

MARK BLAUG

With the possible exception of Karl Marx, no great economist of the past has received so many divergent and even contradictory interpretations as David Ricardo. In the nineteenth century, some argued that Ricardo held an 'iron law of wages', while others denied that he ever advocated any such thing; some condemned Ricardo for totally neglecting the role of demand, while others insisted that he never really lost sight of demand; some were convinced that Ricardo had simply failed to carry the labour theory of value to its logical conclusions, but others were equally sure that he never really believed in the labour theory of value; some deplored the fact that Ricardo had admitted the harmful effects of new machinery on the working class, while others pointed triumphantly to the pages where he said that technical change was not harmful to workers in normal circumstances; some described Ricardo's monetary writings as dogmatic bullionism, but a few gave him high marks for his subtle exposition of the quantity theory of money; some were shocked that Ricardo viewed landlords as the enemies of society, but others took comfort from his failure to call for the immediate and total abolition of agricultural protection—and so on, and so on. On every question, there were at least two, if not three, Ricardos.

By the 1930s or thereabouts, the dust had settled and something like a consensus about Ricardo's meaning had gradually emerged. But the publication of the complete works of Ricardo by Piero Sraffa in the early 1950s, and particularly the appearance of Sraffa's *Production of Commodities by Means of Commodities* in 1960, started a new round of diverse interpretations. Sraffa found a so-called one-sector 'corn model' embedded in Ricardo's early writings and interpreted Ricardo's lifelong obsession with the 'invariable measure of value' as an attempt to work back to the simple logic of this corn model. It took little time for Marxist economists to perceive the significance of this Sraffian reading of Ricardo, and, indeed, a far-reaching re-interpretation of the entire history of economic thought has since been constructed on it. The history of economic thought, we are constantly being told by Cambridge economists, reveals two great branches: a general equilibrium branch leading down from Jevons, Walras and Marshall to the Arrows,

3

Debreus and Samuelsons of today, in which all relevant economic variables are mutually and simultaneously determined, and a Ricardo–Marx–Sraffa branch, in which distribution takes priority over pricing because economic variables are causally determined in a sequential chain starting from a predetermined real wage. Thus, 160 years after his death, Ricardo, that most bourgeois of all bourgeois economists, stands before us as the unwitting founding father of Marxian economics.

This is not the only bone of contention in modern interpretations of Ricardo. At one time, Ricardo was regarded as the virtual inventor of the method of comparative statics and a prime example of the tendency of orthodox economists to emphasize long-run equilibrium values at the expense of any consideration of short-run, disequilibrium adjustments. But developments in modern growth theory have reminded us that Ricardo frequently expressed himself in language that is deeply evocative of steady-state growth theory. It was Pasinetti (1974), in a famous 1960 article, that started us down this track. He made new sense of many puzzling paragraphs in Ricardo's writings by interpreting Ricardo's model as a half-way house to a steady-state growth model: Ricardo writes as if a long-term steady state has been achieved in the labour market via population growth, while at the same time the capital accumulation process is still characterized by disequilibrium adjustments which will achieve stationariness only at some future time; in other words, the 'market price' of labour is, at its 'natural price', determined by the minimum cost of subsistence, but the rate of profit is still above its 'natural' equilibrium level.

At first glance, the Pasinetti interpretation is an attractive one, which resolves many of the difficulties in interpreting the Ricardian system. On the other hand, it leaves unexplained the many passages in which Ricardo declares that population is growing because the 'market price' if labour in fact exceeds its 'natural price'. Hicks and Hollander (1977) therefore reject what they call a 'fixwage theory' in Ricardo and consistently treat the Ricardian system as if it were as much preoccupied with short-run disequilibrium adjustments in both labour and capital markets as with the long-run equilibrium solutions of the stationary state. In a still more radical revision of Pasinetti, Casarosa (1978) rejects the notion that short-run adjustments in Ricardo are tending towards two independent steady-state, long-run equilibrium solutions in labour and capital markets, respectively. He argues that Ricardo's principal reasoning is in terms of a dynamic, 'moving equilibrium' (in the sense of Frisch), in which the rate of growth of population is kept equal to the rate of growth of capital. In short, he plants the idea of a definite interaction between the wages–population mechanism and the investment–profits mechanism, and in one sense that interaction is also at work in the Hicks–Hollander interpretation.

Caravale and Tosato (1980) had arrived at a similar view before either

Hicks and Hollander or Casarosa. All these commentators are concerned to express Ricardo's frequently reiterated dictum that 'profits' vary inversely as 'wages', leaving aside for a moment what Ricardo could have meant by these terms, and the equally frequently reiterated belief that the rate of profit falls 'in the last instance' only because of diminishing returns to agriculture. Pasinetti, however, is unable to account for those passages in which Ricardo more or less clearly says that real wages, or rather wages in terms of a basket of physical commodities, can fall alongside of the falling rate of profit well before the economy has reached the stationary state. The great merit of the 'New View' on Ricardo, meaning interpretations of Caravale–Tosato, Hicks–Hollander and Casarosa, is that they can neatly accommodate those remarks of Ricardo that the 'old' view had to put down as *obiter dicta*.

At the same time, even the 'New View' has difficulty in making sense of passages in which Ricardo declares unambiguously that the rate of profit depends only on the cost of producing wage goods, and on nothing else. Such passages are easy to interpret if we stay with the Pasinetti model. Thus, it may be that Ricardo really operated with three models—a Pasinetti-type, comparative static model ('strong' case 1), a Hicks–Hollander-type disequilibrium growth model ('strong' case 2) and a Casarosa-type, dynamic equilibrium model ('strong' case 3)—adopting one or the other as circumstances warranted. Indeed, I see no way of escaping from this conclusion.[1]

After all, we do need to remind ourselves that it is not possible to square everything that Ricardo said with *any* totally consistent formulation of the entire Ricardian system. For example, Ricardo thought that he had demonstrated that rents rise as a share of total output in the course of economic progress. It is true that Ricardo's *Notes on Malthus* retreated from the proposition that rents must rise as a share of gross output to the weaker proposition that they must rise as a share of net output (after deducting wages). But however we interpret his prediction of a rising rental share, the fact remains that the rental share, and even changes in rents per acre, are indeterminate in Ricardo's model and the same is also true of the other distributive shares. Thus, any totally consistent version of Ricardo must leave some of the things Ricardo said as simply wrong.

[1] Thus Stigler (1981) upheld the Pasinetti-type, subsistence wage interpretation of Ricardo in his review of Hollander's *Economics of David Ricardo*, but Hollander (1983) reiterated his belief in Ricardo's variable wage growth model. Hollander (1983, p. 315) conceded, however, that 'it is probable that there are two Ricardo models—those that are characterized by the versions offered by Hicks and myself, and by Samuelson or Casarosa.' He also conceded that Ricardo's *Principles* is replete with references to the constant wage assumption, and that Ricardo's taxation theorems 'can be interpreted as applying to the case where a subsistence wage rules (Hollander, 1983, p. 316). But this is not a third Ricardo model, according to Hollander, but simply another example of Ricardo's habit of making 'strong' assumptions for the sake of clear exposition. Apart from a play on words, therefore, Hollander accepts the notion that Ricardo is operating with three distinct models of the relation between wages and profits.

Take one further example. It used to be thought—in the bad old days before Sraffa—that Ricardo's habit of expressing all of his economic variables in terms of an 'invariable measure of value', when even he himself admitted that such a hypothetical yardstick did not and could not exist, was simply a terrible confusion; there is no such thing, it was said, as a measuring rod that is itself invariant to changes in factor prices—unless, of course, we are going to assume identical factor-proportions in all industries, and Ricardo was the last author to swallow such a far-fetched assumption. But then Sraffa showed that it is possible to construct a 'standard commodity' in which to express prices such that relative prices are invariant to changes in profits and wages and, moreover, that such a 'standard commodity' is in fact embedded in all normal economic systems. This appeared to rehabilitate Ricardo, showing that he saw further and deeper than many of contemporaries and even later nineteenth-century economists. But Ricardo's 'invariable measure of value' is by no means equivalent to Sraffa's 'standard commodity', because the latter is invariant only to changes in factor prices and to changes in its own methods of production; but there is no numeraire or 'invariable' yardstick that will satisfy both these objectives. That is to say, whatever the merits of Sraffa's notion of a 'standard commodity', it still falls short of solving Ricardo's problem of linking the rate of profit directly and unambiguously to the action of diminishing returns in agriculture (see Caravale and Tosato, 1980, ch. 3). In other words, we cannot exonerate Ricardo from all analytical errors; he was at times inclined to square a circle using only a ruler and compass (which, I need hardly remind you, is impossible).

Samuel Hollander's (1979) book, *The Economics of David Ricardo*, takes strong exceptions to the last remark. For Hollander, Ricardo is never wrong. Moreover, it seems to be Hollander's view that, while Ricardo undoubtedly had some kind of logical model in the back of his head, he never took his own model very seriously. Hollander's book is nothing less than a full-scale frontal attack on the entire body of Ricardian scholarship, arguing that absolutely everybody has more or less misinterpreted Ricardo. Consider just some of the iconoclastic themes of Hollander's book:

(1) Ricardo's method of analysis was identical to that of Adam Smith.
(2) Ricardo's work was basically in the tradition of allocative, general equilibrium analysis and was not in any sense a detour from the mainstream that runs from Smith to Walras; in particular, pricing and distribution are interdependent and not sequential in Ricardo.
(3) Ricardo's profit theory did not originate in a concern over the Corn Laws and Ricardo never employed the corn model that Sraffa detected in the *Essay on Profits*; in particular, Ricardo never believed, even in his early writings, that profits in agriculture determine the general rate of profit in the economy.

(4) Ricardo's value theory was essentially the same as that of Marshall, in that it paid as much attention to the role of demand as to the role of supply, and Ricardo never regarded the invariable measure of value as an important element in his own theory.

(5) Ricardo could have established his 'fundamental theorem of distribution', according to which profits vary inversely with wages, without his invariable yardstick; and, besides, he frequently took the short-cut of assuming identical factor-ratios in all industries to give him the answers he looked for.

(6) Wages in Ricardo are not fixed in commodity terms and they are never conceived as constant or fixed at a subsistence level.

(7) Ricardo never assumed a zero price elasticity of demand for corn, in effect making the demand for agricultural produce a simple function of the size of the population.

(8) Ricardo was not a quantity theorist in the conventional sense, nor a rigid bullionist; nor did he hold a monetary theory that was very different from that of Adam Smith.

(9) Ricardo did not predict a rising rental share, nor did he ever commit himself to any clear-cut predictions; in particular, he did not predict a falling rate of profit if the Corn Laws remained on the statute books, and his opposition to the Corn Laws had more to do with the harmful effects of price fluctuations than with the rate of profit.

(10) Ricardo was never seriously concerned about the possibility of class conflict between landowners on the one hand, and workers and capitalists on the other.

I believe that every one of these ten statements is false.[2] Hollander has flagrantly misread Ricardo's message. I have dealt elsewhere with some of the detailed evidence for and against these startling pronouncements of Hollander (Blaug, 1980); O'Brien (1981, 1982; also Moss, 1979) examines many of them in greater detail. All I can do here is to suggest the root of the problem, which appears to be Hollander's method of textual exegesis. Ricardo is the sort of writer who requires some principle for assigning significance to contradictory statements made on different occasions and under different circumstances. He published a treatise on economics; he also

---

[2] The denial of the third statement requires some qualification. Ricardo did not employ a corn model in the *Essay on Profits* to determine the rate of profit as a purely physical relationship between inputs and output, although much of what he did say is perfectly rationalized by the corn model construction. Hollander is right, therefore, and Sraffa (followed by Eatwell, 1973, and Garegnani, 1982) was wrong. However, Hollander proceeds from the denial of the corn model interpretation to deny that Ricardo ever believed in an 'agricultural' theory of profits, whereas Ricardo clearly held the view, in his early writings, that 'the profits of the farmer' determine the general rate of profit. On all this, see the definitive exegesis by Peach (1984), which should finally lay the ghost of the corn model interpretation. See also Foccarello (1982).

published topical pamphlets on current issues; he wrote unpublished commentaries on other people's writings; he debated in Parliament; and he carried on a voluminous private correspondence on matters of economic theory and policy. Hollander gives equal weight to propositions advanced in Ricardo's *Principles*, in Ricardo's pamphlets, in Ricardo's speeches to Parliament and in his private correspondence, and this makes it all too easy to refute almost everybody else's interpretation of Ricardo. Even if we ignore this difficulty of appraising the context in which some particular statement by Ricardo appears, there is the further difficulty that Ricardo never stopped reworking and revising his own ideas, so that the date at which some proposition is announced also needs to be taken into account.

Stigler once offered a 'rule' of textual exegesis, with particular reference to Ricardo. He suggested that we reconcile problems of interpretation of the great economists of the past by choosing that interpretation which allows us to deduce the maximum number of an author's main conclusions. Hollander seems to reject this rule because, for him, Ricardo never reached any main conclusions. Ricardo had a 'strong' model, or rather a series of models; but according to Hollander Ricardo did not believe in his own models and stepped outside them whenever he was challenged. Indeed, Hollander virtually abandons any attempt to look for a consistent set of models in Ricardo, so that, literally, anything-goes is his answer to any queries about what Ricardo actually meant.

Hollander's Ricardo is one that neither his contemporary nineteenth-century critics nor his twentieth-century critics would have recognized. The doctrine that Ricardo bequeathed to his followers gave rise, and was thought to give rise, to a number of definite predictions: a rising price of corn, a rising rental share of national income, a constant level of real wages and a falling rate of profit. Moreover, given the absence of freely imported corn, these were all positive predictions, not hypothetical ones, because Ricardo boldly denied that countervailing forces could annul them except 'for a time'; under pressure, he committed himself to a 'short run' of about 25 years to exemplify the long-run effects of the causes he postulated—which is not, of course, to say that he advocated waiting for 25 years to see if his theories were true. He conceded that technical progress in agriculture, or 'moral restraint' on the part of the working class, or a shift in workers' consumption patterns towards manufactured goods, might stave off the onset of the 'stationary state'. But these were all face-saving concessions because he had no theory to explain either technical progress, or the disposition of families to control their size, or changes in the composition of the average worker's household budget. In short, Ricardo would never have granted that his theories were capable of being falsified by the actual course of events.

All such considerations disappear in Hollander's interpretation of Ricardo. For Hollander, anything can happen in the Ricardian system. In reacting to

Sraffian and Marxian simplifications of Ricardo, Hollander has simply gone overboard in the opposite direction and turned Ricardo into a peculiarly anaemic forerunner of Marshall and Walras.

All this is not to say that the Ricardo-interpretation industry should be handed over to the model-builders whose only test of a Ricardo interpretation is whether it can be expressed in mathematical equations. There is a real difference, I believe, between making out what Ricardo meant or could have meant and making out what he must have meant if he were truly rigorous, rigour being judged by the standards of modern economics. I think that Pasinetti, Hicks and Hollander, and Casarosa preserve this distinction; I am not at all sure that Caravale and Tosato (1980) do so. Their book spells out not only the equilibrium time-paths of the relevant variables, which Ricardo himself never did, but also the precise disequilibrium behaviour of the model via error adjustment equations—in keeping, no doubt, with the spirit but certainly not with the letter of Ricardo. In their book, we have travelled a long way from what Ricardo actually said to what Ricardo must have meant if he cared as much as modern economists do about the internal consistency of economic models. Is this a cause of alarm, or of congratulation?

REFERENCES

Blaug, M. (1980). 'Marx's Bourgeois Mentor: Review of Hollander's *Economics of David Ricardo*'. *Times Literary Supplement*, April.

Caravale, G. and Tosato, D. (1980). *Ricardo and The Theory of Value, Distribution and Growth*. London: Routledge & Kegan Paul.

Casarosa, C. (1978). 'A New Formulation of the Ricardian System'. *Oxford Economic Papers*, 30, 38–63.

Eatwell, J. (1973). 'The Interpretation of Ricardo's *Essay on Profits*'. *Economica*, 60, 260–82.

Foccarello, G. (1982). 'Sraffa versus Ricardo: The Historical Irrelevance of the "Corn-Profit" Model'. *Economy and Society*, 11, 122–37.

Garegnani, P. (1982). 'On Hollander's Interpretation of Ricardo's Early Theory of Profits'. *Cambridge Journal of Economics*, 6, 65–77.

Hicks, J. R. and Hollander, S. (1977). 'Mr Ricardo and the Moderns'. *Quarterly Journal of Economics*, 91, 351–69.

Hollander, S. (1979). *The Economics of David Ricardo*. Toronto: University of Toronto Press.

Hollander, S. (1982). 'Professor Hollander and Ricardian Economics: A Reply'. *Eastern Economic Journal*, 8, 237–42.

Hollander, S. (1983). 'Professor Garegnani's Reference of Sraffa on the Material Rate of Profit'. *Cambridge Journal of Economics*, 7, 167–74.

Moss, L. S. (1979). 'Professor Hollander and Ricardian Economics'. *Eastern Economic Journal*, 5, 501–12.

O'Brien, D. P. (1981). 'Ricardian Economics and the Economics of David Ricardo'. *Oxford Economic Papers*, 33, 352–86.

O'Brien, D. P. (1982). 'Ricardian Economics'. *Oxford Economic Papers*, 34, 247–52.

Pasinetti, L. L. (1974). *Growth and Income Distribution. Essays in Economic Theory*. London: Cambridge University Press.

Peach, T. (1984). 'David Ricardo's Early Treatment of Profitability: A New Interpretation'. *Economic Journal*, 94, 733–51.

Stigler, C. J. (1981). 'Review of Hollander, *Economics of David Ricardo*'. *Journal of Economic Literature*, 19, 100–1.

PART II

Neoclassical Interpretations

2

On the Substantive Identity of the Ricardian and Neoclassical Conceptions of Economic Organization: the French Connection in British Classicism

SAMUEL HOLLANDER

1 STATEMENT OF ISSUES

My paper is a contribution to the ongoing debate regarding the nature of the neoclassical developments of the 1870s, particularly the legitimacy of the term 'revolution', which implies analytical discontinuity, as a valid description of those developments. This representation has become particularly topical, since the notion of a neoclassical or marginalist economics, contrasting sharply in analytical essentials with Ricardian classicism, constitutes a central theme of the historiography of the modern Cambridge (UK) School. The evidence discussed in this paper suggests, on the contrary, how useful in the present context is the notion of altered 'concentrations of attention' (Hicks, 1976, pp. 208–9), which avoids a revolutionary connotation. For what seems to have occurred in the 1870s was a narrowing of focus, specifically a greater concern with exchange and allocation in their own right; a sharpening of theoretical tools, particularly those relating to consumer choice; and the algebraic formulation of general-equilibrium relationships. These are developments which could have been absorbed by the traditional corpus of analysis, whereas the impatience of the marginalists and their apparent wish to wipe the slate clean meant that much of great import in classical theory for their own chosen and relatively narrow sphere of discourse was not recognized, and spurious analytical distinctions were artificially reinforced. My evidence, in short, suggests how justified was Marshall's insistence, against both Jevons and Walras, upon the essential continuity of nineteenth-century doctrine: 'Under the honest belief that Ricardo and his followers had ren-

---

For their comments and advice thanks are due J. K. Whitaker and Irene M. Spry. I owe a special debt to Tom Kompas for most helpful criticism of the various drafts, particularly the discussion on Walrasian pricing.

dered their account of the causes that determine value hopelessly wrong by omitting to lay stress on the law of satiable wants, [Jevons] led many to think he was correcting great errors; whereas he was really only adding very important explanations' (Marshall, 1920, p. 101n). Indeed Marshall found Ricardo's formulation of pricing preferable to that of Jevons, who 'substitutes a catena of causes for mutual causation' (p. 818). Gerald Shove's estimate of four decades ago stands the test of time:

> The analytical backbone of Marshall's *Principles* is nothing more nor less than a completion and generalization, by means of a mathematical apparatus, of Ricardo's theory of value and distribution as expounded by J. S. Mill. It is not...a conflation of Ricardian notions with those of the 'marginal utility' school. Nor is it an attempt to substitute for Ricardian doctrine a new system of ideas arrived at by a different line of approach...[So] far as its strictly analytical content is concerned, the *Principles* is in the direct line of descent through Mill from Ricardo... (1942, 1960, p. 712).

A preliminary word on the contrary positions may be helpful, first and foremost that of the marginalists themselves. Distribution was envisaged by Jevons (ideally) as a matter of service pricing 'entirely subject to the principles of value and the laws of supply and demand,' with input prices 'the effect and not the cause of the value of the produce'—'I hold labour to be *essentially variable, so that its value must be determined by the value of the produce, not the value of the produce by that of labour*'; and cost of production as a reflection of opportunities foregone (1924, pp. xliii f., 186). He accordingly directed his criticisms at the wage-fund and subsistence approaches to wage-rate deter-mination and the cost approach to value—as he understood them—paying tribute to the French tradition; 'the only hope of attaining a true system of Economics is to fling aside, once and for ever after, the mazy and pre-posterous assumptions of the Ricardian School. Our English Economists have been living in a fool's paradise. The truth is with the French School...' (pp. xliv–v).[1]

Jevons recognized elements of the 'correct' position in Mill's *Principles*—that rent enters into cost where land has alternative uses, that all inequalities (whether natural or artificial) generate economic rents, and the representa-tion of demand and supply as a law 'anterior' to costs (pp. xlviii, li, 197)—but could not resist remarking (in the context of the generalization of the rent concept) that 'those who have studied Mill's philosophic character as long and minutely as I have done, will not for a moment suppose that the

---

[1] Cf. Stigler (1965, p. 304): '[J.B.] Say's approach was fundamentally much more modern than that of his English contemporaries'; for an elaboration of this position, see Hutchison (1978, pp. 84f.)

occurrence of this section of Mill's book tends to establish its consistency with other positions in the same treatise' (p. li).

Walras, whose intellectual origins include par excellence J. B. Say (Schumpeter, 1954, p. 828), similarly objected to the classical pricing and distribution model (as he understood it)—particularly the cost orientation and the natural-wage approach. By neglecting a final demand dimension, and accordingly derived demand, the English had constructed an underdetermined system (1954, pp. 434–5; cf. Jevons, 1924, p. 269).

In more recent times we have the famous criticism of classicism along similar lines by Knight (1956). For Knight, of course, prices depend on the relative subjective appeal to consumers, the flow of goods and thus their marginal utilities governed by cost consideration, where 'costs' reflect alternatives surrendered rather than 'pain' in the sense of labour or abstinence. On this view the economizing principle involves maximizing the total return from any resource, by equalizing the increments of return at the margin to the scarce resource in alternative uses.

It has been suggested (Arrow and Starrett, 1973, pp. 132–3) that once the subsistence theory of wages broke down, 'the most natural alternative was to explain wages by the productivity of labour, an explanation only useful if labor was intrinsically scarce. In short labor had to be treated like land.' Moreover, recognition of the phenomenon of non-competing groups implied a multiplicity of primary factors which, so it is argued, 'required a new theory.' The founders of the neoclassical school 'understood the glaring omission of demand from the classical model'.

In his Nobel lecture (1970) Ragnar Frisch neatly stated precisely that reading of the record that I dispute:

> The classical theory of value—as we find it streamlined in Stuart Mill—was essentially a theory of production costs... there emerges a sort of gravitational force that pulls prices down. The cost of production is so to speak the solid base on to which the prices fall down and remain...
>
> This theory contains, of course, an irrefutable element of truth. But it is too simple to give even a crude presentation of the forces at play. The economic process is an *equilibrium* affair where both technological and subjective forces are at play. The subjective element was nearly left out by the classicists.
>
> On this point economic theory was completely renewed in the years between 1870 and 1890... (1981, p. 5).

As remarked above, the theme of a revolutionary break by the general-equilibrium economists from classicism is also a feature of modern 'Cambridge' historiography. Thus Joan Robinson: 'either there may be a tendency towards uniformity of wages and the rate of profit in different lines of production'—the classical position—'or prices may be governed by supply and demand, but not both. Where supply and demand rule, there is no room for uniform levels of wages and the rate of profits. The Walrasian system makes sense if we interpret it in terms of an artisan economy, where each producer is committed to a particular product, so that his income depends on his output and its price. Each can have a prospective rate of return on investment in his own line, but there is no mechanism to equalize profits between one line and another' (1961, p. 57). This observation is apparently based on the supposition that among the data of the Walrasian system are included the quantities of every specific kind of labour, capital good, and land.

Following Piero Sraffa, Professor Roncaglia (1982, pp. 341–3) similarly represents the analytical core of neoclassicism as 'the model of pure exchange', whereby perfect competition guides us to the optimal allocation of scarce resources. Prices are 'indexes of resource scarcity relative to wants; income distribution comes out as a by-product of price-determination, distributive variables being but the prices for the services of the so-called "factors of production". Production processes are only an intermediate stage connecting final consumers' tastes to the initial scarce resource endowments.' By contrast, 'classicism' is represented as a reproductive process (involving the 'production of commodities by means of commodities') wherein 'at the beginning of the production period, specific quantities of commodities are advanced, as means of production or as subsistence for the workers employed'—both technology (including the structure of production) and wages are exogenously determined—the utilization of which yields outputs exceeding the initial stocks, a surplus 'consisting of heterogeneous set of commodities'. In this system 'relative prices must be such as to allow all sectors a profit inducement to repeat the production sequence'; the spread between product prices and costs must generate a uniform rate of profit in all sectors, the average profit rate itself being determined solely by the exogenously given wage rate and technology.[2]

It is an essential part of the foregoing argument that in the classical system value and output levels are not determined simultaneously by the forces of demand and supply.[3] This separation of value and output precludes the

[2] See also the emphasis upon given endowments of resources as the peculiar characteristic of 'neo-classical' theory, in Walsh and Gram (1980, p. 152). Here, too, Walrasian economics is represented as an *exchange system* extended to allow for production, capital formation, and money, but isomorphically, remaining faithful always to catallactics (p. 123). And a sharp analytical distinction is made between a classical economics concerned with the creation, extraction, and division of the surplus between accumulation and luxury consumption by the capitalist class, and a neo-classical economics, wherein social class is irrelevant, focusing upon the allocation of *given* resources among alternative uses by means of competitive prices (pp. 9–10, 125–6).

[3] Cf. Pasinetti (1974, p. 12) on the absence of a demand theory in the context of profit-rate equalization: '[Ricardo] does not find it useful to enter into complicated details (and in his case they would have been very complicated indeed for him, who did not possess a demand theory).'

possibility that a change in the pattern of consumer demand can influence factor returns, and thus costs, by playing upon the relative scarcity of the factors: The divorce of value and output implies a divorce of value and distribution (cf. Dobb, 1973, p. 261; Garegnani, 1972, p. 278f., 1976, pp. 24–25; Pasinetti, 1974, pp. 43–4; Roncaglia, 1978, pp. 119f).

All this in contrast to Walrasian theory. Indeed, the paradigmatic contrasts have led to the charge that Walras was seriously inconsistent for conceiving the capital endowment of the community as a set of *given* quantities of 'capital-goods proper', yet also (in parts of his *Elements*) adopting the notion of uniformity of profit rates (Garegnani, 1976, pp. 34, 36).

It is my contention that Ricardian economics—the economics of Ricardo and J. S. Mill—in fact comprises in its essentials an exchange system fully consistent with the marginalist elaborations. In particular, their cost-price analysis is pre-eminently an analysis of the allocation of scarce resources, proceeding in terms of general equilibrium, with allowance for final demand, and the interdependence of factor and commodity markets.[4] Serious and long-lived misconceptions regarding classicism flow from a failure to recognize that the classical notions of wages and interest as compensation for effort and abstinence were pertinent only at the macro-economic level where the determinants of aggregate factor supplies are under investigation and not in the micro-economic context where costs referred to forgone opportunities.[5]

My perspective places J. S. Mill directly in the Ricardian theoretical tradition. That we find simultaneously in his *Principles* both 'neoclassical' and 'Ricardian' features implies neither inconsistency (Hollander, 1976)—or no more inconsistency than in Ricardo himself—nor a process of escape, or attempted escape, from his Ricardian heritage, a view expressed recently in the following terms:

> A silent revolution in the direction of the marginalist supply-and-demand theory was brought about [by Marshall] in the course of adopting, extending and transforming some ideas in Mill. As Mill himself had departed considerably from Ricardo, Marshall was thus moving even further from the Ricardian source (Bharadwaj, 1978, p. 254).

It was precisely the beginnings in Mill of considerable deviations from Ricardo's theory of value and distribution that called for and received at Marshall's hands... extensions and refinement; so that Marshall's deli-

---

[4] As far as Ricardo is concerned, my argument here is an elaboration of that given in Hollander (1979, ch. 6). I shall take for granted throughout the demonstration there given of Ricardo's appreciation of the 'demand schedule'—and the variability of the wage rate—although his position in this regard will be apparent in the citations below.

[5] In the sense of forgone *products* alone, and excluding forgone leisure (cf. Robbins, 1970, p. 18).

berations on value and distribution departed systematically from the
questions Ricardo posed and the framework of analysis he
employed.... What Shove regarded as extensions and generalisations of
Ricardo in [Marshall's] *Principles* (the introduction of the demand side,
the functional relation between costs and output, the supply and
demand determination of wages and profits) are radical departures
from the Ricardian standpoint. (p. 269)[6]

My perspective is one that avoids the difficult psychological problems posed
by interpretations that refuse to accept at face value Marshall's statements of
his relationship with his classical forebears, or those of Mill regarding his
intellectual relationship with Ricardo—his repeated insistence that he was
elaborating upon Ricardian themes. The demand side, the functional relation
between cost and output, and the supply and demand determination of wages
and profits, far from being 'radical departures' from Ricardianism, are central
to that doctrine without which neither the cost theory of price nor the inverse
wage-profit relation can be understood.[7]

The second and third sections of this paper will demonstrate the key role
accorded by Ricardo and J. S. Mill to opportunity cost and derived factor
demand: their simultaneous and consistent attachment to cost theories of
value and to the general-equilibrium conception of economic organization as
formulated by J. B. Say and much admired by Walras. Such demonstration
clearly has important implications for the nature of the 'neoclassical' developments of the 1870s.

But we must also consider the reverse side of the coin, from which
perspective it again becomes clear that the term 'revolution' to describe that
doctrine is unhelpful. In his criticisms of Ricardo, Walras wrote that it is 'the

[6] That J. S. Mill in his *Principles* had turned or was in the process of turning his back on
Ricardianism is a widespread belief; cf. for example Schumpeter (1954): 'the economics of
[Mill's] *Principles* are no longer Ricardian.... From Marshall's *Principles* Ricardianism can be
removed without being missed at all. From Mill's *Principles*, it could be dropped without being
missed very greatly' (p. 529).

[7] It is pertinent to refer also to the opinion that Thomas De Quincey *corrected* Ricardian value
theory by stressing the mutual determination of exchange value by 'intrinsic utility' and 'difficulty
of attainment', a 'correction' which 'greatly influenced J. S. Mill's treatment of value in the
Principles and which is in the Hutcheson–Smith tradition of value theory' (Groenewegen, 1974,
p. 193). This is not to my mind a convincing evaluation. The 'mutual determination' of exchange
value by demand and cost considerations was a thoroughly central aspect of Ricardian doctrine.
De Quincey may have believed he was 'correcting' Ricardo, but it is unlikely that Mill was
convinced.

It must be stated that Mill-studies are in a state of confusion. For the literature also provides
assertions to the effect that Mill 'put the clock back' by subscribing to cost of production theories
(Hutchison, 1978, pp. 64–5n, citing Sowell, 1972, a view qualified by admiration for Mill's
contribution to the theory of international trade with its evident demand dimension; Sowell,
1972, pp. 159–60).

price of the products which determines the price of productive services' (1954, p. 425). Similarly, he praised Jevon's statement of the ideal procedure according to which 'the formula of the English school, in any case the school of Ricardo and Mill, must be reversed, for the prices of productive services are determined by the prices of the products, and not the other way round' (p. 45). This clearly does not constitute a picture of mutual interdependence between factor and product markets. It is in fact a statement that emphasizes what the classics had supposedly omitted, and does so by implicitly adopting a short-run perspective. My fourth section is devoted to a demonstration that Walras accepted the 'classical' conception of long-run cost prices—'costs' incorporating profits at a uniform rate on the supply prices of capital goods—employing the Ricardian or Marshallian adjustment mechanism of output response to deviations between demand and supply prices. It also becomes clear that the charge of inconsistency for so doing is unfounded; for he insisted upon profit-rate uniformity, as Ricardo had done and as Marshall was to do, only when allowance is made for changes in the outputs of the different types of capital goods. (The same applies to labour.) Walras adhered to classical cost-price analysis given the appropriate long-run assumptions and, like Ricardo and Marshall, distinguished between maximizing decisions regarding new investments and the actual return on capital goods once constructed.

The fifth section will draw the threads of our analysis together. Brief consideration will then be given to the sources of some of the erroneous views regarding classicism described above.

2 RICARDO ON ECONOMIC ORGANIZATION: THE SAY TRADITION

We set out with J. B. Say's well-known statement in the *Traité d'économie politique* of mutual interdependence between product and factor markets incorporating the principles of opportunity cost and of imputing the values of factors from the values of their products—in broad terms only because of the absence of a marginal conception whereby the physical contributions of individual factors can be isolated:

> It is utility which determines the demand for a commodity, but it is the cost of its production which limits the extent of its demand. When its utility does not elevate its value to the level of the cost of production, the thing is not worth what it cost; it is a proof that the productive services might be employed to create a commodity of a superior value. The possessors of productive funds, that is to say, those who have the disposal of labour, of capital or land, are perpetually occupied in

comparing the cost of production with the value of the things produced, or which comes to the same thing, in comparing the value of different commodities with each other; because the cost of production is nothing else but the value of productive services, consumed in forming a production; and the value of a productive service is nothing else than the value of the commodity, which is the result. The value of a commodity, the value of a productive service, the value of the cost of production are all, then, similar values when every thing is left to its natural course. (Cited in Ricardo, 1951, pp. I, 282–3)

Now Walras certainly believed Say to have been on the right road by this formulation of general interdependency (1954, p. 425). *But so did Ricardo*, who commented on the passage: 'M. Say maintains with scarcely any variation, the doctrine which I hold concerning value.' His sole complaint related to Say's treatment of the services of land on a par with those of capital and labour, in the light of his own (implied) presumption of one-use land (to be elaborated presently) whereby rent is excluded from (marginal) cost (1951, pp. I, 283–4).[8]

Ricardo's subscription to Say's position cannot easily be appreciated in terms of those interpretations that envisage a sharp divergence between the 'British' and the 'French' traditions. Yet the notion of opportunity cost pervades Ricardo's work. Indeed his cost prices make no sense except in these terms. To this matter we now turn.

It is inviting to identify Ricardian cost price with labour embodied, as Malthus in fact did, but it would be incorrect to do so:

It is necessary for me also to remark, that I have not said, because one commodity has so much labour bestowed upon it as will cost 1000 *l*. and another so much as will cost 2000 *l*. that therefore one would be of the value of 1000 *l*. and the other of the value of 2000 *l*. but I have said that their value will be to each other as two to one, and that in those proportions they will be exchanged. (1951, pp. I, 46–7)

Mr. M. . . . misunderstands me . . . I say its whole value will be *in proportion* to a portion of its cost, and I do not say this without allowing for modifications and exceptions—though I consider these of no great magnitude. I have said that the relative value of commodities is in proportion to the quantity of labour bestowed on them. That value may be double what the labour cost. (1951, pp. II, 100–2)

[8] See also Say's (1821, pp. 12f.) doctrine of productive services, regarding which Ricardo wrote to Malthus: 'if he would give up rent, he and I should not differ very materially on that subject' (1951, pp. VIII, 277) and to Say: 'In your doctrine of productive services I almost fully agree, but I submit to you, whether, as rent is the effect of high price, and not the cause of it, it should not be rejected when we estimate the comparative value of commodities' (p. 279).

'Cost of production' or natural price thus includes profits as well as wages each at its average or ordinary rate as Smith had explained (1951, pp. I, 291). Under the appropriate technological conditions defined in the first chapter of the *Principles* (namely uniform factor proportions) a state of general equilibrium, such that prices reflect costs throughout the system, will be one satisfying the principles of profit rate (and wage rate) equalization *and* proportionality of prices to labour inputs. More accurately, under the stated circumstances uniformity of profit rates (and wage rates) require that proportionality. The following passage (drawn from a discussion of subsidized labour for some firms in a manufacturing industry) beautifully summarizes the point, and does so in a context expressing that what is relevant is marginal labour input: 'The manufacturer enjoying none of these facilities might indeed be driven altogether from the market, if the supply afforded by these favored workmen were equal to all the wants of the community; but if he continued in the trade, it would be only on condition that *he should derive from it the usual and general rate of profits on stock, and that could only happen when his commodity sold for a price proportional to the quantity of labor bestowed on its production*' (1951, pp. I, 73n; my emphasis).

Now it is the possibility of capital (and labour) movement between uses or commodity-supply adjustment that assures the tendency to cost price and proportionality to labour input—a matter of great importance that is apparently denied by Cambridge writers and others. This can be illustrated from the discussion of an exogenous change in tastes:

Let us suppose that all commodities are at their natural price, and consequently that the profits of capital in all employments are exactly at the same rate.... Suppose now that a change of fashion should increase the demand for silks, and lessen that of woollens; their natural price, the quantity of labour necessary for their production, would continue unaltered, but the market price of silks would rise, and that of woollens would fall; and consequently the profits of the silk manufacturer would be above, whilst those of the woollen manufacturer would be below, the general and adjusted rate of profits. Not only the profits, but the wages of the workmen, would be affected in these employments. *This increased demand for silks would however soon be supplied, by the transference of capital and labour from the woollen to the silk manufacture*; when the market prices of silks and woollens would again approach their natural prices, and then the usual profits would be obtained by the respective manufacturers of those commodities.

It is then the desire, which every capitalist has, of diverting his funds from a less to a more profitable employment, that prevents the market price of commodities from continuing for any length of time either much above, or much below their natural price. It is this competition, which so adjusts the exchangeable value of commodities, that after paying the wages necessary to their production, and all other expences required to put the capital employed in its original state of efficiency, the remaining value or overplus will in each trade be in proportion to the value of the capital employed. (pp. I, 90–1; my emphasis)

In circumstances of differential factor ratios the same assumption of factor mobility dictates a divergence of (relative) cost prices from (relative) labour inputs as Ricardo explained at length in his first chapter. But the entire notion of cost price presumes factors that have alternative uses; and in all cases, whether or not costs are proportional to labour inputs, *only those returns that reflect alternative opportunities are allowed for in costs.* Embodiment of labour, or for that matter the pain cost attached to labour and abstinence are not in themselves the relevant consideration,[9] as is clear from the fact that since 'it is through the inequality of profits that capital is moved from one employement to another' (p. 119), an economy-wide change in labour productivity or the wage rate or any other disturbance will leave cost prices unaltered should all commodities be impinged upon equally.

The implications of this perspective are legion. For example, from the context of public finance:

From this circumstance [the differential impact on agriculture of the poor rates] it follows, that the farmer will be enabled to raise the price of his produce by the whole difference. For since the tax falls unequally, and peculiarly on his profits, he would have less motive to devote his capital to the land, than to employ it in some other trade, were not the price of raw produce raised. If, on the contrary, the rate had fallen with greater weight on the manufacturer than on the farmer, he would have been enabled to raise the price of his goods by the amount of the difference, for the same reason that the farmer under similar circumstances could raise the price of raw produce...; for there can be no reason why their profits should be reduced below the general rate of profits, when their capitals might be easily removed to agriculture. (pp. 260–1)

The conception in question bears strategically upon the nature of trade: 'If any cause should raise the price of a few manufactured commodities, it would prevent or check their exportation; but if the same cause operated generally on all, the effect would be merely nominal, and would neither interfere with their relative [cost] value, nor in any degree diminish the stimulus to a trade

---

[9] Although a good case can be made whereby Ricardo allowed that the profit rate contains a reward for abstinence and thus acts upon accumulation; Hollander (1979, ch. 7).

of barter, which all commerce, both foreign and domestic really is' (p. 228).
And the principle that cost prices reflect alternative opportunities provides
the rationale for the fundamental theorem of distribution itself—the inverse
wage-profit relation. A *general* wage increase either leaves cost prices entirely
unaffected, thus forcing down profits (the special case of identical factor
proportions), or, by disturbing the structure of profit rates, sets in motion
appropriate supply adjustments that lead to the establishment of a new cost
structure, assuring again uniform profit rates in all industries albeit at a lower
general level (Hollander, 1979, pp. 302f).

One also should not forget that although disturbances to the wage
structure were largely set aside by Ricardo, the rationale for this procedure
was reliance upon the operation of 'competition'—the demand-supply
mechanism—which assured a pattern of relativities reflecting 'the comparative skill of the labourer, and intensity of the labour performed' (1951, p.
I, 20).

It will be apparent that Ricardo's cost prices make no sense except within a
demand-supply framework allowing for alternative uses of resources. Yet
Ricardo is frequently said to have rejected demand-supply analysis (except
perhaps for market price determination). This is a misconception. What he
actually complained of was 'the opinion that the price of commodities
depends *solely* on the proportion of supply to demand or demand to supply'
(1951, pp. I, 382; my emphasis), a complaint alluding to those formulations
that appeared to exclude a role for cost conditions in the mechanism. Thus his
observation to Say: 'You say demand and supply regulates the price of bread;
that is true, but what regulates supply? the cost of production . . .' (1951, p.
IX, 172). Indeed, Ricardo's point (as is apparent from the following reaction to
the treatment by Say of a commodity tax) was precisely that Say had failed to
follow out the logic of his own approach to pricing which runs in terms of
alternative uses:

> It is observed by M. Say, 'that a manufacturer is not enabled to make
> the consumer pay the whole tax levied on his commodity, because its
> increased price will diminish its consumption.' Should this be the case,
> should the consumption be diminished, will not the supply also speedily
> be diminished? Why should the manufacturer continue in the trade if
> his profits are below the general level? M. Say appears here also to have
> forgotten the doctrine which he elsewhere supports, 'that the cost of
> production determines the price, below which commodities cannot fall
> for any length of time, because production would be then either sus-
> pended or diminished.' (1951, p. I, 243n)

The essence of the whole matter is captured exquisitely in a letter to Malthus:
'You say demand and supply regulates value—this I think is saying

nothing...—it is supply which regulates value—and supply is itself controlled by *comparative cost* of production' (1951, p. VIII, 279; my emphasis).

On matters of *principle* Ricardo's line is that of Lausanne: equality of wage rates and of profit rates maximize the return to the factors 'capital' and 'labour'.[10] Moreover, it must be emphatically stated that these average returns themselves are, in principle, variables governed by the relative scarcity of the factors: 'I have invariably insisted, that high or low profits depend on low and high wages, how then can it be justly said of me that the only cause which I have recognized of high or low profits is the facility or difficulty of providing food for the labourer?'—as to this day it is frequently said of Ricardo; 'I contend that I have also recognized the other causes, the relative amount of population to capital, which is another of the great regulators of wages' (1951, pp. II, 264–5).[11] On this view, and keeping in mind Ricardo's further insistence that 'the power of employing labour depends on the increase of a particular part of capital, not on the increase of the whole capital' (1951, p. IX, 127), the way is open for an allowance that the adjustment process following a variation in the pattern of final demand itself will affect the average factor returns. In short, output levels can affect relative cost prices by playing upon the relative scarcity of labour and capital, an outcome in line with neoclassical theorizing.

We can sharpen our understanding of Ricardo's position on the nature of cost price by considering the contrast between costs and rents. I shall first establish Ricardo's awareness that the phenomenon of differential rent, which plays so large a part in his system, is but a special case of a more general phenomenon—land scarcity.

Rent is provisionally defined as the payment to the landlord 'for the use of the original and indestructible powers of the soil' (1951, p. I, 67)—a productivity phenomenon. But in the following passage the ultimate rationale is more specifically expressed in terms of productivity and scarcity (demand and supply):

> On the first settling of a country, in which there is an abundance of rich
> and fertile land, a very small proportion of which is required to be
> cultivated for the support of the actual population, or indeed can be
> cultivated with the capital which the population can command, there
> will be no rent; for no one would pay for the use of land, when there was

[10] This is sometimes conceded by Knight (1956, 41–2n, 63) and Schumpeter (1954, p. 590), despite their generally critical approaches to Ricardian economics from a neoclassical perspective.

[11] And Ricardo himself referred to the relation between wages and profits in terms of 'equilibrium' (1951, p. I, 226).

an abundant quantity not yet appropriated, and, therefore, at the disposal of whosoever might choose to cultivate it.

On the common principles of supply and demand, no rent could be paid for such land, for the reason stated why nothing is given for the use of air and water, or for any other of the gifts of nature which exist in boundless quantity. With a given quantity of materials, and with the assistance of the pressure of the atmosphere, and the elasticity of steam, engines may perform work and abridge human labour to a very great extent; but no charge is made for the use of these natural aids, because they are inexaustible, and at every man's disposal. In the same manner the brewer, the distiller, the dyer, make incessant use of the air and water for the production of their commodities; but as the supply is boundless, they bear no price. (p. 69)

Here J. B. Say is cited to the same effect: 'The earth ... is not the only agent of nature which has a productive power; but it is the only one, or nearly so, that one set of men take to themselves, to the exclusion of others; and of which, consequently, they can appropriate the benefits.'

Using these principles Ricardo rejected physiocratic residues in the *Wealth of Nations*, specifically the notion that in manufactures 'nature does nothing, man does all; and the reproduction must always be in proportion to the strength of the agents that occasion it.' Factor productivity, runs Ricardo's argument, is a necessary but *insufficient* condition for a positive return:

Does nature nothing for man in manufactures? Are the powers of wind and water, which move our machinery, and assist navigation, nothing? The pressure of the atmosphere and the elasticity of steam, which enable us to work the most stupendous engines—are they not the gifts of nature? to say nothing of the effects of the matter of heat in softening and melting metals, of the decomposition of the atmosphere in the process of dyeing and fermentation. There is not a manufacture which can be mentioned, in which nature does not give her assistance to man, and give it too generously and gratuitously. (p. 76n)

Now differential rent (reflecting productivity differentials) is simply a special case of the genus, scarcity rent: 'If all land had the same properties, if it were all unlimited in quantity, and uniform in quality, no charge could be made for its use, unless it possesses peculiar advantages of situation' (p. 69). Similarly: '[if] air, water, the elasticity of steam, and the pressure of the atmosphere, were of various qualities; if they could be appropriated, and each quality existed only in moderate abundance, they, as well as the land, would afford a rent, as the successive qualities were brought into use' (p. 75).

Differential rent is not to be understood as falling outside the general demand-supply framework.

Secondly, Ricardo stated clearly the conditions under which rent would appear even on marginal units of output (absolute rent)—namely, where scarcity manifests itself in an extreme form, the supply curve of agricultural produce becoming, as it were, vertical (the functional relation between output and costs terminating); and he traced through some of the analytical consequences:

> The corn and raw produce of a country may, indeed, for a time sell at a monopoly price; but they can do so permanently only when no more capital can be profitably employed on the lands, and when, therefore, their produce cannot be increased. At such time, every portion of land in cultivation, and every portion of capital employed on the land will yield a rent, differing, indeed, in proportion to the difference in the return. At such time too, any tax which may be imposed on the farmer, will fall on rent, not on the consumer. He cannot raise the price of his corn, because by the supposition, it is already at the highest price at which the purchasers will or can buy it. He will not be satisfied with a lower rate of profits, than that obtained by other capitalists, and, therefore, his only alternative will be to obtain a reduction of rent or to quit his employment. (pp. 250–1)[12]

I spell all this out in order to emphasize Ricardo's comprehension of the general principle of *scarcity* price both where land differentials exist and where they do not; he went along with Buchanan's statement that 'rent is the effect of high price.... It is...from the price which the produce is sold, that the rent is derived; and this price is got not because nature assists in the production, but because it is the price which suits the consumption to the supply' (p. 77n).

To my knowledge Ricardo nowhere *explicitly* states that rent cannot be excluded from cost, notwithstanding the fact that the aggregate supply conditions of land differ from those of capital and labour, in the case of multi-use land. Yet I believe that he appreciated the logic. Consider in particular the generalization of the rent concept from land to capital—the very explicit recognition that once the assumption of capital mobility between uses is abandoned it is the rent analysis that becomes appropriate:

[12] Cf. p. 252: 'I hope I have made it sufficiently clear, that until a country is cultivated in every part' (an allusion to the extensive margin) 'and up to the highest degree' (an allusion to the intensive margin), 'there is always a portion of capital employed on the land which yields no rent, and that it is this portion of capital, the result of which, as in manufactures, is divided between profits and wages that regulates the price of corn.'

As a part of this capital, when once expended in the improvement of a farm, is inseparably amalgamated with the land, and tends to increase its productive powers, the remuneration paid to the landlord for its use is strictly of the nature of rent, and is subject to all the laws of rent. Whether the improvement be made at the expense of the landlord or the tenant, it will not be undertaken in the first instance, unless there is a strong probability that the return will at least be equal to the profit that can be made by the disposition of any other equal capital; but when once made, the return obtained will ever after be wholly of the nature of rent, and will be subject to all the variations of rent. (p. 262)

This principle was in fact utilized in an argument against those who opposed freer corn importation on grounds of capital immobility: 'Suppose,' Ricardo reasoned, 'that the fact be as stated and that no part of the capital could be withdrawn; the farmer would continue to raise corn, and precisely the same quantity too, at whatever price it might sell; for it could not be his interest to produce less, and if he did not so employ his capital, he would obtain from it no return whatever' (p. 269).

There are also the similar effects of a tax on rent (p. 257) and a tax on profits-in-general—in neither case (even allowing capital mobility) can the tax be escaped by way of allocative readjustments. Of course, a fall in the (net) profit rate may subsequently play on the rate of capital accumulation and thus the wage rate, but this is a matter relating to long-run aggregate supply conditions.

Also relevant is the recognition in the context of foreign trade that once the possibility of resource mobility between uses is ruled out, the general rules of cost-price break down. Even assuming uniform capital-labour ratios, commodities will no longer exchange in proportion to relative labour inputs: 'The difference in this respect, between a single country and many, is easily accounted for, by considering the difficulty with which capital moves from one country to another, to seek a more profitable employment, and the activity with which it invariably passes from one province to another in the same country' (pp. 135–6).

We return now to the passage cited above from J. B. Say, which Ricardo applauded: the doctrine of productive services. This passage explicitly spells out the principle of opportunity costs and the closely related argument that the source of factor returns (and the motive for the use of factors) in any use is final demand. While the final demand dimension leaps to the eye in the case of (single-use) land, it is no less pertinent in the case of those returns that enter into cost price.[13] For to refer to cost price is merely to say that demand in any

---

[13] This point is frequently neglected. See below, p. 42.

sector is sufficient to meet the competition of demand elsewhere for the use of resources. There should be no surprise at Ricardo's acceptance of the Say formulation.

What, however, are we to make of Ricardo's subscription to the wages-fund theory and its corollary, as expressed by Mill's fourth proposition on capital, that 'demand for commodities is not demand for labour'? For it was Jevons's complaint precisely that according to this proposition (which he rightly observed originated with Ricardo), capitalists 'maintain and pay for labor whether or not there is a demand for the commodities produced' and 'production goes on independently of the use to which the produce is to be put' (1905, p. 127).

This complaint is unjustified. Nothing in the fourth proposition conflicts with derived demand, since it relates in no way to the individual capitalist's motivation in offering employment. It is a description of the manner in which the aggregate demand for labour and thus the aggregate wage bill (reflecting either higher average earnings or higher employment or both) is expanded. Thus it is that for the reabsorption of labour displaced by machinery Ricardo relied in part upon increased demand for service labour out of net revenue and in part upon net accumulation. That a transfer by capitalists from consumption expenditure to investment raises labour demand is easily demonstrable (Hollander, 1979, pp. 326f). That the same holds true of a transfer from consumption to expenditure on services is clarified in Ricardo's chapter 'On Machinery'. The altered pattern of consumption from commodities to services encourages an expansion of the agricultural sector; labourers displaced in the consumer-goods sector are not, as it were, simply reabsorbed in the service sector but are reabsorbed in expanding agricultural production to meet the consumption requirements of the (additional) service labour, a sequence of events corresponding to that entailed by 'savings from revenue to add to capital' (pp. 373f).

Similarly, it can be shown that Ricardo's discussion of the demand for labour in no way precludes an approach to economic organization in terms of 'synchronized' activity as some writers during the 1870s believed.[14] Ricardo firmly rejected the notion of a literal pre-accumulation of stocks of wage-goods advanced by employers and constituting the demand for labour. Workers, he insisted, are paid in money that is disbursed by them directly at retail in the manner of all consumers, the quantity and character of the commodities produced reflecting that demand: 'I dispute your position,' he

[14] 'It is not necessary to the production of things that cannot be used as subsistence or cannot be immediately utilized, that there should have been a previous production of the wealth required for the maintenance of the labourers while the production is going on. It is only necessary that there should be, somewhere within the circle of exchange, a contemporaneous production of sufficient subsistence for the labourers, and a willingness to exchange this subsistence for the thing on which the labour is being bestowed' (George, 1879, p. 24).

wrote to Malthus, 'that a demand for labour is the same thing as a supply of necessaries' (1951, p. VIII, 258). What was involved, rather, was a direction of activity towards wage-goods production in appropriate response to the volume and pattern of labourers' consumption—the volume alone governed by capitalists' savings decisions.

3 J. S. MILL ON ECONOMIC ORGANIZATION

On all these matters J. S. Mill was entirely at one with Ricardo. The theory of costs was treated from a micro-economic perspective involving relative value and the motives underlying resource allocation; indeed, his appreciation of the relativity of exchange value is nowhere expressed more clearly than in the context of costs of production. 'Value is a relative term,' he wrote in his chapter on the 'Ultimate Analysis of Cost of Production,' 'not a name for an inherent and substantive quality of the thing itself' (1965, p. 479). Accordingly, he defended the emphasis upon labour in Ricardo's treatment of value—despite the fact that the primary costs to be met by the capitalist-employer are wage costs—on the grounds that 'in considering ... the causes of *variations* in value, quantity of labour is the thing of chief importance; for when that varies, it is generally in one or a few commodities at a time, but the variations of wages (except passing fluctuations) are usually general, and have no considerable effect on value' (p. 481). None the less, wage differentials will be reflected in the price structure, as well as relative labour inputs and changes in wage differentials will generate changes in the price structure: 'Although, however, *general* wages, whether high or low, do not affect values, yet if wages are higher in one employment than another, or if they rise and fall permanently in one employment without doing so in others, these inequalities do really operate on values...' (pp. 480, 692).

The same principles applied to profits: 'Values... being purely relative, cannot depend upon absolute profits, no more than upon absolute wages, but upon relative profits only.... Insofar as profits enter into the cost of production of all things [equally] they cannot affect the value of any. It is only by entering in a greater degree into the cost of production of some things than of others, that they can have any influence on value' (p. 482). By this latter allowance Mill had in mind more than the consequence for the price structure of profit-rate differentials reflecting unequal risk and so forth. The allowance covered compensation for differential time periods of production from industry to industry: 'one commodity may be called upon to yield profit during a longer period than the other.'

In consequence of differential factor proportions it followed that 'commodities do not exchange in the ratio simply of the quantities of labour required to produce them.' (p. 484), and this quite apart from the complication created by *partial* wage changes. Even *general* wage changes might influence the structure of prices: 'even a general rise of wages, when it involves a real increase in the cost of labour, does in some degree influence values. It does not affect them in the manner vulgarly supposed, by raising them universally. But an increase in the cost of labour lowers profits; and therefore lowers in natural value the things into which profits enter in a greater proportion than the average, and raises those into which they enter in a less proportion than the average' (p. 485).

We must here have in mind Mill's repeated insistence, always following Ricardo, that changes in production costs exert their influence by way of supply variation. Let us recall the opinion, expressed by Malthus in 1824 (and repeated ever since), that Ricardo had limited demand-supply analysis solely to the market period and cases of monopoly, treating long-run cost price quite independently; the two theories were mutually exclusive (1963, pp. 181–2). Mill rejected Malthus's attribution as soon as it appeared, insisting that in the opinion of the Ricardo school long-run cost prices were arrived at by way of supply variation (1967, pp. 33–4). In the chapter in the *Principles*, 'Of Demand and Supply, in their Relation to Value,' reference is indeed made to 'another law [than that of demand and supply] for that much larger class of things, which admit of indefinite multiplication'; but immediately there-after we find a caution that in dealing with production costs, 'it is not less necessary to conceive distinctly and grasp firmly the theory of this exceptional case' (that of given supplies), which 'will be found to be of great assistance in rendering the more common case intelligible' (1965, p. 468). The point is clear enough: 'The value at any particular time is the result of supply and demand,' but 'unless that value is sufficient to repay the Cost of Production, and to afford, besides, the ordinary expectation of profit, the commodity will not continue to be produced'. Necessary price, in brief, includes a return on capital 'as great...as can be hoped for in any other occupation at that time and place,' and in the event of a return in excess of the going rate 'capital rushes to share in this extra gain, and by increasing the supply of the article, reduces its value'; conversely, in the reverse case output is restricted (pp. 471–2). And it is in this sense that one may easily appreciate the famous reference to 'a law of value anterior to cost of production, and more funda-mental, the law of demand and supply' (p. 583). Here Mill did not intend to deny, any more than Ricardo, that cost of production works its influence by way of supply variations. His point was that demand-supply analysis applied to *all* cases, even where cost analysis was irrelevant—an appropriate perspec-tive in a chapter dealing with 'Some Peculiar Cases of Value'.

The general conclusion regarding the central role of supply variation in the establishment of cost price is scarcely surprising in the light of Mill's observa-tion that the pertinent perspective in cost-price analysis is one involving 'the motives by which the exchange of commodities against one another is immediately determined'.[15] Numerous explicit allusions to relative supply variation will be found precisely in this context; the higher value of commodities produced in industries entailing a relatively high degree of unpleasantness or a relatively longer period of production, or a differential tax are all explained in terms of appropriate supply restraints (pp. 482f). It is indeed in the 'general-equilibrium' context that the dependency of cost price upon demand-supply can be seen most comprehensively. Cost of production, we have already observed, includes normal profit; the equilibrium price structure will thus be one that yields the going return on capital in all sectors. Mill described at great length (p. 407) the institutional arrangements whereby returns, or expectation of returns, are equalized ('the method of accommodating production to demand') leaving no doubt of the conspicuous role accorded supply variation in the establishment of equilibrium prices, following exactly the lines laid down in Ricardo's *Principles*.

Also in line with Ricardo, Mill used the principles of allocation theory in the rationalization of the inverse wage-profit relation. Thus, in contrast to a wage increase affecting one sector, where price will rise to assure equality of profit rates across the board, *there exists no mechanism* whereby general prices would be forced upwards in the event of an economy-wide wage increase, when all firms throughout the system are affected equally by the change. From this perspective the fundamental theorem on distribution is founded squarely upon the theory of allocation:

A general rise of wages would not raise prices but would be taken out of the profits of the employers; always supposing that those profits were sufficient to bear the reduction.

The case is different with a rise of wages confined to a single or a small number of employments. That rise if taken out of profits, would place a particular class of employers at a disadvantage compared with other employers: & as soon as they ceased to hope that the loss would be only temporary, they would withdraw part of their capital, or at all events, all new capital would avoid those trades & go into others. Consequently

[15] In his *Leading Principles* (1874, pp. 48–9) J. E. Cairnes criticized Mill's inclusion of wages and profits within costs, although that position was 'generally accepted by economists'. Wages and profits, he argued, were not 'costs' in the legitimate sense of that term—namely, 'sacrifices incurred by man in productive industry'—but, on the contrary, they constituted 'the return made by nature to man upon that sacrifice'; 'labour' and 'abstinence' were the true costs of production. Mill (who already had some idea of the nature of the criticism) observed to his friend that both forms were legitimate depending on context—whether it involved the economic system as a whole or the motives of the individual participants in activity: 'the cost to society, as a whole, of any production, consists in the labour and abstinence required for it. But, as concerns individuals and their mutual transactions, wages and profits are the measure of that labour and abstinence, and constitute the motives by which the exchange of commodities against one another is immediately determined' (1972, pp. 1894–5).

the supply of these particular articles would fall short, and their prices would rise so as to indemnify the employers for the rise of wages. But this would not happen in case of a rise of all wages, for as all capitalists would be affected nearly alike they could not as a body relieve themselves by turning their capital into another employment. (1972, p. 1735)

Expenses which affect all commodities equally, have no influence on prices. If the maker of broadcloth or cutlery, and nobody else, had to pay higher wages, the price of his commodity would rise, just as it would if he had to employ more labour; because otherwise he would gain less profit than other producers, and nobody would engage in the employment. But if everybody has to pay higher wages, or everybody to employ more labour the loss must be submitted to; as it affects everybody alike, no one can hope to get rid of it by a change of employment, each therefore resigns himself to a diminution of profits and prices remain as they were. In like manner, general low wages, or a general increase in the productiveness of labour, does not make prices low, but profits high. If wages fall, (meaning here by wages the cost of labour), why, on that account, should the producer lower his price? He will be forced, it may be said, by the competition of other capitalists who will crowd into his employment. But other capitalists are also paying lower wages, and by entering into competition with him they would gain nothing but what they are gaining already. (1965, p. 692)

A statement of this position will also be found in the context of Mill's discussion of the nature of costs when focusing upon the distinction between costs from an aggregative and industry perspective. It is indeed precisely in the course of expounding the principles of allocation theory that Mill insisted on the inverse wage-profit relation: 'There is no mode in which capitalists can compensate themselves for a high cost of labour, through any action, on values or prices. It cannot be prevented from taking its place on low profits' (p. 479). It is significant, too, that in his correspondence with Cairnes regarding the nature of costs Mill immediately saw the implications of the argument for the Ricardian inverse wage-profit relationship:

Your discussion of the question whether wages ought in any sense to be considered as cost of production, or whether that term should be exclusively predicated of labour and abstinence, was always likely to be scientifically instructive, but I now perceive that it will have a special value *de circonstance*. You must have been struck as I have been, by the thoroughly confused and erroneous ideas respecting the relation of wages to prices, which have shewn themselves to be almost universal in the discussions of the recent strikes. The notion that a general rise of wages must produce a general rise of prices, is preached universally.... Certainly no one knows, even imperfectly, what the Ricardo political economy is...can suppose this to be it. (1972, pp. 1909–10).

The appreciation of the equilibrating function of price, the extension of demand-supply analysis from the 'market' to the 'long-run' period involving the process of profit-rate equalization, and the application of these principles to the basic theorem of distribution were all part and parcel of Ricardian analysis. In some respects, doubtless, Mill's formulations constituted an improvement in rigour—particularly the formal statement of an *equation* of demand and supply and the distinction between displacements of the demand schedules and movements from one position to another on the same schedule (1965, p. 466). But their merit lies less in substantive content than in their location at a conspicuous juncture among the basic theoretical principles; for Ricardo made many of his statements regarding the theory of allocation in various informal contexts relating to applied problems. No good purpose is served, however, by invidious comparisons regarding 'quality' of analysis. And that is not my concern. *The point is simply that Mill's theory of allocation does not constitute a breakaway from Ricardian doctrine, but is a reiteration thereof.*[16]

I follow the pattern of the previous section by considering Mill's approach to rent. In the aggregate, rent ('the price paid for the use of an appropriated natural agent') differed from the other factor returns in consequence of the conditions of land supply. The agent is 'as indispensable (and even more so) as any implement: but the having to pay a price for it, is not. In the case of the implement (a thing produced by labour) a price of some sort is the necessary condition for its existence: but the land exists by nature. The payment for it, therefore, is not one of the expenses of production...' (1965, p. 58). Allowing for differentials complicated the issue only slightly—'the real expenses of production are those incurred on the worst land, or by the capital employed in the least favourable circumstances' (p. 429). It should be noted also that Mill, following Ricardo, realized that differential rent entails a special case of scarcity value, and that rent might be generated *even in the absence of differentials* in the event of an absolute constraint on farm output: 'It is also distinctly a portion of Ricardo's doctrine, that...the land of a country supposed to be of uniform fertility would, all of it, on a certain supposition,

---

[16] It must at the same time be remembered that in introducing his account of the 'equation of demand and supply' Mill did insist upon his own priority, with the exception of J. B. Say, regarding the solution to the 'paradox, of two things, each depending upon the other.' But what we know of Mill's general reaction to Ricardianism suggests that he regarded—and rightly so—this analysis as a *clarification* of sometimes obscure or ambiguous or incomplete formulations in the original statements of 1817.

pay rent: namely, if the demand of the community required that it should all be cultivated, and cultivated beyond the point at which a further application of capital begins to be attended with a smaller proportionate return' (p. 428).[17]

When Mill focused upon individual sectors—and here Mill made explicit what was only implicit in Ricardo—the picture is a very different one.

> The question... respecting the influence which the appropriation of natural agents produces on values, is often stated in this form: Does Rent enter into Cost of Production? and the answer of the best political economists is in the negative. The temptation is strong to the adoption of these sweeping expressions, even by those who are aware of the restrictions with which they must be taken; for there is no denying that they stamp a general principle more firmly on the mind, than if they were hedged round in theory with all its practical limitations. But they also puzzle and mislead, and create an impression unfavourable to political economy, as if it disregarded the evidence of facts. No one can deny that rent sometimes enters into cost of production. If I buy or rent a piece of ground, and build a cloth manufactory on it, the ground-rent forms legitimately a part of my expenses of production, which must be repaid by the product. And since all factories are built on ground, and most of them in places where ground is peculiarly valuable, the rent for it must, on the average be compensated in the values of all things made in factories. (p. 487).

The consequence of multi-use land for cost pricing is laid down clearly in the 'summary of the theory of value'; namely, that 'when land capable of yielding rent in agriculture is applied to some other purpose, the rent which it would have yielded is an element in the cost of production of the commodity which it is employed to produce' (p. 498; cf. p. 484).

Consistent with Mill's 'Ricardian' approach to cost price is the Say conception of organization, which emphasizes that the ultimate source of factor remuneration is in sales proceeds and the motive for factor employment in the revenue product. We encounter the relationship in question in reference to 'the present system of industrial life, in which employments are minutely subdivided, and all concerned in production depend for their remuneration

---

[17] Pertinent, too, is Mill's early defence of the differential-rent theory against the strictures of Senior and others 'who affect to suppose that Sir Edward West, Mr Malthus, and Mr Ricardo, considered the cultivation of inferior land as the *cause* of a high price of corn'. The reverse was the case Mill insisted in 1828: that 'the cultivation of inferior soils' was the *effect* of high price 'itself the effect of demand' was a doctrine 'explicitly laid down by the distinguished authors previously referred to, and particularly by Mr Ricardo' (1967, p. 174)—a perfectly justified defence of the Ricardian position.

on the price of a particular commodity' (p. 455). The principle is elaborated in a chapter dealing with indirect inputs of labour in lengthy processes of production: 'All these people ultimately derive the remuneration of their labour from the bread, or its price: the ploughmaker as much as the rest; for since ploughs are of no use except for tilling the soil, no one would make or use ploughs for any other reason than because the increased returns thereby obtained from the ground, afforded a source from which an adequate equivalent could be assigned for the labour of the ploughmaker. If the produce is to be used or consumed in the form of bread, it is from the bread that this equivalent must come' (p. 31; it is presumably the *expectation* of future yield that provides the motive for the use of the input).[18] This perspective completely confounds Jevons's reading of his predecessors. And there is no need to repeat what was said above regarding the fourth proposition on capital; Mill was crystal clear about its intended application to aggregate wages and employment alone (p. 87). Finally, Mill's pronouncements on the wages-fund yield a vision of capitalist organization far removed from one wherein workers consume a distinct class of commodities produced in annual jets—a vision fully in line with that of Ricardo elaborated above (cf. Hollander, 1984).

4 WALRAS'S 'CLASSICAL' COST-PRICE ANALYSIS

It is not difficult to show that Walras subscribed to a cost-price analysis of the classical order.[19] In fact, it is the so-called 'Marshallian' adjustment mechanism entailing comparisons of demand and supply prices—the Smith–Ricardo–Mill tradition and also formulated so clearly by Say, as we have seen—rather than the so-called 'Walrasian' adjustment mechanism entailing comparisons of demand and supply quantities (pertinent in the simple exchange model) that he adopted in the production context:

> under free competition, if the selling price of a product exceeds the cost of the productive services for certain firms and a *profit* results, entrepreneurs will flow towards this branch of production or expand their output, so that the quantity of the product [on the market] will increase, its price will fall, and the difference between price and cost will be reduced; and, if [on the contrary], the cost of the productive services exceeds the selling price for certain firms, so that a *loss* results, entrepreneurs will leave this branch of production, or curtail their output, so that the quantity of the product [on the market] will decrease, its price

[18] Cf. p. 32: the labourers producing fixed capital 'do not depend for their remuneration upon the bread made from the produce of a single harvest, but upon that made from the produce of all the harvests which are successively gathered until the plough, or the buildings and fences, are worn out'.

[19] I have found Milgate (1979) most helpful.

will rise and the difference between price and cost will again be reduced. (1954, p. 225)[20]

This process involves not merely the transfer of services between sectors without alteration in the supplies of factors from which they derive, although doubtless to some extent this may be involved. For such transfer would be almost instantaneous, whereas Walras emphasized the slowness of adjustment to disturbance.

We consider first remarks made regarding labour that imply the possibility of altering the *types* of personal capital in response to market pressures, in the long run; that is, upon retraining (or even perhaps with the renewal of the population stock). The case of 'unspecialized productive services' was 'the most frequent case', Walras conceded to the classics, particularly in the market for labour:

> Apart from certain individuals naturally gifted with the voice of a great tenor, the limbs of an acrobat, the eye of a painter or the ear of a musician, the great mass of men are capable of performing a wide variety of tasks, just because they are not especially qualified for the performance of any one of them. A man educated to be a lawyer might often just as well have been a manager; and certainly a person trained as a carpenter could have been a locksmith. What do most men inquire into when they come to choose their occupation? Surely, it is the wages they can earn in it, in other words, the value of their productive services in that occupation. The unspecialized productive services, in contradistinction to specific services have competition to fear. (p. 401)

Clearly there is a long-run tendency towards wage-rate equalization, contingent upon training and education, very much like that of Adam Smith who, of course, had also minimized innate differences of character and ability.

The same conception appears in the famous chapter on the 'Continuous Market', where we find in effect a more general description of the 'tendency' of market to natural price mediated by credit—an account that would have been at home in any classical text. The emphasis is upon the slowness of adjustment to changes in data—including patterns of final demand and technology—having in mind the differential rates of replacement of circulating capital, personal capital and capital goods proper. But that such a 'tendency' is at work, albeit ever disturbed, is quite clear:

> Every hour, nay, every minute, portions of [the] different classes of circulating capital are disappearing and reappearing. Personal capital,

---

[20] I understand 'profit' as super-normal profit in excess of the normal return earned on capital goods proper; cf. p. 267.

capital goods proper and money also disappear and reappear, in a similar manner, but much more slowly. Only landed capital escapes this process of renewal. Such is the continuous market, which is perpetually tending towards equilibrium without ever actually attaining it, because the market has no other way of approaching equilibrium except by groping, and, before the goal is reached, it has to renew its efforts and start over again, all the basic data of the problem, e.g. the initial quantities possessed, the utilities of goods and services, the technical coefficients, the excess of income over consumption, the working capital requirements, etc., having changed in the meantime. Viewed in this way, the market is like a lake agitated by the wind, where the water is incessantly seeking its level without ever reaching it. But whereas there are days when the surface of a lake is almost smooth, there never is a day when the effective demand for products and services equals their effective supply and when the selling price of products equals the cost of productive services used in making them. The diversion of productive services from enterprises that are losing money to profitable enterprises takes place in various ways, the most important being through credit operations, but at best these are slow. (p. 380)

It will be instructive to consider briefly at this point the formal model itself. A feature of Walras's theory of capital is the determination of the rate of net revenue in terms of the exchange of net savings (incomes exceeding consumption and allowance for depreciation) for new additions to the stock of capital goods, the quantities of the different types of capital goods satisfying the condition of equality between their demand and supply prices.[21] This condition also reflects the principle of uniformity of net return on the new investments; for if the condition of uniformity 'is not fulfilled with respect to any two capital goods, it will be advantageous to produce less of the capital good for which the ratio is smaller, and more of the capital good for which this ratio is larger' (p. 276; cf. p. 305).

The emphasis is thus upon uniformity of return on *new* investments; but it would be difficult to appreciate the exclusion of the possibility that a change in the structure of final demand patterns or in technology such as Walras emphasizes, as we have seen, might lower the rentals on certain types of *existing* capital goods and thus require a contraction in their quantities by the non-investment of available depreciation allowances. In short, the principle of

[21] 'New capital goods are exchanged against the excess of income over consumption; and the condition of equality between the value of the new capital goods and the value of the excess gives us the equation required for the determination of the rate of net income and consequently for the determination of the prices of capital goods. Moreover, new capital goods are products; and the condition of equality between their selling price and their cost of production gives us the equations required for the determination of the quantities manufactured' (pp. 269–70).

uniformity of the return on capital extends to investment decisions in general—to replacement demand as well as the net demand for new capital goods—although at any particular moment of time it is highly unlikely that uniformity across-the-board will be satisfied in the light of the disturbances in question: 'In an economy like the one we have imagined, which establishes its economic equilibrium *ab ovo*, it is probable that there would be no equality of rates of net income. Nor would such an equality be likely to exist in an economy which had just been disrupted by a war, a revolution or a business crisis' (p. 308). As we concluded, we are dealing only with a *tendency* to uniformity on capital-in-general.

It is clear that equality of net interest is treated by Walras as a 'point of reference' only. It is in the course of adding to and replacing capital goods that decisions are made with an eye on prospective earnings—as we have seen to be the case also in the labour market—but expectations are continually disappointed, so that actual yields diverge from those expected when the investments are undertaken. This was Marshall's position, too; for he maintained that interest is earned on 'free' or 'floating' capital, and the phrase 'rate of interest is applicable to old investments of capital only in a very limited sense'; given complexes earn quasi-rents, and in the polar extreme case of *permanent* investments the term interest on capital is totally inapplicable (1920, pp. 592–3; also pp. 411–12, 418–19, 533). Nonetheless, the *tendency* to equalization is continually at play to the extent that complexes do wear out more or less rapidly. Indeed Marshall estimated that as much as 25 per cent of existing capital goods is replaced annually 'even in a country in which the prevailing forms of capital are as durable as in England', and was prepared for some analytical purposes (particularly in the context of accumulation) to assume 'that the owners of capital in general have been able in the main to adapt its forms to the normal conditions of the time, so as to derive as good a *net* income from their investments in one way as another' (p. 592).

This has been termed a 'sort of development of Walrasian theory'—that there is uniformity of the rate of profits on 'free capital', which points 'not towards long-run equilibrium analysis (in its stationary state, growth theory sense)' but to 'a sort of long-run equilibrium—in its proper sense of new capital gradually and actually flowing towards where quasi-rents have turned out best' (Harcourt, 1975, p. 351).[22] Surely this is the *Walras–Marshall* line itself?

---

[22] See also Hicks, 1973, pp. 340–1: 'it is quite unnecessary, because we use terms like "capital-intensive" and "rate of profit", to trouble ourselves about the valuation of the capital stock as a whole (as we appeared to have to do in the *production function* method). What matters is not the average rate of profit on the whole capital stock (which cannot be determined without such valuation): what matters is the rate of profit on *new investment*. When the new investment is undertaken, that profit is no more than an expected profit, and what is realized may not be the same as what is expected.'

Now I can discern no difference between this line and that of Ricardo. For some analytical purposes Ricardo certainly presumed across-the-board equality of the return on capital. Thus, to investigate the consequences of a change in demand patterns or in technology he would set off from an assumed state of equilibrium in the sense that we 'suppose that all commodities are at their natural price, and consequently that the profits of capital in all employments are exactly at the same rate . . .' (1951, p. I, 90). But he was perfectly well aware, first, that what matters in the (practical) profitability calculations that govern allocation is the return on *new* investments; for once investments are embodied in an actual capital structure we are dealing with rentals. And secondly that in the polar case of permanent embodiments it is no longer pertinent to talk of a return on *capital* at all (p. 262; see above, pp. 26–7). Finally, like both Walras and Marshall, Ricardo appreciated that adjustments are never instantaneous even where the 'withdrawal of capital' is physically possible: 'it always becomes a matter of calculation, whether these [capital goods] shall continue to be employed on the land, notwithstanding the low [the unexpectedly low] price of corn, or whether they shall be sold, and their value transferred to another employment' (p. 269)—a calculation that is characterized by 'the prejudices and obstinacy with which men persevere in their old employments'; for 'they expect daily a change for the better, and therefore continue to produce commodities for which there is no adequate demand' (1951, p. VIII, 277).

5 SOME IMPLICATIONS FOR THE 'MARGINAL REVOLUTION'

A major implication of the foregoing analysis is that the neoclassical developments of the 1870s involved pre-eminently an altered weighting in the selection of axioms, and in that sense a changed 'focus of attention' as well as a sharpening of analytical tools, but not a paradigmatic displacement. Thus, the principle of marginal utility merely added 'very important explanations' (Marshall, see above, p. 14) for the negative slope of the demand curve; and the marginal productivity principle added to the better understanding of factor demand in particular uses—elaborations required as much by Say as by Ricardo and Mill.

To assert that recognition of a multiplicity of primary factors required a *new* theory based upon the principles of demand (Arrow and Starrett, see above, p. 15) or that classical theory could not solve 'the logical problem of explaining the relative wages of heterogeneous types of labour' (Arrow, cited in Hutchison, 1978, p. 69) is historically unjustified.[23] The wage structure had

---

[23] It may be agreed that the neoclassics 'took as an expository point of departure a model which was the polar opposite of the classical, the model of pure exchange' (Arrow and Starrett, 1973, p. 133). Clear exposition may require extreme assumptions, as Ricardo repeatedly insisted.

long been analysed in terms of demand–supply with recognition of a productivity dimension on the demand side; and while value productivity is more conspicuous the more specialized to a particular use individual factors are, those same considerations are no less relevant when allowance is made for factor mobility between uses, although now strict limits are placed on the extent returns in different uses can diverge. In any event, although factor specificity is indeed a neoclassical preoccupation, both Ricardo and Mill carried this very matter far in their generalizations of the rent doctrine.

If we take into account the matter of foreign trade and classical analysis in that case—the conspicuous role accorded demand considerations where the mobility axioms are abandoned—it becomes yet clearer that the notion of a paradigmatic transformation in the 1870s is not helpful. And while Mill was largely responsible for the analysis, it must be remembered that Ricardo had left the door open by his formulation (see above, pp. 26–7) so that the elaborations, brilliant as they were, were consistent with existing doctrines.

Thus far the neoclassical 'relaxation' of the general (but far from universal) classical assumptions regarding factor mobility between uses. There is also the reverse of the medal to consider—the Ricardian assumption of single-use land. By adopting this assumption Ricardo indicates a preoccupation with the macro dimension; yet the 'class' relationship that concerned him, pre-eminently the inverse wage–profit relationship, could not be understood except in terms of allocation theory. He insisted, as Mill did, upon a micro-foundation for macro-analysis which seems eminently sensible if capitalist-exchange institutions are taken seriously. To trace through the consequences of a variation in the general wage in the case where (marginal) cost price incorporates land rent in the Smith–Say manner would have been technically impossible, given the state of the science. This is also true of J. S. Mill. (It is doubtful whether a specific outcome could be generated in the present day and age, for which reason so much analysis proceeds on the basis of two-factors and two-products.) For all that, the severe problems created for Ricardo's theorem by allowance for multi-use land derive from an analytical model of allocation with which Ricardo himself was familiar. That he did not apply the assumptions of the model universally can be easily appreciated.

That there was indeed no paradigmatic displacement is also quite evident from our investigation of Walras. For when he set aside his own restrictive assumption of factor immobility between uses, he was led to formulations of cost-price identical to those of Ricardo and Mill.

This theme can be extended. The appropriate axiomatic base depends in part on the context. The early and later nineteenth-century economists were concerned (as was Adam Smith) with both growth and allocation, although the weighting of their preoccupations certainly differed. Depending upon the context, it was appropriate to emphasize factor 'scarcity' or factor 'reproducibility' or various combinations. Thus Ricardo frequently dealt with disturbances (demand changes, innovation, taxation) within a static framework, although there is no question of his predominant concern with a broad range of analytical issues relating to the growth process—the aggregate factors (capital and labour) treated as variables. And conversely, Walras extended his own analysis in the *Elements* to the 'Conditions and Consequences of Economic Progress', which deals with the distributional implications of growth in labour and capital supplies (given land): 'What does need to be discussed... in view of its extremely weighty consequences, is the fact... that the quantity of land cannot possibly increase though it is possible to increase the number of persons and the quantity of capital goods proper in an economy that saves and converts its savings into capital' (1954, p. 382).[24] Similarly, he recognized the 'excess of income over consumption in the aggregate'—the matter of surplus and accumulation—as the condition of progress (p. 264). Clearly, the classical growth model was not superannuated by the marginalists.

J. S. Mill's continued preoccupation with growth issues (and with the general profit rate) despite his sharp awareness of the problem of factor immobility, also requires consideration from this perspective. For it is not obviously true that concern with the *general* wage and profit rates dissipates with recognition of the phenomenon of non-competing groups. There may yet be disturbances affecting all types of labour more or less equally, and for analysis of the growth process the standard classical mobility axiom (subject to the qualifications made regarding speed of adjustment) may be most appropriate.

6 A NOTE ON SOURCES OF MISINTERPRETATION

Professor Samuelson has written of the 'sophisticated-anthropomorphic sin' of not recognizing the equivalent content in older writers, because they did not use the same terminology and symbols as we do (1949, p. 373). This certainly explains to a large extent the general failure to recognize a key allocative dimension to British classicism. (To some extent this error was

---

[24] Professor Morishima indeed goes so far as to consider this dynamic part as the *capstone* of the entire general-equilibrium structure (1977), from which perspective he regards the *Elements* as a whole 'as providing a general-equilibrium foundation for the Ricardian neoclassical macroeconomics' (1980, p. 558).

Even W. Jaffé, who denied that part VII was intended as 'an integral part of Walras's general equilibrium edifice', conceded that Walras's intentions were to show 'how the relations analysed in the static theory could be used to elucidate such dynamic tendencies as the rise in land-rent, and the fall in the rate of profit in an expanding economy' (1980, pp. 546–7).

invited by Ricardo's sometimes opaque formulations; but since Ricardo was perhaps the first formally to contrast disturbances that have allocative implications and those that exert influence only at the aggregate level, this is scarcely surprising.)

But there is also a matter of theoretical misunderstanding. It is sometimes presumed that since, in Ricardian theory, 'profits are generated in production,' the kind of perspective we have adopted in this paper must be erroneous (Roncaglia, 1981). This is a non sequitur. Ricardo's achievement was to correct Smith's 'adding-up' approach to cost, whereby a change in either wages or profits (or rents) simply generates a corresponding change in general prices: a wage increase must imply reduced profits since the total is constrained in real terms. Nothing that we have said regarding Ricardo's acceptance of J. B. Say's circular flow conception of economic organization with its allowance for final demand controverts this point. For the volume of final demand itself, of course, is governed by the income flow, which in turn is generated in production.

REFERENCES

Arrow, K. J. and Starrett, D. A. (1973). 'Cost- and Demand-Theoretical Approaches to the Theory of Price Determination'. In J. R. Hicks and W. Weber, *Carl Menger and the Austrian School of Economics*. Oxford: OUP.

Bharadwaj, D. (1978). 'The Subversion of Classical Analysis: Alfred Marshall's Early Writing on Value'. *Cambridge Journal of Economic* II, 253–71.

Cairnes, J. E. (1874). *Some Leading Principles of Political Economy*. London: Macmillan.

Dobb, M. (1973). *Theories of Value and Distribution*. Cambridge: CUP.

Frisch, R. (1981). 'From Utopian Theory to Practical Application: the Case of Econometrics'. *American Economic Review* LXXI, June, 1–16.

Garegnani, P. (1972). 'Heterogeneous Capital, the Production Function and the Theory of Distribution'. In E. K. Hunt and J. G. Schwartz (eds), *A Critique of Economic Theory*. Harmondsworth: Penguin.

Garegnani, P. (1976). 'On a Change in the Notion of Equilibrium in Recent Work on Value and Distribution'. In M. Brown, K. Sato and P. Zarembka (eds), *Essays in Modern Capital Theory*. Amsterdam, New York, Oxford: North-Holland.

George, H. (1879). *Progress and Poverty*, Middleton.

Groenewegen, P. (1974). Review. *Economic Journal* LXXXIII, March, 192–3.

Harcourt, G. C. (1975). 'Decline and Rise: the Revival of (Classical) Political Economy'. *Economic Record* LI, 339–55.

Hicks, John (1973). 'The Mainspring of Economic Growth'. *Swedish Journal of Economics* LXXV, 336–48.

Hicks, John (1976). '"Revolutions" in Economics'. In S. Latsis, *Method and Appraisal in Economics*. Cambridge: CUP.

Hollander, S. (1976). 'Ricardianism, J. S. Mill, and the Neo-Classical Challenge'. In J. M. Robson and M. Laine (eds), *James and John Stuart Mill: Papers on the Centenary Conference*. Toronto: University of Toronto Press.

Hollander, S. (1979). *The Economics of David Ricardo*. Toronto: University of Toronto Press.

Hollander, S. (1984). 'J. S. Mill on "Derived Demand" and the Wage-Fund Treaty Recantation'. *Eastern Economic Journal* x, Jan.–March, 87–98.

Hutchison, T. W. (1978). *On Revolutions and Progress in Economic Knowledge*. Cambridge: CUP.

Jaffé, W. (1980). 'Walras's Economics as Others See it'. *Journal of Economic Literature* xviii, 528–49.

Jevons, W. S. (1905). *Principles of Economics*. London: Macmillan.

Jevons, W. S. (1924). *Theory of Political Economy*, 4th edn. London: Macmillan.

Knight, F. H. (1956). *On the History and Method of Economics*. Chicago: University of Chicago Press.

Malthus, T. R. (1963). 'Political Economy' (1824). In B. Semmel (ed.), *Occasional Papers*. New York: Burt Franklin.

Marshall, Alfred (1920). *Principles of Economics*, 8th edn. London: Macmillan.

Milgate, M. (1979). 'On the Origin of the Notion of "Intertemporal" Equilibrium'. *Economica* xlvi, 1–10.

Mill, J. S. (1965) *Principles of Political Economy. Collected Works of John Stuart Mill*, vols ii, iii. Toronto: University of Toronto Press.

Mill, J. S. (1967). *Essays on Economics and Society. Collected Works of John Stuart Mill*, vols iv, v.

Mill, J. S. (1972). *The Later Letters. Collected Works of John Stuart Mill*, vols xiv–xvii.

Morishima, M. (1980). 'W. Jaffé on Léon Walras'. *Journal of Economic Literature* xviii, 550–8.

Pasinetti, L. L. (1974). *Growth and Income Distribution*. Cambridge: CUP.

Ricardo, David (1951). *Works and Correspondence* (ed.) P. Sraffa. Cambridge: CUP.

Robbins, L. C. (1970). *The Evolution of Modern Economic Theory*. London: Macmillan.

Robinson, Joan (1961). 'Prelude to a Critique of Economic Theory'. *Oxford Economic Papers* xiii, 53–8.

Roncaglia, A. (1978). *Sraffa and the Theory of Prices*. Chichester and New York: Wiley.

Roncaglia, A. (1981). 'Hollander's Ricardo'. *Journal of Post-Keynesian Economics* iv, 339–59.

Samuelson, P. A. (1949). Review, *Economica* xv, 373–4.

Schumpeter, J. A. (1954). *History of Economic Analysis*. New York: Oxford University Press.

Shove, G. (1942). 'The Place of Marshall's *Principles* in the Development of Economic Theory'. In J. J. Spengler and W. R. Allen, *Essays in Economic Thought* (1960). Chicago: Rand McNally.

Sowell, T. (1972). *Say's Law*. Princeton: Princeton University Press.

Sraffa, P. (1960). *Production of Commodities by Means of Commodities*. Cambridge: CUP.

Stigler, G. J. (1965). *Essays in the History of Economics.* Chicago: University of Chicago Press.

Walras, Léon (1954). *Elements of Pure Economics* (ed.) W. Jaffé, 4th definitive edn., 1926. London: Allen and Unwin.

Walsh, V. and Gram, H. (1980). *Classical and Neo-classical Theories of General Equilibrium.* New York: OUP.

3

The 'New View' of the Ricardian Theory of Distribution and Economic Growth

CARLO CASAROSA

1 INTRODUCTION

The traditional 'fix-wage' interpretation of the Ricardian system is based on the idea that Ricardo examined the working of the economic system and the process of growth on the assumption that the wage rate remained constantly at its natural (or subsistence) level. According to this view,[1] Ricardo recognized that the market wage rate might diverge from the natural wage rate, but considered this a wholly transitory situation, since he believed that the population mechanism would rapidly force the market wage rate to converge towards its natural equilibrium level. Therefore he described the process of economic growth *as if* the wage rate remained constantly at the natural level.

In the last few years the fix-wage interpretation has been challenged on the ground that it is incapable of explaining some of Ricardo's most important results, and an alternative interpretation has been put forward.[2] The main elements of evidence against the traditional interpretation are the following propositions of Ricardo, which clearly cannot be accounted for in a fix-wage framework.

(1) During the process of economic growth the wage rate remains above its natural level (Ricardo, 1821, pp. 94–5).
(2) In the early stages of growth the wage rate may rise, but from some point onwards both the wage rate and the rate of profit will certainly fall and

I should like to thank Sir John Hicks for very helpful discussions and comments on an earlier draft and A. Chilosi and A. Gay for useful remarks.

[1] The most rigorous account of this approach is to be found in Pasinetti (1960).
[2] Casarosa (1974, 1976, 1978), Levy (1976), Hicks and Hollander (1977), Costa (1977), Hicks (1979a, 1979b) and Hollander (1979). Johansen (1969) might perhaps be considered the forerunner of the new view of Ricardo, even if his concern was the classical school as a whole. See also Samuelson (1978).

will keep falling until the economy becomes stationary (Ricardo, 1821, pp. 98, 101–4, 112–14, 120, 124–6).

The new formulation of the Ricardian system is an attempt to build a Ricardian model consistent with propositions (1)–(2) and other propositions related to them.[3] The basic idea is that in Ricardo the evolution of the wage rate over time is determined by the contemporaneous working of the population mechanism and of the process of capital accumulation, so that there is no reason why the wage rate should converge towards the natural level unless capital is stationary. Moreover, since capital accumulation depends on the rate of profit, and population growth on the wage rate, and since the rate of profit and the wage rate are (inversely) correlated, it emerges that there is a general interdependence among the economic variables. More precisely, the wage rate, the rate of profit and the rates of growth of population and capital are simultaneously determined by the interplay between the distributive variables, population growth and the accumulation of capital.

In this paper we present a brief outline of the new view of the Ricardian theory of distribution and economic growth and discuss some of the problems it raises, on the basis of a simple one-commodity model.

2 THE MODEL

The model is built on the following 'Ricardian' assumptions.

(1) There are decreasing returns to labour in agriculture.
(2) The marginal product of labour is divided between wages and profits only; rent is the surplus that remains out of total production once workers and capitalists have obtained their income.
(3) Workers accept any wage rather than be unemployed.
(4) Workers and landowners consume all their income.
(5) Entrepreneurs employ labour only if they obtain at least a minimum rate of profit. They save and invest out of profits only if the rate of profit is above the minimum.
(6) There is a natural wage rate which keeps population stationary. Population's growth is an increasing function of the difference between the market and the natural wage rate.

[3] Among these the following appear to be particularly important:
—a reduction in the price of wage-goods, brought about by technical progress or foreign trade, benefits both capitalists and workers (Ricardo, 1815, p. 35; 1821, pp. 79–80);
—taxation causes a reduction both of the wage rate and of the rate of profit (Ricardo, 1821, pp. 222, 225, 226).

To simplify we assume, further, that the system produces only one commodity—corn—and that labour and land are the only inputs to production.

The model consists of six equations:

$$X = f(N) \tag{1}$$

where X = amount of corn produced and N = number of workers employed, with

$$f'(\ ) > 0 \tag{1a}$$

$$f''(\ ) < 0 \tag{1b}$$

$$f'(0) > w_s(1 + r_s) \tag{1c}$$

$$f'(\infty) < w_s(1 + r_s) \tag{1d}$$

where w_s = natural wage rate and r_s = minimum rate of profit.

$$W = wN \tag{2}$$

where W = total wage bill and w = wage rate.

$$K = W \tag{3}$$

where K = stock of capital; with

$$K \leqslant f'(N)N/(1 + r_s). \tag{3a}$$

$$r = \{f'(N) - w\}/w \tag{4}$$

$$\dot{N}/N = G\{(w - w_s)/w_s\} \tag{5}$$

where r = rate of profit, with

$$G(0) = 0 \tag{5a}$$

$$G'(\ ) > 0. \tag{5b}$$

$$\dot{K}/K = F(r - r_s) \tag{6}$$

with:

$$F(0) = 0 \tag{6a}$$

$$F'(\ ) > 0 \tag{6b}$$

if it does not violate (3a). Otherwise:

$$K = f'(N)N/(1 + r_s).$$

Equation (1) is the production function for corn, which we assume twice differentiable with positive, but decreasing, returns; (1c) allows the system to grow and (1d) ensures that economic growth cannot go on indefinitely.

Equation (2) is definitory.

Equation (3) says that capital consists entirely of the wage bill. The meaning of (3a) is the following: since entrepreneurs employ labour only if they obtain at least the minimum rate of profit, for each level of employment there is a maximum wage rate, $\hat{w}$, they are willing to pay. In our model,

$$\hat{w} = f'(N)/(1 + r_s). \tag{7}$$

Correspondingly, for each level of employment there is a maximum amount of capital, $\hat{K}$, that entrepreneurs are willing to invest; from equations (2), (3) and (7) we have:

$$\hat{K} = f'(N)N/(1 + r_s). \tag{8}$$

Condition (3a) says that the amount of capital the entrepreneurs employ cannot be higher than the amount that yields the minimum rate of profit.[4]

Equation (4) follows directly from the Ricardian theory of rent.

The last two equations are the laws of motion of the system. Equation (5) is the so-called law of population, that is, the relationship between the wage rate and the rate of growth of population. Equation (6) summarizes the rules

---

[4] Condition (3a) has been generally overlooked even by those who admit that in Ricardo the rate of profit is the motive behind the accumulation of capital. As a result, it is admitted that the rate of profit might be lower than the minimum even in a circulating capital model. But this is clearly absurd in a system in which the entrepreneurs stop accumulating 'when their profits are so low as not to afford them an adequate compensation for their trouble, and the risk which they must necessarily encounter in employing their capital productively' (Ricardo, 1821, p. 122). In fact, why should such entrepreneurs be ready to advance their (circulating) capital at a wage rate that does not leave them at least the minimum rate of profit? The introduction of condition (3a) disposes, at least for the circulating capital model, of the 'exception' pointed out by Hicks and Hollander (1977, pp. 357–9) and of similar results obtained by Costa (1977). With fixed capital the problem is much more complicated and will not be pursued here.

followed by the entrepreneurs as far as the accumulation of capital is concerned. It says that, if the rate of profit that entrepreneurs obtain from the capital they have advanced is just equal to the minimum rate of profit, they do not save at all and therefore keep their capital constant; while, if the rate of profit is higher than the minimum, their propensity to save (and invest) is positive and is an increasing function of the difference between the rate of profit they have obtained and the minimum rate of profit. However, if the observance of these rules implied the 'advance' of an amount of capital higher than the maximum amount the entrepreneurs are willing to invest at the new level of employment, they will advance just the maximum amount and consume the rest. Otherwise they would get a rate of profit lower than the minimum they are willing to accept.

3 THE WORKING OF THE SYSTEM

We can now study the working of our system in the (N, w) plane (see figure 1).[5] We draw the loci $w = w_s$ and $w = \hat{w}$ (or $r = r_s$). The locus $w = w_s$ is a horizontal line, while locus $r = r_s$ slopes downwards since $\hat{w} = f'(N)/(1 + r_s)$. By (5), on the $w = w_s$ locus population is stationary: above it population grows; and below it population declines. By (6) on the $r = r_s$ locus the rate of capital accumulation is either 0 or negative and below it, positive. Points

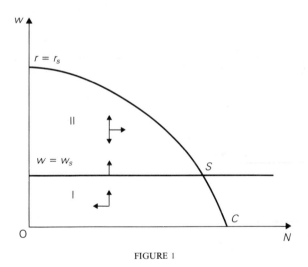

FIGURE 1

[5] This is the approach followed by Hicks and Hollander (1977). The obvious alternative, adopted by Johansen (1969), is to work in the (K, N) plane. Johansen's approach has been followed by Costa (1977).

above this locus are never reached, since in this case the entrepreneurs would get a rate of profit lower than the minimum they are willing to accept.

The two loci intersect when $f'(N)/(1+r_s) = w_s$. Such a point exists since the loci are continuous and we have assumed $f'(0) > w_s(1+r_s)$ and $f'(\infty) < w_s(1+r_s)$. At the intersection point, S, population is obviously stationary. Then capital is also stationary.

What about the wage rate? We first notice that, since from equations (2)–(3) we have $w = K/N$, the rate of change of the wage rate is given by:

$$\dot{w}/w = \dot{K}/K - \dot{N}/N. \tag{9}$$

Now, in region I (below the $w = w_s$ locus) population declines and capital grows. Therefore the wage rate rises. In region II (between the two loci) both population and capital grow. Hence the wage rate may either rise or fall according to which of the two grows faster.

On the $w = w_s$ locus to the left of S the wage rate rises, since population is stationary and capital is growing. On the $r = r_s$ locus to the left of S the wage rate declines, since population is rising and capital remains stationary or declines,[6] to the right of S the wage rate rises, since population declines and capital either is stationary or declines at a lower rate than population.[7] Finally, at S the wage rate is stationary.

We are now ready to describe the possible trajectories of our system. We notice, first, that S is a steady-state position. It is, in fact, the stationary state, since capital, population and the wage rate (and hence also the rate of profit) are all constant.

If we start from a point in region I, population declines and the wage rate rises; the system moves upwards and to the left until it hits the $w = w_s$ locus. Here population becomes stationary but the wage rate goes on rising, so that we enter region II.

We now show that if the system is in region II it cannot get out, and moves continuously to the right until it reaches the stationary state. We have already seen that the system cannot break through the $r = r_s$ locus. But it cannot break through the $w = w_s$ locus either, since when the economy gets on such a locus the wage rate increases and the system goes back to region II. Actually, we can show that once the system is in region II it will never reach the $w = w_s$ locus at a point to the left of S (see Hicks and Hollander, 1977, p. 354). In fact, let us assume that we are in region II, but that the wage rate is declining, because the rate of capital accumulation, although positive, is lower than the rate of growth of population. As the wage rate gets closer to w_s the rate of

---

[6] Capital declines when $d\hat{K}/dN < 0$.

[7] In fact, if capital declines the economy moves along the $r = r_s$ locus. See equation (6).

growth of population declines towards 0, while the rate of capital accumulation rises. Therefore at some $w > w_s$ the rates of growth of population and capital will be equal and the wage rate will stop falling. Hence, as long as we are not in the stationary state, the wage rate cannot be at the natural level and the system moves continuously to the right.

We can therefore conclude that:

(1) the stationary state is globally stable;
(2) after the wage rate has become higher than the natural wage rate, both capital and population keep growing and the wage rate remains above its natural level until the economy falls in the stationary state.

4 THE DYNAMIC EQUILIBRIUM PATH

The results we have just obtained are obviously important for a better understanding of Ricardo's theory. In fact, from the working of our model we have explicitly derived the first of Ricardo's propositions mentioned in the introductory section. Moreover, since we have shown that the process of economic growth must end up in the stationary state, and that during the process of growth the wage rate remains above the natural level, we have also shown that, at least in some neighbourhood of the stationary state, the wage rate must fall. The latter result is clearly consistent with Ricardo's proposition (2), even if we must admit that proposition (2) is more specific, since it says that the wage rate must fall all along during the process of growth, with the possible exception of an initial phase, while in the model we have just considered the wage rate might go up and down several times before falling to the natural level.

Can we get closer to the Ricardian results?

Some of the proponents of the new formulation of the Ricardian system[8] have found the answer in the notion of dynamic or balanced equilibrium path, that is, a path along which capital and population change at the same rate. Formally, this implies the addition to the system (1)–(6) of the following equation:

$$\dot{K}/K = \dot{N}/N. \tag{10}$$

From the analysis of the previous paragraph, we know that this condition can be satisfied only in region II and at the stationary point. And since in region II the rate of growth of population is positive, we can use (5) and (6) to rewrite the dynamic equilibrium condition as:

[8] See, in particular, Casarosa (1974, 1976, 1978), Levy (1976) and Samuelson (1978).

Carlo Casarosa

$$F[\{f'(N)-w\}/w-r_s] - G\{(w-w_s)/w_s\} = 0. \tag{10'}$$

(10') is an equation with two unknowns, w and N, and therefore it gives us, for every N, the level of the wage rate that ensures that capital and population grow at the same rate. We may call it the dynamic equilibrium wage rate, w^*, and from what we have said above it is clear that:[9]

(a) as long as $f'(N)/(1+r_s) > w_s$, $w_s < w^* < f'(N)/(1+r_s)$;
(b) when $f'(N)/(1+r_s) = w_s$, $w^* = w_s$.

Moreover, by differentiating (10') and solving, we have:

(c) $dw^*/dN < 0$.

Therefore the dynamic equilibrium path of the wage rate is a downwards-sloping curve such as DS in figure 2.

As for the evolution of the other variables along the dynamic equilibrium path, it should be evident from equations (5), (6) and (10') that, as employ-

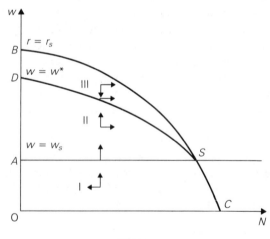

FIGURE 2

[9] Caravale and Tosato (1974, 1980) presented a model very similar to the dynamic equilibrium model, but made the surprising assumption that the wage rate that keeps capital and population growing at the same rate (which they call the natural wage rate) remains constant in the course of growth. As we have just seen in the text, with decreasing returns the wage rate that keeps capital and population growing at the same rate *cannot* remain constant and actually must continuously fall as growth proceeds. Therefore the assumption of a constant natural wage rate is incompatible with the other features of the Caravale–Tosato model.

ment increases, the rate of growth of capital and population and the rate of profit must all fall.

According to some authors (see, e.g. Samuelson, 1978, pp. 1422, 1427–8), the dynamic equilibrium path is a path that can be followed by the economic system during the process of growth and can be shown to be stable. If this view were correct our task would be completed, since the dynamic equilibrium path complies fully with both of Ricardo's propositions mentioned in the introductory section. Unfortunately, our Ricardian system cannot move along the dynamic equilibrium path. In fact, when the economy is on such a path the market wage rate remains constant (see equation (9)), while the dynamic equilibrium wage rate falls. Therefore the system gets off the dynamic equilibrium path.

One way to save the dynamic equilibrium analysis is to assume that the marginal productivity of labour in agriculture decreases not continuously but in steps, and that the steps are sufficiently long (Casarosa, 1978).[10] As long as the marginal product of labour remains constant, the dynamic equilibrium wage rate is also constant and therefore the system can move along the dynamic equilibrium path. As we pass from one step to the following, the dynamic equilibrium wage rate declines to a new level and the economic system gets off the equilibrium path. However, it can be shown that the dynamic laws of the system bring about its convergence to the new dynamic equilibrium position. The possible trajectories followed by the economic system are of the type indicated by the arrows in figure 3. Hence we can

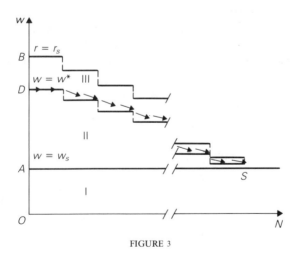

FIGURE 3

---

[10] For a discussion of this 'solution' see Hicks (1979a; 1979b, p. 54). The step model has been adopted also by Pasinetti (1981).

describe the motion of the system over time as a sequence of dynamic equilibria (the last of which is the stationary state), even if the economy cannot be in dynamic equilibrium all the time.

If we are not ready to make the step assumption, we must give up the idea of describing the motion of the system as a steady equilibrium motion. This does not mean, however, that we must abandon the notion of a 'dynamic equilibrium' path altogether, since it can still be useful to restrict the possible trajectories followed by the system in the course of growth. Let us see how.

The dynamic equilibrium path divides the region between the $w = w_s$ and the $r = r_s$ loci into two regions (see figure 2). In region II (below the dynamic equilibrium path and above the $w = w_s$ locus) the wage rate is lower than the dynamic equilibrium wage rate and hence the rate of profit is higher than the dynamic equilibrium rate of profit. Therefore the rate of capital accumulation is higher than the rate of growth of population. Consequently the wage rate rises. In region III (above the dynamic equilibrium path and below the $r = r_s$ locus) it is the other way round and the wage rate falls.

Now, if the system starts from a point in region II, it moves upwards and to the right and sooner or later reaches the dynamic equilibrium path. Here the system moves horizontally to the right and therefore gets into region III. In region III the system moves downwards to the right. It may well converge towards the dynamic equilibrium path, but in no case can it break through the dynamic equilibrium path and move into region II, since, if the system reached the dynamic equilibrium path, it would be repelled back into region III. Actually, we could easily show that, once in region III, the system cannot go back to the dynamic equilibrium path before the stationary state.

We can therefore say that in the initial stages of growth the wage rate may rise for a while, until the system reaches the dynamic equilibrium path. Thereafter it falls and keeps falling until it gets into the stationary position.

For the other variables of the system we come to similar results: once the economy has crossed the dynamic equilibrium line, the rate of profit and the rates of growth of capital and population go on falling until the economy enters the stationary state.

These results are obviously stronger than the ones we were able to establish without the dynamic equilibrium notion, and, what is more important, are exactly the same as Ricardo's results contained in proposition (2).

At this point the presentation of the new view of the Ricardian system is practically completed. However, before concluding, we would like to point out the possibility that, in the analysis of the motion of the economic system, the dynamic equilibrium path plays an even more central role than the one we have just considered.

From our analysis we know that, if the economy is initially below the dynamic equilibrium path, the actual path rises towards the former and at some point crosses it; while, when the economy is above the dynamic equilibrium path, the actual path slopes down to the right as the dynamic equilibrium path does. Now, if in region III the actual path were everywhere steeper than the dynamic equilibrium path, we could well work *as if* the system moved along the dynamic equilibrium path, especially if the initial position of the economy were below the dynamic equilibrium path or not very far from it. In fact, in this case the economic system would most of the time be in a very close neighbourhood of the dynamic equilibrium path, and clearly it would not make much difference to work with the actual path or with the dynamic equilibrium path.

The question is, of course, whether we can assume that in region III the actual path is everywhere steeper than the dynamic equilibrium path. Since both paths must end up in the stationary state, there is surely at least one phase in which the actual path is steeper. But this is not enough for our purpose. However, since the slope of the dynamic equilibrium path depends on the slope of the marginal product curve, while the slope of the actual path depends on the difference between the rates of growth of capital and population, we can say that, the stronger the influence of the rate of profit on the propensity to accumulate, and the flatter the slope of the marginal product, the higher the probability that the actual path will approach continuously the dynamic equilibrium path. This, of course, should be expected from what we have said in the framework of the 'step' model.

5 CARAVALE'S NATURAL EQUILIBRIUM MODEL

Recently there have been some attempts to rescue the natural equilibrium interpretation of Ricardo. In this section I shall comment briefly upon Caravale's attempt, which is based on previous work by Caravale and Tosato (1974, 1980).

Caravale admits that Ricardo's definition of natural wage rate is not appropriate for a growing economy but maintains that the idea of a constant wage rate, determined by 'outside' circumstances such as sociological or political forces, is central to Ricardo's thought. Therefore Caravale proposes a new dynamic definition of natural wage rate which, according to him, makes it possible to explain Ricardo's view of the dynamics of the economic system in terms of a natural equilibrium path, seen as the centre of gravitation of the economic system. The proposed definition is as follows: 'The natural wage rate is a real wage rate [above the subsistence level and] constant over time, in a situation in which the rates of growth of population and capital are equal' (Caravale, 1982, p. 147).

At first sight Caravale's definition of natural wage rate seems identical to our notion of dynamic equilibrium wage rate, and in fact Caravale's model and the dynamic equilibrium model have the same dynamic equilibrium

C

condition. However, the role of the equilibrium condition in the two models is radically different, since in the dynamic equilibrium model it determines the level of the wage rate which guarantees that capital and population grow at the same rate, while in Caravale's model it determines the rate of growth of population, since the wage rate is given (at the natural level). In other words, in Caravale's model the rate of growth of population depends not on the real wage rate but on the rate of growth of capital; and the dynamic equilibrium condition simply says that, whatever the rate of capital accumulation, the rate of growth of population adjusts to it.

In my opinion Caravale's model is unsatisfactory both theoretically and as an interpretation of Ricardo.

From the first point of view, I simply note that Caravale's 'law of population' does not seem to have any theoretical basis; in fact, Caravale himself finds it difficult to give a justification to his 'law'.

As for the capability of Caravale's model to represent Ricardo's views, not only is Ricardo's law of population completely different from Caravale's law, but also Caravale's model cannot explain one of Ricardo's central propositions; it cannot explain Ricardo's statement that during the process of economic growth the wage rate tends to fall together with the rate of profit. In fact, since in Caravale's model the market wage rate gravitates continuously towards the natural wage rate, which is constant over time, it is impossible to hold this model and at the same time state that the wage rate falls over time.

We can therefore conclude that Caravale's attempt to rescue the natural equilibrium interpretation of Ricardo is no more convincing than the conventional natural equilibrium interpretation.

6 CONCLUDING REMARKS

The natural equilibrium (fix-wage) interpretation of the Ricardian theory is incapable of explaining some of Ricardo's most important results. For this reason a number of economists have recently proposed to abandon the fix-wage assumption and to accept the idea that in Ricardo the evolution of the wage rate during the process of growth is determined by the simultaneous working of the mechanisms of population growth and capital accumulation.

In this paper I have presented a simple model of the new formulation of the Ricardian system and discussed the two main approaches that have been followed: the market equilibrium and the dynamic equilibrium approach. I have shown that, although the Ricardian economy cannot move along a steady-growth path because of decreasing returns, the notion of dynamic equilibrium turns out to be quite useful for restricting the possible trajectories that the economic system might follow during the process of growth. I have even shown that, if the marginal product of labour decreases slowly enough, the actual path of the economic system is likely to remain most of the time in a very close neighbourhood of the dynamic equilibrium path, so that we could describe the motion of the system *as if* it followed the dynamic equilibrium path.[11]

From the analysis of the working of this model I have derived Ricardo's results, which are incompatible with the natural equilibrium interpretation of his theory. I therefore conclude that the new formulation of the Ricardian system should supersede the traditional one on the ground of its greater explanatory capacity.

REFERENCES

Caravale, G. (1982). 'Note sulla teoria ricardiana del valore, della distribuzione e dello sviluppo'. *Giornale degli Economisti*, 41, 141–83.

Caravale, G. and Tosato, D. (1974). *Un modello ricardiano di sviluppo economico.* Turin: Boringhieri.

Caravale, G. and Tosato, D. (1980). *Ricardo and the Theory of Value, Distribution and Growth.* London: Routledge & Kegan Paul.

Casarosa, C. (1974). 'La teoria ricardiana della distribuzione e dello sviluppo econo- mico'. *Rivista di Politica Economica*, 44, 959–1015.

Casarosa, C. (1976). 'Imposte e distribuzione del reddito nell'analisi ricardiana'. *Giornale degli Economisti*, 35, 171–200.

Casarosa, C. (1978). 'A New Formulation of the Ricardian System'. *Oxford Economic Papers*, 30, 38–63.

Costa, G. (1977). 'La convergenza allo stato stazionario di un'economia di tipo ricardiano'. In P. Sylos Labini and F. De Cindio (eds), *Saggi di economia in onore di Antonio Pesenti.* Milan: Giuffrè.

Hicks, J. (1979a). 'The Ricardian System: A Comment'. *Oxford Economic Papers*, 31, 133–4.

Hicks, J. (1979b). *Causality in Economics.* Oxford: Basil Blackwell.

Hicks, J. and Hollander, S. (1977). 'Mr Ricardo and the Moderns'. *Quarterly Journal of Economics*, 91, 351–69.

Hollander, S. (1979). *The Economics of David Ricardo.* London: Heinemann.

Johansen, L. (1969). 'A Classical Model of Economic Growth'. In C. H. Feinstein (ed.), *Socialism, Capitalism and Economic Growth, Essays in Honour of M. Dobb.* Cam- bridge: CUP, pp. 13–29.

Levy, D. (1976). 'Ricardo and the Iron Law: A Correction of the Record'. *History of Political Economy*, 8, 235–51.

Pasinetti, L. (1960). 'A Mathematical Formulation of the Ricardian System'. *Review of Economic Studies*, 27, 78–98.

Pasinetti, L. (1981). 'On the Ricardian Theory of Value: A Note'. *Review of Economic Studies*, 48, 673–5.

[11] It should be noticed that the role played by the dynamic equilibrium path is in this case exactly the same as the role played by the natural equilibrium path in Pasinetti's model.

Ricardo, D. (1815). 'An Essay on the Influence of a Low Price of Corn on the Profits of Stock'. In P. Sraffa (ed.), *The Works and Correspondence of David Ricardo*, vol. IV. Cambridge: CUP, 1951.

Ricardo, D. (1821). *On the Principles of Political Economy and Taxation*. In P. Sraffa (ed.), *The Works and Correspondence of David Ricardo*, vol. I. Cambridge: CUP, 1951.

Samuelson, P. (1978). 'The Canonical Classical Model of Political Economy'. *Journal of Economic Literature*, 16, 1415–34.

4

Time in Ricardian Models: Some Critical Observations and Some New Results

GIACOMO COSTA

1 INTRODUCTION

The initial motivation for writing this paper was a certain dissatisfaction with the following features of the *standard* versions of the Ricardian model.[1]

(1) *Circulating capital* The fact that, in Ricardian theory, production requires the use of capital is verbally but not formally recognized.[2] As a consequence, the relationship between the rate of profit and the rate of interest remains obscure, and so does the nature of the Ricardian 'profits'. Moreover, the failure to distinguish between wage goods ('corn') available at the beginning of the period and those that will become available at the end leads to a certain vagueness about the timing of transactions within the period. But it is precisely the peculiarity of the assumptions explicitly made with respect to the timing of transactions and settlements that accounts for some of the most striking differences between the classical and the neoclassical economists—and between properly built Ricardian and modern growth models.[3] Once the assumptions made or implied in the verbal accounts of Ricardo's period model of a capitalist economy with respect to the timing of production and transactions are spelled out, one is also in the position to evaluate the well-known Kaldor–Pasinetti claim that in Ricardian theory distribution is logically prior to value, and that it is based on a 'surplus principle' which is foreign and alternative to the 'marginal principle' of neoclassical theory (see Kaldor, 1956, p. 84; Pasinetti, 1960, p. 81).

(2) *The distinction between 'investment' and 'saving' decisions* It is easy to

---

[1] By 'standard version of the Ricardian model' I mean that first set out by Kaldor (1956), and then more fully developed by Pasinetti (1960). Pasinetti's formulation has been adopted to a very large extent in the very influential work by Blaug (1978) as well as by the more recent builders of Ricardian models. It is indeed surprising how little the more recent versions of the Ricardian model, such as those by Casarosa (1978, 1981) and by Caravale and Tosato (1980), have deviated from Pasinetti's, at least with respect to the points raised in the present paper.

[2] A partial exception is the paper by Hicks and Hollander (1977).

[3] On this, see the very interesting discussion by Malinvaud (1976), pp. 275–86.

see that in both the two-sector and the one-sector versions of the standard Ricardian model the market equilibrium rate of interest is an index of the scarcity of capital. (This will be shown in section 3 below.) For a large enough initial capital stock—given the size of the labour force—the market equilibrium rate of interest will be negative. There is nothing wrong with this possibility—a negative rate of interest may still represent the highest possible rate at which capitalists may be able to transform corn available at the beginning of the period into corn available at the end—but surely the model should provide for the existence of a lower bound to the market rate of interest, in the form of a physical rate of depreciation of corn. On the other hand, this rate of depreciation—the least rate of interest at which capitalists may be willing to lend or employ their corn for productive use—should be clearly distinguished from the level of the rate of interest, usually assumed to be non-negative (see for example Pasinetti, 1960, p. 87), at which the capitalists' propensity to save out of their interest income becomes zero. Not only are these two sets of decisions conceptually distinct, but it is implied in the time-structure of the Ricardian models that they are also carried out at different instants of the period—the former at the beginning, the latter at the end of it.

(3) *Existence proofs of market, natural, stationary equilibria* These are simply not provided in the literature, even if some authors claim that they have given proofs (see Pasinetti, 1960, pp. 92, 93–4; Casarosa, 1978, pp. 42–3). This is somewhat surprising, since one of the main problems discussed in the literature is that of the dynamic relationship between different sorts of equilibrium positions!

(4) *Different dynamic properties of the two- and one-sector models* The fact that existence problems have not been seriously studied may explain why it has not been noticed—indeed, the opposite has been maintained (by Pasinetti, 1960, p. 95)—that the two- and one-sector models have different dynamic properties.

(5) *Differential or difference equations?* Ricardian dynamics has been studied so far exclusively in terms of differential equations. Whether and under what conditions this is legitimate, given the explicit or implicit assumptions made about the nature and timing of production and transaction during the Ricardian period, is far from obvious. It is by now well known that 'going to the limit' may not be innocuous from an economic point of view.[4] What is surprising in the literature on Ricardian models is that, not even in the more up-to-date contributions (such as those by Caravale and Tosato, 1980, or Casarosa, 1981), is this problem recognized, let alone solved in a satisfactory manner.

[4] A point that was first brought up in the literature, in the context of growth models, by Kennedy (1968). Another striking example of this general circumstance is given with reference to the theory of the transaction demand for money by Hellwig (1975).

The purpose of this paper is to come to grips with these five groups of problems. In section 2 a new version of the two-sector Ricardian model is presented. It is as close to the standard formulations as possible, subject to the condition of satisfying the theoretical requirements discussed under headings (1) and (2) above. The exposition is fairly detailed, so that the section can also serve as a critical summary of the standard literature. In section 3 a proof of existence and uniqueness of market equilibrium is provided, and the possibility of under-investment of capital clearly identified. In section 4 it is shown that the stationary state is stable in the large for the two-sector market equilibrium Ricardian model—when this is formulated in terms of differential equations. In section 5 the standard one-sector model is introduced, and its dynamic properties compared with those of the two-sector model. The standard one-sector model may exhibit a tendency to a periodic over-accumulation of capital and fall in the rate of interest which the two-sector model does not have. An economic interpretation of this circumstance is provided in terms of a distinction between unproductive consumption and unproductive labour. A final curious finding reported in section 5 is that, if the landlords' consumption takes place, like the workers', at the beginning and not at the end of the period, then the dynamic difference between the two- and the one-sector model vanishes.

In section 6 the problem of the transition from the 'naturally' discrete to the continuous version of the Ricardian dynamic system is taken up. It is argued that this transition—if it is at all logically possible—implies an assumption to the effect that production is a steady flow which accumulates gradually during the period, and hence implies an implicit change in the description of the productive conditions assumed in the model. In section 7 there is a short discussion of the local stability properties of the stationary state for the discrete-time Ricardian systems.

Although some or all of this work may seem rather technical, it does afford some new perspectives from which to comment on several interesting problems of Ricardian interpretation. These are: the differences between Ricardian and neoclassical theories of value and distribution, the relevance of the concepts of natural and dynamic equilibria for the study of Ricardian dynamics and the 'anti-Keynesianism' of Ricardo. Some comments are also offered on the role of formal models in the study of economic thought.

2 THE TWO-SECTOR RICARDIAN MODEL

The Goods

These are: two produced commodities ('corn' and 'gold'), labour, and the services of lands of various degrees of fertility. Corn is produced by deploying workers on the lands, while gold is produced by labour alone. Somehow, gold vanishes from sight as soon as it is produced and is transferred to its buyers, so there never is any stock of it. In spite of its being often called 'money',[5] therefore, it is neither a store of value nor a means of payment. The stock of accumulated corn provides the real capital of the economy. If stored by its owners, corn wastes at a rate of δ (where, of course, $-1 < -\delta \leq 0$) per period.

The Social Classes

The capitalists own the capital stock, and no piece of land; the landlords own the lands and do not hold any corn. The workers own nothing. The entrepreneurs (who may be conceived as a sub-class of the capitalists[6]) rent the lands and hire the workers in order to produce the two commodities, corn and gold.

The Markets

There are markets for labour, for the services of land, for corn for immediate delivery, corn for future delivery and gold for future delivery. They are all held at the beginning of the period, and competition prevails in each of them. Therefore, rent on the lands of the marginal degree of fertility and net profits are zero.

Habits and Tastes

Capitalists consume and accumulate corn. Landlords are interested only in gold. Workers need corn to support themselves and their families. Entrepreneurs would like to make net profits, but their very eagerness prevents them from ever succeeding in doing so.

The Timing of Production and Transaction

Workers are hired at the beginning of the period, and work for the whole duration of it. The new corn and gold pop up all at once at the end of the period. Workers, however, need to be fed *during* the period. This is why they have to be paid at the beginning of it and also why the economy needs capital.[7] The capitalists' and landlords' consumption takes place at the end of the period.

---

[5] See Pasinetti (1960, pp. 82–3) and Casarosa (1978, p. 58).

[6] The analytical convenience of this distinction—a distinction between socio-economic roles which may be played by the same individuals—will become apparent in the sequel.

[7] On this point both Kaldor (1956, p. 85) and Pasinetti (1960, pp. 82–3) are as clear and explicit as can ever be desired.

Production Conditions in the Two Sectors

$$X_1 = f(N_1) \tag{1}$$

$$f(0) \geqq 0 \tag{1a}$$

$$\lim_{N_1 \to 0} f'(N_1) > (1+\bar{r})u \tag{1b}$$

$$f''(N_1) < 0 \tag{1c}$$

$$\lim_{N_1 \to \infty} f'(N_1) < (1+\bar{r})u \tag{1d}$$

$$X_2 = aN_2. \tag{2}$$

where

X_1 = output of corn per period;
N_1 = number of workers employed in the production of corn;
u = subsistence real-wage rate;
$\bar{r}$ = rate of interest at which the capitalists' saving propensity
    is zero: $\bar{r} \geqq 0$;
X_2 = output of gold per period;
N_2 = number of workers employed in the gold-producing sector.

Prices, the Rate of Interest, the Rates of Return

p_1^0 = price of corn for immediate delivery;
p_1^1 = price of corn for future (end of period) delivery;
p_2^1 = price of gold for future delivery;
w = wage rate.

(All these prices are expressed in an abstract unit of account.[8]) We then define

$$r \equiv (p_1^0/p_1^1 - 1) = \text{corn rate of interest.} \tag{3}$$

---

[8] For failing to distinguish between corn available at the beginning and corn available at the end of the period, and hence between our p_1^0 and p_1^1, Kaldor (1956, pp. 85–6) and Pasinetti (1960, pp. 82–4) translate their verbal account of a capitalistic economy into a model where production turns out to be simple rather than capitalistic; for workers are paid out of the period's production and not out of capital! Consider for example Pasinetti's equation (11) on p. 83: total profits π are expressed as the difference between the value of the social output net of rent, $p_1 X_1 + p_2 X_2 - p_1 R$, and the value of the wage bill, $p_1 W$, as if the quantities involved in this expression referred to goods available at the same instant! This equation, and others of the same type, occur in Blaug (1978, p. 104), Casarosa (1978, p. 58), Caravale and Tosato (1980, pp. 97–8, 103). The problem of the nature of these 'profits' is discussed in section 8 below.

Because of competition, commodity prices are equal to marginal production costs. Thus

$$p_1^1 = w/f'(N_1) \tag{4}$$

$$p_2^1 = w/a. \tag{5}$$

Notice that (4) and (5) embody, in some sense, the labour theory of value, for they imply that the ratio of the price of corn for future delivery to the price of gold for future delivery equals the ratio of the amount of labour necessary (on the marginal land) to produce a unit of corn to the amount of labour necessary to produce a unit of gold.

There is another, equivalent, way to express conditions (4) and (5). Let r_1 and r_2 denote the corn marginal rates of return of investing capital in the production of corn and gold, respectively. Then the following two equalities are definitional:

$$r_1 = \frac{f'(N_1)}{w/p_1^0} - 1 \tag{3'}$$

$$r_2 = \frac{p_2^1}{p_1^1} \frac{a}{w/p_1^0} - 1 \tag{3''}$$

while the conditions

$$r_1 = r \tag{4'}$$

$$r_2 = r \tag{5'}$$

are necessary if there is to be equilibrium in the spot market for corn. Of course, (4') and (5') ensure also that there is no incentive to 'move capital' from one sector to the other. Given the definitional equalities (3), (3') and (3''), it is easy to see that (4) and (5) imply (4') and (5'), and conversely. Notice also that, using (3), (4) and (5) can be written

$$\frac{w}{p_1^0} = \frac{f'(N_1)}{1+r} \tag{4''}$$

$$\frac{(p_2^1/p_1^1)a}{1+r}. \tag{5''}$$

In words, the real wage expressed in spot corn must be equal to the *discounted* marginal product of labour in corn production and to the discounted value in terms of future corn of the marginal product of labour in gold production.

Rent and the Demand for Gold

The Ricardian theory of rent can be expressed by the equation

$$R = f(N_1) - N_1 f'(N_1) \tag{6}$$

where R = rent in terms of corn for future delivery; while the landlords' budget constraint is

$$p_1^1 R = p_2^1 X_2^d \tag{7}$$

where X_2^d = demand for gold for future delivery.

The Behaviour of Capitalists

The capitalists' aim is to transform their initial stock of corn, H, into the largest possible corn stock at the end of the period. They may achieve this by selling their corn spot to, and buying it forward from, the entrepreneurs (i.e., by lending their capital to the entrepreneurs), provided the rate of interest implicitly defined by these transactions is not below $-\delta$. The capitalists' desired rate of saving is assumed to be an increasing function of the rate of interest only. We let

H = initial capital stock;
K = the amount of capital 'invested' in the production process, i.e. lent by the capitalists to the entrepreneurs;
s = the capitalists' desired rate of saving.

With this notation, the above assumptions[9] on the capitalists' behaviour may be expressed as follows:

---

[9] In the standard formulation of the Ricardian one- and two-sector models, no distinction is made between initial capital (our H) and capital employed in production, K. In these models it may happen, as was shown in section 3 of the text, that the market equilibrium rate of interest, r^*, is below the rate of interest at which savings is zero, $\bar{r}$. There is really nothing strange in this circumstance, but for some reason Casarosa (1981, pp. 226–30) feels that it has to be prevented. In order to do so, he proposes to modify *the saving equation* (9) as follows: 'If the observance of these rules [i.e., if saving behaviour according to (9)] implied the "advance" of an amount of capital higher than the maximum amount the entrepreneurs are willing to invest at the new level of employment, they will advance just the maximum amount and consume the rest.'

But how can savings decisions, in the context of the standard one-sector Ricardian model (which is Casarosa's own chosen context), ever 'imply' anything with respect to the amount of capital 'advanced' by the entrepreneurs? They might, if (1) the capitalists' consumption were carried out at the beginning of the period, i.e. if it were 'out of capital'; and (2) r^* depended on some parameter of the saving function (9); *and* (3) K, as distinct from H, depended on r. None of these conditions holds in the standard Ricardian models. It may well be, of course, that there is a specification of the saving function (9) such that, if it assumed that the capitalists' consumption, like the workers', takes place at the *beginning* of the period, it affords the conclusion that $r^* \geqq \bar{r}$. But this is not what Casarosa is saying in the above quotation.

If, for $K = H$, $r \geqq -\delta$,   then $K = H$.   (8a)

If, for $K = H$, $r < -\delta$,   then K is such that $r = -\delta$.   (8b)

$$\Delta H = s(r) \cdot H$$ (9)

where the function s is thus characterized:

$s(r) \leqq r$ for all r.   (9a)

$s'(r) > 0$.   (9b)

$s(r) = 0$ for $r = \bar{r}$,   (9c)

where $\bar{r}$ is some non-negative real number. In the special case $s(r) \equiv r$, we get the simple accumulation rule

$$\Delta H = rH$$ (9′)

which is often adopted in the literature (see for example Pasinetti, 1960, p. 87, equation (18), and Caravale and Tosato, 1980, pp. 98, 107).

The Market Equilibrium Conditions

We need only consider explicitly the labour market:

$$N_1 + N_2 = N$$ (10)

where N = total number of workers at the beginning of the period; the gold market:[10]

$$X_2^d = X_2$$ (11)

and the spot corn market:

$$p_1^0 K = w(N_1 + N_2).$$ (12)

The description of the market equilibrium two-sector model is thus completed.

---

[10] Casarosa (1978, pp. 53–6) gives convincing evidence that according to Ricardo the capitalists' consumption demand is also mainly for luxuries. In the text, we adhere to the simpler assumption that only the landlords consume gold not to depart from the *standard* formulation of the Ricardian model. With the more accurate assumption suggested by Casarosa, the system would become more interdependent. But, as will be pointed out in section 8, the system is to some degree interdependent anyway.

The Concepts of Natural and Stationary Equilibrium

In the market equilibrium model, H and N represent given initial conditions, the size of the stock of capital and the size of the working population, respectively, inherited from the past. If we add the condition

$$w/p_1^0 = u \tag{13}$$

we must be willing to re-classify either H or N from the exogenous to the endogenous variables of the system. With these alterations, the market equilibrium has been specialized to a *natural* equilibrium, i.e., to a special type of market equilibrium where the values taken up by H and N are so adjusted to each other that the market real wage equals the natural real wage. The importance of this type of position lies in the fact that, according to the Malthusian population law assumed by Ricardo, namely

$$\Delta N/N = g(w/p_1^0) \tag{14}$$

with

$$g' > 0 \tag{14a}$$

and

$$g(u) = 0, \tag{14b}$$

then, once the economy has reached such a position, the labour force will not change over time.

Let us now consider a market equilibrium position where H and N are such as to satisfy the condition

$$r = \bar{r} \tag{15}$$

in addition to (13). According to (9c) and (14b), (13) and (15) imply that both the population and capital are in fact stationary, i.e. are invariant with respect to time. This is then the concept of *stationary* equilibrium.

3 EXISTENCE AND UNIQUENESS OF MARKET EQUILIBRIUM

From equations (4), (5), (6), (7), (10) and (11), we get

$$N = \frac{f(N_1)}{f'(N_1)} \equiv n(N_1). \tag{16}$$

By an easy but rather tedious argument (given in the appendix), it can be shown that the inverse of the function $N = n(N_1)$, which we shall call $N_1 = n_1(N)$, is characterized as follows.

(i) The function $N_1 = n_1(N)$ is defined and continuous for all non-negative values of N, and $n_1(0) = 0$.

(ii) Its derivative exists for all positive N, and $dn_1/dN < 1$, $\lim_{N \to 0}(dn_1/dN) = 1$.

(iii) If

$$\lim_{N_1 \to \infty} f'(N_1) \geq 0, \quad \text{then} \lim_{N \to \infty} n_1(N) = \infty.$$

If instead there is a (necessarily unique) N_1^0 such that $f'(N_1^0) = 0$, then

$$\lim_{N \to \infty} n_1(N) = N_1^0.$$

(iv) For each positive N, $0 < n_1(N) < N$.

Thus, the existence and uniqueness of a positive value of N_1, N_1^* that solves (16) for any given value of N is guaranteed. But this implies that the market equilibrium values of N_2, R, X_1, X_2, and p_1^1/p_2^1 are also unique and positive. For example, for the market equilibrium value of R, R^*, we have from (6), and the fact that N_1^* is the unique positive solution to (16),

$$R^* = f(N_1^*) - N_1^* f'(N_1^*) = Nf'(N_1^*) - N_1^* f'(N_1^*) > 0.$$

As to the market equilibrium rate of interest, from equations (3), (4), (10), (12) and (16), we get

$$r = \frac{N}{K} \cdot f'\{n_1(N)\} - 1 = \frac{1}{K} \cdot f\{n_1(N)\} - 1. \tag{17}$$

It is easy to see that the function on the right-hand side of (17) is increasing with N, decreasing with K. In this sense, then, the market equilibrium rate of interest is an index of capital scarcity.

For, given N, equation (17) shows that r is a function of K only. Set $K = H$ in it: if the corresponding value of r is no less than $-\delta$, then by (8a) we have $K^* = H$ and $r^* = (1/H)f\{n_1(N)\}$ in market equilibrium; if not, then the market equilibrium value of K, K^* is determined by the equation

$$-\delta = \frac{1}{K} \cdot f\{n_1(N)\} - 1. \tag{18}$$

Since $\delta < 1$, and the first term on the right hand side of equation (18) is a monotonically decreasing function of K, ranging between 0 and $+\infty$ as K varies between $+\infty$ and 0, there is a unique positive solution to this equation, and $K^* < H$. Once the equilibrium value of K is known, then the equilibrium value of the last remaining variable, the market real-wage rate w/p_1^0, can also be found from equations (10) and (12).

4 EXISTENCE, UNIQUENESS AND STABILITY OF THE STATIONARY STATE FOR THE TWO-SECTOR MODEL IN CONTINUOUS TIME

If to the accumulation equation

$$\dot{H} = s(r) \cdot H \tag{19}$$

(the continuous-time version of (9)) we add the equation

$$\dot{N} = g(w/p_1^0) \cdot N \tag{20}$$

(the continuous-time version of (14)), we obtain a system of two differential equations which describes the evolution of the Ricardian two-sector market equilibrium model over time. We study the existence, uniqueness and stability of the stationary state by drawing the phase diagram of system (19)–(20) with respect to a (N, H) pair of axes (see figure 1).

The locus $\dot{N} = 0$ is simply the straight line $K = uN$. The locus $\dot{H} = 0 = \dot{K}$ is the graph of the function implicitly defined by the condition

$$r = \frac{1}{K} f\{n_1(N)\} - 1 = \bar{r} \tag{21}$$

while the locus $r = -\delta$ is given by

$$-\delta = \frac{1}{K} f\{n_1(N)\} - 1. \tag{22}$$

From (21) and (22) we get

$$K = \frac{1}{1 + \bar{r}} \cdot f\{n_1(N)\} \equiv k(N) \tag{21'}$$

and, respectively,

$$K = \frac{1}{1 - \delta} \cdot f\{n_1(N)\} = \frac{1 + \bar{r}}{1 - \delta} \cdot k(N). \tag{22'}$$

We note that, since $df\{n_1(N)\}/dN = f'(N) \cdot n_1'(N) > 0$, the functions (21') and (22′) are increasing, while since by (ii)

$$\lim_{N \to 0} \{df(n_1(N))/dN\} = \lim_{N_1 \to 0} f'(N_1),$$

by equation (1b) we have

$$\lim_{N \to 0} \frac{dk(N)}{dN} > u.$$

The stationary-state population, N_s, can be found by setting $K = uN$ in equation (21′). We then have

$$uN = \frac{1}{1+\bar{r}} f\{n_1(N)\} \equiv \frac{1}{1+\bar{r}} N \cdot f'\{n_1(N)\}$$

an equation with the trivial solution $N = 0$. If there is another solution, this will have to satisfy the equation

$$(1+\bar{r})u = f'\{n_1(N)\}.$$

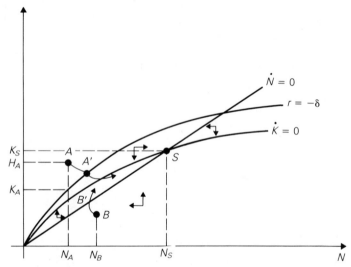

FIGURE 1 At point B, $r > \bar{r}$ and $w/p_1^0 < u$, so that for a while population decreases. Once the system reaches point B', where the market real wage equals the subsistence real wage, the real wage goes on increasing, and stays above u along the path to S. Paths starting from points above the locus $r = \delta$, such as point A, undergo a change of regime. During the first phase—from A to A'—not all capital is advanced, and the existing capital decreases at the rate δ; i.e., $\dot{H}/H = -\delta$. Once a point of the locus $r = -\delta$ is reached, then all capital is advanced, and capital accumulation is again ruled by equation (19).

By assumption (1b), $f'\{n_1(N)\} > (1+r)u$ for N small enough. Moreover, $f'\{n_1(N)\}$ is decreasing and by assumption (1d) it is smaller than $(1+r)u$ for large enough N. Therefore a positive solution exists and is unique. The phase diagram is largely self-explanatory. The main fact, of course, is that the stationary state is basically stable, and that, if initially the market real-wage rate is above u, it stays above u along the whole of its path to the stationary state.

5 TWO ONE-SECTOR RICARDIAN MODELS, AND THEIR DYNAMIC PROPERTIES

There is a one-sector model nested in the two-sector model. By (a) suppressing equations (2), (5), (7) and (11) and the variables X_2, N_2, p_2^1, r_2, X_2^d; (b) letting X_1^{1d} denote the landlords' demand for corn (there is now nothing else they can consume); and (c) modifying their budget constraint accordingly,

$$R = X_1^{1d}, \tag{7'}$$

we arrive at the standard one-sector Ricardian model discussed in the literature. In the context of this model, it is easy to see that

$$r = \frac{N}{K} f'(N) - 1 \tag{23}$$

a relation that should be compared to (17). The changes in the structure of the phase diagram when (23) is substituted to (17) are not insignificant, since the locus $\dot{K} = 0$ no longer needs to be an increasing function of N. In this section, however, we will carry out a comparison between the local stability properties of the stationary state for the standard two- and one-sector models.

We proceed in the usual way, by considering the linearized version of the dynamic system (19)–(20), where the approximation is taken at the stationary state. The characteristic equation turns out to be

$$\begin{vmatrix} -s'(1+\bar{r})-\lambda & s'u(1+\bar{r})n_1' \\ g' & -g'u-\lambda \end{vmatrix} = 0 \tag{24}$$

where of course s', g', and n_1' stand for $s'(\bar{r})$, $g'(u)$ and $n_1'(N_s)$, respectively. The characteristic roots are

$$\left.\begin{array}{c} \lambda_1 \\ \lambda_2 \end{array}\right\} = \tfrac{1}{2}[-\{s'(1+\bar{r})+g'u\} \mp \sqrt{d_2}] \tag{25}$$

where

$$d_2 = \{s'(1+\bar{r})+g'u\}^2 - 4s'(1+\bar{r})ug'(1-n'_1).$$

It then follows at once from property (ii) of the function $n_1(N)$, given in section 3, that

$$\{s'(1+\bar{r})-g'u\}^2 < d_2 < \{s'(1+\bar{r})+g'u\}^2.$$

The characteristic roots are therefore real and negative. In the standard one-sector model, the only difference is that in (24) the term $s'u(1+\bar{r})n'_1$ is replaced by $s'u(1+\bar{r})+N_s f''(N_s)$. Accordingly, in (25) the term d_1 is substituted for d_2, where

$$d_1 = \{s'(1+\bar{r})+g'u\}^2 + 4s'g'N_s f''(N_s) < \{s'(1+\bar{r})+g'u\}^2.$$

Contrary to d_2, d_1 need not be positive. The real part of the roots is still negative, but they are not necessarily real. Let us consider the following example: $s(r) \equiv r$, so that $\bar{r} = 0$; $f(N) = -(1/2)aN^2 + 4aN + c$, so that $f'(N) = -aN + 4a$, $f''(N) = -a$. Let us also choose units so that $u = 1$. We then find $N_s = K_s = (4a-1)/a$, and

$$d_1 = (1+g')^2 - 4g'(4a-1). \tag{26}$$

And clearly in (26) d_1 can be made negative by choosing a large enough value for the parameter a.

One might perhaps express the difference in the structure of the two models by saying that, while in both of them there is unproductive consumption, only in the two-sector model is there unproductive *labour*. And one would then be able to conclude that what saves the system from periodic falls in r below $\bar{r}$ is the presence of unproductive labour. If the above line of reasoning is correct, however, a redistribution of an increasing labour force in favour of the gold sector should be only *one* way to put a parachute on r: instead of slowing down the fall in $f'(N_1)$, one might think of a way to speed up the fall in w/p_1^0. Could this not happen if the landlords spent their rents in the spot rather than in the future market for corn—if the rents, like the wages, were paid 'out of capital' rather than 'out of product'?

Let X_1^{0d} be the landlords' demand for spot corn. Their budget constraint takes now the form

$$p_1^1 R = p_1^0 X_1^{0d} \tag{7''}$$

and we can verify our conjecture by considering this new one-sector model. It is easy to see that, when (7″) is substituted for (7′),

$$r = \frac{f(N)}{K} - 1$$

so that the $\dot{K} = 0$ locus is increasing with N. For this new one-sector model the stationary state has the same stability properties as for the two-sector model.

6 SOME PERPLEXITIES ON CONTINUOUS-TIME RICARDIAN MODELS

The accumulation relations we have been using so far have been differential equations—even if, in the exposition of the market equilibrium model, much has been made of the discreteness of the production period. For simplicity, we will consider the very simple accumulation equation (9′), which, using (17), can be written as

$$K(t+1) - K(t) = f[n_1\{N(t)\}] - K(t). \tag{9″}$$

We want to consider how a differential equation of the form

$$\dot{K}(t) = f[n_1\{N(t)\}] - K(t) \tag{9‴}$$

may be derived from (9″). (This question is apparently regarded so trivial in the literature that it is never raised.) A possible line of argument might be as follows. Let the period of production start at time t, with initial capital $K(t)$. How much capital will society have at an intermediate moment $(t+h)$, with $0 < h < 1$, of the production period? At time $(t+h)$ the workers will have consumed a fraction h of the initial capital stock, $K(t)$. On the other hand, if the production $f\{n_1(N)\}$ per unit period is an even, steady flow, such that at time $(t+h)$ there·already is an accumulated stock of it, $h \cdot f\{n_1(N)\}$, then it will be true that

$$K(t+h) - K(t) = h \cdot f[n_1\{N(t)\}] - hK(t)$$

from which, by letting $h \to 0$, one reaches (9‴).

If this is the justification that can be given for replacing (9″) with (9‴), then, quite apart from its doubtful mathematical validity, it appears to imply an assumption as to the time-profile of the output flow during the period, which is completely at variance with the 'point-output' nature of corn and even of gold production that is verbally emphasized by all writers on the Ricardian system. If under this assumption circulating capital is still needed, this can only be due to the fact that, while there is really no production period, there still is assumed to be a *market* period. Capital then would appear to be needed not because 'production takes time' but because wages are paid at discretely spaced instants rather than continuously.

7 LOCAL STABILITY PROPERTIES OF THE STATIONARY STATE IN DISCRETE RICARDIAN MODELS

It may be that the doubts expressed in the previous section are unfounded. Even if they were, it would still be of some interest to report a few results concerning the dynamic properties of the 'natural', difference equation, versions of our models. If we start from the system of equations (9) and (14), linearize it at the stationary solution, and let μ_1, μ_2, be the roots of *its* characteristic equation, we find $\mu_i = 1 + \lambda_i$, i = 1, 2. Since, as was seen in section 5, λ_1 and λ_2 are real and negative, λ_1 and λ_2 are certainly real and bounded above by $+1$. A necessary and sufficient condition for stability is then that $-1 < \mu_1$, or $-2 < \lambda_1$. It is easy to produce a simple numerical example where this condition does not hold. Even if it does hold, μ_1 (or both μ_1 and μ_2) may ne negative, so that even if stable the two-sector discrete model may exhibit alternations.

Let us consider the following example: $s(r) \equiv r$ (which implies $\bar{r} = 0$); $u = 1$ by appropriate choice of physical units; $X_1 = f(N_1) = \sqrt{N_1}$. It is easy to check that in this case $N_1 = n_1(N) \equiv \frac{1}{2}N$. We then find

$$\left.\begin{array}{r}\lambda_1\\\lambda_2\end{array}\right\} = \tfrac{1}{2}\{-(1+g')\mp\sqrt{d_2}\}$$

where

$$d_2 = (1+g')^2 - 4g'(1-\tfrac{1}{2}) = 1+(g')^2$$

and hence

$$(1-g')^2 < d_2 < (1+g')^2.$$

From these relations one can see that

$$\lambda_1 < \tfrac{1}{2}\{-(1+g')-(1-g')\} = -1$$

$$\lambda_1 < -2 \quad \text{if} \quad g' \geqq \sqrt{3}.$$

Thus in our example, provided the population mechanism reacts to a discrepancy between market and natural real wage sufficiently fast, there will be instability. Even in the more normal case in which there is stability, the system alternates (because $\lambda_1 < -1$).

The one-sector discrete model inherits from its continuous analogue the latter's oscillatory tendency: if λ_1, λ_2 are complex, so will be μ_1, μ_2. The stability condition is now $|\mu_1| < 1$, and by taking up again the example already introduced in section 5, we can easily show that it may be violated. We have

$$\left.\begin{matrix} \mu_1 \\ \mu_2 \end{matrix}\right\} = 1 + \left\{\begin{matrix} \lambda_1 \\ \lambda_2 \end{matrix}\right\} = 1 + \tfrac{1}{2}\{-(1+g')\mp\sqrt{d_1}\} = \tfrac{1}{2}\{(1-g')\mp\sqrt{d_1}\}$$

where d_1 is given in (26).

We are interested in the case where $d_1 < 0$. We have then

$$|\mu_1| = |\mu_2| = \tfrac{1}{4}\{(1-g')^2 - d_1\} = \tfrac{1}{4}\{(1-g')^2 - (1+g')^2 + 4g'(4a-1)\}$$
$$= \tfrac{1}{4}\{-4g' + 4g'(4a-1)\} = 2g'(4a-1)$$

an expression which is necessarily larger than 1 if $d_1 < 0$.

We can summarize these findings thus. The difference in the dynamic properties of the standard two- and one-sector model carries over from the continuous to the discrete version. The two-sector discrete system is likely to be stable (unless population growth is much faster than capital accumulation) but may exhibit alternations. The one-sector model may oscillate, and if it does these oscillations may be explosive rather than dampened. (Farther away from the stationary state there is likely to be a limit-cycle.)

8 RICARDIAN MODELS AND RICARDO'S THOUGHT: SOME COMMENTS ON ALTERNATIVE INTERPRETATIONS AND RECONSTRUCTIONS

Against the background of the formal work carried out in the preceding sections, we can now proceed to comment on some of the interpretations of and contentions on Ricardo's theory at present outstanding.

Value and Distribution

Let us first of all consider the following summary statement of the well-known Kaldor–Pasinetti rendition of Ricardo's theory of value and distribution, a summary exclusively made up of quotations from their articles. (It should be kept in mind that *both* authors are referring to the two-sector natural equilibrium system.)

(1) Ricardo's theory was based on two separate principles, which we may term the 'marginal principle' and the 'surplus principle'.... The 'marginal principle' serves to explain the share of rent, and the 'surplus principle' the division of the residue between wages and profits. (Kaldor, 1956, p. 84)

(2) Rent...is determined by technical factors. (Pasinetti, 1960, p. 80)

(3) The marginal product of labour...is not...equal to the wage, but to the sum of wages and profits. The rate of wages is determined quite independently of marginal productivity by the supply price of labour which Ricardo assumed to be constant in terms of corn. (Kaldor, 1956, p. 84)

(4) Profits...represent a residual. Rent being determined by the produce of the marginal land put into cultivation, and the wage rate by non-economic factors, what remains of the total production is retained, under the form of profit, by the capitalists, who are the organizers of the process of production. (Pasinetti, 1960, p. 81)

(5) The Ricardian model...contains a theory of value which is completely... independent of distribution. (Pasinetti, 1960, p. 84–5)

What, then, is Kaldor's 'surplus principle' or 'surplus theory'? Since no independent definition or explanation is given by him of these terms, it would appear that the economic content of this 'principle' is to be found in the following two properties which both Kaldor (in (3)) and Pasinetti (in (4)) attribute to Ricardian theory:

(a) The validity of the 'marginal principle' is suspended as far as the distribution of income between wages and profits is concerned; for this 'principle' would require the equality of the marginal product of labour to the real wage, and this equality is not observed in the Ricardian model.

(b) On the other hand, given the conditions determining rent and the real wage, no new condition is needed to determine profits; for they are simply 'what is left' to the entrepreneurs once the rent and the wages have been paid out to the landlords and the workers, respectively.

Now, the question that (b) immediately prompts is: why should 'what is left' be appropriated by the entrepreneurs? It might appear that an answer is provided by Pasinetti in (4): it is appropriated by them because they are 'the organizers of the process of production'. But this will not do. Either the Ricardian economy needs capital—in which case the so-called 'profits' are claimed in their entirety by the owners of capital as interest, and what Kaldor and Pasinetti call payment of wages is in fact repayment of capital—or it does not. But if, contrary to all explicit verbal stipulations made by Kaldor and

Pasinetti,[11] it does not—i.e. if workers *can* be paid 'out of product'—then the 'organizers of the process of production' won't be able to 'retain' anything, even if they formed a monopoly; for why then should any worker accept a real wage w/p_1^1 smaller than $f'(N_1)$?

The workers could of course *be forced* to work for less than $f'(N_1)$ by some sort of institutionalized coercion: but this sort of slave or feudal economy is not the one described by Ricardo, where social relationships take place through markets! In this connection it can also be noticed that the statement in (4) above, that 'the wage rate is determined by non-economic factors', is also in danger of conjuring up the image of a feudal economy. In actual fact, what in the Ricardian theory is 'determined by non-economic factors' is the *natural* or subsistence real wage, u, not the market real wage, w/p_1^0. Whether the latter (a variable) equals the former (a constant) or not depends on H, K and N, the determinants of the latter.

If then part (b) of the 'surplus principle' consists of the proposition that in Ricardian theory the 'organizers of the process of production' are allowed by the structure of the economy to retain *net* profits, it appears to be untenable, both in the case of a capitalistic economy (because then the 'residual' is totally absorbed by the actual or imputed contractual payment, interest) and in the case where the workers, like the landlords, can 'wait' (because then the competition among the entrepreneurs will bid the real wage up to $f(N_1)$; and, even if there were no competition among them, $f(N_1)$ would clearly be the 'reservation real supply price' of labour). As to part (a) of the 'surplus principle', it appears to be based on a misunderstanding of what the 'marginal principle' implies when it is applied to a *lagged* production process: the equality of the real wage not to the marginal product of labour, but to the discounted marginal product of labour.[12] Indeed, Kaldor's statement, in (3) above, that 'the marginal product of labour...is...equal...to the sum of wages and profits', far from being incompatible with the 'marginal principle', is an obvious consequence of that form of it, which is relevant to the 'point-input, point-output' nature of the production process assumed by Ricardo.

As to Pasinetti's claim, in (5) above, that distribution is logically prior to valuation, this is also plainly false, even leaving aside the fact that, in an economy where production takes time, the determination of the value of future product in terms of present product, $p_1^1/p_1^0 \equiv 1/(1+r)$, is itself a crucial part of the valuation problem. The basic fact here is that, contrary to what

---

[11] But in complete agreement with Pasinetti's algebraic expression for π, 'profits'. See also note 8 above.

[12] See equations (4″) and (5″) above. As was shown in section 2 of the text, an alternative way to formulate the 'marginal principle' is to require that the marginal rate of return be equal to the rate of interest in both sectors of the economy. See also Hicks and Hollander (1977, p. 356), where the condition is formally laid down that the real wage rate be equal to 'the *discounted* marginal product of labour'.

Pasinetti in (2) might perhaps suggest, rent is not determined if N_1 is not known. And in order to find N_1 one needs to know N_2, while in order to find N_2 one needs to know p_1^1/p_2^1 and R .... This is, of course, no 'circular indeterminacy', but merely a verbal illustration of the fact that there is a core of interdependent equations in the standard two-sector Ricardian model, made-up equations (4), (5), (6), (7), (10) and (11).

Distribution and Growth

Can the Ricardian growth process be described by a sequence of natural rather than market equilibria? There are two aspects to this question, which had better be kept separate. The first is: do the various relevant passages from Ricardo that can be (and have been[13]) amassed warrant the above proposition, or the similar one (Pasinetti, 1960, p. 88) that Ricardo 'concentrates on describing the changing characteristics of his system in terms of *natural* behaviour of the variables in a process of capital accumulation'? The second is: what are the mathematical properties of the growth models that we can agree to consider Ricardian?

On the first question, it seems to me that Kaldor and Pasinetti are perhaps less categorical in answering in the positive than the proponents of the 'New View' have made them out to be. Notice however that, if the answer is in the negative, as, given the evidence, it appears that it is bound to be, then this should imply a shift in emphasis from natural to market equilibrium in the presentation of the Ricardian theory of value and distribution: the focus should be, as it has been in this paper, on the *market* equilibrium position.

On the second question, one of the basic facts a model-builder will recognize (although Kaldor, 1956, pp. 85–6, apparently did not) is that, if 'the rate of population growth itself is adapted to a certain rate of capital accumulation which has been going on for some time' while the market real wage remains at its natural level, then this process of demographic growth cannot be Malthusian. This recognition is the departure point of both Caravale–Tosato (1974, 1980), who give up the Malthusian law, and Casarosa (1978), who keeps the Malthusian mechanism and has a market real wage sufficiently higher than the natural real wage to maintain the rate of population growth equal to a certain (positive) rate of capital accumulation. A market equilibrium that also satisfies the additional condition of equality between the rate of capital accumulation and the rate of population growth is called by Casarosa 'dynamic equilibrium', and he argues that a sequence of market equilibria would converge to a dynamic equilibrium if $f'(N_1)$ were constant. He also points out that, according to Ricardo, $f'(N_1)$, although a decreasing function of N_1, is not a continuous but rather a step function, and

---

[13] By Casarosa (1978, 1981), and by Hicks and Hollander (1977).

he appears to maintain that the notion of dynamic equilibrium may still retain its importance as an 'attractor' of market equilibria if 'the steps are sufficiently long', an assumption whose precise mathematical meaning is not further elucidated and about which Casarosa himself in a later article (Casarosa, 1981) appears to be doubtful.

Why not then pursue the study of the combined action of capital accumulation and population growth without prejudicing the issue of the nature of the trajectories generated by the dynamic model thus obtained? This type of study, begun by Pasinetti (1960) in the mathematical appendix of his article, has been carried by Trezza (1969), Costa (1977) and Hicks and Hollander (1977). Pasinetti himself argued that there are no differences in the dynamic properties of the one- and two-sector models, and he concentrated on the one-sector model. The later papers have all been concerned with the standard one-sector model. Costa (1977) shows that the stationary state is stable in the large, but that there may be oscillations around it. In order to prove this stability property, a crucial step is the ruling out of the possibility of limit-cycles round the stationary state. It is here that Hicks and Hollander fail to produce a convincing argument.[14]

However, it has been shown above that the two-sector market equilibrium model behaves differently: a sequence of market equilibria starting off from an arbitrary initial position converges monotonically to the stationary state. The same is true of the trajectories generated not by the standard one-sector model, but by that variant of the one-sector model in which rent is paid out of capital (as Wicksell and Schumpeter, for example, would have it) and not out of product.

Notice that all the work surveyed above has been carried out in terms of differential equations. Whether, and under what assumption, this is feasible, given the crucial production lag built in the Ricardian model (or rather, that should be built in it), is a question that has been raised for the first time in this paper.

Effective Demand in Ricardian Theory

Did Ricardo have to 'assume that all incomes are spent (Say's law)' (Pasinetti, 1960, p. 84)? Was he 'unable to grasp the importance of effective demand'

---

[14] In the crucial n. 7 on p. 359 of their article, Hicks and Hollander recognize the possibility that 'the path might converge, asymptotically, to a fixed circuit around E [the stationary state point] never actually reaching E.' They think that it can be 'ruled out', since, 'if there were such a circuit, there would be a "forbidden zone" around E, which the path could not enter'. But this is impossible, they argue, for 'though E is a "singular point" of the path', at which the slope of the path is not defined, 'it is clear that at any point indefinitely near E the slope is determinate and is *real*, in the mathematical sense.' But of course, the fact that the slope of the path is well defined near the critical point E is an indication of the existence of trajectories *inside* the 'closed circuit': in no way does it help to 'rule out' the existence of the circuit itself.

(Pasinetti, 1974, p. 29)? These propositions might be taken to mean that Ricardo failed to take into account in his theory some factor which could be easily fitted in once its importance was recognized. But if 'Say's law' is taken to mean that 'all incomes are spent *in produced goods*', then it is no new and independent assumption, but an implication of the (other) assumptions upon which the model is built. So it would appear that the proper question to ask should be: is there any room in a model on whose Ricardian features we can agree, for those possibilities that we would now describe as 'effective demand failures'?

Most people would feel inclined to answer that, to the extent to which the standard Ricardian models are basically non-monetary, there can be no effective demand deficiencies in them. But, as has been shown in sections 2 and 3 above, a careful analysis of the market equilibrium shows that, if 'Say's law' is taken to imply that 'all capital is invested *in the production process*', then it does not necessarily hold in the Ricardian model: for if capital is very abundant relative to labour, so that the rate of interest is lower than $-\delta$, the capitalists will find it convenient to store some of their corn. So the suggestion advanced by Hicks (1965, pp. 40–2) that the classical economists failed to identify the problem of effective demand because they were working with a single-capital good model, is perhaps of the mark. Even if there is only one store of value available, different uses can be made of it!

According to some authors (see for example Corry, 1959), the famous Ricardo–Malthus controversy was really not about 'effective demand', in our modern sense, but about the possibility that an excessive accumulation of capital might lead to a progressive fall in the rate of interest. This is indeed what can happen in the standard one-sector model, but not, as was shown in sections 4 and 5 above, in the two-sector model. We can interpret this result, and the similar one obtained in section 5, by saying that it is not unproductive consumption *per se* that puts a floor on the rate of profit, but either an unproductive consumption that reflects itself in unproductive labour or an unproductive consumption that is a direct subtraction from the wage fund.

Model-building in the Interpretation of Ricardo

We can agree with Blaug (this volume, pp. 3–10) that it may be pointless to try to impose on Ricardo our modern concern with rigour and consistency. This does not, of course, mean that *we* can afford not to be rigorous and consistent when speaking about him. Blaug himself is able to give examples of Ricardian propositions that cannot be covered by '*any*...formulation of Ricardo's system' only on the strength of his knowledge of the truth about the various logical relations involved. As I see it, the purpose of model-building should be not to encapsulate Ricardo in a single hard-and-fast formal construction, but rather to develop a sort of logical grammar in terms of which to describe and clarify whatever aspect of his theoretical writings is being discussed. That there was a need for such a conceptual tool is what explains the success of Pasinetti's article, even among people who did not—and do not—agree with his substantive theses on Ricardo, 'marginalism', 'causality', etc. The basic elements of this grammar are very likely to remain the concepts of market, natural and stationary equilibria and the dynamic relationships between them. (In this respect, the present paper is a direct continuation of Pasinetti's.)

On the other hand, the type of formal knowledge achieved through building and analysing models should not be regarded as equivalent to an interpretation. For the purpose of interpretation, all the tools of historical and economic scholarship are required.

APPENDIX

In this appendix the properties (i)–(iv) of the function $N_1 = n_1(N)$, listed in section 3 above, are established.

From (16), which for convenience we rewrite here as

$$N = f(N_1)/f'(N_1) \equiv n(N_1),$$
(A1)

it is easy to see that $n(N_1)$, where defined, is an increasing function of N_1. Indeed,

$$\frac{dn}{dN_1} = \frac{1}{(f')^2}\{(f')^2 - ff''\} > 1.$$
(A2)

It follows that the inverse function, $N_1 = n_1(N)$, exists and that

$$0 < \frac{dn_1}{dN} = \frac{1}{dn/dN_1} < 1.$$
(A3)

We now want to identify the domain and range of n (range and domain of n_1). For $N_1 = 0$, one of the following three situations may occur:

(a) $f(0) = 0$, and

$$\lim_{N_1 \to 0} f'(N_1) = f'(0) = \bar{f}' < +\infty.$$

Here then the function n is well defined at $N_1 = 0$, and we have $n(0) = 0$, $n_1(0) = 0$.

(b) $f(0) \geq 0$, and $\lim_{N_1 \to 0} f'(N_1) = +\infty$. (A function that gives rise to this situation is $X_1 = \sqrt{N_1}$). Here n is not defined at $N_1 = 0$. However, since

Giacomo Costa

$\lim_{N_1 \to 0} n(N_1) = 0$ we can *set* $n(0) = 0$, thus maintaining the continuity of the function at 0. We then have, again, $n_1(0) = 0$.

(c) $f(0) = \bar{f} > 0$, and

$$\lim_{N_1 \to 0} f'(N_1) = \bar{f}' < +\infty.$$

Here $n(0) = \bar{f}/\bar{f}'$, so the function $N_1 = n_1(N)$ is defined only for $N \geq \bar{f}/\bar{f}'$, and $n_1(f/f') = 0$.

Does the domain of n (range of n_1) have an upper bound? There are two possibilities:

(a') $\lim_{N_1 \to +\infty} f'(N_1) \geq 0$. It is easy to see that in this case $\lim_{N_1 \to +\infty} n(N_1) = +\infty$, hence $\lim_{N \to +\infty} n_1(N) = +\infty$.

(b') $\lim_{N_1 \to +\infty} f'(N_1) < 0$. Since, by equation (1c), $f''(N_1) < 0$, there is a unique positive value for N_1, let us say, N_1^0, such that $f'(N_1^0 = 0$. We then have $\lim_{N_1 \to N_1^0} n(N_1) = +\infty$, and hence $\lim_{N \to +\infty} n_1(N) = N_1^0$.

In that follows, we will disregard (c). (The alterations in the argument necessary in order to consider situation (c) are on the other hand almost trivial.) We can summarize the information gathered on the function $n_1(N)$, thus: the function is defined on the non-negative reals; it is continuous where defined; its range is $[0, +\infty)$ or $[0, N_1^0)$; its derivative exists everywhere except possibly at $N = 0$ and is given by (A3). It can be seen at once from (A2) that

$$\lim_{N \to 0} n_1'(N) = 1. \tag{A4}$$

We can now show that, for each positive N, $n_1(N) < N$. Assume not. Then for some positive N, say, $\bar{N}$, we would have

$$1 \leq \frac{n_1(\bar{N})}{\bar{N}} = \frac{n_1(\bar{N}) - n_1(0)}{\bar{N} - 0} = n_1'(\bar{\bar{N}}), \text{ where } 0 < \bar{\bar{N}} < \bar{N},$$

thus contradicting (A3).

REFERENCES

Blaug, M. (1978). *Economic Theory in Retrospect* (3rd edn). Cambridge: CUP.
Caravale, G. A. and Tosato, D. A. (1974). *Un modello ricardiano di sviluppo*. Turin: Boringhieri.

Caravale, G. A. and Tosato, D. A. (1980). *Ricardo and the Theory of Value, Distribution, and Growth.* London: Routledge & Kegan Paul.

Casarosa, C. (1978). 'A New Formulation of the Ricardian System'. *Oxford Economic Papers*, 30, 38–63.

Casarosa, C. (1981). 'The New View of the Ricardian Theory of Distribution and Economic Growth'. In M. Baranzini (ed.), *Essays on the Foundations of Economics.* Oxford: Blackwell, 225–38.

Corry, B. A. (1959). 'Malthus and Keynes: A Reconsideration'. *Economic Journal*, LXIX, 717–24.

Costa, G. (1977). 'La convergenza allo stato stazionario di un'economia di tipo ricardiano'. In F. de Cindio and P. Sylos Labini (eds), *Saggi di Economia in Onore di Antonio Pesenti.* Milan: Giuffrè, pp. 57–76.

Hellwig, M. (1975). 'The Demand for Money and Bonds in Continuous-time Models'. *Journal of Economic Theory*, 8, 462–4.

Hicks, J. R. (1965). *Capital and Growth.* Oxford: OUP.

Hicks, J. R. and Hollander, S. (1977). 'Mr Ricardo and the Moderns'. *Quarterly Journal of Economics*, 91, 351–69.

Kaldor, N. (1956). 'Alternative Theories of Distribution'. *Review of Economic Studies*, 23, 83–100.

Kennedy, C. (1968). 'Time, Interest, and the Production Function'. In T. N. Wolfe (ed.), *Value, Capital and Growth.* Edinburgh: University Press, pp. 275–89.

Malinvaud, E. (1976). *Leçons de théorie microéconomique* (3rd ed.). Paris: Dunod.

Pasinetti, L. L. (1960). 'A Mathematical Formulation of the Ricardian System'. *Review of Economic Studies*, 27, 78–98.

Pasinetti, L. L. (1974). *Growth and Income Distribution: Essays in Economic Theory.* London: CUP.

Trezza, B. (1969). 'Sull'esistenza di fenomeni ciclici e sulla stabilità globale del processo di sviluppo del sistema ricardiano'. *Giornale degli Economisti*, 28, 326–39.

PART III

Sraffa-based Interpretations: the Separation of Prices and Quantities

5

On Hollander's Interpretation of Ricardo's Early Theory of Profits

PIERANGELO GAREGNANI

1 INTRODUCTION

Sraffa's well-known suggestion regarding the 'rational foundation' of Ricardo's early principle that 'the profits of the farmer ... regulate the profits of all other trades' (present both in the 1814–15 correspondence and in the *Essay on Profits*) has been challenged by Samuel Hollander in his articles of 1973 and 1975.[1] According to Sraffa (1951), Ricardo based that principle on the argument that:

> in agriculture the same commodity namely corn, forms both the capital (conceived as composed of the subsistence necessary for workers) and the product, so that the determination of profit by the difference between total product and capital advanced, and also the determination of the ratio of this profit to the capital is done directly between quantities of corn, without any question of valuation.

Then:

> if there is to be a uniform rate of profit in all trades it is the exchangeable values of the product of *other* trades relatively to their own capitals (i.e. relatively to corn) that must be adjusted so as to yield the same rate of profit as has been established in the growing of corn. (Sraffa, 1951, pp. xxxi–xxxii)

[Samuel Hollander's comment on the present article and a rejoinder by Pierangelo Garegnani are published in the *Cambridge Journal of Economics* (Garegnani, 1983a; Hollander, 1983). Passages from the rejoinder are included in the 'Summing up' below, which, for brevity's sake, replaces Appendix I of the original paper.]

I wish to thank K. Bharadwaj, A. Campus, M. Pivetti, A. Roncaglia and F. Vianello who read and commented on an early draft of this paper. Financial assistance from the Consiglio Nazionale delle Ricerche is gratefully acknowledged.

[1] The argument of those two articles reappears with no substantial change in chapter 4 of *The Economics of David Ricardo* (Hollander, 1979). (However, see section 2 for the role Hollander seems to attribute in his 1979 book to the quantity theory of money in the origin of Ricardo's theory of profits.)

D

Thus, according to Sraffa, the simplification that wages consist only of corn allowed the Ricardo of that early period to reach his theory of profits without dealing with the problem of prices.

In opposition to this interpretation, Hollander (1973, p. 260) has argued that, in the *Essay on Profits* and his earlier correspondence, Ricardo held 'substantially the same position as that ultimately appearing in the *Principles*',[2] i.e. that Ricardo based his reasoning upon 'variations of the money-wage in consequence of changing prices of wage goods' and accordingly reached his conclusions on the associated 'inverse movements' of the general rate of profits without relying upon physical corn quantities.

I shall argue here that Hollander's contention suffers from some serious shortcomings. In particular: (1) Hollander fails to explain how the Ricardo of 1813–14 arrived at the inverse relation between the wage and the profit rate; (2) it is only by ascribing to Ricardo an uncommon use of language that Hollander can account for the presence of the principle of the determining role of farmers' profits in the *Essay*; (3) Hollander's criticism of the two main pieces of direct textual evidence which Sraffa brought to support his interpretation (i.e. Malthus's letter of 5 August 1814, criticizing Ricardo for assuming 'a material rate of produce' in agriculture, and Ricardo's correspondence with Malthus in Spring 1815) is seriously deficient. More generally, Hollander appears at times to forget that the reasoning based on the assumption of an agricultural capital consisting exclusively of corn is claimed by Sraffa as the 'rational foundation' of Ricardo's early conclusions on profits, i.e. to be the *logical basis* of Ricardo's argument and not its explicit content. Ricardo had to support these conclusions in relation to a reality where the agricultural capital consisted mostly, though not entirely, of corn. He would accordingly admit the non-corn elements of agricultural capital and generally conduct his arguments in terms of *value* quantities, the treatment of which, taken together with other elements, reveals the underlying physical quantities of the 'rational foundation'. The following section will deal with point (1) above, whereas point (2) will be taken up in section 3. Sections 4 and 5 will then be devoted to point (3).

I may conclude this introduction by noting that the controversy may be of more interest than merely for the history of economic thought. Thus, Hollander apparently sees it as bearing upon whether Ricardo can be placed on a continuous line of development leading to Marshall and the marginalist theories that became dominant at the end of the century,[3] or whether 'he was in fact developing an alternative basic theory' (Hollander, 1973a, p. 14), a

[2] Cf. also the following passage: 'According to my argument, the position adopted in the *Essay*—indeed earlier—is precisely that of the *Principles*' (Hollander, 1975, p. 189).

[3] Hollander refers to the 'theory of economic equilibrium via the market mechanism' (1979, p. 657), in which we find 'a demand and supply analysis which was for Ricardo as for ... the neoclassicals ... the vehicle of determination in his general system'.

question of some importance for us today in the face of the deficiencies that have lately appeared in the former kind of theories. Indeed, Ricardo's determination of the rate of profit r as it emerges from Sraffa's interpretation clearly takes P, the corn produced on the no-rent land, and N, 'the consumption necessary to such production',[4] i.e. the corn wages, as the two *independent* variables in the equation $r = (P - N)/N$. This in turn strongly suggests a wage determined independently of P and *vice versa*[5] rather than a demand and supply analysis of wages and profits where P and N would be *dependent* variables no less than r is.

2 THE ORIGIN OF RICARDO'S THEORY OF PROFITS

We may begin by considering the question inevitably raised by Hollander's denial that Ricardo reached his theory of profits by reasoning in terms of physical corn quantities. The question is: by what other means does Hollander suggest that Ricardo reached, by 1813, that theory of profits which contrasted so sharply with the generally accepted one, running in terms of the 'competition' of capitals?[6] An argument based on the effect on the rate of profit of 'variations in the money-wage rate'[7] relative to the money prices of the products would have met, as Hollander himself states, the 'serious stumbling block' (1973b, p. 265) represented by the view Ricardo entertained at the time that a rise in corn prices, through its effect upon wages, would be followed by a rise of *all* other prices, thus leaving the effect on the profit rate indeterminate.

In his 1975 *Economica* article (p. 189), however, Hollander refers to an argument advanced by Ricardo which 'depended upon the supposition that changes in the money-wage rate (as the price of corn changes) *do not generate changes in final price*', and describes this as 'the position adopted in the *Essay*,

---

[4] We are here following Hollander and Sraffa in conceiving capital in Ricardo as reducible ultimately to wages (see e.g., Hollander, 1973b, p. 269, and for Sraffa, the passage quoted above).

[5] This would be the case when the wage is seen as determined by circumstances (whether economic or more broadly social) that are best studied *separately* from those affecting the social product and the other shares in it. Such a separate determination of the wage—and the consequent determination of the other shares in the product as the 'surplus' of the product over the wages—seems evident when, as in Quesnay or Ricardo, the wage is explained in terms of a customary subsistence; but it also emerges in Marx and Smith, who admitted a larger influence on the wage of other economic conditions (see Garegnani, 1960, p. 4).

[6] Adam Smith had written: 'when the stocks of many rich merchants are turned into the same trade, their mutual competition naturally tends to lower its profit, and when there is a like increase of stock in all the different trades carried on in the same society, the same competition must produce the same effect in them all' (Smith, 1910, vol. I, p. 78).

[7] Cf. the passage by Hollander quoted on p. 88 above.

indeed earlier.[8] As an indication of how Ricardo could have *reached* his theory of profits, this remark would be clearly unwarranted. It is true that in the *Essay* Ricardo had come to reject the generally accepted view that 'the price of corn regulates the prices of all other things' (*Works*, vol. IV, p. 21n; see also pp. 34–5). But the evidence tells us that Ricardo arrived at that rejection no less than one year after arriving at his theory of profits,[9] which cannot therefore have been reached on such a basis.

Hollander, in his later book, does come back to the point and speculates about what he there describes as a 'very attractive reconstruction' of the origin of Ricardo's theory of profits (Hollander, 1979, p. 118). According to this reconstruction, by 1813 Ricardo found that the general rise in money-prices consequent upon a rise in the price of corn, and hence in the money-wage, could not occur because it would require an increase in the quantity of money. Ricardo would then have concluded that money-prices of com-modities other than corn remain constant as the price of corn rises, and that the rise in money-wages would have to lower the rate of profit. Here, it seems unnecessary to enter into the doubts that the pure logic of this argument may raise:[10] as Hollander himself admits, such a 'reconstruction' again contradicts the fact that, even in 1814, Ricardo *still* adhered to Smith's view of general prices rising with corn prices.[11]

It seems, therefore, that Hollander provides no answer as to how a Ricardo reasoning purely in terms of money-wages and prices could have reached his theory of profits despite the 'serious stumbling block' of the assumed general price rise. The available evidence indicates, on the contrary, that in his theory

---

[8] My italics. A similar passage referring however to the *Essay*, and not to any earlier period, occurs in Hollander (1973b, p. 276).

[9] The first statements of Ricardo's theory of profits can be traced in his letters to Malthus of 10 and 17 August 1813 (*Works*, vol. VI, pp. 93–5), whereas Ricardo's change of opinion about the effect of a rise in the price of corn on the prices of all other commodities must have occurred sometime between 11 August 1814, when in a letter to Malthus he was *still* supposing such an effect (p. 120), and February 1815, when he rejected it in the *Essay*.

[10] See, however, Appendix I of original paper (*Cambridge Journal of Economics*, 6(1), 1982).

[11] It is however difficult to understand why, in spite of this admission, Hollander should imply elsewhere in the same book just *that* reconstruction of the origin of Ricardo's theory of profits (see e.g. Hollander, 1979, p. 656; also, pp. 242, 648, 655, 661, 687). A clue might perhaps be found when in 1973 Hollander writes that Ricardo's attempt to deal with Malthus's contentions 'led him to adopt', in a letter of 25 July 1814, the view that the prices of manufactured products would also rise (1973b, p. 265; my italics). In fact, the wording of Hollander's passage as to Ricardo being 'led to adopt' the view in question is surprising, since the evidence is that Ricardo already held that view three years earlier, in the bullion papers of 1811. Hollander's wording might therefore be meant to suggest that, as a result of his discussion with Malthus in the summer of 1814, Ricardo had *returned* to such a view, which he would somehow have abandoned in the period between 1811 and 1814. As far as I can see, this suggestion would lack any textual basis: Ricardo's views on the question in his letters of 1814 appear to be the same as those we find in his bullion papers of 1811 (see n. 10).

of prices Ricardo had no basis for his novel analysis of profits until some time between August 1814 and February 1815, when he began to realize he had been incorrect in following Smith and received opinion on such a general price rise. We shall, however, return to this question at the end of the paper, after examining Hollander's attempt to invalidate the direct evidence in favour of Sraffa's interpretation.

3 THE PRINCIPLE OF THE DETERMINING ROLE OF FARMERS' PROFITS

Hollander (1973b) describes Ricardo's proposition that 'the profits of the farmer... can regulate the profits of all other trades' (e.g. *Works*, vol. VI, p. 104) in terms of: 'a more sophisticated variation thereof that the *state of agricultural productivity* on the margin of cultivation is the unique determinant of the general profit rate' (Hollander, 1973b, p. 275; my italics). As can be seen, Hollander's 'variation' consists of taking Ricardo's expression 'profits of the farmer' as *equivalent* to the expression 'state of agricultural productivity' in describing the determination of the general rate of profit. The two expressions are, however, by no means equivalent.

Thus, for example, the 'profits of the farmer' change with the corn wage rate quite independently of a change in the 'state of agricultural productivity'. And, what matters most here, while Ricardo's own proposition can find a 'rational foundation' only in the argument described by Sraffa, the same is not true for Hollander's variation. One could in fact reach the conclusion that (with wages consisting entirely of corn) 'the state of agricultural productivity' is the unique determinant of the profit rate without necessarily becoming aware that the profits of the farmer must then regulate those of all other trades because they are independent of relative prices. Indeed, this is what Hollander must claim happened to Ricardo himself. And it is because of this claim that he must interpret Ricardo's farmer's profits principle in terms of the 'variation' we are discussing.

In this way, however, Hollander is compelled to ascribe to Ricardo an incorrect use of words ('profits of the farmer' as a synonym for 'state of agricultural productivity')[12] and to do so in a case (that of wages consisting entirely of corn) in which those words could mean exactly what they say.[13]

---

[12] This emerges very plainly in Hollander's use of the words 'literally' or 'strictly' or 'formal' in numerous passages (see, e.g. 1975, p. 189; 1979, pp. 132, 138–9, 145).

[13] The case for Hollander's interpretation is made even more difficult by the fact that, as we shall see in section 4 below, he has to admit that, at one moment at least (i.e. in the letter to Malthus of 25 July 1814), Ricardo *did* use the corn argument of Sraffa's interpretation. Why then should we interpret Ricardo's words as incorrect, when they could be correct and, at one time at least, Ricardo used the argument corresponding to the straightforward reading of those words?

But this is not all: Hollander's suggested reading of Ricardo's proposition on the determining role of farmers' profits meets a second difficulty. The proposition disappears in the *Principles*, where we only find the more general statement that the productivity of labour on the land which pays no rent is fundamental in determining general profits (Sraffa, 1951, p. xxxiii). Why, we may ask, does it disappear if, as Hollander contends, Ricardo's argument in the *Principles* is 'substantially the same' as that of the *Essay*?

As far as I can see, Hollander provides no explicit answer to this question. But the answer is probably implicit in the distinction he attempts to trace between two different propositions on profits in Ricardo. The first, or 'strong', proposition would assert that agricultural productivity is the *unique* determinant of the general rate of profit and would thus include the farmers' profits principle interpreted in the way we saw. The second, or 'weak', proposition would be the more general proposition according to which 'the state of agricultural productivity exerts an influence on the general profit rate, although not to the exclusion of other forces' (Hollander, 1973b, p. 275). The two propositions would be distinguished by, respectively, the presence or absence in Ricardo of the (implicit) assumption of wages consisting entirely of corn.

On the basis of that distinction, Hollander argues that: 'in the *Essay*, unlike the early correspondence, Ricardo reverted in general to the assumption that corn alone enters the wage basket' (1975, p. 190), and hence to the 'strong' proposition. Following this line of thought, we would have to think that in the *Principles* Ricardo had *again* changed his position by returning to the pre-*Essay* 'weak' proposition, dropping 'the assumption that corn alone enters the wage basket': hence, the disappearance there of the principle of the determining role of farmers' profits.

If this were Hollander's explanation for that disappearance it would not be satisfactory. In Ricardo we cannot in fact find the succession from a 'strong' proposition held in early 1814 at the time of his letter to Trower to a 'weak' one held in his correspondence with Malthus during the rest of 1814, and then to the 'strong' one to which Ricardo is supposed to have 'reverted' in the *Essay*. The principle of the determining role of the farmers' profits, described as the 'strong' proposition, is present in Ricardo's correspondence *all through 1814*, and thus, contrary to what Hollander asserts, was held *simultaneously* with, and not before and after, the proposition described as 'weak' by Hollander.[14] Should we conclude that, in 1814–15, Ricardo held both pro-

---

[14] The presence of the so-called 'weak' proposition in the 'early correspondence' mentioned by Hollander in the quoted passage can be traced in Ricardo's letters to Malthus of 23 October and 18 December 1814 (*Works*, vol. VI, pp. 145 and 162 respectively) with their references to improvements in 'machinery' increasing the rate of profit. Earlier, the proposition was present in the implicit reference to non-corn constituents in the letter of 25 July, which will be discussed in section 4 below, and in the letter of 16 September, in which the state of the cultivation of the land

positions at once, i.e. that agricultural productivity both *is* and *is not* the 'unique' determinant of the profit rate?

The inconsistency disappears however when we leave aside *Hollander's* distinction between a 'weak' and a 'strong' proposition on profits, based merely on whether the neat assumption that wages consist entirely of corn is or is not made by Ricardo, and revert instead to *Sraffa's* distinction, which is that between two different *logical bases* which Ricardo used in succession for his analysis of profits. In the letters of 1814, no less than in the *Essay*, the *basis* of Ricardo's argument lay in the physical corn quantities of agriculture and therefore, implicitly, on the simplification of wages consisting entirely of corn with its approximate correspondence to reality. An analogy with the corn argument would, however, allow Ricardo to see easily, and occasionally admit, that productivity in the non-agricultural wage goods sectors could *also* influence the rate of profit. In fact, the fall in the general profit rate resulting from decreasing agricultural productivity, which Ricardo could determine on the basis of the quantities of corn in agriculture, would have to óperate through a fall in the ratio between *value* of product and *value* of wages: it was then easy for Ricardo to think that the analogous changes in labour productivity in non-corn wage goods would act similarly.

However, this analogy would in no way alter Ricardo's need to hold on to the argument founded on physical corn quantities—and therefore to the principle of the determining role of farmers' profits—as the only firm logical foundation of his admittedly approximate conclusions. Hence, the *simultaneous presence* in Ricardo of what Hollander misleadingly distinguishes as his 'strong' and 'weak' propositions on profits—a simultaneity that continues until, after the *Essay*, the logical basis of his argument is altered and he no longer needs to rely ultimately on physical corn quantities. It seems, therefore, that the disappearance of the farmers' profits proposition in the *Principles* is

---

is only allowed to be *'almost* the only great permanent cause' of the level of the rate of profit (*Works*, vol. VI, p. 133; my italics). However, what Hollander describes as the 'strong proposition, i.e. the determining role of farmers' profits, which had been stated in the letter to Trower of 8 March 1814 (*Works*, vol. VI, p. 104), and was to reappear one year later in the *Essay*, is in fact present all through the Ricardo–Malthus correspondence of those months. Malthus continues to attack Ricardo's principle of the determining role of farmers' profits (see Malthus's letters of 5 August, 9 October, 23 November, 29 December; vol. VI, pp. 117–18, 139–40, 153, 167), and Ricardo continues to counter Malthus's arguments. (See, e.g., his letter to Malthus of 16 September 1814: 'the state of production from the land compared with the means necessary to make it produce operates in all [trades], and is *alone* lasting in its effects' (vol. VI, p. 133: a letter which, it should be noted, also contains the hint at the 'weak' proposition mentioned above.) The same simultaneity between 'weak' and 'strong' propositions emerges, on the other hand, in the *Essay* itself, where the so called 'strong' proposition of the determining role of farmers' profits goes together with the 'weak' statements implied when Ricardo lists manufactured products in agricultural capital (*Works*, vol. IV, p. 10, for example).

explicable in terms of a change in the logical basis of Ricardo's argument and not by the last swing in a supposed early oscillation on the assumption that wages consist entirely of corn—an assumption that could not in fact be strictly adhered to by Ricardo, who had to answer Malthus's challenge.

4 MALTHUS'S LETTER OF 5 AUGUST 1814 CONCERNING RICARDO'S 'MATERIAL RATE OF PRODUCE'

But besides having to explain the principle of the determining role of farmer's profits, Hollander's interpretation of Ricardo's early argument on profits has to overcome the hurdle represented by two pieces of direct evidence with which Sraffa buttressed his interpretation.

The one we shall consider in this section is Malthus's letter of 5 August 1814. In this letter, Malthus writes to Ricardo: 'In no case of production *is the produce exactly of the same nature as the capital advanced*. Consequently we can never properly refer to a *material rate of produce*, independent of demand, and of the abundance or scarcity of capital...', thus ascribing to Ricardo precisely the corn argument of Sraffa's interpretation. Moreover, Malthus connects this argument with Ricardo's principle of the determining role of farmers' profits by deducing from the above passage that: 'It is the state of capital, or the general profits of stock and interest of money, which determines the particular profits upon the land; and...it is not the particular profits or *rate of produce* upon the land which determines the general profits of stock and the interest of money' (*Works*, vol. VI, p. 117–18; my italics).

Faced with this letter, Hollander does not in fact deny that Ricardo did *at some stage* hold the corn argument of Sraffa's interpretation. What Hollander attempts to do is to confine this argument to a single letter of Ricardo, that of 25 July 1814, which Malthus was answering on 5 August. He then proceeds to describe such an argument as 'a rather *casual* and *inadequate* restatement—the significance of which should not be exaggerated—of his basic and consistently maintained position [on profits]' (Hollander, 1973b, p. 266–7; my italics), where the 'consistently maintained position' would be the reasoning based on the money-wage rate that Hollander attributes to Ricardo (p. 88 above).

Let us look at Hollander's position in more detail. The passage from Ricardo's letter of 25 July reads: 'The capitalist who may find it necessary to employ a hundred days labour instead of fifty in order to produce a certain quantity of corn cannot retain the same share for himself unless the labourers who are employed for a hundred days will be satisfied with the same quantity of corn for their subsistence that the labourers employed for fifty had before' (*Works*, vol. VI, pp. 114–15). Hollander's evidence for describing this argument by Ricardo as 'casual'[15] lies in the fact that, both in the preceding and the following letters (26 June and 10 August 1814, respectively), Ricardo did not refer to quantities of corn, but only 'to upward pressure on money wages due to the rising costs of wage goods' (Hollander, 1973b, p. 262).

A first difficulty of Hollander's interpretation of Malthus's reference to the 'material rate of produce' is that the passage in Ricardo's letter of 25 July does not constitute that *one* instance of the corn argument which Hollander needs it to be for his argument. The quoted passage in fact continues with 'if you suppose the price of corn doubled, the capital to be employed estimated in money will probably be also *nearly* doubled—*or at any rate will be greatly augmented*' (my italics), where the phrase 'nearly doubled, or at any rate greatly augmented' appears to imply that capital consists *chiefly*, but not exclusively, of corn.[16] Thus, the argument does not seem to differ in any substantial respect from the one we find elsewhere, including the Table of the *Essay*.[17] It then seems unlikely that Ricardo's July letter could be the only basis of Malthus's strikingly explicit statements about 'produce exactly of the same nature as the capital advanced' and 'material rate of produce': it seems more plausible that the July letter came to Malthus as a reminder of Ricardo's earlier, more explicit, statements which Sraffa suspects to have existed (Sraffa, 1951, p. xxxi).

However, the deficiency of Hollander's interpretation of the origin of Malthus's statement about the 'material rate of produce' as relating to a 'casual' argument of Ricardo can be seen in a second respect. Hollander's opinion as to the conflict between the corn argument of 25 July and the argument in terms of money-wages of the immediately preceding and following letters appears in fact to be based upon an inexact understanding of the role of the corn argument in Ricardo's reasoning.

To the extent to which the argument in terms of a 'material rate of produce' allowed Ricardo to determine the rate of profit, it also allowed him to

---

[15] The 'inadequacy' of the corn argument which supposedly induced Ricardo to abandon it soon after stumbling on it on 25 July (see Hollander's passage above) is, on the other hand, contradicted by Hollander himself when he elsewhere contends that, over the entire period 1813–15, Ricardo often relied on the assumption of wages consisting entirely of corn (see above p. 92)—an assumption that is sufficient to validate fully the corn argument.

[16] Ricardo's phrase could alternatively refer to a fall in the *real* wage, but this possibility is hardly ever implied by him when dealing with an extension of cultivation. Hollander himself adopts the interpretation we have given in the text when he refers to that phrase in the context of 'falling per capita corn wages due to a relative rise in the price of corn' (Hollander, 1975, pp. 189–90, referring back to Hollander, 1973b, p. 266; see also Hollander, 1979, p. 129)—although by doing so he contradicts his own interpretation of the letter of 25 July as containing Ricardo's argument based on a 'material rate of produce'.

[17] Accordingly, Ricardo's July letter does not seem to contradict Sraffa's statement according to which the corn argument 'is never stated by Ricardo in his extant letters and papers', contrary to what Hollander implies in 1973b, p. 265.

determine the ratio between value of the product and value of capital (whether the two value quantities were to be expressed in corn or in money). This being so, we should expect Ricardo's explicit statements to be generally in terms of value quantities. He was, in fact, concerned with conclusions applicable to reality, and not merely with correct deductions from an assumption—that of wages consisting entirely of corn—the realism of which could, and would, be immediately disputed. Given the decisive importance of agricultural products in agricultural capital, he would feel confident that conclusions reached by adopting the simplification of wages consisting entirely of 'corn' would be of general validity: and he would argue these conclusions with reference to a reality where agricultural capital consisted mostly, though not exclusively, of corn. Indeed, as we already noticed in section 3 above, he never rigorously adhered to the simplification of corn wages and, occasionally, even went on to consider the effects on the rate of profit of improvements in the production of wage goods other than corn.

Thus, in particular, we should expect that, even when corn quantities emerge as capital in Ricardo's writings, they would not explicitly be physical quantities, but rather value quantities (as in the Table of the *Essay*, or in the letter of 25 July 1814)—although the choice of corn as the value unit renders transparent the limited role of value measurements for aggregates that consist largely of corn.

This peculiar role played by physical quantities of corn in Ricardo's early reasoning does imply that Ricardo would easily pass from ratios between corn quantities to ratios between values, and vice versa. It is this connection between physical and value magnitudes that Hollander appears to overlook when he quotes Ricardo's letters of 26 June and 11 August 1814 as evidence of the 'casual' character of the corn argument in the letter of 25 July.

Thus, the letter of 26 June is that in which we read: 'the rate of profits and of interest must depend on the proportion of production to the consumption necessary to such production' (*Works*, vol. VI, p. 108), the 'striking passage' which, Sraffa suggests (1951, p. xxxii), is 'the nearest Ricardo comes to an explicit statement' of the rate of profit as a 'material rate of produce'. Now, Hollander disputes this interpretation and points to the ensuing phrases— 'this [proportion] again essentially depends upon the *cheapness* of provisions, which is... *the great regulator of the wages of labour*'—in order to argue that the 'proportion' referred to by Ricardo involves *money-wages* and is therefore a proportion between *value* quantities (Hollander, 1973b, p. 262). Hollander seems here to forget that it is just in order to explain this 'proportion' that, in the subsequent letter of 25 July, Ricardo will introduce what Hollander takes as *the* statement of the corn argument. Thus, what the two letters when taken together in fact show is the ease with which Ricardo would pass from the physical quantities of his underlying reasoning to the corresponding value quantities and vice versa in order to explain the behaviour of the latter by means of that of the former. This is also shown by the fact that the reference to corn *values*, which we have argued Ricardo's letter of 25 July in fact contains (p. 95 above), did not in the least prevent Malthus from objecting, on 5 August, to the conception that in agriculture 'the produce [is not] exactly of the same nature as the capital advanced'—from objecting, that is, to a conception which he evidently knew to underlie Ricardo's argument, apparently conducted in terms of value quantities.

As for Ricardo's letter of 11 August, the one after that of 25 July, it is true that, there, we read the following passage unambiguously referring to money prices and wages: 'the rise of his goods [of the woollen or cotton manufacturer] *will not be in the same proportion* as the rise of labour' (letter of 11 August 1814: *Works*, vol. VI, p. 120; my italics). But the question we should ask ourselves is: how could Ricardo so confidently state, in contrast with Adam Smith, that prices would rise, but not 'in the same proportion as the rise of labour,[18] if not by *assuming* a fall in the rate of profit which he had independently determined by reasoning on the basis of the physical quantities of agriculture?

5 THE RICARDO—MALTHUS CORRESPONDENCE OF SPRING 1815

No more convincing is the way in which Hollander deals with a second main piece of direct evidence for Sraffa's interpretation, namely the Ricardo–Malthus correspondence of spring 1815. In these letters Malthus develops an argument which, as Ricardo has to admit, is 'very ingenious' and 'carries a great deal of plausibility with it' (*Works*, vol. VI, p. 192). The argument is as follows. As cultivation extends to inferior lands, could not the consequent fall in the corn value of the manufactures included in agricultural capital reverse Ricardo's conclusion in the *Essay*; i.e., by causing a greater corn surplus from the land, allow for a rise, and not a fall, of the rate of profit in agriculture and hence in the whole economy?[19]

The discussion of this argument in the intense correspondence of the two months between 10 March and 5 May 1815 appears to contradict Hollander's

---

[18] Adam Smith, whom Ricardo was here following in the general notion that all prices would rise with a rise in the price of corn, had in fact written: 'the money price of labour, and of every thing that is the produce of either land or labour, must necessarily rise or fall *in proportion* to the money price of corn' (1910, vol. II, pp. 11–12; my italics), a passage which Ricardo himself will single out later when he comes to reject the entire notion of such a general rise (*Works*, vol. I, p. 308).

[19] Cf. Malthus's letter to Horner in *Works*, vol. VI, p. 187. It should be noticed that the problem now raised by Malthus differs from the earlier problem concerning the effect on profits of improvements in the production of manufactured items of wages—with which, as we argued in section 4, Ricardo could deal by means of an analogy with the effect of similar improvements in corn production and thus without facing the problem of the value of corn relative to manufactures.

interpretation by indicating how unprepared Ricardo was as yet for any reasoning based on the relative value of commodities (corn and manufactures), as opposed to the argument based on physical quantities of corn, implied when in the Table of the *Essay* he treated the corn capital of the old lands as a constant. The inconclusiveness of this second line of reasoning against Malthus's argument only induces Ricardo to start feeling his way towards the alternative line to be developed later in the *Principles*, and this clear process of transition provides further evidence against Hollander's idea that, in the *Essay* and his earlier correspondence, Ricardo held 'substantially the same position' ultimately appearing in the *Principles*.

In the *Essay*, Ricardo had already rejected Smith's idea of a general rise in prices following a rise in the price of corn and, hence, in money-wages; moreover, in one passage he had even used the *constancy* in the price of manufactures in the face of rising corn prices and money-wages to argue the fall of the rate of profit with 'the progress of wealth'. However, in the first few letters of this exchange with Malthus, Ricardo does *not* resort to the easy answer that this new line of reasoning would have afforded against Malthus's contention that the rate of profit might rise *together with the price of corn* as cultivation is extended to inferior lands. And even when in the later letters this answer does emerge, Ricardo appears most reluctant to rely on such a comparatively new argument, implying as it does a drastic switch of attention away from agricultural, and towards manufacturing, profits. He still keeps his focus on agricultural profits, even though this only leads him to the inconclusive proposition that the rate of profit may fall or rise, depending on the size of the rise in the price of corn relative to manufactures (letter of 17 April). (For a more detailed account of Ricardo's argument on profits in this correspondence, see Appendix below.)

Indeed, with respect to determining the size of the rise in the price of corn, the Ricardo of spring 1815 still appears to be far from the labour theory of the *Principles*, and it is only in one of the last letters of this exchange (21 April) that he finally hints that the price of corn will rise in proportion to the labour required on the no-rent land. (For an account of Ricardo's position on relative values in this correspondence see Appendix below.)

Now, to Eatwell's citation of these letters Hollander has surprisingly responded (1975, p. 188) by taking them as additional evidence for his own interpretation. He finds this evidence in the fact that Ricardo's consideration of manufactured wage goods and the corresponding value calculations 'makes it clear that he did not base his table [in the *Essay*] upon the assumption that corn is the only wage good' (Hollander, 1975, p. 192). This response is surprising in two respects. In the first place, why should Ricardo's value calculations concerning non-corn elements of the wage in spring 1815 ever prove that Ricardo's earlier argument in the *Essay* did not have the simplification of corn wages as its 'rational foundation'? Ricardo was con-corned with conclusions applicable to reality, and just as he had always admitted the presence in reality of manufactured elements of agricultural capital (see pp. 92–3 above), he would also be ready to consider the complications raised by such elements when faced with them by Malthus.

In the second place, we saw in section 3 that it is Hollander rather than Sraffa who attributes to Ricardo a strict assumption of corn wages whenever the latter states the 'strong' proposition of the determining role of farmers' profits, as Ricardo undoubtedly does in the *Essay*. So, if the letters of spring 1815 in fact showed that Ricardo had not ultimately based his reasoning in the *Essay* on corn wages, it is Hollander's interpretation of the 'strong' proposition that would be contradicted, at least as much as Sraffa's.

This correspondence in fact shows Ricardo's need in spring 1815, and his readiness, to face systematically the problem of relative values. It is the same need that is demonstrated when, in his letter to James Mill of 30 December 1815, Ricardo writes: 'I know I shall soon be stopped by the word price' (*Works*, vol. VI, p. 348). This would indeed be a surprising statement if Hollander's interpretation were correct. How could Ricardo expect to be 'soon stopped by the word price' nearly one year *after* publishing the *Essay* if, as Hollander holds, his position there had been 'substantially the same' as that of the *Principles*, where 'the word price' is present at the very beginning of the argument? He could hardly be stopped *now* by the word 'price'.

What the letter to Mill, taken together with the correspondence of the preceding spring, in fact bears witness to is Ricardo's transition to a new logical basis for his theory of profits, thus showing that the corn measurements of the *Essay* were much more than merely 'a convenient method of portraying some of the principles in simple arithmetical form' (Hollander, 1973b, p. 282). These measurements were, as we argued in section 4, the natural way to exhibit, without open, forced assumptions, the logical ground on which rests the constancy of the relevant quantities in the table as cultivation is supposed to extend to less fertile lands. Such measurements were therefore just as naturally abandoned when that logical ground could be replaced with the one provided by a general theory of relative values.

We saw in section 2 above that Hollander fails to explain how Ricardo could have reached his theory of profits by 1813, if not by means of an argument based upon quantities of corn. Indeed, it seems plausible that it was this early argument and the resulting theory of profits that also led Ricardo to recognize, with the error of the 'popular view of the effect of wages on prices' (Sraffa, 1951, p. xxxv), what he called 'Adam Smith's original error respecting value' (*Works*, vol. VII, p. 100), i.e. that the price of commodities is arrived at by a process of adding up the wages, profit and rent and hence led him to develop the theory of value of the *Principles*. Ricardo's originality and profundity show in precisely this: that he could see through the difficulties of what we would today describe as the solution of a system of n simultaneous price equations in the $(n-1)$ unknown relative prices and in the rate of profit, by means of simplifications like the 'material rate of produce' or, later, the proportionality between values and quantities of embodied labour, which, as it turned out, could be dropped without affecting the essence of his conclusions.

6 SUMMING UP

It may help the reader if, in conclusion, I sum up the four main arguments I have brought against Samuel Hollander's interpretation of Ricardo's early theory of profits.

(1) In section 2 here I argued that, contrary to what Hollander claimed, Ricardo could not *arrive at* his novel theory of profits by relying upon variations in the money wage rate relative to the money prices of the products. This is so because, at the time, Ricardo shared the accepted opinion that, through its effect upon money wages, a rise in corn prices would be followed by a rise of all other prices, the effect on the profit rate remaining indeterminate (see above, pp. 89–91). On the other hand, I pointed out (p. 90) that Professor Hollander's 'attractive reconstruction' according to which Ricardo's theory of profits originated from an application of the quantity theory of money to deny such a general rise in money prices, contradicts the fact that Ricardo shared the common opinion at least until August 1814—a full year after August 1813, when we have evidence he had already arrived at his theory of profits. I also pointed out that, though Hollander admits this contradiction, he seems elsewhere to imply precisely that 'reconstruction' (above p. 90, n. 11).

(2) In section 4 here I contended that Professor Hollander is incorrect in claiming that Malthus was only reacting to the immediately preceding letter by Ricardo when, on 5 August 1814, he ascribes to Ricardo's argument on profits exactly the 'rational foundation' pointed out by Sraffa. According to Hollander, Ricardo would in fact have casually stumbled on the corn argument in that letter (25 July 1814), only to abandon it soon after as 'inadequate' (Hollander, 1973, pp. 266–267): this would be demonstrated by the previous and subsequent letters by Ricardo (26 July and 11 August 1814). Against this I argued that the corn argument is no more explicit in Ricardo's letter of 25 July than it is in numerous other passages of his writings during those years. Also, I argued more generally that the claim as to the singularity of that letter, compared with the ones which preceded and followed it, rests on a misunderstanding of the nature of Ricardo's 'material rate' reasoning, which could only be the 'rational foundation' of his explicit argument and not the argument itself.

(3) In connection with his denial that Ricardo had reached his theory of

profits by means of the corn argument, Professor Hollander has to take Ricardo's phrase that 'the profits of the farmer' regulate the profits of all other trades as meaning that 'agricultural productivity' regulates profits. In this, I argued, Hollander ascribes to Ricardo an incorrect use of words in a case in which those words could mean exactly what they say (above p. 91).

(4) Finally, I have argued that the correspondence with Malthus in the spring of 1815 shows Ricardo still unprepared for any reasoning relying on the relative prices of commodities and provides clear evidence of the transition from an early line of reasoning, based on the physical quantities of agriculture, to the line developed later in the *Principles*. I also noticed that this is the same process of transition which we witness when, in December 1815, Ricardo writes to Mill: 'I know I shall soon be stopped by the word price' (section 5 above; cf. Appendix).

APPENDIX

In the letters of 14, 17 and 21 March 1815, the first three since Malthus had advanced his new argument, Ricardo conducts his entire reasoning along the lines of the Table of the *Essay*, i.e. in terms of the comparison between corn production and the expenses estimated in corn incurred for that production, and argues that the total agricultural expenses of production evaluated in corn cannot fall either in the absolute (see *Works*, vol. VI, p. 189) or as a proportion of the whole corn produce (vol. VI, pp. 192–3; 196), when cultivation is extended and the wage rate falls in terms of corn because of the fall of the corn value of its manufactured components.[20]

It is only in his letter of 27 March, the fourth from his side, that Ricardo hints at the argument—based on the proposition that the money-prices of manufactures cannot 'materially rise or fall' in the face of a rise of the price of corn and of money-wages—indicated in the *Essay* (vol. IV, pp. 35, 36), which would be quite decisive against Malthus's present argument. After denying that money-prices in general would rise because of a rise in the price of corn, he writes: 'I am of the opinion that a rise in the price of corn always lowers general profits by increasing wages' (vol. VI, p. 205). However, in the preceding lines of even this letter he had followed the old line of argument concerning a fall in the rate of profit arising from the fact that, as cultivation is extended, 'the whole *corn* cost of production on the land' will bear a larger proportion to 'the whole corn produce' (vol. VI, p. 204). In the subsequent

---

[20] Ricardo is mistaken here, since, if the proportionate decline in the productivity of labour on inferior lands is sufficiently steep, and the price of corn rises relative to manufactures in proportion to the quantity of labour required on the no-rent land, then such an absolute or relative decline may indeed occur over some interval of the extension of cultivation.

letter of 4 April Ricardo, while mentioning the constancy of other money-prices as the price of corn rises (pp. 210–11), continues to centre his attention on the *agricultural* rate of profit, although the only thing he can then do is to throw the argument back at Malthus: 'before my theory is affected it must be shown that the whole [additional surplus] will not remain with the landlord' (vol. VI, p. 209).

Even more significant for the fact that Ricardo still feels uneasy over an argument centred on manufacturing profits is the succeeding letter of 17 April. There, it is true, Ricardo states his new line of argument more fully than on 27 March or 4 April: 'I think that the price of commodities will be very slightly affected either by a rise or fall in the price of corn. If so, every rise in the price of corn must affect profits on manufactures, and it is impossible that agricultural profits can materially deviate from them' (vol. VI, p. 213), a line of argument which, at the cost of neatly turning upside down the principle of the determining role of agricultural profits (as Malthus was quick to point out — vol. VI, p. 207), would seem decisive against Malthus. But instead of relying on this argument, Ricardo again turns to the agricultural profit rate in an independent attempt to show how this could fall in spite of the fall in the corn-price of the manufactures entering the wage, only to arrive at the following inconclusive close: 'if . . . we had supposed the price of corn to rise to £6 then profits would be *increased* and would be much more than 25%, but some adequate cause must be shown for such rise and it cannot be arbitrarily assumed' (vol. VI, p. 214, my italics). And, what is more, instead of appealing back at this point to the previous *conclusive* argument, he goes on to plead with Malthus: 'the whole appears to me a labyrinth of difficulties; one is no sooner got over one than another presents itself, and so in the endless succession. Let me entreat you to give my simple doctrine fair consideration (vol. VI, p. 214), where, as the context and Malthus's answer (vol. VI, pp. 216–17) show, the 'simple doctrine' is that embodied in the Table of the *Essay* where such value changes are ignored and agricultural capital is treated *as if* it consisted entirely of corn.

The following two letters, which are the last dealing with Malthus's 'ingenious argument', consider then the case in which 'a large tract of rich land were added to the Island'. In the first (21 April) Ricardo coordinates the two lines of argument as follows:

> a given quantity of food only being required, that quantity could be raised in the rich land added to the Island, with much less capital than was employed on the old . . ., and *profits on the land* would rise at the expense of the rent of the landlord, whilst the cheaper price of corn would raise the profits on all manufacturing capital (vol. VI, pp. 220–1),

where he still relies *primarily* on agricultural profits. The same is done even more strongly in the last letter (8 May). There we in fact find a good example of what we contended earlier (section 4): of how an underlying reasoning in physical terms is used to argue about the behaviour of money values:

> If then the money value of the produce from the land should fall, from facility of production, it must ever continue to bear a greater ratio to the whole money value of the capital employed on the land, for there will be a great increase of average produce per acre, *whilst the fall in money value will be common to both capital and produce.* (Vol. VI, p. 226; my italics)

As we stated earlier, the Ricardo of this correspondence still appears to be far from the labour theory of the *Principles*. Thus, in his early letters he assumes that the price of corn, relative to money and manufactures, will only rise in proportion to the *corn expenses* incurred, and not in proportion to the quantity of labour required. As he makes clear in the letter of 17 March, where he writes, 'the price of corn would not, I think, rise in proportion to the greater number of men employed but to the greater amount of [corn] wages paid:' (vol. VI, p. 193),[21] the corn expenses for wages rise in a lower proportion than the quantity of labour required to produce the corn, because the rate of wages, valued in corn, falls together with the lower corn value of its manufactured components. It may also be observed that in the first two letters of this exchange Ricardo incorrectly relates the rise in the price of corn to the rise in the *average* corn expenses of production, and not to the expenses incurred on the no-rent land (pp. 193, 197), though he corrects his error in the succeeding letter of 21 March (p. 198).

It is in his letter of 17 April that Ricardo appears finally to abandon the supposition of a rise in the money price of corn proportionate to its costs in terms of corn. In that letter he seems, however, uncertain as to what will in fact regulate the size of the rise in the price of corn. Thus, in the arithmetical example he gives, he assumes a rise in the price of corn which is in fact *higher* than in proportion to the labour required (vol. VI, pp. 213–14)[22] only to conclude with the passage already quoted in this Appendix about the 'labyrinth of difficulties' which the question raises. It is only in the subsequent

---

[21] See also the preceding letters of 14 March (*Works*, vol. VI, p. 189) and Ricardo's correction of the phrase 'less labour' with 'less cost of labour' in the letter of 21 March (p. 197). See finally the expression 'corn and labour' entering the value of the money-commodity, and the expression 'labour and expense' of bringing that same money commodity to market in, respectively, the letters of 27 March (p. 203) and 4 April (p. 211).

[22] Hollander, 1979, p. 161, argues that the rise is there calculated by Ricardo in proportion to the *money*-costs of producing the corn on the no-rent land. This is not true (the price rises in the proportion 1/8, smaller than the proportion $(289 - 256)/258$ in which these costs rise): indeed, if Hollander were correct, the rate of profit could not have fallen.

letter (21 April) that Ricardo seems to find again some firmer ground by indicating this time a rise in the money-price of corn which is in proportion to the labour required on the no-rent land. He writes there: 'it appears to me that my table is applicable to all cases in which the relative price of corn rises from more labour being required to produce it *and under no other circumstances can there be a rise*... unless commodities fall in value from less labour being required for their production (vol. VI, p. 220; my italics).

REFERENCES

Eatwell, J. (1973). 'The Interpretation of Ricardo's *Essay on Profits*'. *Economica*, 40, 260–82.
Garegnani, P. (1960). *Il capitale nelle teorie della distribuzione*. Milan: Giuffré.
Garegnani, P. (1983a). 'Ricardo's Early Theory of Profits and its Rational Foundation: A Reply to Professor Hollander'. *Cambridge Journal of Economics*, 7, 175–8.
Garegnani, P. (1983b). 'The Classical Theory of Wages and the Role of Demand Schedules in the Determination of Relative Prices'. *American Economic Review*, 309–13.
Hollander, S. (1973a). *The Economics of Adam Smith*. London: Heinemann.
Hollander, S. (1973b). 'Ricardo's Analysis of the Profit Rate, 1813–15'. *Economica*, 40, 260–82.
Hollander, S. (1975). 'Ricardo and the Corn Profit Model: Reply to Eatwell'. *Economica*, 42, 188–202.
Hollander, S. (1979). *The Economics of David Ricardo*. London: Heinemann.
Hollander, S. (1983). 'Professor Garegnani's Defence of Sraffa on the Material Rate of Profit'. *Cambridge Journal of Economics*, 7, 167–74.
Ricardo, D. (1951–73). *Works and Correspondence* (11 vols), ed. P. Sraffa. Cambridge: CUP.
Samuelson, P. (1962). 'Parable and Realism in Capital Theory'. *Review of Economic Studies*, 29, 193–206.
Smith, A. (1910). *An Inquiry into the Nature and Causes of the Wealth of Nations*, vols I and II. London: Dent and Sons (first published in 1776).
Sraffa, P. (1951). 'Introduction to Ricardo's *Principles*'. In Ricardo's *Works*, vol. I. Cambridge: CUP.

6

Hollander's Ricardo

ALESSANDRO RONCAGLIA

In the current debate on the interpretation of David Ricardo's economic thought, Sraffa's edition of Ricardo's *Works and Correspondence* undoubtedly is the central point of reference. My aim in this paper is to confront it with those interpretations which Sraffa's edition of Ricardo was meant to supersede, and with those interpretations that have been put forward in opposition to it. In doing this, I will use as my term of comparison Samuel Hollander's book on *The Economics of David Ricardo* (1979a), which is the culmination of many papers (cf. Hollander, 1971, 1973b, 1975, 1977a, 1977b, 1977c, 1979b; Hicks and Hollander, 1977). It is also a sequel to his book on Adam Smith (1973a). It is intended to be 'the definitive work for decades' (according to the publisher's description), and part of a far-reaching reconstruction of the history of economic thought.

Hollander's Ricardo stresses the interdependence of distributive and pricing problems, and the market as an allocative mechanism. Ricardo emerges as fully integrated in the tradition of general equilibrium theorists, descending from Adam Smith to the neoclassical writers. This assessment challenges the view of Sraffa and restores the previous judgement of Alfred Marshall (1961, appendix I). On this basis the history of economic thought would appear as a continuous homogeneous line, centred on the market as an allocative mechanism and revolving around supply-and-demand equilibrium and general interdependence.

Hollander's views dispute, therefore, any clear-cut distinction (methodological, conceptual and analytical) between classical political economy and neoclassical marginalist economics. For Hollander, if dividing lines are introduced, they should separate the classical and neoclassical tradition mainly from the ('modern') Cambridge position:

Thanks (but no implication) are due to K. Bharadwaj, G. Caravale, J. Eatwell, P. Garegnani, P. Groenewegen, G. Harcourt, J. Kregel, G. Montani, A. Rosselli, B. Schefold, I. Steedman, P. Sylos Labini, M. Tonveronachi for useful comments on a previous draft.

The modern 'Cambridge' school of economists finds little merit in general equilibrium procedure, and champions, rather, an approach involving the treatment of prices, production levels, and distribution by means of separate models with an eye upon the isolation of 'one-way-direction' relationships or the 'causal ordering' of variables. [Pasinetti, 1974; Roncaglia, 1978; Garegnani, 1970; and Dobb, 1973, are cited as instances.]

This is a method commonly attributed to Ricardo and Sraffa (as well as to Marx and Keynes). The conclusion to which I am led by the evidence presented in this book is that Ricardo's method has much more in common with that of the general equilibrium theorists. (Hollander, 1979a, p. 689; 1979b, p. 458)

Thus, Hollander's interpretation of Ricardo is also an attack on the Sraffian reconstruction of political economy which offers a fully consistent solution to some problems classical economists had left open (centring on the relationship between prices and distribution), while remaining within their conceptual framework. As Hollander (1979a, p. 4) stresses, 'each generation rewrites its own history of economics': the debate on alternative interpretations of the history of economic thought, at its best, is nothing else but a debate on fundamentals among competing theoretical schools (on this, see also Roncaglia, 1978, pp. xiii–xiv).

A discussion of Hollander's interpretation compels some reference to the basic background for this debate. Thereafter Hollander's conception of the analytical core of the Ricardian system and the relationships connecting income distribution to population growth and capital accumulation will be examined. On this basis Hollander's account of Ricardo's theory of profits will be discussed, and his position will be argued to be unwarranted. Scepticism follows on his more general reconsideration of the classical and the marginalist approaches.

1 THE CLASSICAL AND MARGINALIST APPROACH

The thesis of a clear-cut distinction between classical and marginalist economists is widespread: Hollander cites both Schumpeter (1954) and Knight (1956). Marshall's reconciliation attempt, with which Hollander explicitly identifies himself, did not succeed in overturning the general feelings expressed by Jevons (1879, preface to the 2nd edn) in his biting phrase on 'that able but wrong-headed man, David Ricardo, [who] shunted the car of economic science onto a wrong line.'

Sraffa (1960, p. 93), in placing his analysis in the context of the classical 'picture of the system of production and consumption as a circular process', stresses that 'it stands in striking contrast to the view presented by modern [that is, marginalist] theory, of a one-way avenue that leads from "factors of production" to "consumption goods".' This is probably the most synthetic way of separating the two approaches, based on the very conception of the economic process and implying a basic analytical difference relating to the choice of data. As a consequence of this choice, the two different lines of analysis acquire different meaning and interpretative power, so that they cannot be considered as alternatives for exposing the same phenomena. There are the following differences.

(1) As Sraffa stresses, within the classical (or 'surplus') approach, the economic process is one of continuous reproduction (and enlargement) of the material bases of human societies, as 'production of commodities by means of commodities'. At the beginning of the production period, specific quantities of commodities are advanced, as means of production or as subsistence for the workers employed. In a 'productive' system the productive utilization of these commodities yields outputs in excess of the initial stocks: the excess constitutes the surplus, consisting of a heterogeneous set of goods.

From this picture of the events, a number of analytical issues are derived. Central in a capitalist society is the *distribution* of the surplus among the various social classes (also because distribution exerts a decisive influence over accumulation). There is also the related influence of income distribution on relative prices. These ratios must allow all sectors a profit inducement to repeat the production sequence. Prices must at least cover production costs, and in a competitive situation the difference between product prices and costs must be such as to generate a uniform rate of profits in all productive sectors.

In dealing with distribution, Ricardo found himself deeply entangled with relative prices. Analogous involvement would take place, by logical necessity, with other analytical issues such as the growth of the system in time, induced technical change and so on. It is because of these ramifications that the problem of relative prices and their relationship with distribution is said to be the 'core' of the Ricardian system, and generally of the classical 'surplus' approach (see Garegnani, 1970, section 8; and Garegnani, 1978, section 4). Also, from this 'core' the way is open to the identification of causal chains, even to the recognition of the historical evolution of economic variables: many consider the 'openness to history' a decisive virtue of the 'surplus' approach over the marginalist one.

Ricardo's 'core' contribution is regarded as a substantial advance over Smithian analysis. Technology and the real wage rate are the necessary and sufficient data for determining the rate of profits (and 'exchange values'). As a major consequence, profits appear as generated in *production* (and not in exchange, through 'sale over costs', as the 'mercantilists' maintained). The rate of profits was therefore not determined by other forces (such as the Smithian 'competition of capitals', already present, e.g., in Massie (1750) and Hume (1752), and defended by Malthus in his discussions with Ricardo) independent of technology and the wage rate. Finally, an inverse relationship between the wage rate and rate of profits was established for any given set of technological conditions.

(2) The marginalist (or neoclassical) approach generally characterizes economic activity as the rational (i.e., optimizing) utilization of scarce resources for the satisfaction of human wants and desires. Following Robbins's (1935) well-known definition, 'Economics is the science which studies human behaviour as a relationship between ends and scarce means which have alternative uses' (p. 16). This is more than simply asserting that 'consumption is the sole end and purpose of all production' (which is all Hollander can find in Ricardo: see 1979a, pp. 544–50). It implies a different functioning of an economic system from that specified by Ricardo. For marginalist economists, at any moment in time each economic subject has definite amounts of resources at command and a certain set of preferences denoting alternative modes of consumption. On the basis of these data, the optimizing individual acts in order to maximize his satisfaction through exchange and through production, where resources are transformed into final outputs. Technological knowledge—but not the choice of the technology to be used—is included among the data.

The 'analytical core' of the marginalist approach thus appears to be the model of pure exchange, whereby perfect competition is depicted as the solution to the problem of the optimal allocation of scarce resources. Prices are interpreted as indexes of resource scarcity relative to wants; income distribution comes out as a by-product of price determination, distributive variables being but the prices for the services of the so-called 'factors of production'. Production processes are only an intermediate stage connecting final consumers' tastes to the initial endowments of scarce original resources.

The distinction between the classical surplus and the marginalist neo-classical approach has been characterized as a counterposition of reproducibility versus scarcity (e.g., Pasinetti, 1965). Yet, both aspects are present in each approach: in the classical theory scarcity is a prerequisite for a good to be a commodity, i.e., to be economically relevant—air is not a commodity. For marginalists the transformation of primary resources into useful goods through production is taken into account as a complication which does not imply substantial modification of the structure of the analysis. None the less, scarcity and reproducibility play a different part within each schema.

Analogously, we might illustrate the counterposition of the respective 'subjective' and 'objective' theories of value. The subjective element dominates marginalism through the stress on consumers' tastes in settling relative values. For the classical theory relative values are attributed to the objective 'difficulty of production', be it represented by a single magnitude (labour-contained) or the set of technical coefficients of production.

This sketch should not be construed as merely parading a simple choice between differing viewpoints. In fact, as the recent (Cambridge–Cambridge) capital theory debates have shown, the structure of the analytical core of marginalism is such as to limit it to the study of 'temporary equilibria': it is impossible for it to deal in a consistent way with such a basic capitalist phenomenon as the long-run class division of income. Too, the rate of profit cannot be determined on a supply-and-demand analysis of a 'factor of production' called capital (in either aggregate or disaggregate models), since capital contains produced and reproducible commodities whose endowments cannot be taken as 'given' in a long-run context, and whose prices depend on income distribution (see Sraffa, 1960; Garegnani, 1960; and, for a summary, Harcourt, 1972, or Roncaglia, 1978, ch. 6).

This outline of the main characteristics of the respective conceptions provides a reference ground for testing Hollander's attempt at portraying Ricardo in a homogeneous stream culminating in marginalist economists.

2 MARSHALL AND JACOB HOLLANDER ON RICARDO: THE EARLY RECONCILIATION

Well antedating Samuel Hollander, there were two significant attempts to narrow the Ricardo and marginalist breach. Marshall was first in time and influence, and he observed: 'We must interpret [Ricardo] generously, more generously than he himself interpreted Adam Smith' (1961, p. 813). This 'generosity' (which is also adopted by Hollander, 1973a) meant discarding Ricardo's 'surplus' approach, a disposal fostered by its dilution by 'Ricardians' (see Bharadwaj, 1978b); then short sentences, when taken out of context, were interpreted as gestures to vaguely shaped marginalist notions.

In point is Ricardo's 'discussion of the difference between "Value and Riches",' where 'he seems to be feeling his way towards the distinction between marginal and total utility', notwithstanding the immediately pre-ceding recognition by Ricardo that utility is simply a *prerequisite* of value, and not a measurable element determining its magnitude, even in the sense of comparisons between different commodities. No meaning, therefore, can be attributed within Ricardo's analysis to 'marginal' and 'total' utility.

The same can be said with respect to Ricardo's recognition of the influence of changes in the rate of profits on relative prices. This is read by Marshall as proof of a commitment to 'the fact that Time or Waiting as well as Labour is an element of cost of production'. (On the same lines, see Edelberg, 1933). However, this reading is gratuitous, since Ricardo neither says nor implies anything about the explanation, even less the determination, of the profit rate in terms of Time or Waiting; nor does he recognize a specific 'factor of production' called capital.

In general, as is well known, Marshall maintained that objective and subjective theories complemented each other, as the two blades of the scissor, representing 'component parts of the one all-ruling law of supply and demand', with supply stressed by classical economists, while the demand represents the marginalist contribution (1961, p. 820). This reading of price determination is often supported (Hollander, 1979a, ch. 6, or Rankin, 1980) with references to Ricardo's analysis of market prices changes; but the analysis of the adjustment process has little to do with Ricardo's main theoretical preoccupation, the determination of 'natural' or 'normal' prices. In passing, Marshall is also wrong in maintaining that Ricardo was able to overlook the influence of demand on natural prices only thanks to an implicit assumption of constant returns to scale. Shove (1942, pp. 296–7) pointed out that Marshall's interpretation is contradicted by Ricardo's stress on diminishing returns in the then dominant economic sector, agriculture.

Samuel Hollander accords Marshall's interpretation a cordial reception. He admits that 'Ricardo failed to appreciate the conception of marginal utility' (1979a, p. 277) and 'could see no way that "utility"...could be measured, and denied interpersonal comparability' (p. 278; see also p. 596). Hollander nevertheless hastens to add that 'the distinction between total and marginal utility and the conception of diminishing marginal utility could easily have been accommodated' in Ricardo (p. 279; also p. 659, where Ricardo's—and Smith's—concern for real per capita income is read as a concern for utility). This is equivalent to saying that it is easy to add a teaspoon of salt to a cup of tea (and to equate taste for tea with support for the British Empire).

Marshall's 'Time or Waiting' is also adopted by Hollander (pp. 211, 317, 671–2). He speaks of 'compensation for the postponement of present consumption' (p. 211), based on a passage in which Ricardo is merely stating that profits must be computed over the whole length of the production period: 'The price of the commodity must also compensate for the length of time that must elapse before it can be brought to market.' Similarly, for Hollander, in Ricardo's writings 'profits appear to be a necessary payment to assure that time-consuming processes are undertaken' (p. 317). This interpretation is also attributed to Schumpeter, who knew better—for Ricardo is only saying that, *given* the existence of profits *and the level* of the rate of profits, prices must behave to accommodate them, without implying anything on the explanation of the level of profits and the rate of profits. Analogously, Ricardo's recognition of 'the effect of a declining profit rate on accumulation' is connected to 'the time preference notion' (p. 672), without recognizing that in marginalist analysis it is time preference that (simultaneously) determines the rate of growth and the rate of interest; in Ricardo the rate of profits determines the rate of capital accumulation.

Marshall's third point, concerning supply and demand in Ricardo's analysis, will be considered later. More subtle, in comparison with Marshall, is Jacob Hollander's (1904, 1910) reading of Ricardo, followed most notably by Cannan (1929, ch. VII, section 3). According to J. Hollander, Ricardo's analysis moves away, in the successive editions of the *Principles* (1817, 1819, 1821), from a stricter adhesion to a labour-contained theory of value to a more general cost-of-production theory, similar to the Smithian adding-up-of-components theory. Ricardo's analysis thus appears less prone to 'socialist' development, and (with the help of Marshall's 'Time or Waiting') a possible starting point for the construction of marginal productivity theories, especially if one takes the theory of differential rent as the historical root of the marginal principle.

The picture of a progressive retreat of Ricardo from a labour-contained theory of value back to a Smithian-like adding-up-of-components theory is demolished by Sraffa (1951), to the general satisfaction of following interpreters (including Samuel Hollander, 1979a, p. 103n, who however minimizes the importance of the issue). Such a characterization can be attributed to Ricardians from McCulloch to John Stuart Mill. Through these changes the ground is laid for the development of a theoretical position such as that propagated in Marshall's *Principles* (see Bharadwaj, 1978a). Samuel Hollander (1977c) tries to maintain a stricter adhesion of the disciples to the ideas of the master, but his arguments are based on the interpretation of Ricardo as a marginalist precursor and on a juxtaposition of quotations unsupported by the underlying analytical structure (on DeQuincey's position in particular, and then for a criticism of Hollander's position in this respect, see Groenewegen, 1974, and mimeo, 1977).

Ricardo's position can be briefly stated on the basis of Sraffa's 1951 contribution.

(1) The labour-contained theory of value does not represent a complete theory of relative prices because of sectoral differences in the ratio of fixed to circulating capital, in the length of the production period, and in the durability of fixed capital.

(2) However, the major proposition on the relationship between distributive variables identifiable in the 'corn (one commodity) model' or of the labour-contained theory of value nevertheless holds: an increase in the wage rate implies a decrease in the rate of profits, and not (contrarily to what Smith seems to imply, at least on Ricardo's reading) a general price increase; certain prices will increase and others diminish, and a case can even be imagined (in which the commodity chosen as a standard of measure is produced by unassisted labour in the shortest production period) in which *all* prices fall. This is true whether the wage rate be expressed in 'real' terms, i.e., in terms of

the labour contained in the basket of commodities consumed by the workers, or in 'money' terms, as in gold when used as the general standard of measure.

3 POPULATION AND WAGES: SUPPLY AND DEMAND IN RICARDO'S ANALYSIS OF DISTRIBUTION

Hollander (1979a) follows Sraffa (1951) in considering the inverse relationship between rate of profits and rate of wages as the analytical core of the Ricardian theory. In his words, where the Ricardian terminology of the rate of profits is replaced by the misleading expression on the 'rate of return on capital', which throws a marginalist flavour on the subject,

> The entire Ricardian scheme is designed to relate the rate of return on capital to the 'value' of per capita wages (Ricardian 'real' wages)— which in effect amounts simply to the proportion of the work-day devoted to the production of wages—and variations in the rate of return to (inverse) variations in the 'real' wage rate. This relationship will be referred to as 'the fundamental theorem on distribution.' (Hollander, 1979a, p. 7)

This thesis implies the rejection of a possible alternative interpretation of Ricardo, according to which Ricardo's main theme involves the description of the evolution in time of the economy toward a stationary state (see, for instance, Stigler, 1952; Kaldor, 1955; Samuelson, 1959; Blaug, 1968; and, even if with a stronger stress on the role of the theory of value, Caravale and Tosato, 1980). In fact, for Ricardo the stationary state appears as an aside (see, e.g., *Works*, vol. I, p. 109), so much so that the term 'stationary state' is absent from Sraffa's index (*Works*, vol. XI). The stationary state theme can rather be said to derive from J. S. Mill's lengthy treatment in his *Principles of Political Economy* (1848, bk IV). Hollander is explicit on this point:

> To single out the theorem relating to a declining rate of return on capital is to exaggerate the import of a particular application of the basic theory.... Ricardo paid more careful attention to the general principle of the inverse wage–profit relationship than to the particular issue of a falling profit rate. (Hollander, 1979a, p. 12)

In fact, even if one were to accept that this 'particular application' was regarded by Ricardo as of fundamental political relevance, Hollander would be correct in separating this issue from the analytical role played by the various elements in Ricardo's theoretical construction, and in asserting the dominance of the wage–profit relationship within the Ricardian scheme. While we may be justified in attributing to Ricardo a 'value judgement' on which every obstacle to accumulation must be condemned, his analytical premise of the strict connection between profits and investments allows us to locate a 'political' bias on the analytical prominence of distribution. But for the reconstruction of his analytical model, the weight of the wage–profit relationship cannot be denied. Even after dropping his value judgement on accumulation, or the equating of profits and investments, the wage–profit relationship still retains its crucial position in the conceptual classical framework, as in the modern Sraffa revival.

There is, however, another way of hurdling the importance often attributed to Ricardo's acceptance (possibly for deriving certain politically relevant deductions from his theory) of the Malthusian population principle. Connecting by means of functional relationships the rate of growth of population to the wage rate, and the rate of capital accumulation to the rate of profits, allows some commentators (see Hicks and Hollander, 1977; Hicks, 1979; and especially Casarosa, 1974 and 1978) to impute to Ricardo a supply-and-demand mechanism for the determination of income distribution different but parallel to the typical neoclassical practice. In this vein the rate of interest—the price of the 'factor of production' capital—balances demand and supply of capital, while the wage rate weighs off the disutility of work against labour's marginal productivity (supply and demand of labour).

In Ricardo, where the rate of accumulation depends on the rate of profits (the two are equal when profits are fully reinvested and non-capitalists' savings are nil), if the Malthusian rate of growth of population is made to rest on the wage rate, we will have an 'equilibrium' wage rate, and rate of profits on the wage–profit frontier corresponding to a growth rate of population that equals the rate of capital accumulation. For higher wage rates (and, correspondingly, profit rates below the equilibrium level) the population 'supply' would outrun the 'demand', so a real wage reduction will result from a stable equilibrium adjustment process whereby income distribution becomes endogenous, within a supply and demand mechanism. The assumption of decreasing returns in agriculture allows a tracing of an equilibrium path (a 'dynamic' or 'moving' equilibrium: see Casarosa, 1978, pp. 41 and 50) for the distributive variables, which in the limit is the stationary economy (see Hicks and Hollander, 1977, p. 367).

However, the legitimacy of this extrapolation from Ricardo's writings is dubious. It is certainly true that, according to Ricardo (*Works*, vol. I, p. 93), 'the natural price of labor is that price which is necessary to enable the laborers, one with another, to subsist and to perpetuate their race, without either increase or diminution', so that the subsistence wage corresponds to a well specified (zero) growth rate of population. As a consequence, the wage rate may be higher than the natural price of labour for an indefinite length of time in a country in which population and wealth are increasing (Ricardo, *Works*, vol. I, pp. 94–5). However, there is a long swath from this to a model based on the functional relationships summarized above.

Ricardo does *not* state that the greater the difference between actual and subsistence wage rates, the higher the growth of population: he avoids even a hint at a precise functional relationship between the real wage and population growth.

Moreover, the growth of population induced by a wage rate above the subsistence level has a small and very delayed bearing on the labour supply: in so far as it entails a lower death rate for old or retired people, it does not affect the size of the labour force; in so far as it involves a diminution of infantile mortality, or an increase in the birth rate, it will only affect the size of active population after many years—Malthus himself, stressing the importance of this element, spoke of a lag of sixteen to eighteen years; Ricardo did not find anything to criticize in this assertion (*Works*, vol. II, p. 225). Furthermore, as Kregel (1977) shows, international mobility of labour cannot help: 'If the natural price of labor is different in different countries ... spatial mobility of labor can do nothing to affect these differences; it cannot even assure that market wages will correspond more closely to natural wages' (p. 218).

Besides, there are some other reservations on the implied relationship between the rate of capital accumulation and rate of growth of the demand for labour, namely, the implicit assumption of a constant (or constant rate of change in the) capital–labour ratio, which would be a restrictive assumption on technology and technical change and on the quality of different plots of land. (It is true that Ricardo sometimes sweeps away these complications—see, e.g., *Works*, vol. IV, p. 12—but he is conscious of their reality—see vol. IV, p. 11—so that the simplifying nature of the assumption is known to limit the generality of the deductions following from it. Something analogous can be said for the influence over the wage rate of supply and demand of labour.)

In general, one must recall Ricardo's scepticism of the study of production levels, and of their movements in time, and his idea of the limited scope of the real strength of political economy. In a letter to Malthus (9 October 1820), he writes:

> Political Economy you think is an enquiry into the nature and causes of wealth—I think it should rather be called an enquiry into the laws which determine the division of the produce of industry among the classes who concur in its formation. No law can be laid down respecting quantity, but a tolerably correct one can be laid down respecting proportions. Every day I am more satisfied that the former enquiry is vain and delusive, and the latter only the true objects of the science. (*Works*, vol. VIII, pp. 278–9)

This passage not only confirms Hollander's thesis about 'the entire Ricardian scheme [being] designed [to prove] the fundamental theorem on distribution'. It does something more: it points to a certain problem, and a certain set of analytical propositions, as being considered not simply the most relevant ones, but somehow separable from the others as the analytical 'core' to which alone the term science is fully applicable. The cobweb of deductions that can be built around it for dealing with a whole series of other problems (notably, all problems on the size of the economic system and its movements in time) should methodologically be deflected on to a different plane.

4 HOLLANDER AND THE 'PHYSICAL' THEORY OF THE RATE OF PROFITS

Hollander's main argument for assimilating Ricardian to marginalist analysis (in contrast to Sraffa's 1960 analysis) must therefore stem from the 'core' of the Ricardian system. Here are two distinct (obviously related) aspects: (1) Sraffa's reading of a 'physical' theory of the rate of profits in Ricardo, and (2) the role of supply and demand, and the relationship between distribution and pricing.

All interpreters of Ricardo now agree that he initially accepts the Smithian theory of the rate of profits as determined by the 'competition of capitals', but then refutes it with an original theory of his own in a decisive contribution to economic analysis. According to Sraffa (1951, pp. xxxi–xxxii), Ricardo's 'new theory' takes shape in early 1814 (the lost 'papers on the profits of Capital'), where the rate of profits is determined within the agricultural sector as a 'physical' ratio of surplus product to capital advanced. In the *Essay on Profits* (1815) the new theory is already put to work, together with the principle of diminishing returns on land for the derivation of politically relevant conclusions. Hollander (1973b, 1975, 1979a, ch. 3) argues that Sraffa's interpretation fails on at least three (related and substantial) points: (1) the interpretation of the rate of profits as a 'physical' ratio; (2) the secondary role of the distinction between 'money' and 'real' wage rates; (3) the role of the quantity theory of money in the 'fundamental theorem on distribution'. Let us consider briefly these points.

(1) As is well-known, classical economists considered profits (together with rents and eventually that part of wages exceeding subsistence) as the surplus produce of society. Also, classical economists display a general agreement in assuming the ('natural') wage as dependent on long-run social habits. Ricardo adds (Malthusian) differential rent, which, as Wicksteed reminds us, is not based on 'genuine margins' (see Roncaglia, 1978, pp. 105–6) and so is excluded from marginalist theory. Profits can be determined as a residual so that no additional element, beyond those entering into wages,

rents and the size of the surplus (which depends on the technological conditions of production), affects profits. The rate of profits is then defined as the ratio of profits to capital advances. It is a pure number, independent of the choice of the unit of measure; Hollander's (1979a, p. 22) distinction between 'the real or corn rate, of profits' and the 'nominal or silver rate' is thereby a false issue. Obviously, it is necessary that numerator and denominator of the ratio be expressed in homogeneous terms.

According to Sraffa, this is done by Ricardo (initially in the lost 'papers on the profits of Capital', and then in the *Essay on Profits*) with the so-called 'corn model': in the agricultural sector, and in a conscious simplification, both output and capital advances can be considered as made up of a unique commodity, corn, which is used as seed and as subsistence for the employed workers. The rate of profits is thus determined within the agricultural sector as a ratio of homogeneous physical quantities (as a 'physical ratio'): rates of profit in all other sectors thereby adjust to it. In a second stage (with the *Principles*, 1817) Ricardo is obliged to abandon this simplification, not because of the sudden recognition of its nature, but because of Malthus's criticisms of its analytical relevance. He then shifts to a labour theory of value (which is also recognized as a simplification of reality) whereby profits and capital advances are expressed in terms of labour contained.

Hollander's criticisms of the 'corn model' and the 'physical' rate of profits has been aptly refuted by Eatwell (1975) and, more recently and vigorously, by Garegnani (1982). I thus leave aside the question of the dependence of the general profit rate on the agricultural rate, which is a logical corollary of the 'corn model'.

(2) Sraffa's identification of the 'physical' rate of profits has thus a clear logical and a sound textual foundation. Hollander's denial must imply some alternative logic. Two points can be singled out: namely, the importance attributed by Hollander to the distinction between 'money' and 'real' wages, and that attributed to the quantity theory of money.

Ricardo's 'money' wages are obviously wages expressed in money; 'real' wages commonly signify the commodities which the worker buys with his income or, under a labour theory of value, the labour content of such commodities. (In Ricardo's own definition, 'real wages' are the worker's share in the value of his product; but we can retain the common usage, since our reasoning still holds under Ricardo's definition.) Real wages may then be expressed in terms of 'corn', as in the 'physical' model of the *Essay on Profits*, or in terms of labour embodied in these commodities when, as in the *Principles*, a labour theory of value is adopted. However, Ricardo's money is commodity-money; even 'money wages' emerge as 'real'. In general, with commodity-money a rise in money wages is a rise in real wages and implies a reduced surplus to be shared between profits and rents, and a fall in the rate of profits (provided production techniques do not change).

Hollander (1979a) thus exaggerates the distinction. It fogs communication to charge that what Ricardo criticizes is 'Smith's failure to distinguish ... between nominal and relative value' (p. 648). Smith is perfectly aware of this distinction. Ricardo's main target, as remarked, is Smith's theory of profits as determined by the competition of capitals.

As a logical corollary there is Ricardo's criticism of Smith that a rise in money wages can be 'passed on' into a general rise of money prices of all products. (This outcome is typical in a regime of non convertible paper money where the real and money wage discrepancy becomes vital.) Here Hollander compares deductions from alternative analytical schemas and departs from their own main contours (see pp. 138ff, or 160ff, where Ricardo's 'concessions' to Malthus are inherently derivable from both alternative analytical visions).

The distinction between money and real wages, however logically irrelevant within the context of the problem of value as discussed above, serves Hollander in suggesting that income distribution is but a pricing problem, as understood by the marginalists. This distinction also opens the way to attributing a central role to the quantity theory of money.

(3) The stress on the quantity theory of money is the main implication of Hollander's backdating Ricardo's 'new' theory to the Napoleonic era currency controversies (see 1979a, pp. 108ff; there is no reference to this argument in 1973b and 1975). Hollander's thesis of an analytical connection between the quantity theory of money and the inverse wage–profit relationship differs substantially from Tucker's (1954) suggestion that Ricardo's 'new theory' might have originated from his involvement in the currency debate rather than from the debate on the Corn Laws.

In fact, at the time of the currency debates, and up to the *Essay on Profits*, Ricardo still accepted the Smithian thesis that higher money wages compelled a general increase of money prices. Hollander notes, however, that Ricardo became increasingly aware that an increase in the money supply was required for a general increase in the price level. But Ricardo's abandonment of the Smithian thesis was due to his pondering the logical contradiction between it and his 'new theory' of the rate of profits (see Sraffa, 1951, pp. xxxiii–xxxiv).

It was typical of classical theory to visualize money as but a veil; for in the long run the supply of gold and/or convertible paper money automatically adjusts to the needs of the economic system, while gold output and the general level of gold standard prices were related to the cost of production of gold. There is thus neither a textual nor a logical basis for Hollander's (rather tentative) statement that, 'although we cannot be positive about the matter, it is most likely that the statements alluding to the profit rate and those relating to the monetary mechanism are connected rather than independent' (1979a, p. 115).

5 CONFUSING THE CLASSICAL ADJUSTMENT PROCESS WITH THE MARGINALIST ALLOCATION PROBLEM

Hollander's interpretation of Ricardo's abandonment of the Smithian theory of profits can be considered as mainly an abortive attack on the 'surplus' approach. The more 'positive' aspect is Hollander's attempt to tie Ricardian and marginalist economics in a supply and demand package and to reassert the formal identification of distribution and pricing. Thus, Hollander maintains, Ricardianism and neoclassicism share 'a common heritage or "central core", which amounts largely to allocation theory and the mechanism of demand-supply analysis' (1979a, p. 684).

Ricardo's attitude towards supply and demand is reflected in his rejection of Smith's theory of profits. Malthus, while defending this theory, attributes a decisive role to demand in determining the level of money prices in relation to costs, and hence profits (see the passages quoted by Hollander, 1979a, pp. 152–3); Ricardo considers the profit rate as emanating from technology and the wage rate. For Ricardo the supply-and-demand relation only affects market prices; natural prices are traced to the difficulty of production:

> It is the cost of production which must ultimately regulate the price of commodities, and not, as has been often said, the proportion between the supply and demand: the proportion between supply and demand may, indeed, for a time, affect the market value of a commodity, until it is supplied in greater or less abundance, according as the demand may have increased or diminished; but this effect will be only of temporary duration. (*Works*, vol. I, p. 382; see also quotations in Hollander, 1979a, ch. 6)

Yet Hollander claims (1979a, p. 10), 'demand–supply analysis for Ricardo—as for Smith and the neoclassicists—was the vehicle of determination in his general system.' This is not a reference to an adjustment process of actual to theoretical variables, but is Hollander's distillation of the very essence of the Ricardian system. Curiously, in opposing Ricardo's 'modern' interpreters, Hollander chides Malthus, who 'believed *quite erroneously* that Ricardo maintained his cost theory of exchange value as an *alternative* to demand–supply theory' (p. 663; my italics). To make the point means that Hollander overlooks the evidence: (1) that for Ricardo, as for so many other economists, market prices are those actually prevailing in reality, while natural prices are the theoretical variables; (2) that neither Ricardo nor Smith uses supply and demand schedules; (3) that the classical adjustment process is very different from marginalist allocation theory.

On the first point Ricardo's statement (quoted above) should suffice. On the second point, Hollander (1979a, p. 278) explicitly recognizes that 'Ricardo rejected the possibility of specifying precisely the price–quantity relationship': it is a pity that, among so many quotations, Ricardo's statement is not submitted to the reader (*Works*, vol. IV, p. 220). He observes: 'No general rule can be laid down for the variations of price in proportion to quantity.' Thus Hollander's (1979a, pp. 273ff) attempts to find in some of Ricardo's numerical examples instances of demand curves are an equivocal superimposition of a marginalist frame over a non-marginalist position.

On the third point, the misidentification arises from Hollander's misleading use of the allocation term to apply to Ricardo's description of the adjustment process. 'Allocation' aspects refer to the marginalist problem of the optimal utilization of scarce resources confronted with alternative uses; the allocational problem is typically solved by the simultaneous determination of equilibrium prices and quantities. In the classical ('surplus') approach the economic system reproduces itself over time, and the study of the factors modifying the structure of production is severed from the study of the analytical 'core' of the system. Ricardo, in particular, does not consider as a theoretical problem the 'choice' of the structure of production, which is visualized as a *historical* problem, with the production structure adapting to evolving social habits and to technological developments. In fact, what Ricardo discusses is simply the effect on the *market* price of a difference between supply and 'effectual' demand (i.e., the demand corresponding to natural prices); the deviation of the market price from its 'natural' level then induces a tendency of supply to adjust to effectual demand, followed by a tendency of the market price to return to the natural price. Natural prices and production structure are clearly considered as previously determined data for the adjustment process.

Be it noted, in passing, that the clash Hollander (pp. 10, 684–9) perceives between Ricardo's and Sraffa's (1960) analyses dissolves. Sraffa (p. 9), like Ricardo, preserves the classical distinction between market and natural prices. This shared distinction is not abolished by the fact that Ricardo elaborates the adjustment mechanism while Sraffa does not. It is certainly not conclusive evidence of a discrepancy about the analytical mechanism determining natural prices.

Another Hollander thesis to pour Ricardo into marginalism is in asserting that in the Ricardian, 'as in the Smithian and the neoclassical systems, distribution and pricing are interdependent', and that 'changes in the pattern of final demand can affect the wage rate' (1979a, p. 10; see also pp. 680–1). This is correct, within certain limits: in the Ricardian and 'surplus' approach, distribution can be affected by the pattern of final demand (1) through its effect on the 'exogenous' wage rate in the classical tradition or the rate of profits, as suggested by Sraffa (1960, p. 33; 'exogenous' here means 'external to the analytical core'); (2) through its effect on the level of production in the various sectors and, hence, out of the constant returns case, over technology, and as a consequence over the whole wage rate–profits rate curve.

What is wrong is what Hollander conveys as a similarity between the classical and the marginalist *theory* of distribution and pricing. In the Walrasian model, which Hollander recalls (1979a, p. 683), once technology, consumers' tastes and the initial endowments of resources are given, all prices, including the services of the factors of production, are obtained as the solution to a general equilibrium system. Here 'distribution and pricing are interdependent' for they are one and the same thing.

There is no ground for imputing this position to Ricardo; but Hollander does so in discussing the determination of the rate of profits as a problem of pricing and in invoking supply and demand of capital notions (1979a, pp. 250–5, 680–3). We also have Hollander describing profits as compensation for saving, or deferring present consumption (see above, p. 110). Hollander is in good company: no less an authority than Samuelson, after having under-played the analytical individualism of Smith and Ricardo by a marginalist lumping of their theories (see 1959, 1978), leans over to the Smithian theory of profits based on the competition of capitals as against Ricardo's criticisms (1980, p. 577) of a supply-and-demand analysis of distribution. But it is precisely in this reference that marginalism shows its limits: the capital theory controversies of the 1960s established the *impossibility* of determining the rate of profits with a supply-and-demand mechanism. Ricardo's 'surplus' approach is vindicated against all attempts at 'modernizing' it in a marginalist mould.

6 THE CONNECTION BETWEEN THEORY AND THE HISTORY OF ECONOMIC THOUGHT

Hollander's mass of quotations sometimes shows Ricardo, especially in his occasional speeches or letters, including elements and causal relationships that 'modify' or 'complicate' his central thought structure. These papers can be used for exonerating Ricardo from the 'Ricardian vice' of applying theory to reality without the necessary qualifications. Ricardo surely was well aware that 'There are more things in heaven and earth than are dreamt of in [his analysis].' But the provisos and the zeal of modern terminology cannot transform Ricardo into a general equilibrium Walrasian. Hollander's erudition is a very welcome contribution to the clarification of a number of important specific issues, such as the relative importance, within Ricardo's analytical framework, of the tendency to a stationary state in comparison to the 'fundamental theorem on distribution'.

One must also agree with Hollander that the whole set of issues discussed above reveals the impossibility of separating the debates in the history of economic thought from theoretical debates. This intellectual division of labour, common at universities all over the world, on the one hand carries risks of leaving us unable to establish a rational 'string' connecting or separating past authors, often limiting us to anecdotal history and an inconclusive barrage of quotations; on the other hand, without reference to the historical background, theoreticians cannot understand the conceptual frame which alone gives a concrete meaning to otherwise purely formal analytical schemes.

REFERENCES

Bharadwaj, K. (1978a). 'The Subversion of Classical Theory: Alfred Marshall's Early Writings on Value'. *Cambridge Journal of Economics*, 2, 253–71.

Bharadwaj, K. (1978b). *Classical Political Economy and Rise to Dominance of Supply and Demand Theory*. New Delhi: Orient Longman.

Blaug, M. (1968). *Economic Theory in Retrospect* (2nd edn). Homewood, Ill.: Irwin.

Cannan, F. (1929). *A Review of Economic Theory*. Reprinted in London: Frank Cass, 1964.

Caravale, G. and Tosato, D. (1980). *Ricardo and the Theory of Value, Distribution and Growth*. London: Routledge & Kegan Paul.

Casarosa, C. (1974). 'La teoria ricardiana della distribuzione e dello sviluppo economico'. *Rivista di politica economica*, 44, 959–1015.

Casarosa, C. (1978). 'A New Formulation of the Ricardian System'. *Oxford Economic Papers*, 30, 38–63.

Dobb, M. (1973). *Theories of Value and Distribution Since Adam Smith*. London: Cambridge University Press.

Eatwell, J. (1975). 'The Interpretation of Ricardo's *Essay on Profits*'. *Economica*, 42, 182–7.

Edelberg, V. (1933). 'The Ricardian Theory of Profits'. *Economica*, 13, 51–74.

Garegnani, P. (1960). *Il capitale nelle teorie della distribuzione*. Milan: Giuffré.

Garegnani, P. (1970). 'Heterogeneous Capital, the Production Function and the Theory of Distribution'. *Review of Economic Studies*, 37, 407–36.

Garegnani, P. (1978). 'La realtà dello sfruttamento.' *Rinascita*, 35, 31–2.

Garegnani, P. (1982). 'On Hollander's Interpretation of Ricardo's Early Theory of Profits'. *Cambridge Journal of Economics*, 6, no. 1.

Groenewegen, P. (1974). 'Review of *Theories of Value and Distribution since Adam Smith* by M. Dobb'. *Economic Journal*, 84, 192–3.

Groenewegen, P. (1977). 'Thomas DeQuincey: Faithful Disciple of Ricardo?' Unpublished paper.

Harcourt, G. C. (1972). *Some Cambridge Controversies in the Theory of Capital*. London: CUP.

Hicks, J. (1979). 'The Ricardian System: a Comment'. *Oxford Economic Papers*, 31, 133–4.

Hicks, J. and Hollander, S. (1977). 'Mr Ricardo and the Moderns'. *Quarterly Journal of Economics*, 91, 351–69.

Hollander, J. (1904). 'The Development of Ricardo's Theory of Value'. *Quarterly Journal of Economics*, 18, 455–91.

Hollander, J. (1910). *David Ricardo—A Centenary Estimate*. Reprinted in New York: McKelley 1968.

Hollander, S. (1971). 'The Development of Ricardo's Position on Machinery'. *History of Political Economy*, 3, 105–35.

Hollander, S. (1973a). *The Economics of Adam Smith*. London: Heinemann.

Hollander, S. (1973b). 'Ricardo's Analysis of the Profit Rate, 1813–15'. *Economica*, 40, 260–82.

Hollander, S. (1975). 'Ricardo and the Corn Profit Model: Reply to Eatwell'. *Economica*, 42, 188–202.

Hollander, S. (1977a). 'Ricardo and the Corn Laws: A Revision'. *History of Political Economy*, 9, 1–47.

Hollander, S. (1977b). 'Smith and Ricardo: Aspects of the Nineteenth Century Legacy'. *American Economic Review*, 67, 37–41.

Hollander, S. (1977c). 'The Reception of Ricardian Economics'. *Oxford Economic Papers*, 20, 221–57.

Hollander, S. (1979a). *The Economics of David Ricardo*. Toronto: University of Toronto Press.

Hollander, S. (1979b). 'Review of *Sraffa and the Theory of Prices*, by A. Roncaglia'. *History of Political Economy*, 11, 454–58.

Hume, D. (1752). 'On Interest'. First published in *Political Discourses*. Reprinted in *Essays: Moral, Political and Literary*. London: Longmans, 1875.

Jevons, W. S. (1879). *The Theory of Political Economy* (2nd edn). London: Macmillan.

Kaldor, N. (1955). 'Alternative Theories of Distribution'. *Review of Economic Studies*, 23, 83–100.

Knight, F. H. (1956). *On the History and Method of Economics*. Chicago: University of Chicago Press.

Kregel, J. A. (1977). 'Ricardo, Trade and Factor Mobility'. *Economia Internazionale*, 30, 215–25.

Malthus, R. (1820). *Principles of Political Economy*. In Ricardo, *Works*, vol. II.

Marshall, A. (1961). *Principles of Economics*, vol. I. (9th (variorum) edn). Ed. C. W. Guillebaud. London: Macmillan.

Massie, J. (1750). *An Essay on the Governing Causes of the Natural Rate of Interest*. Reprint ed. J. Hollander. Baltimore: Johns Hopkins Press, 1912.

Mill, J. S. (1848). *Principles of Political Economy*. London.

Pasinetti, L. (1965). 'A New Theoretical Approach to the Problems of Economic Growth'. *Pontificiae Academiae Scientiarum Scripta Varia*. Amsterdam: North Holland, 571–696.

Pasinetti, L. (1974). *Growth and Income Distribution—Essays in Economic Theory*. London: Cambridge University Press.

Rankin, S. C. (1980). 'Supply and Demand in Ricardian Price Theory: A Reinterpretation'. *Oxford Economic Papers*, 32, 241–62.

Ricardo, D. (1951–73). *Works and Correspondence* (11 vols), ed. P. Sraffa. Cambridge and London: CUP.

Robbins, L. (1935), *An Essay on the Nature and Significance of Economic Science* (2nd edn). London: Macmillan.

Roncaglia, A. (1978). *Sraffa and the Theory of Prices*. London: John Wiley.

Samuelson, P. A. (1959). 'A Modern Treatment of the Ricardian Economy'. *Quarterly Journal of Economics*, 73, 1–35 and 217–31.

Samuelson, P. A. (1978). 'The Canonical Classical Model of Political Economy'. *Journal of Economic Literature*, 16, 1415–34.

Samuelson, P. A. (1980). 'Noise and Signal in Debates among Classical Economists: A Reply'. *Journal of Economic Literature*, 18, 575–8.

Schumpeter, J. A. (1954). *History of Economic Analysis*. New York: Oxford University Press.

Shove, G. (1942). 'The Place of Marshall's *Principles* in the Development of Economic Theory'. *Economic Journal*, 52, 294–329.

Sraffa, P. (1951). 'Introduction to Ricardo's *Principles of Political Economy*'. In Ricardo, *Works*, vol. I, pp. xiii–lxii.

Sraffa, P. (1960). *Production of Commodities by Means of Commodities*. Cambridge: CUP.

Stigler, G. J. (1952). 'The Ricardian Theory of Value and Distribution'. *Journal of Political Economy*, 60, 187–207.

Tucker, G. S. L. (1954). 'The Origin of Ricardo's Theory of Profits'. *Economica*, 21, 320–31.

PART IV

Sraffa-based Interpretations:
An Integrated Approach to Value
and Growth

7

Diminishing Returns and Accumulation in Ricardo

GIOVANNI A. CARAVALE

1 SCOPE AND PLAN OF THE WORK

The aim of this paper is threefold. First, it presents a unifying interpretative schema for Ricardo's problems of value, distribution and growth centred on the relation between diminishing returns and accumulation. Second, it brings out the analogy between this schema and some previous interpretations of Ricardo's theory. Finally, it compares the interpretative schema with two relevant contributions to the field.

In particular, sections 2–6, after recalling Ricardo's 'scientific programme', lay out the foundations for the interpretation here suggested: on the one hand the centrality, for Ricardo, of the concept of natural equilibrium, and on the other the close connection between variations in technology and changes in distribution. Ricardo's treatment of wages is considered in this context. Subsequently some of the implications of the interpretative schema are discussed: in particular, the relation between Ricardo's and Smith's theories of prices, and the role played by the labour theory of value in Ricardo's theoretical construction.

Section 7, on the other hand, tends to emphasize what appears to be a striking similarity between the interpretative schema that is suggested in sections 2–6 and some past interpretations of Ricardo's theory which, for different reasons, seem to be of great relevance. The striking aspect of the analogy is that, whereas the interpretative schema suggested in sections 2–6 benefits from the analytical results of contemporary economic theory, no such support was available to the economists of the past whose contributions are briefly examined.

A first draft of this paper was presented at the Perugia Workshop on Ricardo, while a subsequent version appeared in *Giornale degli Economisti* (March–April 1982). The text published here, while retaining the essential argument of the previous versions, presents several additions as well as some expansions and modifications. In the various stages the work has benefited from comments of G. Lunghini, P. Garegnani, I. Steedman, S. Hollander, D. Tosato, A. Rosselli, G. Calzoni, A. Roncaglia, M. Blaug, A. Boitani and M. Sebastiani, whom I would like to thank. Responsibility for the opinions expressed in the paper is of course entirely my own.

The final two sections consider, in the light of the foregoing analysis, the recent contributions of Garegnani and Hollander to the interpretation of Ricardo's thought. Although these authors draw inspiration from opposite theoretical conceptions, their contributions seem to have a common feature in that the interpretation of Ricardo's thought is in mainly 'static' terms. After some critical observations as to the relevance, for Ricardian analysis, of Garegnani's theory of the 'core', it is suggested that the attempts, of which Hollander's work is the most significant example, to 're-absorb' Ricardo into the tradition of neoclassical economic thought lack solid foundations and are therefore unacceptable.

2 RICARDO'S 'SCIENTIFIC PROGRAMME'

The Ricardian problems of value, distribution and growth are often presented as susceptible of separate treatment, or—even worse—as susceptible of treatment only in so far as they are separate. This paper seeks to demonstrate that these problems, instead, form part of a continuum extending from diminishing returns to the laws of motion of the system and including the problems of relative prices, distribution, circularity and the 'invariable standard of value'. These problems, in other words, cannot be fully understood unless they are placed in an analytical context capable of revealing the connections running between them.

That such an approach is legitimate and necessary can be deduced from what may well be considered Ricardo's scientific programme, as lucidly expounded in the 'Preface' to the *Principles* (the passage is very well known but its importance is not always sufficiently grasped):

> The produce of the earth—all that is derived from its surface by the united application of labour, machinery, and capital, is divided among three classes of the community; namely, the proprietor of the land, the owner of the stock or capital necessary for its cultivation, and the labourers by whose industry it is cultivated.
>
> *But in different stages of society, the proportions of the whole produce of the earth which will be allotted to each of these classes, under the names of rent, profit, and wages, will be essentially different; depending mainly on the actual fertility of the soil, on the accumulation of capital and population, and on the skill, ingenuity, and instruments employed in agriculture.*
>
> *To determine the laws which regulate this distribution, is the principal problem in Political Economy:* much as the science has been improved by the writings of Turgot, Stuart, Smith, Say, Sismondi, and others, they afford very little satisfactory information respecting *the natural course of rent, profit, and wages.*

In 1815 Mr Malthus... and a Fellow of University College, Oxford [Edward West] ... presented to the world, nearly at the same moment, *the true doctrine of rent; without a knowledge of which, it is impossible to understand the effect of the progress of wealth on profits and wages... . Adam Smith, and the other able writers to whom I have alluded, not having viewed correctly the principles of rent, have, it appears to me, overlooked many important truths, which can only be discovered after the subject of rent is thouroughly understood.* (*Works*, vol. I, pp. 5–6; italics added)

The passage is so clear that any comment might seem superfluous. Let me however briefly emphasize few essential points.

(1) The objective of the analysis is clearly that of the *natural course*—that is, of the laws of motion along what will be called the natural equilibrium path of rent, profits and wages.[1] In modern terminology this is clearly a dynamic type of problem. With respect to this problem, the questions concerning *value*, here not explicitly mentioned, evidently assume an instrumental role.

(2) The identification of those categories of phenomena that may determine changes in distribution during the process of economic growth is clear: they are the laws of returns in agriculture, the accumulation of capital, population growth and the role of technical progress.

(3) The fundamental importance of the theory of rent in the study of the above-mentioned phenomena is evident. (It is particularly noteworthy that the concept is mentioned three times within the space of a few lines in the same paragraph.) Without it, Ricardo insists, it is not possible to grasp the essential nature of the problem, or to discover 'many important truths' about it. This point seems particularly relevant in relation to some recent interpretations of Ricardo's analysis (see below, in particular section 8 on Garegnani, 1981).

The building blocks of the unifying interpretative schema which is here suggested for the analysis of Ricardian theory—and which, it may be said, alone seems able to attain the targets set out in the 'Preface'—are, on the one hand, the concept of natural equilibrium, closely linked with the idea of a natural wage rate, which constitutes the pivot of the analysis both from the 'static' point of view (determination of prices and of the profit rate with a given technology) and from a 'dynamic' one (determination of the natural equilibrium growth path in the face of a changing agricultural 'technology'); and, on the other hand, the inseparable link between changes in technology (deriving from the phenomena of diminishing returns in agriculture) and changes in distribution. This means that, in the context of the natural equilibrium approach—i.e. in a context in which the level of the real natural

---

[1] Ricardo's main concern for distribution, in spite of the use of the term 'proportions', is with the rate of profit and with the rate of money wages in relation to the 'progress of rent'.

wage, or its law of motion through time, is taken as exogenously given—it is impossible to conceive of a change in distributive variables not deriving from a technological change occurring somewhere in the system.

Let us consider these two points in some detail.

3 THE CONCEPT OF NATURAL EQUILIBRIUM

Ricardo recognizes that the forces of supply and demand may bring about market situations which differ from those of natural equilibrium—the basis of the distinction having been laid down by Adam Smith with his definition of 'natural' and 'market' prices. But, in line with Smith, Ricardo believes that market prices represent only transitory departures from natural prices, which are conceived of as a centre towards which 'the prices of all commodities are continually gravitating' (Smith, 1954, p. 51).

Referring directly to the *Wealth of Nations*, Ricardo concludes his chapter 'On Natural and Market Prices' of the *Principles* by stressing, beyond all doubt, his fundamental theoretical interest for the study of natural values:

> Having fully acknowledged the temporary effects which, in particular employments of capital, may be produced on the prices of commodities, as well as on the wages of labour, and the profits of stock, by accidental causes, without influencing the general price of commodities, wages, or profits, since these effects are equally operative in all stages of society, we will leave them entirely out of our consideration, whilst we are treating of the laws which regulate natural prices, natural wages, and natural profits, effects totally independent of these accidental causes. In speaking then of the exchangeable value of commodities, or the power of purchasing possessed by any one commodity, I mean always that power which it would possess, if not disturbed by any temporary or accidental cause and which is its natural price. (*Works*, vol. I, pp. 91–2)

It is important to stress:

(1) the close connection between natural prices and natural wages: the two are presented as two aspects of the same theoretical concept;
(2) the reason Ricardo gives for the exclusion from the analysis of the deviations of market values from natural values (the term 'value' refers here to prices, wages, and profits); the reason is the *accidental and temporary nature* of the deviation, as opposed to the *permanent* nature of the changes with which Ricardo was concerned ('lasting changes').

In particular, the connection between natural prices and the natural wage rate is clearly evidenced in the following passage from the *Notes on Malthus* (in which Ricardo refers to Malthus's criticism of his—Ricardo's—definition of the natural price of labour in the *Principles*): 'I have done so that we have one common language to apply to all causes which are similar' (*Works*, vol. II, p. 227).

The lack of interest in the 'deviations' of the market from natural values resulting from accidental and temporary causes contrasts with the strong interest in the non-temporary and non-accidental causes which act on natural values.

What did Ricardo mean by this expression? The answer is important and can be found by referring to numerous passages of his writings.[2] One, from the *Notes on Malthus*, is particularly significant (Ricardo is commenting on a hypothesis advanced by Malthus on changes in the rate of profit):

> The supply [of corn] may have diminished from a bad season, the [decreased] farmer's profits are then *accidental and temporary*, and are besides counteracted by his obtaining the increased price for a smaller quantity. *The only permanent cause* [of a fall of profits] *then is increased cost of production.* (*Works*, vol. II, p. 282; italics added)

Another relevant passage appears in the 1822 essay *On Protection to Agriculture*, in the context of Ricardo's discussion of the notion of 'remunerative price':

> It is now universally admitted, that rent is the effect of the rise in the price of corn, and not the cause; *it is also admitted, that the only permanent cause of rise in the value of corn, is an increased charge on its production, caused by the necessity of cultivating poorer lands; on which, by the expenditure of the same quantity of labour, the same quantity of produce cannot be obtained.* (*Works*, vol. IV, p. 212; italics added)

The terminology used by Ricardo is the same as that in the previously cited passage from the *Principles*: on the one hand, 'accidental and temporary causes' which are not of interest to him; on the other, 'permanent causes',

---

[2] See for example *Principles* (*Works*, vol. I, p. 189, italics added): 'no accumulation of capital will *permanently* lower profits, unless there be some *permanent* cause for the rise of wages .... If the necessaries of the workman could be constantly increased with the same facility, there could be no *permanent* alteration in the rate of profits or wages, to whatever amount capital might be accumulated.' See also *Principles* (*Works*, vol. I, pp. 110–11; *Essay on Profits* (*Works*, vol. IV, pp.35–6); and Ricardo's letter to Malthus of 6 September 1814 (*Works*, vol. VI, p. 143). The same type of interpretation of Ricardo's *permanent* cause of change in natural values is given by Marx (1969, vol. II, pp. 213–15).

represented by the increased cost of production in agriculture (here, as often in Ricardo, typified by corn)—that is, the 'lasting changes', in the technology of the agricultural sector, which form the focal point of Ricardo's analytical interest.

In other words, these lasting changes can be conceived only as a result of changes in the 'difficulty of production' arising from diminishing returns. It is therefore clear that, when Ricardo speaks of the laws that govern natural values, he has in mind a theory of the behaviour of these values over time. He considers, that is, a sequence of natural equilibrium positions along a path generated by non-accidental and non-temporary causes, which are summarized in the continuous increases in the cost of producing agricultural commodities. (See, in the same sense, Lunghini, 1977, pp. 39–40.)

Ricardo's thought can therefore be interpreted in terms of a *natural equilibrium path*, which represents a centre of gravity for the development of the system (cf. Eatwell, 1977–8, pp. 31–2), and with respect to which the actual behaviour of the economy represents a deviation (a 'departure') in the same way in which the market values of prices, wages and profits represent a deviation from their corresponding natural equilibrium values.[3]

For the identification of this natural equilibrium path, a notion of the natural wage rate compatible with an active accumulation process, and a consequent redefinition of the Malthusian mechanisms of population adjustment, become necessary.

This point is relevant and appears to require specific attention.

4 THE THEORY OF WAGES IN RICARDO: A CENTRAL AND CONTROVERSIAL ISSUE

The problem concerning Ricardo's theory of wages is at the same time central and controversial.

It is central in the sense that the way in which it is posed and resolved determines in the last analysis both the position of Ricardo's whole theoretical construction in one tradition of thought rather than the other, and the analytical deductions that can be made from that construction—the relationship between diminishing returns and the rate of accumulation, within a *natural* equilibrium approach; or, instead, the inverse relation between the market wage rate and the rate of profit; or, instead, the distributive antagonism between wages and profits in a 'static' framework.

---

[3] The natural equilibrium path is not thought of here as resulting from an empirically observed tendency, but instead is defined on the basis of the analytical framework and its basic hypothesis (including those regarding technology). It is also clear that actual growth will not necessarily and continuously proceed along the *natural equilibrium path* but can fluctuate, though always around the latter, its centre of gravity.

It is a very controversial issue from the double viewpoint of the presence of a certain degree of 'ambiguity' in Ricardo's writings, coupled with the circumstance that, precisely for all the motives indicated above, it is substantially on this ground that the different and contrasting interpretations of Ricardo's thought come to light.

From this latter angle it seems necessary to emphasize that, contrary to what some authors (e.g. Hollander, 1983, pp. 314–18) seem to believe, the most relevant distinction in the interpretations of Ricardo's thought is not that between fix-wage models and non-fix-wage models, but rather that between interpretations based on the notion of the natural wage rate and those based on the notion of the market wage rate.

This latter distinction does not coincide with the former one. On the one hand, the central question here is the relative importance of one or the other of the two concepts of wage rate in the reconstruction of Ricardo's thought—natural wage rate and market wage rate—and not that of the fixity or non-fixity of only one type of wage rate considered in the theory.[4] On the other hand, as will be shown below, only the second type of distinction can accommodate the assumptions explicitly considered by Ricardo as to the possibility of changes in the natural wage rate through time (according to some exogenously given law)—in addition to the possibility of different levels (and/or different laws of motion) in various countries in the same historical period (see *Works*, vol. I, pp. 96–7).

This section seeks to define the position of the present analysis in terms of the distinction between *natural wage models* and *market wage models*, and to find out which of the two definitions of natural wage rate given by Ricardo in his writings is consistent with the main analytical conclusions of his theoretical construction. The implications of the choice made will then be briefly discussed.

The relation between the interpretative schema suggested in this paper and other interpretations of Ricardo will, hopefully, thus emerge, and an overall evaluation of Ricardo's treatment of wages will be possible.

As to the first point, it is clear that, in line with what has been said above as to the centrality for Ricardo of the concept of natural equilibrium, the present analysis of Ricardo's treatment of wages belongs to what have been called the 'natural wage interpretations'. In other words, the interpretation here suggested, although explicitly considering *two* notions of the wage rate (the natural and the market wage rate), assigns the central analytical role to the

---

[4] Pasinetti (1982, p. 240), for instance, writes: 'The Pasinetti–Sraffa view—if I may be allowed the presumption of calling it so—of the Ricardian system is *not* a "fix-wage interpretation" ... . Two notions of the wage rate are explicitly considered: "natural" wage rate, which is an exogenous magnitude (and which, by the way, is *not* a subsistence wage rate ...), and a "market wage rate", which is an observable magnitude and emerges from the interaction of the forces of supply and demand ...'.

natural wage rate, determined by circumstances exogenous to the model, and intimately connected with the central notion of natural prices and natural equilibrium. In this perspective the market wage rate represents a variable whose oscillations, brought about by supply and demand interaction, express the gravitational tendency towards the natural wage rate. In Ricardo's words,

> The market price of labour is the price which is really paid for it, from the natural operation of the proportion of the supply to the demand; labour is dear when it is scarce, and cheap when it is plentiful. However much the market price of labour may deviate from its natural price, it has, like commodities, a tendency to conform to it. (*Works*, vol. I, p. 94)

As has been pointed out above, the basic difference between the natural and market wage rate is that, while the former is determined by 'external' circumstances, the latter is determined within the model by the interaction of supply and demand forces:

> It is not to be understood that the natural price of labour, estimated ... in food and necessaries, is absolutely fixed and constant. It varies at different times in the same country, and very materially differs in different countries. *It essentially depends on the habits and customs of the people.* An English labourer would consider his wages under their natural rate ... if they enabled him to purchase no other food than potatoes, and to live in no better habitation than a mud cabin.... Many of the conveniences now enjoyed in an English cottage, would have been thought luxuries at an earlier period of our history. (*Works*, vol. I, pp. 96–7; italics added)

Clearly, the notion of the natural wage rate does not coincide with that of biological subsistence;[5] it can vary through time, and can assume different values from country to country: it depends on 'institutional factors' which may be studied *before* the analytical solution of the model of natural prices, and thus independently of these (Garegnani, 1983, p. 311).[6]

[5] See n. 4 above. See also Garegnani, 1983, p. 310: 'It seems ... that what characterizes these authors [Adam Smith and Ricardo] was not the idea of a wage determined by subsistence, even less that of a subsistence constant over time. It was more generally the ... *separate determination* [of the natural wage rate which] found expression in the fact that these authors took the real wage as given when approaching the determination of relative prices.'

[6] Although the relevance of what follows will become clearer in the following pages, it may be interesting to comment here on the different implications that the assumption of a given real wage has in different contexts. For this purpose a distinction can perhaps be introduced between the concept of *parametric constant* and that of *predetermined constant*. Both are treated as 'givens' in the model; but, while no specific number is assigned to the first, which can thus take virtually any value with reference to a given situation, to the second there is assigned one and only one value, on the basis of which the model is analysed. This means that in the first case alternative

It must be observed that the hypothesis that the *level* of the natural wage rate is given in terms of commodities is, from a methodological point of view, totally equivalent to the assumption that what is exogeneously given is the *law of motion of the natural wage rate through time*, in line with what Ricardo explicitly says about the variations of the 'habits and customs of the people' from period to period. The structure of the model, in other words, would not change. The only difference would be represented by a different numerical value of the solutions of the model for natural prices and for the general rate of profit[7]: the assumption of a given percentage rate of growth of the natural wage rate, for instance, would imply, with diminishing returns in agriculture, a reduction in the rate of profit more marked than the one that would result from the assumption of a given *level* of the natural wage rate.

It is now necessary to tackle the thorny problem of the presence, in Ricardo's writings, of two different notions of the natural wage rate: the markedly dynamic concept given in the *Essay on Profits*, and the definition—strictly associated with the idea of a constant level of the population—of the same wage rate given in the chapter 'On Wages' in the *Principles*.

A precise dynamic notion of natural wage, as that real-wage rate which remains constant in presence of a situation of continuous equality between the rates of growth of population and of capital, is in fact given by Ricardo in the *Essay*:

> We will, however, suppose that no improvements take place in agri-culture, and that *capital and population advance in the proper proportion, so that the real wages of labour, continue uniformly the same;*—that we may know what peculiar effects are to be ascribed to the growth of capital, the increase of population, and the extension of cultivation, to the more remote, and less fertile land. (*Works*, vol. IV, p. 12; italics added)

Again, in the *Essay* Ricardo writes:

> The rise or fall of wages is common to all states of society, whether it be the stationary, the advancing, or the retrograde state. In the stationary

---

values of the real wage are admissible with reference to a given situation, and the analysis concentrates on the solutions associated with each of these. In the second case, instead, alternative values of the real wage are *not* admissible, and the freedom of choice, so to speak, ends with the choice itself of the specific value suggested by the relevant socio-historical data of the situation. The analysis, on the basis of this 'once-and-for-all' choice, thus concentrates on the solutions of the model associated with different levels of other significant coefficients of the model—e.g., those expressing the technological requirements of a crucial productive sector. The latter approach characterizes the present paper.

[7] The same is true if we assume to know the law of motion of the natural wage's rate of growth through time.

state, it is regulated wholly by the increase or falling off of the population. In the advancing state, it depends on whether the capital or the population advance at the more rapid course. In the retrograde state, it depends on whether population or capital decrease with the greater rapidity. As experience demonstrates that capital and population alternately take the lead, and wages in consequence are liberal or scanty, nothing can be positively laid down, respecting profits, as far as wages are concerned. *But I think it may be most satisfactorily proved, that in every society advancing in wealth and population, independently of the effect produced by liberal or scanty wages, general profits must fall, unless there be improvements in agriculture, or corn can be imported at a cheaper price.* It seems the necessary result of the principles which have been stated to regulate the progress of rent. (*Works*, vol. IV, pp. 22–3; italics added)

It is quite clear that Ricardo, speaking here of real wages, is reasoning in purely dynamic terms; and that the frame of reference of his argument is perfectly in line with the above-mentioned notion of the natural wage. In other words, it seems absolutely natural that Ricardo—in order to *concentrate* on what he believes to be the most important (dominant and permanent) cause of changes in the 'general profits on capital', represented by the phenomenon of diminishing returns, i.e. in order to eliminate, so to speak, from his picture the non-systematic, occasional, temporary factors influencing the rate of profit—should centre his analysis on the definition of natural wage as that wage rate in correspondence with which the rates of growth of capital and population coincide. It is in fact only when this special condition prevails that the real wages can remain constant at their natural level, and *the working of the permanent and dominant factor of agricultural diminishing returns can come into full light as the cause of the progressive fall in the general rate of profits.*[8]

It seems important to emphasize that a conception of this type also appears to underlie Ricardo's analysis in two relevant chapters of his *Principles*— chapter VI, 'On Profits' (termed 'strategic' by Hollander, 1979, p. 395), and chapter XXI, 'Effects of Accumulation on Profits and Interest'—centred as they are on the thesis that 'there is no other [permanent] reason for a fall of profit but a rise of wages, and ... [that] the only adequate and permanent cause for the rise of wages is the increasing difficulty of providing food and necessaries for the increasing number of workmen' (*Works*, vol. I, p. 296); here in fact both the numerical examples and the argument are developed on the assumption that during the process of growth the natural wage rate is given in

---

[8] This is recognized by Hollander (1979, p. 395), who writes, referring to the first of the two passages of the *Essay* cited above, 'Ricardo thus consciously restricted the analysis of growth in order to focus upon the effects of diminishing returns *alone*.'

commodity terms while the 'dynamic mechanisms' of accumulation and population growth are at work.

It is however quite evident that the above definition given by Ricardo in the *Essay on Profits* significantly differs from that he gave later in the chapter 'On Wages' of the *Principles*: 'The natural price of labour is that price which is necessary to enable the labourers, one with another, to subsist and to perpetuate their race, without either increase or diminution' (vol. I, p. 93). Here the notion of natural wage is strictly associated with that of a constant level of the population. The problem thus arises, in this context, of the compatibility of this notion with the presence of an active process of accumulation.

In what follows it will be argued that, since it is necessary to choose between these two contrasting notions of natural wage, it is the former that should be given preference. It will be in fact emphasized (1) that Ricardo shows a considerable amount of 'flexibility' as regards his own definition of the chapter 'On Wages' in the *Principles*; and (2) more important, that what Stigler (1965, pp. 447–50) calls the 'principle of scientific exegisis'[9] indicates that the dynamic notion of natural wage given by Ricardo in the *Essay* is the only one consistent with the main analytical conclusions of his system of thought.

As to the first point, it must be said that Ricardo's 'flexibility' with respect to his own definition of natural wage given in the chapter 'On Wages' of the *Principles* is apparent in the *Notes on Malthus*, when he writes: 'I am however very little solicitous to retain my definition of the natural price of labour. Mr Malthus's will do as well for my purpose' (*Works*, vol. II, p. 228).[10]

It is important to stress that Malthus's definition to which Ricardo refers is developed, in purely dynamic terms, in the context of the criticism addressed by Malthus to Ricardo's definition of the *Principles*—a criticism that relates precisely to its logical consistency in the analysis of the growth process:

> Mr Ricardo has defined the natural price of labour to be 'that price which is necessary to enable the labourers one with another to subsist, and to perpetuate their race, without either increase or diminution'. This

[9] See also on this point Marshall and Marshall (1879), especially the 'Introduction' (p. xx), where the Marshalls point out that what really matters is not finding out what an author has 'really said'—since it is well known that each author says and writes many things conflicting with one another—but, rather, *assessing what was relevant for him*. The Marshalls' criterion evidently coincides with Stigler's principle of scientific exegesis.

[10] The sentence is extremely illuminating, although it belongs to a paragraph that Ricardo, in order to avoid repetitions, replaced with another one. It is clear that this type of 'flexibility' does not coincide with that relating to the constancy (or inconstancy) of the level of natural wages through time. See on this point Garegnani (1983, p. 311), who however seems to juxtapose this last issue with that of the Malthusian-type mechanisms of adjustment capable of explaining the tendency of market wages towards their natural level.

price I should really be disposed to call a most unnatural price; because in a natural state of things, that is, without great impediments to the progress of wealth and population, such a price could not generally occur for hundreds of years. But if this price be really rare, and, in an ordinary state of things, at so great a distance in point of time, it must evidently lead to great errors to consider the market-prices of labour as only temporary deviations above and below that fixed price to which they will very soon return.

The natural or necessary price of labour in any country I should define to be, 'that price which, in the actual circumstances of the society, is necessary to occasion an average supply of labourers, sufficient to meet the average demand'. (*Works*, vol. II, pp. 227–8)

Again, in the *Notes on Malthus*, Ricardo shows his awareness of the mechanism of mutual functional dependence between wages and accumulation—which is central for the point here examined—and in particular of the idea, already expressed in the *Essay*, that, if the growth of capital is faster than that of population, wages increase, determining a reduction in the rate of profit (and in the rate of growth)—a circumstance that would 'obscure', so to speak, the systematic depressive effect exerted by diminishing returns on the rate of profit:

if population did not keep pace with capital, labour would rise, and the quantity of corn which I should annually obtain, instead of increasing in the proportions of 1,000, 1,300, 1,700 and so on, might, by the sacrifices I should be obliged to make to obtain the labour required, increase my capital only in the proportions 1,000, 1,200, 1,300, etc. etc. The precise reason then that my accumulation goes on at a slow pace, is that there is a scarcity of labour. (*Works*, vol. II, p. 321)

And in his chapter 'On Wages' of the *Principles*, Ricardo seems to get very close to his former dynamic definition, as it is shown by the fact that his argument runs in terms of rates of growth:

It has been calculated, that under favourable circumstances population may be doubled in twenty-five years; but under the same favourable circumstances, the whole capital of a country might possibly be doubled in a shorter period. In that case, wages ... would have a tendency to rise, because the demand for labour would increase still faster than the supply. (*Works*, vol. I, p. 98)

in long settled countries, where, from the diminishing rate of the supply of raw produce, all the evils of a crowded population are experienced ...

the population increases faster than the funds required for its support. *Every exertion of industry, unless accompanied by a diminished rate of increase in the population, will add to the evil, for production cannot keep pace with it.* (*Works*, vol. I, p. 99; italics added)

Thus the idea of a constant natural real wage in the presence of appropriate conditions regarding the rates of growth of capital and population is not in the least inconsistent with the theoretical conception developed by Ricardo after the *Essay on Profits*—even if he did not explicitly revert to it in his writings. It is, on the contrary, the only one capable of throwing full light on the 'permanent and dominant' cause of the fall in the rate of profit: the phenomenon of diminishing returns in agriculture.

As to the second point—that concerning the solution of problems of interpretation arising from divergent textual evidence—it is clear that reference to Stigler's criterion of *scientific exegisis* (1965, p. 448) which takes as 'the test of an interpretation ... its consistency with the main analytical conclusions of the system of thought under consideration',[11] makes it necessary, first, to recall, however briefly, Ricardo's main analytical conclusions, and, second, to discuss the 'problem of consistency'.

Ricardo's *main analytical conclusions*, in line with what has been said above, may be briefly summarized as follows.

(1) The working of the economic system can be significantly analysed in terms of natural equilibrium; i.e., the situation deserving the greatest analytical attention is that associated with natural prices (and natural wages) reflecting the dominant conditions of production. As these change, new natural equilibrium positions prevail. This, as has been pointed out, does not imply that market equilibrium positions are ignored: they are considered on a different plane. Not only are they viewed as transient situations, but—what matters most—they are assigned a substantially instrumental role in the realization of the tendency of the system towards its natural equilibrium.

(2) The key problem is that of the growth prospects of the economic system when diminishing returns prevail in agriculture, the sector producing the wage goods *par excellence*;[12] in other words, of the relation between decreasing productivity in agriculture and the general rate of profit—which coincides with, or is proportional to, the accumulation rate. As it will be pointed out, this implies a study of the relation between changes in the conditions of production and the ensuing variations in distribution. *The*

[11] See also O'Brien (1981).

[12] The circumstance that in Ricardo 'the natural wage rate [is] specified as a (given) physical quantity of food, plus a physical quantity of manufactures' (Eltis, 1984, pp. 188–9) does not imply substantive modifications, since it is clear that, taken as a whole, the given basket of wage goods requires, with diminishing returns in agriculture and constant returns elsewhere, an increased level of money wage to be purchased.

analysis of the growth process in terms of natural equilibrium can thus be said to represent Ricardo's main theoretical concern.

The 'problem of consistency' can be examined through a study of the theoretical difficulties that would ensue, for Ricardo's analytical model, from the acceptance of the definition of natural wages given in the chapter 'On Wages' of the *Principles*—a definition, it is important to recall, that strictly associates the concept of natural wage with that of a constant level of population through time.

These difficulties can be briefly indicated in terms of the following alternatives.

(1) The first alternative would be the limitation of the *natural equilibrium analysis* to the situation of the stationary state, to the exclusion of the whole phase of accumulation: it would thus be impossible to study the main analytical object of Ricardo's theoretical attention (the growth process) in terms of Ricardo's own methodology (natural equilibrium analysis). In other words, the phase during which the process of accumulation is active and the levels of production and employment expand through time could be analysed *only in terms of market equilibrium*, along a path in which the market values of wages, prices, etc., would *not* coincide, except by accident, with their natural counterparts.

This is in fact the type of approach followed by a whole class of interpretative models,[13] centred, in purely neoclassical spirit, on the notion of *market* equilibrium and on the interaction between demand and supply. But this approach seems a complete reversal of Ricardo's emphasis on natural values and is therefore an unacceptable alteration of the fundamental characteristics of his analysis.

(2) The second alternative is represented by limiting the analysis to a substantially *static* context, although, on the basis of a totally different view of Ricardo's analysis, the need to stick to the letter of the *Principles* is met in some natural wage interpretations at the very high cost of substantially giving up the rigorous examination of the working of Ricardian *dynamic* mechanisms and of their interaction through time—a central theme in Ricardo's research. This is in fact what happens on the one hand in Pasinetti's (1960) *point natural equilibrium* analysis and on the other hand in Garegnani's (1981) study of the wages–profit distribution of a *given* level of output. The former has been examined at some length elsewhere (see Caravale and Tosato, 1980), while the latter will be taken up in some detail in section 7 below. Suffice it here to add that the acceptance of the (straight jacket) definition of the *Principles* forces Pasinetti to admit that: 'in an economy with population

---

[13] See for example Hicks and Hollander (1977), Hollander (1979), Casarosa (1978, 1982) and Samuelson (1978). See also section 9 below, where Hollander's contribution is examined in greater detail.

growth ... the actual wage rate will normally be above its "natural" level (Pasinetti, 1982, p. 241), a circumstance that appears to conflict with Pasinetti's perfectly correct general approach to the interpretation of Ricardo in terms of natural equilibrium and in particular with his correct thesis concerning the fact that the 'notion of a *natural* wage rate' is, for Ricardo, 'much more fundamental' than that of *market* wage rate (Pasinetti, 1982, p. 241).

(3) A third alternative would be to renounce altogether the claim to supply a rigorous reconstruction of Ricardo's theory. This would happen, for instance, when, in the effort to reconcile the notion of natural wage given in the chapter 'On Wages' with the necessity of developing a natural equilibrium analysis of the process of growth, the interpreter is forced (a) to formulate the assumptions regarding the initial volume of population in necessarily vague terms, and (b) to neglect the influence that vast (though decreasing through time) amounts of unemployment may exert on the level of the natural wage in the course of the accumulation process. It would, in point of fact, be necessary to assume that, at the beginning of the story, in connection with a given level of the natural (real) wage rate, the (given and constant) amount of potential workers available for the production process is high enough to 'feed', so to speak, the economy during the whole 'progressive' phase until the system reaches the stationary state. It would also be necessary to assume that the presence of such a relevant 'reserve army of labour' does not determine any change in the key variable of the system, the natural wage rate; i.e., that the 'reserve army' can subsist without any cost to the economic system and without exerting a depressive influence upon 'the habits and customs of the people'. In the words of Joan Robinson, 'either the population is growing at just the right rate or there is an indefinite reserve of potential labour, *living on nuts in the jungles, ready to take employment when the standard real wage is offered*' (Robinson, 1972, p. 40; italics added).

The difficulty of accepting the assumption that the given reserve army of labour does not determine any reduction in the natural wage is all the stronger, as its presence would not represent a temporary feature of the economy, but would instead, by definition, be a *permanent* characteristic of it, up to the attainment of the stationary state. (On this point see Picchio del Mercato, 1981, pp. 85–116.)

We may therefore conclude that Ricardo's natural equilibrium analysis of the growth process is incompatible with the definition of natural wage given in the chapter 'On Wages', while it can be legitimately carried out in terms of the *Essay's* dynamic definition. It is in fact this latter definition that makes it possible to bring out the inverse relation between diminishing returns (expressed indifferently by the increase either in the labour content of 'corn' or in the *nominal*, or money, wage rate, with a given natural *real* wage) and the accumulation process (see Caravale and Tosato, 1980, ch. 2).

Any other analytical conception of the natural wage rate would end up by having Marshallian-type implications in the interpretation of Ricardo's theory, and would thus represent a substantial break with the essence of his theory. As Lunghini (1977, pp. 14–15) aptly points out, '[Marshall's] silent conclusion is that the classical doctrine is valid only in the stationary state ... because the economic forces have time to work out fully their effects.'[14] Now, *without* the dynamic definition of natural wage discussed above, it would be impossible to define an analytically rigorous construction of the accumulation process founded on the notion of natural equilibrium.[15] In other words, it would be necessary to conclude, with Marshall, that Ricardo has built a theory of natural prices valid *only* for the stationary state—a conclusion that clearly does not do justice to Ricardo and opens the way at the same time to a re-absorption of his theory in the neoclassical tradition.

The implications of this conclusion for the Ricardian case of diminishing returns must now be carefully specified. In his chapter 'On Wages' Ricardo writes:

> If, for instance, *wages were regulated* by a yearly increase of capital, at the rate of 2 per cent, they would fall when it accumulated only at the rate of $1\frac{1}{2}$ per cent. They would fall still lower when it increased only at the rate of 1, or $\frac{1}{2}$ per cent, and would continue to do so until the capital became stationary ... and be only sufficient to keep up the numbers of the actual population. (*Works*, vol. I, p. 101; italics added)

It seems clear that the idea of wages being 'regulated' by the rate of increase of capital means in this context, as in the above cited passage of the *Essay*, that, if the rate of increase of population is taken as given and does not change through time, the wage rate can remain *constant* if and only if the rate of accumulation keeps constant at that very same rate. If, on the contrary, diminishing returns determine a progressive decline in the rate of growth of capital, while the rate of increase of population is insensitive to the progressive reduction of the rate of accumulation (this is the instance considered by Ricardo here), then the wage rate cannot remain constant, but will instead continually diminish. This reduction, Ricardo says, is the consequence that the working of diminishing returns will tend to bring about 'unless [the exertion of industry] is accompanied by a diminished rate of increase in the population' (vol. I, p. 99). The constancy of the wage rate is thus compatible,

---

[14] See Marshall (1966, p. 298): '[the] much quoted and much misunderstood doctrine of Adam Smith and other economists [is] that the normal, or natural value of a commodity is that which economic forces tend to bring about if the general conditions of life were stationary for a run of time long enough to enable them to work out their full effect.'

[15] According to Hollander (1982), the hypothesis discussed in the text is attributable not to Ricardo, but to J. S. Mill.

in the case of diminishing returns, only with a reduction in the rate of population growth *parallel* to that of capital growth.

The exact level at which the wage rate is supposed to remain constant when the two relevant growth rates (of capital and population) coincide remains to be ascertained. If it were the natural wage rate, then we would back to the dynamic definition of the *Essay*; if on the contrary, as seems more likely in the context of the passage, the constant wage rate referred to is not a natural, but a market wage rate, then we would be again in presence of the analytical difficulties pointed out above, in the sense that—before the attainment of the stationary state—it would be impossible to analyse the system in terms of *natural equilibrium*.

The whole chapter 'On Wages', in fact, suffers from Ricardo's considerable difficulty in reconciling the typically dynamic character of his analysis with the definition of natural wage rate given at the outset of the same chapter. An act of analytical courage, in the spirit of Stigler's principle of scientific exegesis and of the Marshalls' criterion of relevance, seems essential: namely, the explicit resumption of the *Essay's* definition of natural wage rate as that constant level of the wage in correspondence with which the rates of growth of population and of capital coincide.[16] In a Ricardian context, with diminishing returns, this equilibrium condition is realized only if the rate of increase of population *instantaneously copies* the (declining) rate of accumulation; contrary to what happens in most contemporary growth models, the former rate thus assumes the role of a purely endogenous variable.[17]

It seems worthwhile to emphasize:

(1) that only with reference to this particular equilibrium condition is it possible to define the system of natural prices for any one of the infinite points that constitute the ideal growth path of the economy in its tendency towards stationarity; i.e., only with reference to this hypothetical equilibrium condition is it possible to carry out the kind of (natural equilibrium) analysis that Ricardo explicitly says constitutes the object of his research;

(2) that this equilibrium condition is just a hypothetical one, and no explanation is therefore required as to the practical possibility of its realization in the real world (or in Ricardo's world).

[16] It is obvious that in this case the Malthusian-type adjustment mechanism should be redefined in terms of modifications in the *rate of change* of population; in other words, the tendency of the market wage rate to 'conform to its natural level' can no longer be worked out in terms of changes in the *level* of population. On this point see Caravale and Tosato (1980, ch. 5).

[17] If the rate of population growth were considered an exogenous constant, coincidence between this rate and that of capital growth could occur only in correspondence with a *single* point (or instant) of the whole process of growth. Before this point, the economic system would be characterized by a progressive absorption of excess population in the production process; after it, on the contrary, continuous increases in the 'reserve army of labour' would tend to occur.

If, nevertheless, one wished to think in these latter terms, one could perhaps mention (1) the idea that the rate of increase of population may be thought of as a decreasing function of the absolute level of the population itself—a sort of collective and spontaneous birth control motivated, for instance, by ecological reasons (a suggestion that has been recently misinterpreted by Casarosa, 1983, pp. 112–15, as an indication of actually existing tendencies or forces, and has been criticized as such), or (2) the hypothesis that progressively increasing standards of living per capita may be connected with a progressive reduction in the size of families.

As a matter of fact, the equilibrium condition consisting of the equality of the growth rates of capital and population—which, by the way, is nothing new in the 'history' of modern Ricardian models: see Little (1957, pp. 156–7) and Findlay (1974, p. 1)—is found in Casarosa (1978, 1983) and echoed in Samuelson (1978), though in terms that seem basically incompatible with the basic features of Ricardo's theory as they have been described above.

Casarosa believes that what he calls the 'traditional view' of Ricardian theory (that based on the notion of natural equilibrium) is seriously deficient in that it fails to explain some basic characteristics of the Ricardian system (see esp. Casarosa, 1978, pp. 38–63)—in particular, the fact that during the process of growth the wage rate remains above its natural level and tends, from some point onwards, to fall with the rate of profit—and should therefore be replaced by a 'New View' of the Ricardian theory. This latter interpretation has strong analogies with the market equilibrium interpretations of Ricardo (see Casarosa, 1983; also Hicks, 1979, pp. 133–4), but presents the peculiar characteristic of making the centre of attraction of market values a position called *dynamic equilibrium*, which is defined as that in which the rate of growth of capital equals that of population, and is (however) kept distinct from the position of natural equilibrium.

The idea is that, if it can be proved that market equilibrium is continuously attracted towards 'dynamic equilibrium', it is legitimate to study the system's evolution *as if* it followed the dynamic equilibrium path.

The logical consistency and the interpretative value of this proposition, however, seem extremely weak.

First of all, the concept of dynamic equilibrium itself as defined by Casarosa does not seem to have any right of citizenship within Ricardo's theory. In fact, this concept is neither a *market* situation, brought about by supply and demand interaction, nor a *natural* situation, reflecting (with a given natural wage rate) the prevailing conditions of production: it is only an interpretative superstructure, which may be taken to represent an indication of the malaise stemming from the effort to reconcile the definition of natural wage given in the chapter 'On Wages' with the dynamic problems arising in Ricardo's theory of growth.

Second, in spite of appearances, Casarosa's dynamic equilibrium wage rate does not coincide with the dynamic definition of natural wage given by Ricardo in the *Essay on Profits* (i.e., the definition that the foregoing analysis indicates as the only one compatible with Ricardo's main analytical conclusions. In the former it is the (market) wage rate that makes the rate of population growth equal to the declining rate of accumulation; while in the *Essay*, and in the analytical interpretation given above, maintenance of the natural wage rate—given from outside the model by the 'habits and customs of the people'—implies the condition that the two relevant growth rates coincide. In other words, the assumption is made that the wage rate can remain constant over time at the natural level—thus shedding full light on the dominant phenomenon of diminishing returns—only if the two relevant rates of growth coincide; and as the rate of accumulation declines because of the progressive reduction in agricultural productivity, the condition can be realized only if the rate of population growth adjusts to it without delay. Reference to this particular condition makes it possible to define a *natural equilibrium path*, each point of which will be characterized by a different set of natural prices and a (natural) value of the general profit rate which will be decreasing through time. When the equilibrium condition is not realized, the path will instead move along a market equilibrium path which, as it has been shown (see Caravale and Tosato, 1980, chs 5–7), will tend in general to be attracted by the natural equilibrium path.

It can be said, incidentally, that, as, in the latter case, the model can give origin to a whole series of market paths according to the choice of the initial situation and of the reaction parameters, the natural wage interpretation given above appears to be more general than those supplied by the class of market wage models, concentrated as they are on specific (market) paths of a system tending towards a situation of stationarity.

It is clear that the difference between the two conceptions goes back to that between the two types of interpretation mentioned above, stressing respectively the role of exogenous factors and the role of supply and demand forces in the determination of the wage rate.[18] Since on this point Samuelson's 'canonical model' is more explicit than Casarosa's analysis, it is useful to refer to the former.

---

[18] Hollander (1983, p. 316) admits that 'Ricardo's *Principles* and his *Essay* are replete with references to the constant wages assumption', but he believes that these are only to be considered as representing a 'simplifying assumption [made] for the sake of a clear exposition'. According to Hollander, 'Ricardo's typical "first approximation" [should not be mistaken] for a full growth model—the man's style for the substance.'

Hollander's thesis of the 'strong cases'—which is a leitmotiv of his interpretation of Ricardo—would obviously deserve a more detailed analysis; it must however be emphasized that what Hollander calls strong cases are nothing more than the essential features of a model, or of a theory. This cannot aim, as Joan Robinson has taught us, at mapping the world (or any portion of it) in a one-to-one scale, but on the contrary must concentrate on those characteristics that appear to play an essential role in that portion of the world which it sets out to describe.

Samuelson distinguishes two cases. In the first (called the 'short-circuited' version of Ricardian dynamics), population growth adjusts instantly to the declining rate of capital growth so that 'the wage rate falls or rises immediately to the ... subsistence wage rate' (this is what Samuelson, 1978, pp. 1421–2, calls the 'unrealistic polar Ricardian assumption'). In the second case, considered the central one, the adjustment of population growth is not instantaneous; with diminishing returns the market wage rate tends to decline through time (and the difference between this latter and the subsistence wage rate is consequently progressively reduced), either as a consequence of the fact that the rate of growth of population lags behind the declining rate of growth of capital, implying an excess of supply over demand of labour in each period, or as a consequence of the fact that the equilibrium condition—that the two relevant growth rates should always be equal—is 'imposed', as it is by Samuelson and Casarosa.

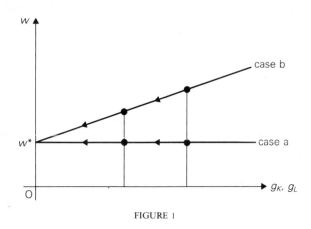

FIGURE 1

The situation could be illustrated, for the two cases (a and b, respectively), in figure 1, where the growth rates of capital (g_K) and population (g_L) are drawn on the horizontal axis, and the values of the market wage (w) and of the 'subsistence wage' (w^*) are drawn on the vertical axis. It seems clear, however, (1) that the first case implies the substantial abandonment of the definition of *natural* wage given by Ricardo in the chapter 'On Wages' since population growth, until the attainment of the stationary state, is positive while the market wage rate constantly coincides with the *natural* wage rate;[19] and (2) that on the other hand the second case—with the equilibrium condition of the equality of the two growth rates—implies the consequence, highly peculiar

[19] This consequence could be avoided only if the adjustment were formulated in terms of rate of growth of *employment* with a given and 'abundant' (in sense specified above) population. But this assumption would again be opened to the analytical difficulties mentioned above.

from a strictly neoclassical point of view, that the labour market would always be in perfect equilibrium (given appropriate initial conditions) in the sense that supply would always equal demand, but that the price (the market wage rate) would continuously decline.[20] It is in fact this reduction in the market wage rate that is supposed to bring about the *required* reduction in the population growth rate—as if, in a rigidly planned economy, a central authority, enlightened with perfect foresight, could announce at the beginning of each period what the lower rate of increase of capital (and the number of new job opportunities) would be, and at the same time could fix the lower market wage rate to be capable of making the rate of increase of population exactly equal to that of capital. The extent to which this conception can appear logically more sound—and more 'realistic', if this is the ground chosen for judgement—than the natural equilibrium approach remains an open question.

A final criticism relates to the working of Casarosa's model. His interpretation crucially depends on the possibility of proving that, in a Ricardian context, market equilibrium continually tends towards the above-defined concept of dynamic equilibrium—a problem that on the logical plane could, *strictu sensu*, be tackled only if the answer to the question of 'the right of citizenship' of this latter concept for Ricardo's theory could be proved to be positive.

Anyway, Casarosa here distinguishes two cases: (1) the case in which labour productivity in agriculture declines not continuously but *in steps*, which are 'sufficiently long' to legitimate the study of the convergence problem with reference to a *constant* level of such labour productivity; and (2) the more general case, in which diminishing returns determine a *continuous* reduction in labour productivity in agriculture. The arguments put forward by Casarosa to prove his thesis do not seem convincing in either case.

The first case, for which Casarosa supplies an indication of the convergence process, amounts to nothing less than an assuming-away of the central phenomenon on which Ricardo's analysis is based: diminishing returns in agriculture. In the words of an authoritative and benevolent critic (Hicks, 1979, p. 134), this amounts to 'reducing the non-steady-state sequence to a sequence of steady states', a procedure of which 'the justification ... from the text of Ricardo, seems rather slight' (p. 134), and which makes the analysis of this point of little relevance for the interpretation of Ricardo's theory.

As for the second case, the one relevant for Ricardo's theory, Casarosa admits, on the other hand, that the 'justifications of the dynamic equilibrium model are a *little less solid*' since—although this *may* happen—'the economic

---

[20] Samuelson's approach is so neoclassical, in the interpretation of classical growth problems, that he states, for instance: 'if we begin with redundant L/K, *labour will be a free good with zero competitive price or wage*' (1978, p. 1423, italics added).

system does not *necessarily* tend towards the dynamic equilibrium path' (Casarosa, 1983, pp. 106–10)—two circumstances that inflict lethal blows to the interpretative value of Casarosa's suggested model of dynamic equilibrium.

Much of the confusion surrounding the interpretation of Ricardo's treatment of wages stems from the fact that this treatment is characterized by the simultaneous presence of three elements which must be kept quite distinct (a fourth element—the change in the value of money—is assumed away from the start; see *Works*, vol. I, p. 46):

(1) the role of 'the habits and customs of the people' in the determination of the real natural wage rate—either in its level or in its law of motion;
(2) the role of supply and demand conditions in the labour market in the determination of the market real wage rate;[21]
(3) the role of the ever-increasing difficulties in the production of 'the necessaries of the workman', with a *given* commodity natural wage rate in the configuration of the growth process, through the resulting effects on the price of the wage goods, on the money wage rate and on the profit rate.

Confusion is certain if these three elements are not carefully distinguished from each other.

For Ricardo, recognition of the first element plays the role of giving the theory general validity, in a double sense: (1) it is applicable in principle to all phases of a country's historical development as well as to all countries; and (2) it may refer (as it has been pointed out above) both to the level of the natural wage rate and to its law of motion through time. Beyond the illustration of this basic point—which in fact impresses the hallmark on to his whole theoretical conception (the natural equilibrium approach)—Ricardo said, and could hardly have had to say, very little.

The second element, on the other hand, summarizes the 'temporary and accidental' causes that may determine changes in the level of real wages: that is, wages being 'liberal or scanty'. As this element is likely to introduce 'disturbances' in the determination of the rate of profit—enhancing or, on the contrary, reducing the effects of the continuous increase in the price of corn (with a constant real natural wage)—it becomes essential to keep the effects of supply and demand—respectively, population growth and capital growth— *quite distinct* from the 'non-temporary', 'non-accidental', but instead 'dominant and persistent' causes affecting the rate of profit and the pace of expansion of the economy. This is the analytical *raison d'être* of the dynamic definition of natural real wage discussed above.

---

[21] The market wage is normally expressed in monetary terms. It may thus be thought of as *real* only in the sense of purchasing power, not in the sense of a bundle of commodities definable prior to the determination of prices.

The third element belongs to the true core of Ricardo's analysis; it is represented by the study, in terms of natural equilibrium, of the growth prospects of the economic system when diminishing returns prevail in agriculture and workers need to be paid rising money wages in order to purchase *a given* physical amount of food and manufactured goods (the natural wage rate).

The *leitmotiv* of this section has been to show how this analytical objective could only be achieved through an *appropriate* conception of the natural wage rate, and in particular of the connection between such a wage rate and the growth rates of capital and population.

5 THE CONNECTION BETWEEN CHANGES IN TECHNOLOGY AND CHANGES IN DISTRIBUTION

The second building block of the interpretative schema here proposed is the intimate connection between distribution and technology. In fact, within the framework of analysis briefly outlined above it becomes impossible to distinguish, in Ricardo, the problem of alternative distributive setups from that of changes in technology. In other words, changes in distribution can be analysed in a significant way only as a consequence of changes in the technical coefficients of the system, which in turn are determined by the working of the law of diminishing returns under the pressure of population growth (see Caravale and Tosato, 1980, chs 2–3).

Indeed, even when Ricardo seems to consider the possibility of changes in distribution *un*accompanied by changes in technology (*Works*, vol. I, p. 45; vol. IX, pp. 335–6; vol. IV, p. 403), he may be said to be actually considering a change in the relative price of two commodities (both produced under conditions of constant returns) brought about by a change in distribution, consequent upon a change in the production conditions of 'corn'. Of course, this outcome depends crucially on the assumption that the two commodities whose relative prices have changed are produced with different fixed capital–labour ratios (see Caravale and Tosato, 1980, esp. ch. 3).

The other possible interpretation—that based on the ruling out of *all* possible changes in technology—would have to admit alternative values of the *real* (commodity) wage, in the presence of a given technology; this would conflict with Ricardo's notion of a *given* natural wage, and would therefore lie totally outside his main line of analysis.

The above-mentioned connection between distribution and technology stems from the simple fact that, given the *natural wage*, each state of technology (i.e. each given matrix of technical coefficients) generates a unique set of natural equilibrium values of the prices of commodities and of the profit rate. Changes in income distribution and changes in methods of production (of wage goods) are therefore, in Ricardo's theory, one and the same thing.[22]

The uniqueness of the price vector generated by each set of technological conditions, on the one hand, and the inadmissibility of alternative levels of real wages, on the other, make it possible to conclude that a (neoclassical-type) problem of *hypothetical* changes in distribution for a given technology finds no room in Ricardo's analytical framework.

This conclusion has relevant methodological implications, since it means that no distinction can be drawn, in Ricardo, between a realm of statics (to which the problem of alternative distributive setups would belong) and a realm of dynamics (to which the question of the effects on growth of changes in agricultural productive methods would belong).

On the analytical plane, Ricardo's problem finds a *general* solution (i.e. a solution not limited to the sphere of validity of the labour theory of value), since it can be shown, with reference to a model with m sectors with different 'organic compositions of capital', that an increase in the labour time necessary for the production of one unit of 'corn' is invariably accompanied by a decrease in the rate of profits and therefore—given the hypotheses as to the behaviour of the various social classes—in the rate of accumulation.

More specifically, for each 'state' of technology, that is at each level of the labour content of corn, natural prices and the rate of profit are unequivocally determined. But each of these solutions is, to put it figuratively, no more than one frame from a film sequence showing the gradual fall in the rate of profit as a consequence of diminishing returns, that is, of the continuous rise in labour input required by the characteristics of the agricultural technology hypothesized in the model (Caravale and Tosato, 1980, ch. 2 and appendix).

This analytic solution clearly owes a great deal to Sraffa's theory of prices and can thus be called a 'Ricardo after Sraffa' solution.[23]

---

[22] The text obviously refers to a 'closed' economy. Consideration of international trade would not however affect the argument. For example, imports of wage goods (typically, corn) produced at home under diminishing returns would cause the abandonment of 'marginal' lands whose cultivation would no longer be necessary: the fall in the price of agricultural products and the corresponding rise in the rate of profit, given the natural wage, would reflect, in terms of the basic model, a change in the 'state of technology' (i.e. a fall in the labour content of corn). Ricardo explicitly recognizes the analogy, from this point of view, between technical progress and foreign trade in his chapter XIX ('On Sudden Changes in the Channels of Trade' of the *Principles*, see, e.g., *Works*, vol. I, p. 271). The argument would be similar in the case of the introduction of, or changes in, taxes—see n. 56 below.

[23] An implicit reference to an analytical solution of this type (i.e. of the 'Ricardo after Sraffa' type) seems to be contained in the following passage by Garegnani: 'Ricardo's originality and profoundity show precisely in this: that he could see through the difficulties of what we would now describe as the solution of a system of n simultaneous price equations in the $(n-1)$ unknown relative prices and in the rate of profit, by means of simplifications like the "material rate of produce" or, later, the proportionality between values and quantities of embodied labour, which *as it turned out*, could be dropped without affecting *the essence of his conclusion*' (Garegnani, p. 100 above; italics added).

Population growth, the cultivation of less fertile lands, the emergence of diminishing returns in terms of the increased difficulty of producing agricultural goods, the increase of the prices of the wage goods, the increase of *nominal* wages (with a constant natural commodity wage rate), the consequent decrease of the rate of profit and the progressive reduction of the rate of growth of the economy—these are the logical steps of Ricardo's line of theoretical argument, a line to which even seemingly independent research topics, for instance the invariable standard of value, can be shown strictly to belong (see Caravale and Tosato, 1980, esp. ch. 3).

6 SOME IMPLICATIONS

It is perhaps worthwhile briefly to discuss some implications of the interpretative schema here proposed, especially as regards (1) Ricardo's position *vis-à-vis* Smith's theory of prices, and (2) the role of the labour theory of value in the Ricardian context.

As to the first point, it should be made clear that Ricardo's criticism of Smith's theory concerned the assertion that, even after the accumulation of capital, *relative natural prices do not necessarily differ from relative labour quantities*; in other words, that even with positive profits it is possible, under specific circumstances, for relative natural prices to coincide with relative quantities of labour. These specific circumstances, Ricardo then argued, are not those prevailing in general; therefore, *relative natural prices do not necessarily coincide with relative labour quantities* (even if the latter are the most important determinant of relative natural prices):

Adam Smith thought...that accumulation, necessarily, without any regard to the different degrees of durability of capital, or any other circumstance whatever, raised the prices or exchangeable value of commodities, and consequently that their value was no longer regulated by the quantity of labour necessary to their production. In opposition to him, I maintain that it is not because of [the] division into profits and wages,—it is not because capital accumulates, that exchangeable value

---

It should however be made clear that the 'essence of his [Ricardo's] conclusion' should refer to the relation between diminishing returns and the process of accumulation, through the rate of profit—in a perspective in which the strict connection between technology and distribution plays a central role—rather than to the study of alternative ways of distributing a *given* amount of production between wages and profits. It is precisely the former conclusion that—to my knowledge for the first time—is analytically proved, for the *general version* of the Ricardian model (that is, for the case of different capital–labour ratios in the various sectors of the economy), in Caravale and Tosato (1980, ch. 2 and appendix).

varies, but it is in all stages of society, owing only to two causes: one, the more or less quantity of labour required, the other, the greater or less durability of capital:—that the former is never superseded by the latter, but is only modified by it. (*Works*, vol. VII, p. 377)

Ricardo's general conception of natural prices has been discussed above. What has not been made explicitly clear is the analytical definition that he gives of natural price. Some relevant passages from the *Principles* and from the *Notes on Malthus* may help to clarify the point (see also, e.g., chapter xxx of the *Principles* (*Works*, vol. I, p. 385)).

Mr Malthus appears to think that it is a part of my doctrine, that the cost and value of a thing should be the same;—it is, if he means by cost, 'cost of production' including profits. (*Works*, vol. I, p. 47)

Mr Malthus accuses me of confounding the very important distinction between cost and value. If by cost, Mr Malthus means the wages paid for labour, I do not confound cost and value .... *If by cost Mr Malthus means cost of production, he must include profits as well as labour; he must mean what Adam Smith calls natural prices, which is synonymous with value.* (*Works*, vol. II, pp. 34–5; italics added)

Ricardo thus identifies the notions of 'natural price', 'cost of production' and 'value'.

By cost of production I invariably mean wages and profits, Adam Smith includes rent. I may have two loaves on my table, one obtained from very fertile land, the other from the very worst in cultivation; in the latter there will not be any rent, the whole of its value will be only sufficient to pay wages and profit. It is this loaf which will regulate the value of all loaves .... *In truth then in the cost of production* [i.e. natural price] *of all agricultural produce there is no rent, for the value of that produced from the capital last employed yields a compensation for wages, and a compensation for profits on capital, but no compensation for rent. In this sense only do I differ from Adam Smith.* (*Works*, vol. II, pp. 42–5)

Like Sraffa 150 years later, Ricardo defines natural prices as equal to the cost of production, and makes this cost equal to the sum of two elements.[24]

---

[24] The 'doubts' that Sraffa as a young man attributed to Ricardo as to the inclusion of profits in the notion of cost are thus clearly not present in Ricardo's theory: 'Ricardo, ... reduces cost to a single element, labour, with some *doubts* as to whether to include the services of capital' (Sraffa, 1928–9, p. 31; italics added).

Thus Ricardo can be thought to oppose a Smith-type adding-up approach only in so far as this is taken to mean that the rate of profit and the wage rate are determined in a totally independent fashion, so that a rise in wages invariably determines an increase of prices without affecting the rate of profit. In other words, when Ricardo speaks of Adam Smith's 'original error respecting value' (vol. VII, p. 100), he cannot have in mind the presence of various component parts of the natural price, but only the lack of the interdependence of these parts and the mechanism through which relative natural prices are determined.[25]

The second point refers to the role of the labour theory of value in Ricardo's theoretical construction. It is suggested here that the labour theory is relevant in Ricardo only as a theory of exchange and that its role is thus exclusively an analytical one.

Ricardo's letter to Mill of 28 December 1818 (vol. VII, p. 337), after the so often quoted passage recalled above, continues with a passage that is much less quoted but which appears of great import for the problem here discussed:

> But, say my opposers, Torrens and Malthus, capital is always of unequal durability in different trades, and therefore of what practical use is your enquiry? Of none, I answer, if I pretended to shew that cloth should be at such a price,—shoes at such another—muslins at such another and so on—*this I have never attempted to do,—but I contend it is of essential use to determine what the causes are which regulate exchangeable value.* (*Works*, vol. VII, pp. 377–8; italics added)

And in a letter to J. B. Say of 11 January 1820 Ricardo writes:

> In that chapter [Ricardo here refers to Say's (1819) chapter on value] you appear to have mishapprehended a position of mine. I do not say that it is the value of labour which regulates the value of commodities, for that is an opinion I do all in my power to overthrow; but I say that it

[25] See, on this point, Steedman's analysis (1982, pp. 126ff.) of Marx's criticism of Ricardo for his acceptance of Smith's thesis of the 'resolution' of prices in a sum of incomes. Whereas Marx considered that only by excluding non-wage capital could the prices of goods be 'resolved' in wages and profits, modern theorists, in particular Sraffa, have shown that it is possible to conceive 'a resolution' of this type even in the presence of non-wage capital (circulating capital goods used as inputs in the productive process).

An example of the risks of overemphasizing the differences between Ricardo and Sraffa on this ground is supplied by the following passage by Garegnani: 'Indeed, it seems plausible that it was this early argument [the one based upon quantities of corn] and the resulting theory of profits that also led Ricardo to recognize, with the error of the "popular view of the effect of wages on prices" ..., what he called "Adam Smith's original error respecting value" ... i.e. that the price of commodities is arrived at by a process of adding up the wages, profit and rent, and hence led him to develop the theory of value of the *Principles*' (p. 99 above).

is the comparative quantity of labour necessary to the production of commodities, which regulates their relative value. (*Works*, vol. VIII, p. 149)

Beyond all possible doubts, Ricardo makes it clear that his theory of value is *not* a theory of 'absolute' prices (i.e. prices in terms of a chosen numeraire), but a theory of relative prices (i.e. an attempt to identify the ratios of exchange between any two commodities produced in the system).

And in the chapter 'On Value' of the *Principles:*

It is necessary for me also to remark, that I have not said, because one commodity has so much labour bestowed upon it as will cost £1,000 and another so much as will cost £2,000, that, therefore, one would be of the value of £1,000 and the other of the value of £2,000; but I have said that their value will be to each other as two to one, and that in those proportions they will be exchanged. It is of no importance to the truth of this doctrine whether one of these commodities sells for £1,100 and the other for £2,200; or one for £1,500 and the other for £3,000; *into that question I do not at present inquire. I affirm only that their relative values will be governed by the relative quantities of labour bestowed on their production.* (*Works*, vol. I, pp. 46–7; italics added)

It is clear that Ricardo here assumes that the specific conditions for the validity of the labour theory of value prevail and that, therefore, no 'modification' of the connected rule of exchange occurs. It is also clear that Ricardo's main interest is represented by relative prices and that the labour theory of value was never conceived by him as a means of ascertaining the ultimate source of value.

The quarrel between the two views of Ricardo's supposed theory of the *causes* of value is a misrepresentation of his analytical efforts.[26] Ricardo was not searching for a philosophical or metaphysical explanation of the causes of value, for the ultimate origin of value. He wanted instead to define an analytically sound theory of exchange, capable of making it possible for the

[26] See Sraffa (1951). The misunderstandings in this field go back to Samuel Bailey (1967). Bailey, after affirming that 'value denotes ... nothing positive or intrinsic, but merely the relation in which two objects stand to each other as exchangeable commodities' (pp. 4–5), attributes to Ricardo the idea that 'the value of an object [is] something intrinsic and independent of other commodities' (p. 15) 'because the quantity of labour ... is the cause of value' (p. 18).

The anonymous review of Bailey's *Critical Dissertation*, attributed to James Mill and published in *Westminster Review* in January 1826, clarified Ricardo's intentions: 'Cost of production, by preventing demand from raising value above its own level, limits and determines value; and, therefore may, with great correctness, be denominated the Regulator of Value. To call it the Cause [of value], is a metaphysical blunder' (Bailey, 1967, p. 186). On this point, see also Nazzani (1883, pp. 575–80).

general case (in modern parlance, multi-sector model with different capital–labour ratios) to draw the same direct and unambiguous relationship between diminishing returns and the rate of profit that the 'corn model' of the *Essay on Profits* had made it possible to draw for a very special case. This is the real 'core' of Ricardo's analysis: *the inverse relation between the number of time-units of labour necessary for the production of one unit of agricultural product and the general rate of profit.*

The labour theory of value, conceived by Ricardo only as a theory of exchange, made it possible—within a sphere of validity which was wider than that of the corn model, but still limited (i.e. not general)—to eliminate the disturbances arising from distribution, and thus served to show without ambiguity that the cultivation of progressively poorer lands implied the reduction of the general profit rate. Awareness of the limits of validity of this theory of exchange led Ricardo to the life-long and unsuccessful search for an invariable measure of value.

And this search could not be otherwise than unsuccessful: the problem as Ricardo posed it had no satisfactory solution, in the sense that the 'standard measure' could have been defined *only* if conditions occurred that made it possible to do without it. (This point is clarified in Caravale and Tosato, 1980, ch. 3.)

To the unsuccessful search for the 'standard measure' strictly belongs Ricardo's last essay, *Absolute and Exchangeable Value*, written in 1823 soon before his death (see *Works*, vol. IV). In fact, the analytical content of this essay, both in the draft and in the final unfinished version, perfectly coincides with Ricardo's argument in section VI of the chapter 'On Value' of the *Principles* and in his above mentioned letter to Mill of 28 December 1818:

> there can be no perfect measure of the variations in the value of commodities arising from an alteration in these proportions [the proportions into which commodities are divided for wages and profits], as the proportions will themselves differ according as the commodity employed for the measure may be produced in a shorter or longer time. It must then be confessed that there is no such thing in nature as a perfect measure of value, and that all that is left to the Political Economist is to admit that the great cause of the variation of commodities is the greater or less quantity of labour that may be necessary to produce them, but that there is also another though much less powerful cause of their variation which arises from the different proportions in which finished commodities may be distributed between master and workman in consequence of either the amended or deteriorated condition of the labourer, or of the greater difficulty or facility of producing the necessaries essential to his subsistence. (*Works*, vol. IV, pp. 404–5)

Ricardo's 1823 essay may thus be taken to confirm:

(1) the analytical nature (and therefore the instrumental role) of the standard of measure Ricardo sought: this was, in other words, always conceived by Ricardo as an analytical tool capable of restoring the general validity of the labour theory of value and consequently making it possible to identify a direct and unambiguous relation between diminishing returns and the rate of profit;
(2) the recognition that the definition of a truly perfect measure of value is impossible;
(3) the clear identification of the reason of this impossibility, namely the 'unequal durability of capital in different trades';
(4) the settlement on an approximate, admittedly imperfect, solution.

The problems Ricardo tackles in this essay do not therefore represent a *new* line of research. In particular, the discussion on 'absolute value' should not be taken to mean an enquiry into the origin of value, a circumstance that is explicitly recognized by Marx (1979, vol. I, p. 651): 'Ricardo never concerns himself with the origin of surplus-value',[27] but rather as a different way of identifying the argument relating to the first of the two requisites of the invariable standard.[28] The 1823 essay is consequently nothing but a continuation of Ricardo's previous line of research.

In fact, in what are presumably his last words, in a letter to Mill dated 5 September 1823 (the day of the onset of his fatal illness), Ricardo writes:

> I have been thinking a good deal on this subject lately, but without much improvement. I see the same difficulties as before and am more confirmed than ever that, strictly speaking, *there is not in nature any correct measure of value nor can any ingenuity suggest one, for what constitutes a correct measure for some things is a reason why it cannot be a correct one for others. (Works,* vol. IX, p. 387; italics added)

In the light of the above, Napoleoni's (1977) thesis of the 'dramatic contraposition' of two irreconcilable elements in Ricardo cannot therefore be accepted. According to Napoleoni, there would be a 'dramatic contra-

---

[27] Marx continues: 'He [Ricardo] treats it [surplus-value] as an entity inherent in the capitalist mode of production, and in his eyes the latter is the natural form of social production. *Whenever he discusses the productivity of labour, he seeks in it not the cause of the existence of surplus-value, but the cause that determines the magnitude of that value* (1979, vol. I, p. 651; italics added).

[28] Cf. section 6 of the chapter 'On Value'. As is well known, the requirements postulated in 'a perfect measure of value' are (1) that it requires the same quantity of labour for its production at all times; (2) that the prices of other commodities expressed in terms of this unit do not change as a consequence of distributive changes.

position' between 'the two principles that remain unreconciled in Ricardo': 'absolute value', that is, the labour embodied in each commodity, and 'exchangeable value', that is, the exchange ratio between one commodity and every other one. Shortly before his death, Ricardo was obliged to admit explicitly, Napoleoni concludes, that there is no way of passing from the one to the other.

This 'dramatic contraposition' disappears as soon as it is recognized that Ricardo's work was directed not at the identification of the original source of value but, on the contrary, at the forging of a tool—the labour theory of value *qua* theory of exchange—with which to define an unambiguous relationship between diminishing returns and the rate of profit. But, as Ricardo came to realize, the tool proved unsuited to the task.

It is true that some passages in Ricardo might give the impression that he thought of the labour content of commodities as the source of value of the national production. For example, in chapter XX of the *Principles* ('Value and Riches, Their Distinctive Properties': *Works*, vol. I, pp. 273–88), Ricardo distinguishes between *value* and *riches* and discusses the effect of a sudden increase in productivity arising from technological progress, so that the same input of labour results in a larger output. In this case, he says, the nation's wealth would increase, but not the value of the output:

> By the invention of machinery, by improvements in skill, by a better division of labour, or by the discovery of new markets . . . , a million men may produce double, or treble the amount of riches . . . , but they will not on that account add anything to value; for every thing rises or falls in value, in proportion to the facility or difficulty of producing it, or, in other words, in proportion to the quantity of labour employed on its production. (*Works*, vol. I, p. 273)

In fact the argument relates once again to the specific analytical problems of the evaluation of production in terms of the chosen numeraire and the identification of the exchange ratios between commodities. Supposing the labour theory of value is valid, and choosing for convenience as numeraire the labour content of one unit of gold (so the prices of all commodities coincide with their respective labour contents; see Caravale and Tosato, 1980, ch. 2), a sudden and uniform increase in productivity concerning *all* the sectors would obviously cause an increase in physical outputs, while it would leave unaltered the prices of goods expressed in terms of the commodity numeraire, the exchange ratios between the various commodities as well as the value of the summation, for the whole economy, of the price-quantity products. In this case, however, the national product measured in terms of the chosen numeraire (whose conditions of production have changed) would appear to have increased. This 'paradoxical' circumstance seems to account for Ricardo's assumption that the productive conditions of the commodity numeraire are unchanged.[29] With this hypothesis the value of the national product remains constant in terms of the numeraire; relative prices are also constant, while prices in terms of the commodity numeraire diminish. Ricardo's main analytical interest seems to be (*see* above), the identification of the exchange ratios of each commodity with the numeraire on the one hand, and with every other commodity on the other—rather than the affirmation of the principle that the expense of a certain amount of labour on a commodity confers upon it once-and-for-all a certain 'value':

> an effect is also produced on the portion of goods still unconsumed, which were manufactured previously to the improvement; the value of those goods will be reduced, inasmuch as they must fall to the level, quantity for quantity, of the goods produced under all the advantages of the improvement (*Works*, vol. I, p. 274)

In fact, being the 'new' prices (in terms of the commodity numeraire) reduced by the 'improvement', the 'old' goods must fall in price (in terms of the same numeraire) if they are to be sold in the market.

It seems clear, however, that Ricardo's argument, in fact, applies only if two conditions are simultaneously verified:

(1) the increase in labour productivity must not be associated with the introduction (or substitution) of 'machinery' but must be due exclusively to 'improvements in skill' and/or 'a better division of labour';
(2) the basic premise of the labour theory of value must be verified; i.e. the 'organic composition of capital' must be the same throughout the various productive sectors.

Since these two conditions are not in general verified, the effects of technological progress on the 'riches' of the economic system and on relative prices are more complex than Ricardo seems here to have thought.[30]

7 SOME SIGNIFICANT ANALOGIES IN THE INTERPRETATION OF RICARDO

There is an interesting analogy between the interpretation given above, which benefits from the analytical results of contemporary economic theory, and

[29] Significantly, Ricardo, in this chapter, again stresses the first of the two conditions identified in the chapter 'On Value' as necessary for an invariable measure of value: 'That commodity is alone invariable, which at all times requires the same sacrifice of toil and labour to produce it' (*Works*, vol. I, p. 275).

[30] An indication of the difficulties that arise from the systematic consideration of 'machinery'—though in a much simplified context—is offered in Caravale and Tosato (1980, appendix to ch. 6). On the other hand, the reduction in some technical coefficients as a consequence of technological innovation (in the conditions indicated in the text) would imply a change in the 'state of technology', expressed analytically by the matrix of technical coefficients and, therefore, a new set of relative prices and of the related rate of profit (see Caravale and Tosato, 1980, ch. 2).

that of some important earlier writers whose analysis has no base other than their apprehension of the essential features of Ricardo's theory from the reading of his writings.

Marx

Marx's analytical interpretation of Ricardo's theory—that is, the analytical model that Marx thought Ricardo had in mind in his theoretical works (not to be confused with the criticism that Marx addressed to Ricardo[31])—appears to be based on the attribution of a central role to the notion of *natural equilibrium*, and on the strict and systematic connection between changes in technology (diminishing returns) and changes in distribution. The following passages, from Marx's *Theories of Surplus Value* and from *Grundisse*, respectively, seem particularly relevant (see also Marx, 1969, vol. II, pp. 446, 438–9, 466):

> Ricardo defends the proposition that the permanent price is determined by the *cost-price*, and not by *supply or demand*: that, therefore, the permanent price is determined by the *value* of the commodities only in so far as this value determines the cost-price. Provided that the prices of the commodities are so adjusted that they all yield a profit of 10 per cent, then every lasting change in these prices will be determined by a change in their values, in the labour-time required for their production. As this value continues to determine the general rate of profit, so the changes in it continue to determine the variations in cost-prices.
>
> ... Once the cost-prices of the commodities in the various branches of production are established, they rise or fall relatively to each other with any change in the values of the commodities. If the productivity of labour rises, the labour-time required for the production of a *particular commodity* decreases and therefore its *value falls*.... The *absolute amount of labour employed on it* has been reduced, hence also the amount of paid labour it contains and the amount of wages expended on it, even though the rate of wages has remained the same. If the commodity were sold at its former cost-price, then it would yield a higher profit than the general rate of profit, since formerly, this profit was equal to 10 per cent on the higher outlay. It would therefore be now more than 10 per cent on the diminished outlay. If ... the productivity of labour decreases, the real values of the commodities rise. When the rate of profit is given—or, which is the same thing, the cost-prices are given—the relative rise or fall of the cost-prices is dependent on the rise

---

[31] Steedman (1982) has shown—again, in the light of contemporary theoretical results—that most of Marx's criticisms of Ricardo (for Ricardo's identification of values and cost prices, his determination of the rate of profit, etc.) were unjustified.

or fall, the variation, in the real values of the commodities. *As a result of this variation, new cost-prices or, as Ricardo says, following Smith, 'new natural prices' take the place of the old.* (Marx, 1969, vol. II, pp. 213–15; final italics added)

A. Smith explained the fall of the rate of profit, as capital grows, by the competition among capitals. To which Ricardo replied that competition can indeed reduce profits in the various branches of business to an average level, can equalize the rate, but cannot depress this average rate itself. A. Smith's phrase ... is false in the sense in which he understands it, as if competition imposed laws on capital from the outside, laws not its own. Competition can permanently depress the rate of profit in all branches of industry, i.e. the average rate of profit, only if and in so far as a general and permanent fall of the rate of profit, having the force of a law, is conceivable *prior to* competition and regardless of competition. Competition executes the inner laws of capital; makes them into compulsory laws towards the individual capital, but it does not invent them. It realizes them. To try to explain them simply as results of competition therefore means to concede that one does not understand them. Ricardo, for his part, says: 'No accumulation of capitals can *permanently* reduce profits unless an equally permanent cause raises wages.... *He finds this cause in the growing ... unproductivity of agriculture, 'the growing difficulty of increasing the quantity of subsistence', i.e. in the growth of proportionate wages, so that labour's real wage is no greater, but the product obtains more labour; in a word, a greater portion of necessary labour is required for the production of agricultural products. The falling rate of profit hence corresponds, with him, to the nominal growth of wages and real growth of ground rent.* (Marx, 1977, pp. 751–2; final italics added)

Natural prices (natural equilibrium with a uniform rate of profit), the continuous change in the set of these prices as a consequence of the progressive decline in agricultural productivity, the reduction in the rate of profit following the working of diminishing returns in agriculture, and the distributive antagonism between profit-receivers and *rentiers* are thus the cornerstones of Marx's analytical interpretation of Ricardo—an interpretation, it may be observed, that differs widely from that suggested by some contemporary authors, who draw inspiration from Marx's 'constructive' work and tend to read Ricardo's theory mainly in terms of a distributive antagonism between capitalists and workers.

It is interesting to emphasize the coincidence between the above interpretation and two others: that of Ricardo's friend and most faithful follower, J. R.

McCulloch; and that suggested by the author of the first mathematical formulation of the Ricardian system, W. Whewell.

McCulloch

In his review of the *Principles* published in the *Edinburgh Review* of 1818 — almost an 'authentic interpretation', in the legal sense of the word[32] — McCulloch (1818) treats extensively a number of points that are crucial for Ricardo's analytical construction. In particular, the distinction between market prices and natural prices and the central role attributed to the latter are thus clarified:

> A very great, if not the principal source, of the errors into which political economists have been betrayed, appears to have originated in their confounding together the Natural and the Market price of commodities. But the laws by which these prices are regulated, are essentially different. Should the supply of any necessary or desirable commodity be increased beyond the effectual demand, or the demand of those who are able and willing to pay the expense of its production, including in that expense the ordinary rate of profit on the capital employed, its price will decline....
>
> ...In the same way, when the supply of any commodity falls short of the quantity usually demanded, the competition on the part of the buyers becomes greater than that on the part of the sellers, and an increase of its ordinary price is the consequence....

[32] In his letter to McCulloch of 22 August 1818, Ricardo comments upon this review in the following terms: 'I know not whether I ought to thank you, but I have been exceedingly gratified. My own doctrines appear doubly convincing as explained by your able pen, and I have already heard in this retreat that those who could not understand *me*, most clearly comprehend *you*. For this service I may thank you, and I may also be permitted to express my satisfaction that I have succeeded in impressing you with the same view of the general principles of Political Economy which I myself entertain. I have not many converts of which to boast, but when I can number amongst them yourself and Mr Mill I think mine is no mean triumph. The latter gentleman is now on a visit to me here, and I am sure you will be pleased to know that he thinks your review a masterly essay on the science, and will very much assist to disseminate correct views on a very intricate part of it' (*Works*, vol. VII, p. 286). And, in a letter to Trower of 18 September 1818, Ricardo, again referring to McCulloch's review, writes: 'I am glad to hear that you are pleased with the review of my book in the *Edinburgh Review*. It gives me great satisfaction, and principally because the writer [McCulloch] appears to have well understood me, and to have explained my doctrines with great clearness and perspicuity' (*Works*, vol. VII, p. 296).

'In this review [McCulloch's review of the *Principles*]', Piero Sraffa writes in his 'Introductory Notes' to Ricardo's *Correspondence* (vol. VI, pp. xxi–xxii), 'which was decisive in establishing Ricardo's fame and popularizing his doctrines, he [McCulloch] showed himself the most complete convert and disciple of Ricardo's theories, and he was to become the main defender of his doctrines against criticism.'

...It is *the cost of production*, which is the permanent and ultimate regulator of the exchangeable value of every commodity. The occasional variations, arising from an excess or deficiency of supply, or from a variation in the demand, are mere temporary oscillations on one side or the other of this given quantity. It is but seldom, indeed, that the market price and the real price of a commodity entirely correspond; but, except in cases of monopoly, the one can never permanently continue either much above or much below the other ... .

...No rise [in the market price of any commodity] can continue, except where the cost of production has been proportionably increased. If that cost has remained stationary, or has not increased in a corresponding ratio, prices will decline as soon as the causes of temporary enhancement are removed. (McCulloch, 1818, pp. 60–2)

On the other hand, Ricardo's concept of the cost of production as the foundation of the theory of relative natural prices, and the 'dynamic' concept of rent, is thus clearly expounded (particularly in relation to Smith's views):

The theory, however, which teaches that the exchangeable value of a commodity can only be increased by an increase in the quantity of labour necessarily expended on its production, would not be complete, if it could be shown that Rent entered as a component part into price; for if this were really the case, it would follow, that prices must vary as rents vary, or that the one must rise and fall with every rise and fall of the other. It is therefore necessary briefly to inquire into the *nature and causes of rent*.

... On the first settling of any country abounding with rich and fertile land, there is never any rent; and it is only because land is of different qualities with respect to its productive powers; and because, in the progress of population, the supply of rich and fertile land becomes exhausted, and land of an inferior quality, or less advantageously situated, must be brought into cultivation, that rent is ever paid for the use of it.

... Now, the sole reason why rent begins to be paid on land of the first quality, whenever land of a secondary quality is taken into cultivation, is, because on the inferior land a greater expenditure of capital and labour is necessary to afford the same produce. When the wants of society force us to have recourse to poorer soils, rent immediately begins to be paid on land of the first quality, just because there cannot, in the same country, be *two rates* of *profit*.

... The price, therefore, at which raw produce sells in the market, is its *natural* price; it is the price which is necessary to procure the requisite supply, and is not in the slightest degree influenced by either high or low rents. Rents are only paid by those lands which yield an excess of produce after paying the expenses of labour and the ordinary profits of stock; but in every progressive country, lands are always taken into cultivation, which yield at the time nothing but the profits of stock, and for which there can be no rent paid. Hence, it is evident, rent does not enter into the price of raw produce; for *the price of that produce is regulated by the price of the portion raised on the very worst lands in cultivation, and which pay no rent.* (McCulloch, 1818, pp. 72–6)

The connection is then stressed between the laws that regulate rent and those that regulate profits; correct conclusions are drawn by McCulloch both as to the ensuing distributive conflict and as to the growth prospects for the economy:

a proper understanding of the nature and causes of rent, is but a step, though a very material one, towards ascertaining the laws by which the *profits of stock* are regulated.

...It is not...the competition caused by an increase of capital which reduces profits as society advances, but it is the necessity of having recourse to inferior soils to obtain the necessary supplies of food. (McCulloch, 1818, pp. 79–80)

It follows, from these principles, that the interest of the landlord is always opposed to that of every other class in the community.

...High rents are invariably accompanied by a high price of raw produce, and consequently by high wages, and a low rate of profit. Every increase of rent is, therefore, a proof that society is becoming clogged in its progress. It shows, that the power to accumulate capital and population, or to increase that fund, by whose extent the extent of the productive industry of the country must ever be regulated, is diminished.

...High rent and low profits, for they are inseparably connected, ought never to be made the subject of complaint, if they occur in the natural progress of society, and under a system of perfectly free inter-course with other nations. But if they are caused by an exclusive commercial system, or by restrictions which prevent the importation of cheap foreign corn, and which, therefore, force the cultivation of inferior soils at home, they are highly to be deprecated. (McCulloch, 1818, pp. 81–2)

Whewell

In spite of the critical attitude that pervades W. Whewell's (1831) *Memoir* on Ricardo,[33] the central analytical points of Ricardo's theoretical construction ('the postulates which seem to form the foundations of Mr Ricardo's doctrines') are grasped with lucidity.

As for the notion of rent, Whewell writes:

> the farmer will not consent to make less than the average rate of profits; also, competition will not allow him to make more: and therefore the excess of the produce of the land above that amount which is necessary to realize such profits, will be transferred to the landlord as *rent*. Hence, ... rent is the excess of the produce of capital employed on land, above the produce of the same capital otherwise employed.
>
> It is also supposed that there are soils of different degrees of fertility, which form a continuous decreasing series: and that the lowest degree of fertility on which the cultivator can obtain ... profit without paying rent, will be cultivated. (Whewell, 1831, p. 3)

The 'dynamic' notion of natural wages and the definition of the adjustment mechanism in terms of rates of growth (rather than absolute levels of the relevant variables) are given in the following terms:

> Mr Ricardo assumes that the natural rate of wages is invariable; that is, that the labourer's command of food and other necessaries is never permanently augmented or diminished. Hence, if the price of corn (or whatever is the main article of food) rises or falls, a rise or fall in wages shortly follows and compensates this charge.
>
> This opinion is supposed to be established by the ascertained laws of the progress of population. It is conceived that, if the demand for labour, and consequently the reward of it, is diminished, the encouragement to population being thus weakened, *a retardation in its advance* will occur, which will, after a certain period, restore the original standard of wages: and that these effects inverted will occur in the case of an increase of wages. (Whewell, 1831, p. 5; italics added)

---

[33] See in particular Whewell (1831, pp. 2–3): 'For my own part, I do not concieve that we are at all justified in asserting the principles which form the basis of Mr Ricardo's system, either to be steady and universal in their operation, or to be of such paramount and predominant influence, that other principles which oppose and control them, may be neglected in comparison. Some of them appear to be absolutely false in general, and others to be inapplicable in almost all particular cases. Perhaps, however, to trace their consequences may be one of the most obvious modes of verifying or correcting them.'

The definitions of *natural* and *market* prices are then correctly specified:

> [Ricardo's]... principle... [can be] expressed by saying, that the price must be such as to pay the cost of production with profits.
>
> This *natural price* may often be different from the *market price*, which is affected by another principle, that of *supply* and *demand*. According to the principle of supply and demand, the price increases by an increase of the demand, or by a diminution of the supply, and *vice versa*.
>
> ... the market price, determined by the immediate action of demand and supply, may be very different from the natural price, determined ... by the cost of production: this latter price being however that under which the equilibrium obtains, and to which the other perpetually tends. (Whewell, 1831, pp. 163–6)

The concept of natural equilibrium, central for Ricardo, is described in terms that show a considerable inclination on the part of Whewell to share Ricardo's stand on the subject, being replete with observations of the greatest interest to today's economists:

> Supposing the preceding postulates true, the problems in which they are applied are much simplified by assuming such an equilibrium to obtain: but... [i]n reality, this equilibrium is never attained: probably in most cases it is never approximated to. There is a constant tendency towards the state of things in which the elements of wealth are in this exact balance, but this is a tendency like that which the waters at the source of a river have to descend towards its mouth.... .
>
> We are to recollect, therefore, that even if our principles were exact, deductions from them made according to the method we are now following, would give us only a faint and distant resemblance of the state of things produced by the perpetual struggle and conflict of such principles with variable circumstances. Such deductions however would probably have some resemblance, in the general outline of their results, to the true state of things. They would offer to us a *first approximation*... .
>
> In order however that solutions of this nature may have any value, it is requisite that the principles, of which we estimate the operation, should include *all* the *predominant* causes which really influence the result. We necessarily reject some of the circumstances and tendencies which really exist: but we can do this with propriety, only when the effects of these latter agents are, from their small amount or short duration, inconsiderable modifications only of the general results. The quantities which we neglect must be of an inferior *order* to those which

we take into account; otherwise we obtain no approximation at all. (Whewell, 1831, pp. 166–7)

On the other hand, Whewell clarifies the crucial phenomenon of diminishing returns in agriculture in its relation with distribution:

> If we suppose the population of a country to go on increasing, and the powers of agriculture to remain stationary, it will, in order that the increased numbers may be provided with subsistence, be necessary that more and more capital and labour should be applied to the task of raising food. If we suppose these to be employed on new land, more and more land will be perpetually cultivated; and if we make the supposition ... that the land of the country consists of a progression of soils of decreasing fertility, each new soil cultivated will yield less surplus produce to the labour employed upon it.
>
> This increase of population, and consequent extension of agricultural labour to less productive soils, Mr Ricardo conceived to have been the progress of things in this country: and apparently he conceived it also to be the necessary and universal progress of nations. On this supposition his first main problem was to trace the distribution of the various portions of the produce, as wages, rent, and profits, which takes place in the course of this progress. (Whewell, 1831, pp. 166–7)

The ensuing reduction of profits is then discussed in mathematical terms (1831, pp. 170–3), while the remaining part of the *Memoir* is devoted to the analysis of the problem of fixed capital,[34] the economic effects of taxation within a Ricardian context, the question of foreign trade and the rate of exchange.

8 GAREGNANI'S THEORY OF THE 'CORE'

Sections 2–6 above have suggested a framework for a unified interpretation of the problems relating to value, distribution and growth discussed by Ricardo, problems that are often considered substantially separate fields of his research, while section 7 has emphasized certain analogies between the interpretation suggested and that supplied by some important authors of the past.

On the basis of the conclusions reached thus far, the final two sections of the paper aim at evaluating the hypotheses and implications of Garegnani's and Hollander's contributions to the interpretation of Ricardo's theoretical work.

---

[34] On this question see also Campanelli (1980).

Garegnani (1981, esp Part I) maintains that the classical authors (from Quesnay to Smith, Ricardo and Marx) 'shared not so much the idea of a wage determined by the level of subsistence as the more general concept of a wage determined by economic and social forces *before and independently of* the other shares of the social product' (1981, p. 12).

These authors, working from the premise that the volume of social product depends basically on the stage of capital accumulation attained and on the technical conditions of production, consider 'the quantities produced as data (or independent variables) when the shares of the social product other than wages are determined' (p. 13). They construct their theoretical models on the basis 'of the conception according to which real wages and social product are *data* when the determination of the shares of the social product other than wages is considered—these shares are therefore determined by subtraction' (p. 13). Classical economic theory, centred on the idea of surplus,

> presents, so to speak, a *core* separated from the rest of the analysis by the fact that the wage, the social product and the technical conditions of production there appear as previously determined. This 'core' ... includes the determination of the shares other than wages of the social product, as the difference between the given social product and—again given—necessary subsistence[35] ... this determination also entails that of the relative prices of commodities which thus becomes an integral part of the 'core'. In the same 'core' we find, as a natural extension, the analysis of the *relationships* between, on the one hand, real wages, the social product and the technical conditions of production—the *independent* variables—and, on the other, the surplus and the relative prices of commodities—the *dependent* variables. (Garegnani, 1981, pp. 13–14)

From the point of view of its structure, classical theory thus appears to be characterized by 'the separation of the analysis into distinct logical stages' (1981, p. 15) and, in fact, by the existence of a limited 'core' consisting of the determination of prices and non-wage incomes. This circumstance, according to Garegnani, makes the analysis of the classical economists very different from that of the marginalists, for in the latter real wages, the prices of commodities and of the factors of production, and the social product are determined simultaneously. In other words, 'the determination of prices and of non-wage incomes is no longer the limited "core" of surplus theories, but comes to embrace practically the whole sphere of economic theory' (1981, p. 16).

---

[35] From the fact that the social product and productive techniques are given, it follows that the number of workers is also given. 'Subsistence consumption' is therefore obtained by multiplying the number of workers by the real wage.

It is important to note, in relation to the discussion that will follow, that for Garegnani 'the characteristic premise of surplus theories ... [is that] the real wage and the social product are given *before* prices and the rate of profit are determined' (1981, p. 36).

In fact, the problem which can arise here, and which did arise for Ricardo, is that, 'If [social product and necessary consumption are not previously known when expressed in value terms] and the value of even one of these magnitudes depends on the rate of profit, determination of the latter rate on their basis risks running into a vicious circle' (1981, p. 20).

The essential characteristic of surplus theories in general is thus represented by the possibility of solving this problem through the determination of the social product and necessary consumption before the determination of the rate of profit and prices. This is the circumstance that makes it possible, according to Garegnani, to shed light on the residual nature of profits.

Applying this interpretative schema to Ricardo's theory, Garegnani makes two relevant simplifying assumptions:

(1) that 'fertile lands abound and that rent can therefore be ignored' (1981, p. 18); and
(2) that, since Ricardo develops his analysis *as if* capital consists only of the wages advanced to the workers each year, non-wage capital can be disregarded.

As should become clear from what follows, the degree of relevance of these two hypotheses is different in the sense that only the former seems to be essential to the interpretative schema suggested by Garegnani and to the analytical inferences drawn from it. It should be added, however, that both of these assumptions seem to make it difficult to grasp fully a relevant portion of Ricardo's theoretical research.

The first hypothesis, regarding the elimination of rent, implies the exclusion of decreasing returns from the analysis. The concept that Ricardo so much emphasizes in his 'scientific programme' is thus left out of the picture (and of the 'core'). This implies the impossibility of analysing the true essence of Ricardian theory, the inverse relation, that is, between the labour content of 'corn' and the general rate of profit—a relationship that expresses the basic class antagonism between *rentiers* and capitalists (with a given real commodity wage).

The only possible antagonism remaining in Garegnani's interpretative context is that between *real* wages and profits, a circumstance that sharply contrasts with Garegnani's own clear perception that 'the specific analysis of the relationship between capital and wage labour made by Marx could not have been made by *Ricardo, interested as he mainly was in the relationship between capital and landed property at a time when the conflict between capital and labour was not yet concretely manifest*' (1981, p. x; italics added). (In this sense, see Caravale and Tosato, 1980, p. 12.) P. Sraffa, in his 1928–9 manuscript, writes in the same vein: 'Ricardo's theory lays great emphasis on the distinction between rent on one side and all the other shares on the other; but he left in the background the question [of] ... the distribution ... between capital and labour [which] ... became the central issue [soon after his death]' (pp. 9–10). But while the antagonism between *rentiers* and capitalists has its foundation in the working of diminishing returns and is therefore an essential expression of the 'laws of motion' of the economic system as Ricardo saw them, that between workers and capitalists is essentially *hypothetical* (with a given technology) in character, and is consequently totally unconnected from such laws.

It is also useful to add that, within Ricardo's natural equilibrium approach, the assumption of *alternative values* of the real wage seems basically incompatible with the hypothesis that the 'situation is given'. More specifically, even when population is taken as a datum, the former assumption appears to conflict with the idea of a given level and composition of output and, in one instance, with that of a given technology of the system. The study of alternative distributive setups *in a given situation* would thus seem to have no room in Ricardo's natural equilibrium analysis. Among other things, this implies that, in a typically Ricardian context with diminishing returns in agriculture, different levels and compositions of natural equilibrium values of the social product may be associated with the same set of technological coefficients (and vice versa). Contrary to what one might be led to think,[36] speaking of a given technology of the system is thus not necessarily the same thing as speaking of a given level and composition of output.

To elucidate this point, two cases must be distinguished. The first is represented by the assumption that a higher level of real natural wages is associated with a higher demand for agricultural products; the second by the assumption that, instead, a higher natural wage rate, with an unchanged level of population, would correspond to an increase in the demand for 'luxuries and conveniences' (the assumption favoured by Ricardo).

(1) If a higher level of the real natural wage rate implied, with an unchanged population, an increased demand for agricultural commodities, this would be associated with a *new* position of natural equilibrium, that is, with a new level of agricultural production and, under diminishing returns, with a reduction of labour productivity at the margin and an increase in the labour content of 'corn'. The consideration of alternative values of the real natural wage rate would thus conflict both with the assumption that the state of technology is given, and with the hypothesis that the size and composition of

[36] See for instance Eatwell (1977–8, 1977). It must be observed that the *given* natural equilibrium position, with reference to which the problem of the possible wage–profit rate configurations would be studied, cannot possibly be that of the stationary state, since here the rate of profit would by definition be zero (or a minimum equivalent to zero).

output is given.[37] In other words, it would be incorrect to think of a movement along a given wage–profit inverse relation, since each level of the real wage rate would be associated with a different state of technology, a different wage–profit relation and a different set of natural prices.

(2) Ricardo, however, makes it clear that he believes that a higher level of real natural wages would *per se* imply not an increase in the demand for corn—a consequence that can arise in his view only from an increase in population after a certain time lag—but, rather, an increase in the demand for 'luxuries and conveniences'.[38]

If these latter commodities are supposed to be produced under conditions of constant returns to scale, the new position of natural equilibrium with which the higher level of wages would be associated would be characterized *not* by a changed state of technology, but by a modification in the set of natural prices, in the size and composition of output, and in distribution (a lower rate of profit would in fact correspond to the higher real wage rate). The assumption of constant returns to scale in the production of non-agricultural commodities would in this case play an essential role in making it possible to think of a movement along the wage–profit inverse relation.

The state of technology would 'change' only in the first case, while the size and composition of output would 'change' in both.

The analysis 'of the possible wage–profit rate configurations for a given system of production and for a given composition and scale of output' (Eatwell, 1977, p. 64), which (on the basis of a different conception of the wage that here participates in division of the surplus) is perfectly consistent in Sraffa's theory, is thus inconsistent in Ricardo's theory.

Even if Garegnani's main theoretical reference point is obviously the hypothesis of no change in quantities produced that characterizes *Production Of Commodities By Means Of Commodities* (Sraffa, 1960), it may be noted in passing that an interpretation of Ricardo based on the substantial exclusion of decreasing returns is to be found in Sraffa's early writings (1925, 1926). (K. Bharadwaj reads Ricardo in the same sense—see 1978, esp. pp. 44ff.)

In his criticism of Marshallian theory, Sraffa maintained that the 'law of non-proportional productivity'—that is, the functional link between quantity produced and cost of production—has no empirical content but is 'the consequence of the shifting of the basis of the theory of value from the cost of production to utility' (1925, p. 279). In other words, it is only the counterpart,

[37] In a two-sector Ricardian model an increased level of the production of 'corn' would be associated with an increased level of rents and with a greater level of the production of 'gold' (the luxury good) thus also implying an increase in employment. See Caravale and Tosato (1980, ch. 2, para. 2.5).

[38] See in particular Ricardo's letters to Trower of 15 September 1820 (*Works*, vol. VII, pp. 235–6), of 26 September 1820 (p. 258), and of 3 October 1820 (pp. 272–5). See also chapter XXI of the *Principles* (vol. I, p. 292).

on the production side, of the hypothesis of the consumer's decreasing utility on the demand side. According to Sraffa, the classical economists, notably Smith and Ricardo, did not share this position:

> The idea of interdependence between quantity produced and the cost of production of a commodity produced under competitive conditions is not suggested by experience at all and could not arise spontaneously. It can be said that *all classical writers accept implicitly, as an obvious fact, that cost is independent of quantity [constant returns], and they do not bother to discuss the contrary hypothesis.* (Sraffa, 1925, p. 279; italics added)

Both Ricardo and Smith had analysed diminishing and increasing productivity; but, says Sraffa, the theory of diminishing productivity was taken into account only from the viewpoint of distribution, while that of rising productivity was discussed, on the production side, in relation to the problem of the division of labour:

> The theory of decreasing productivity was always dealt with by classical writers in relation to the rent of land, and was therefore included, according to the traditional division of economics, in the theory of 'distribution'. Increasing returns on the other hand was discussed in relation to the division of labour, that is in the analysis of 'production'. But nobody, until comparatively recently, had thought of unifying these two tendencies in one single law of non-proportional productivity, and considering these as one of the bases of the theory of price.... *It is true ... that the law of diminishing productivity of the land gave prominence to a connection of this type, but recognition of the fact that greater output of necessity carried with it greater cost led only to consideration of the resulting variations in distribution. Moreover, this effect could not be considered a normal cause of variation of the relative price of individual commodities, for the increase in cost involved all, or almost all, commodities together, since almost all, in the final analysis, were derived from agricultural production and hence the action of decreasing productivity increased proportionately the cost of each.* (Sraffa, 1925, p. 279; italics added)[39]

The same view is reiterated in the *Economic Journal* article of 1926—a 'sadly truncated form' of the original paper written in Italian for *Annali di Economia* (Sraffa, 1925), according to Kahn (1979, p. 23):

[39] I thank Alessandro Roncaglia and John Eatwell for having supplied their translation of these two passages.

The law of diminishing returns has long been associated mainly with the problem of rent, and from this point of view the law as formulated by the classical economists with reference to land was entirely adequate. It had always been perfectly obvious that its operation affected, not merely rent, but also the *cost of the product; but this was not emphasised as a cause of variation in the relative price of the individual commodities produced, because the operation of diminishing returns increased in a like measure the cost of all.* This remained true even when the English classical economists applied the law to the production of corn, for, as Marshall has shown, 'the term "corn" was used by them as short for agricultural produce in general' (Sraffa, 1926, p. 182; italics added)

Sraffa is even more explicit in a letter to Keynes written in June 1926:[40]

Marshall's theory assumes that variable returns (either diminishing or increasing) predominate, *as opposed to Ricardo's theory, which implies universal constant returns.* Originally the two laws were designed for quite different uses: diminishing returns for the analysis of rent, increasing returns for division of labour.... Now, the Ricardian form of diminishing returns affects, not only a single commodity, but the whole of commodities in whose production enters the factor of production (say, 'land') which gives rise to the diminution of returns: as to increasing returns, external economies 'can seldom be allocated exactly to any one industry: they are in great measure attached to groups, often large groups, of correlated industries', as Marshall himself recognizes (Industry and Trade, p. 188). *In both cases variations in the conditions of production of the commodity concerned and of the 'other' commodities are of the same order of magnitude, so that it is not legitimate to consider the first and neglect the latter.* (italics added)[41]

We can sum up as follows.

(1) The young Sraffa's overall interpretation of Ricardo is in terms of constant returns.

(2) The role of the principle of diminishing returns in agriculture is here confined to the theory of distribution; i.e., this principle is taken into account

---

[40] The letter is to be found in Roncaglia (1978, p. 11).

[41] Sraffa's cautious attitude towards the *general* problem of the theory of competition must be borne in mind. The 'preliminary approximation to reality' of the 1925 article ('we must then concede that, in general, commodities are produced under conditions of constant costs'), Sraffa continues in the above letter, 'has been misunderstood and taken to imply that in actual life constant returns prevail: *although I believe that Ricardo's assumption* [constant returns] *is the best available for a simple theory of competition* (viz. a first approximation); of course in reality the connection between cost and quantity produced is obvious' (see Roncaglia [1978], p. 12; italics added).

only to prove—as Sraffa himself writes in his 1928–9 manuscript (pp. 8–9), 'that rent does not enter into the cost of production of that final part of the product which regulates value', thus opening the way to the incorrect attribution to Ricardo of the conception, which is *not* to be found in Ricardo, that the fundamental distributive problem concerned the distribution of a *given* product between wages and profits.

(3) Changes in distribution (arising from changes in the cost of production connected with changes in the quantity produced) are *not* considered a normal cause of changes in relative prices, because the movement is thought to concern all commodities and therefore to affect the cost of each proportionally.

Now, when we recognize the central importance of the hypothesis of diminishing returns in Ricardo's analysis, it is Sraffa's own analytical framework of *Production of Commodities* that makes it possible to show that, for the general case, an increase in the quantity of labour required to produce the wage goods will lead to a fall in the general rate of profit and to a change in the whole system of relative prices (the direction of each change will depend on the technical production conditions of each commodity in relation to those of the commodity chosen as numeraire) (see Caravale and Tosato, 1980, ch. 2 and its appendix).[42] In other words, if we admit, as did Sraffa in his early writings, the working of diminishing returns in agriculture, we must also recognize that the link between quantity produced and cost of production does not affect distribution *alone*, but constitutes instead a normal cause of changes in the relative prices of the commodities produced in the economic system.

Sraffa's position in 1925–6 therefore seems to be closer to Smith's view of the effects of a change in wages on prices than to Ricardo's tormented reflections on the effect of changes in wages on the rate of profit in the presence of different productive conditions (capital–labour ratios, or 'organic compositions of capital') in the various sectors.[43]

---

[42] This implicitly contradicts the common thesis, based on the hypothesized absence of a relationship between quantity and prices, of the *separation* of the theory of value from the theory of production in classical economic analysis. See for example Eatwell (1977–8, p. 41): 'Since output is a *datum* there is no place in the theory of value for functional relationships between quantities and prices, or between saving, investment and the rate of profit. Changes in output will, in general, lead to changes in prices and the rate of profit, but nothing can be said, *a priori*, about the form of such changes, which reflect variations in the conditions of production. So the theory of value and the theory of output are formally *separable* from one another.'

[43] Marshall, who is the most important point of reference in Sraffa's early work, clearly grasped the importance of diminishing returns in Ricardo's theory and, in general, the influence of the supply conditions of the various commodities on prices when an increase in demand elicits an increase in production. See Marshall (1920, pp. 140–3 and 383–7).

Marx clearly perceives the link between diminishing returns and relative prices in Ricardo's theory (1969, pp. 133, 43).

Garegnani's second hypothesis regards the absence of non-wage capital:

> In order to interpret Ricardo's theory of profit at once coherently and faithfully we shall assume that the raw materials and implements available at the start of the productive cycle are of little account and that capital can thus be identified with the wages advanced each year. (Garegnani, 1981, p. 19)

This is justified, according to Garegnani, 'because Ricardo tends to identify the entire stock of social capital with the wages advanced for the year' (p. 19), and thus to develop his analysis '*as if*, for the community as a whole, capital consists only of the wages advanced for the year' (p. 27).

This interpretation, which coincides with Marx's reading of Ricardo on this particular ground,[44] seems incapable of adequately reflecting Ricardo's position;[45] a notable portion of his analysis stems from his clear awareness of the problems arising from the presence, in the economy considered as a whole, of non-wage capital, and in particular from the different relationships between this type of capital and labour in the various sectors.

It is true that at times Ricardo, in order to simplify his numerical examples (e.g. in the *Principles: Works*, vol. I, p. 33), occasionally either disregards non-wage capital or assumes that it is equal (in relation to labour) in the various sectors; the fact remains that a considerable part of the problems discussed in the chapter 'On Value' in the *Principles* (a chapter that Ricardo altered

---

[44] As is well known, Marx accuses Ricardo of failing to analyse the role of non-wage capital in the economic system as a whole, and also criticizes him for identifying the rate of profit with the rate of surplus value, as well as for accepting Smith's view that the price of every commodity in the last analysis resolves itself into a sum of incomes (excluding rent, a sum of wages and profits). In fact, if all production in a unit period is the fruit of the work of 'unassisted' labour, paid in advance, capital would be represented by wages, the rate of profit and that of surplus value would coincide, and they in their turn would coincide with the ratio between profits and wages; the price of every commodity could be immediately resolved into wages and profits. See Marx (1969, vol. II, pp. 373ff.). See also Steedman (1982, pp. 126ff.). From Marx's point of view there is a curious coexistence between the hypothesis he attributes to Ricardo ('He [Ricardo] treats the matter as though the entire capital were laid out directly in wages': Marx, 1969, p. 373) and the detailed discussion that Marx works out of Ricardo's treatment of relative natural values. In this latter, Marx devotes specific attention to the analytical consequences arising from the presence, in the various sectors of the economy, of 'capitals with different periods of turnover and containing different proportions of the various forms of capital' (p. 174)—i.e., the crucial importance of the 'essential question of the transformation of values into cost-prices' (p. 192).

[45] Steedman rightly points out that, though his terminology is 'a potential source of confusion', Ricardo does not neglect the presence of aggregate non-wage capital in either the *Esssay on Profits* or the *Principles*: 'It has... been shown both that there is direct evidence that Ricardo did not ignore non-wage capital at the economy level and that, once careful allowance is made for Ricardo's shifting and rather confusing use of terms, all his apparent denials of aggregate non-wage capital can be seen to be just that—merely apparent. Just as Marx was too ready to take Ricardo's "value" to be his own (Marx's), so he was over-hasty in taking Ricardo's "whole produce" to mean what he (Marx) meant by that term' (Steedman, 1982, p. 137).

several times as the book went through its successive editions) would make little sense if read with the assumption that Ricardo excluded the existence of non-wage capital.

But even if non-wage capital is assumed to be non-existent, it would not be legitimate to rule out the possibility of divergences—which could be due to differences in the time-structure of the various commodities—between (natural) relative prices and relative quantities of labour embodied in the various commodities.

Garegnani in fact recalls that Ricardo admitted the existence of 'exceptions' to the rule of exchange dictated by the labour theory of value, and that 'he ... thought about this problem until the end of his life without ... reaching a solution he could consider satisfactory' (Garegnani, 1981, p. 28).[46]

The presence (in Ricardo as well as in Marx) of insoluble problems arising from the 'modifications' of the principle of the relative labour input quantities would seem to invalidate the theory of the core, because the determination of the rate of profit crucially depends on the system of prices. It is however not so, emphasizes Garegnani: the solution is provided by recent theoretical contributions. Garegnani classifies these under two headings: the 'surplus equation method' and the 'price equations method'. The first refers to Sraffa's 'standard system' and to Garegnani's 'wage-goods sector'; the second to Sraffa's general solution of the model of natural prices.

Now, with reference to Sraffa's contribution *only*, the following sketchy observations can perhaps be made.

(1) The surplus equation method, through the construction of the very special numeraire represented by the 'standard commodity', makes it possible to determine the rate of profit before, and independently of, prices; the requisites of the theory of the core are thus met.[47] The context of Sraffa's

---

[46] Garegnani (1981) also writes, in this respect, (1) that Ricardo's 'determination of the rate of profit remains based on it' (i.e., the rule according to which commodities are exchanged in proportion to the quantity of labour embodied in them) (p. 28) and (2) that 'Ricardo's great merit has been ... to overcome the circularity into which the determination of non-wage incomes seems to twist as soon as the various magnitudes are expressed in value terms. And this contribution of the *Principles* to economics results from the hypothesis that commodities are exchanged according to the quantity of labour required to produce them' (p. 24). These statements hardly seem compatible with Garegnani's recognition that Ricardo does not succeed in finding an analytically satisfactory solution to the problem. Also, though at the risk of splitting hairs, it should be stressed that Ricardo put the problem in terms of 'modifications' and not 'exceptions'.

[47] There remains the problem, for the actual system as well as for the standard system, of what role to assign to what may be called the 'institutional rules' in the formation of prices (e.g. wages being paid in advance or instead, at the end of each productive cycle). In other words, should these rules be considered as once-and-for-all, given data for the solution of the problem, or as hypotheses with some degree of freedom in their definition? The rate of profit would be completely independent of prices only in the former case. See Caravale and Tosato (1980, pp. 70–2).

analysis is however different from that of Ricardo's: the former is centred on the study of the distribution alternatives with a given technology, while the latter concentrates on the analysis of the effects of changes in technology. It has been shown elsewhere (Caravale and Tosato, 1980, ch. 4) that the transposition of an analytical tool—the standard commodity—conceived within the former logical framework to the latter is by no means automatic (see Caravale and Tosato, 1980, pp. 82–5). A significant use of Sraffa's standard commodity in the Ricardian context should therefore be excluded.

(2) On the other hand, the price equations method can be shown (Caravale and Tosato, 1980, ch. 3) to be of the greatest help in finding an analytically satisfactory solution of Ricardo's central problem (i.e. the inverse relation between labour content of corn and the rate of profit)—that *general* solution for which Ricardo searched in vain until the end of his life.

The problem is, however, that, with the price equations method, the rate of profit (whether in a context in which changes in technology are explicitly considered or in a context with a given technology) is determined simultaneously with prices, so that the requisites of the theory of the core no longer seem to be met[48]—at least, not unless we read Garegnani's position here in

---

[48] There is an interesting analogy between the problems discussed in the text and those on which Marx criticizes Ricardo on the subject of the rate of profit. Particularly in vol. II of his *Theories of Surplus Value*, Marx repeatedly criticizes Ricardo for having, in his opinion, *presumed* a general rate of profit instead of examining how far its existence is compatible with the determination of value on the basis of labour-time (1969, vol. II, p. 174). In other words, Marx considers that Ricardo errs both because he does not explain the general rate of profit in terms of labour-time (i.e. as relation between total surplus S and total capital $C + V$) and because he does not analyse the divergences between relative production prices and relative labour quantities in terms of the 'essential question of the transformation of values into cost-prices' (1969, vol. II, p. 192). Outside this structure, says Marx, the rate of profit and production prices are completely incomprehensible. 'If one did not take the definition of value [labour-time] as the basis, the average profit, and therefore also the cost-prices, would be purely imaginary and untenable' (1969, p. 190); the cost-prices remain unintelligible without values determined by labour-time' (p. 194).

Some recent and important theoretical work now shows that, in this criticism of Ricardo, Marx is mistaken: 'with the benefit of hindsight and of the works of Dmitriev, Bortkiewicz and Sraffa, we can see clearly that Marx's criticism of Ricardo on this score was ill-judged. We know, first, that Marx's structure of explanation proved unsuccessful; he was not able to construct a coherent theory of the rate of profit and of prices of production by starting from labour-times, moving on to the rate of profit and then deriving, finally, the cost-prices. *And we also know, more fundamentally, that Marx's failure in this regard was not, so to speak, a "personal" failure, a failure to carry through a possible line of theoretical argument. It was Marx's proposed structure of argument itself that was inherently flawed. The general rate of profit and the price of production must be determined simultaneously within the theory and Marx's proposed "linear" structure of argument is a dead-end*' (Steedman, 1982, p. 124; italics added). 'From a formal standpoint, Marx's error lay in trying to determine first the rate of profit and then the normal prices of commodities (or "prices of production" as Marx called them); the fact is that the profit rate and the prices of production have to be treated *simultaneously* within the theory' (Steedman, 1981, pp. 14–15). This argument of Steedman's is clearly linked to his analysis in *Marx after Sraffa*

terms of a *weak* concept of the core (social product and subsistence consumption only given in physical terms), to be contrasted with a *strong* concept of the core (social product and subsistence consumption known in terms of a homogeneous measure). It must however be stressed that this 'weak' interpretation would leave undefined the precise meaning of a theoretical core in which the difference between social product and subsistence consumption could be thought of only in terms of a sort of warehouse inventory (whose value could not be previously known): the 'weak' interpretation would in point of fact totally coincide with the correct and accepted proposition that, given production techniques and the real wage, the rate of profit and prices are determined together and, with them, the social product and necessary consumption (and the difference between the latter two).[49]

In other words, in the case considered, the requirements of the core theory seem to be satisfied only if the theory itself is conceived of as one of the ways in which to express the basic 'assymetry' of the distributive variables (one of which is exogenously given and the other, instead, is determined as solution of the model), and not as a methodological framework on which to test, for the general case, the possibility of a meaningful determination of profits as the difference between social product and subsistence consumption *before* the rate of profit is determined. In Garegnani's interpretation this latter would seem *the* characteristic of surplus theories in that it would be capable of evidencing the idea of a 'product of known magnitude to share out between wages and profits, with the rate of profits deriving then from the proportional distribution of the profits over the capital employed' (1981, p. 38)—in other words, of 'a product to apportion between wages and profits, a product known independently of such apportionment and of the prices corresponding to it' (1981, p. 52).

It should be emphasized that this conclusion has no implication whatsoever for what concerns the difference in analytical structure between classical and marginalist theory; and, in particular, that the breaking of the rigid 'separation' between distribution and the determination of natural prices

---

(1977), and appears relevant to Garegnani's theory of the core in the sense that it seems to negate its general validity. See also Shibata (1939).

[49] Garegnani stresses that 'within these equations [the price equations of Sraffa's general system], to represent profits as the *difference* between the value of the product on the one hand and that of wages and of the means of production on the other is no more meaningful than to consider the value of a product as the sum of profits, wages and the value of the means of production' (1981, p. 36); and that, moreover, the 'amount of profits is not determined until their rate is determined' (p. 37). Garegnani however considers these circumstances only as reasons for a *lack of transparency* in the fundamental characteristics of the surplus theories (the conception of profits as a residual, and the properties associated with this idea); these characteristics, in his view, would remain unaltered owing to the unquestionable fact that real wages and the rate of profit cannot change independently of each other and are inversely correlated.

does *not* imply that Ricardo is to be re-interpreted according to marginalist supply and demand theory. But it does imply that the radical difference between classical and marginalist theory is seen more clearly, from a methodological point of view, in terms of wage determination (a social–historical datum for the classicists, a dependent variable for the marginalists) and in terms of the reference point selected for the analysis (natural prices for classical theory, supply–demand equilibrium prices for marginalist theory).

With regard to the problem of the so-called 'separation' of distribution and prices, it should finally be emphasized that, given the real commodity wage, any change in distribution inevitably reflects (with diminishing returns) a change in the technology of the economic system; this latter, in its turn, is connected with a change in the volume of goods produced *and* with a new price vector, through a mechanism that is totally independent of marginalist supply and demand theory and strictly belongs, instead, to the theory of natural prices.

9 THE 'NEW VIEW' AND HOLLANDER'S RICARDO

The preceding pages have made it clear, I hope, that the present approach differs radically from that of the so-called 'New View' of the Ricardian theory (see Hicks and Hollander, 1977, pp. 351–69; Casarosa, 1978, pp. 38–63; 1982), the latter concentrating on the notion of *market* wage rate to the substantial neglect of Ricardo's notion of *natural* wage rate.[50]

This view, which, as Pasinetti (1982) aptly points out, is not really 'new', risks disregarding the essence of Ricardo's theory by shifting attention towards problems that can better be treated in terms of 'departures' from the natural equilibrium values of the variables or from the natural equilibrium path of the economy.

As regards, in particular, Hollander's (1979) recent and monumental book on Ricardo's economic theory—a book that deserves much more space and attention than that can be given here[51]—it seems necessary to comment at least on a few points. These points, which are obviously closely connected, concern:

(1) the problem of the 'separation' of distribution and prices;
(2) the discussion of the presence, in Ricardo's basic model, of the two hypotheses of (a) an identical organic composition of capital throughout the various sectors of the economy and (b) a given and constant wage;

[50] This only plays the external role of a *boundary floor* in the analysis of the evolution of the system over time.

[51] Hollander's (1979) position is reiterated, and to a certain extent made more extreme, in his paper in this volume.

(3) the nature of the 'fundamental theorem of distribution';
(4) the relation between Ricardo and Sraffa;
(5) Hollander's main thesis of the substantial continuity of thought from Ricardo, to Marshall, Walras and the neoclassical school in general.

Response to the problem of the relationships between the distributive framework and the determination of prices has been used, Hollander recalls, as the shibboleth by which to divide the development of economic thought into two approaches: on the one hand, that based on the simultaneous determination of distribution, commodity and factor prices (Smith, J. S. Mill and the neoclassicists); on the other, that based on the idea of distribution as 'separate' from the determination of prices and logically prior to it (Ricardo, Marx and, later, Sraffa). Now, Hollander believes that there is no evidence on which to attribute the 'divorce' between distribution and prices to Ricardo; classicists and neoclassicists do not differ sufficiently to be considered as two distinct schools of economic thought.

> a dual development of nineteenth-century analysis is perceived, one line emanating from Smith, carried further by J. S. Mill and the so-called 'dissenters', and culminating with Walras and Marshall, in whose models 'product prices and income distribution [are] assimilated into one system of mutual and simultaneous determination of product-prices and factor-prices'; and a second line, including Ricardo and Marx and carried further by the 'neo-Ricardian' critics of orthodox neoclassical doctrine (including Sraffa), according to which distribution is divorced from the general pricing process, having logical priority over prices or exchange values. (Hollander, 1981, p. 2)

> Demand–supply analysis for Ricardo, as for Smith and the neoclassicists, was the *vehicle of determination* of his general system, extending to long-run price in both product and factor markets. There is, in particular, a symmetrical explanation of the returns to labour and capital in terms of equilibrium between demand and supply for the factors, reflecting an interdependence of the two systems of markets. Specifically: consumer choices (and hence outputs) can influence relative prices by affecting the relative scarcity of labour and capital, and thus the wage and the rate of interest; conversely, distributional changes can alter relative prices by way of changes exerted upon output levels given the pattern of demand schedules. (Hollander, 1981, pp. 3–4)

Hollander's interpretation of Ricardo depends on (1) practically eliminating Ricardo's identification of social categories, or classes, each disposing of its income in a specific fashion (the 'classical savings function'), and substituting for it the far less precise, and strict neoclassical, concept of a *consumer* with a given structure of preferences; and (2) attributing to Ricardo the idea that the wage is not a socio-historical datum, but a variable determined by the forces of supply and demand.

Both of these hypotheses represent a profound alteration of Ricardo's thought. If they are accepted, any conclusions are possible: Ricardo can be classed with economists very different from him, working in an entirely different way, on entirely different problems, within entirely different frames of reference. In particular, for the problem of wage determination—where, according to Hollander (1981, p. 11) Ricardo 'often' assumes constant wages for reasons of analytic or didactic expediency—I hope that sections 2–6 of this paper sufficiently demonstrated the central importance for Ricardo of the idea of a natural equilibrium closely connected with the concept of a (natural) wage, in each social and historical context (given in terms of commodities). Supply and demand, according to Ricardo, affect *only* market values and therefore concern only those aspects that Ricardo intended to 'leave entirely out of [his] consideration' (*Works*, vol. 1, pp. 91–2).

More generally, it must be remembered that Ricardo carefully defined the limited role he attributed to the working of demand and supply mechanisms in the determination of prices, and rejected—drastically and explicitly—any interpretation of his analysis in terms of demand and supply. In chapter XXX ('On the Influence of Demand and Supply on Prices') of the *Principles*, for instance, he writes:

> It is the cost of production which must ultimately regulate the price of commodities, and not, as has been often said, the proportion between the supply and demand: the proportion between the supply and demand may, indeed, for a time, affect the market value of a commodity, until it is supplied in greater or less abundance, according as the demand may have increased or diminished; but this effect will only be of temporary duration... The opinion that the price of commodities depends solely on the proportion of supply to demand, or demand to supply, has become almost an axiom in political economy, and has been the source of much error in that science. (*Works*, vol. I, p. 382)

The chapter concludes:

> Commodities which are monopolized, either by an individual or by a company ... fall in proportion as the sellers augment their quantity, and rise in proportion to the eagerness of the buyers to purchase them; their price has no necessary connexion with their natural value: but the prices of commodities, which are subject to competition, and whose quantity may be increased in any moderate degree, will ultimately depend, not on the state of demand and supply, but on the increased or diminished cost of their production. (*Works*, vol. I, p. 385)

In a letter to Malthus of 30 January 1818, Ricardo writes with an unusual degree of impatience:

> Lord King, Mr Whishaw and you have done me a great deal of honour in making my work the subject of your discussion, but *I confess it fills me with astonishment* to find that you think, and from what you say they appear to agree with you, that ... *natural price*, as well as *market price*, is determined by the demand and supply,—the only difference being that the former is governed by the average and permanent demand and supply, the latter by the accidental and temporary—In saying this do you mean to deny that the facility of production will lower natural price and difficulty of production raise it? Will not these effects be produced; after a very short interval, although the absolute demand and supply, or the proportion of one to the other, should remain permanently the same?... It seems natural therefore to seek for the cause of the variation of permanent price in the expenses of production. Diminish these and the commodity must finally fall, increase them and it must as certainly rise. What has this to do with demand? ... I cannot help viewing this question as a truth which admits of demonstration and *I am full of wonder that it should admit of a doubt. If indeed this fundamental doctrine of mine were proved false I admit that my whole theory falls with it ....* (*Works*, vol. VII, pp. 250–1; the first and last italics are added)[52]

The point is forcefully made, and its fundamental importance for the whole analytical construction is stressed by Ricardo in terms that leave very little room for doubt.

The concept is repeated in a letter to Trower of 21 July 1820, where Ricardo refers to a comment, made by Trower, on Malthus's *Principles*:

> I am pleased ... with the observations you make on what he [Malthus] has said respecting my doctrine, of price, being ultimately regulated by cost of production. By the very definition of *natural price, it is wholly*

---

[52] An anonymous review of (McCulloch's) 'Essay on Political Economy', published in the *Quarterly Review* of January 1824 (pp. 297–334) and attributed to Malthus (see *The Dictionary of National Biography*, Oxford University Press, vol. XII, pp. 886–90), clearly summarizes 'the main principles' of 'the new school of political economy', i.e. of Ricardo's theory: '(1) That the quantity of labour worked up in commodities determines their exchangeable value. (2) That the demand and supply have no effect upon prices and values, except in cases of monopoly or for short periods of time. (3) That the difficulty of production on the land is the regulator of profits, to the entire exclusion of the cause stated by Adam Smith, namely, the relative abundance and competition of capital' (pp. 307–8). If the attribution is correct, it seems noteworthy that Malthus, after a life-long basic miscomprehension of Ricardo's 'fundamental doctrine', especially as far as the determination of prices is concerned, should show such a precise grasp of Ricardo's basic tenets only a few months after the latter's death.

*dependent on cost of production and has nothing to do with supply and
demand. (Works, vol. VIII, p. 207; italics added)*

Moreover, if the classical and neoclassical schools are most easily distinguished by their respective views of wages—a social and historical datum for
the former, a variable determined within an interdependent system for the
latter—the breaking of the rigid separation between distribution and price
determination (see pp. 177–8 above) does *not* imply, in contrast to Hollander's view (and as has been pointed out above), the necessity of a neoclassical re-interpretation based on supply and demand mechanisms.

In fact, with a given commodity wage, every change in distribution is
inextricably linked, via the operation of diminishing returns, with a technological change (see pp. 149–51 above); and this, in its turn, is linked with a
change in the quantity of commodities produced and in the price vector of the
system (Caravale and Tosato, 1980, ch. 2).

In other words, if we recognize the central importance of the law of
diminishing returns in Ricardian analysis, while keeping clear the distinction
between the latter and that of later neoclassical economists, a precise
functional link emerges between changes in the matrix of technological
coefficients in distribution, changes in the price system and changes in the
quantities of commodities produced. The direction of change of all these
variables is, as has been said, *precisely identifiable* (see Caravale and Tosato,
1980, esp. appendix to ch. 2).

Hollander maintains that 'the difference between Ricardian and Marshallian
economics involves not matters of principle but only matters of detail,
allowing us to transfer from one to the other by way of minor revisions'
(Hollander, 1981, p. 12), and that it is therefore necessary to distinguish
between differences that constitute 'alternative simplifying hypotheses' and
differences involving matters of principle.

In Ricardo, the hypothesis of an identical structure of capital ('uniform
factor ratios', in Hollander's neoclassical terminology) and of a constant
wage are not part of his 'basic model' and therefore are not to be considered
as fundamental discriminants, i.e. involving a difference of principle with
respect to, for example, Marshall. According to Hollander, in fact, 'on matters
of fundamental import, and not merely casually, Ricardo himself released
the two simplifying assumptions [uniform factor ratios and constant wages]'
(Hollander, 1981, p. 12). Hollander thus stresses that Ricardo's basic model is
characterized by the idea that the wage is not exogenously given and by the
assumption of different capital–labour ratios in the various sectors; this
latter, in particular, with its implications for the allocative mechanism and for
interpretation of the price–quantity relation, would bring Ricardo's analysis
close to general equilibrium theory.

Now, while recalling what has been said above on the problem of wages in

Ricardo, it must be admitted that the most significant part of his analysis of value and distribution stems from his keen awareness of the diverse structure of capital in the various economic sectors and of the problems—which he did not resolve—arising from it. Hollander hits the mark in saying that the assumption of different *factor ratios* belongs to Ricardo's basic model and that it is difficult even to conceive of a Ricardian model in its absence. Without it, large parts of Ricardo's work would not have been written at all. But this does not imply that Hollander is right as regards the central question of Ricardo's position in the history of economic thought. As has been pointed out above, Hollander's choice is based on profound alterations of Ricardo's main analytical features.

The third point touches the problem, in Hollander's reworking of Ricardo, of the relation between the 'fundamental theory of distribution' and his view that Ricardo attached little importance to 'the particular question of the fall in the rate of profit', i.e. to the problem of economic growth.

Hollander's view of the relation between the wage and the rate of profit (the 'fundamental theorem') is not very clear. It is a relation between the rate of profit and wages, but, since it is not clear whether Hollander accepts that the Ricardian real wage is made up of a *given* basket of commodities,[53] it is equally not clear whether the wage is the *money* wage, which Hollander measures in gold (given the real wage), or the *real wage*, which he measures in terms of commodities.

What has been said above tends to show that Hollander's definition of the 'analytical core' of Ricardo's economic theory would be correct only in the first case, certainly not in the second.[54] But in this first case, how is the

[53] While Hollander several times refutes the attribution of such a hypothesis to Ricardo, at other times (Hollander, 1979, pp. 395–6) he states that Ricardo occasionally accepted precisely this hypothesis for analytical purposes. Moreover, in discussing the problems raised by the accumulation process, Hollander maintains that the secular increase in money wages is accompanied in Ricardo both by a fall in the rate of profit and by a fall in the real commodity wage. A concept of wage analogous to that discussed in the text from the analytical point of view would be that of a wage measured in terms of the labour content of the commodities included in the given basket representing the natural wage.

[54] In his criticism of Sraffa's and Garegnani's positions on Ricardo's 'early theory of profits'—the analysis carried out by Ricardo as regards the determination and tendency of the rate of profit—Hollander (1973, 1975 and 1979) denies that Ricardo may have based his argument upon the 'corn model' where the rate of profit is determined without reference to prices. Hollander believes instead that Ricardo based his reasoning upon variations of the money wage in consequence of changing prices of wage goods and reached his conclusions on the 'inverse movements' of the general rate of profits without relying on physical corn quantities (along lines substantially identical to those followed in the *Principles*). It seems of some interest to observe that, in order to oppose his interpretation to the Sraffa–Garegnani view of the 'early theory of profits', Hollander, in this specific context, implicitly makes the assumption that the real wage is given. His own market-oriented general interpretation of Ricardo appears then to give up a good deal to the (opposite) natural equilibrium 'dynamic' interpretation of Ricardo's theory, based on the inverse relation between diminishing returns and the accumulation rate.

G

'fundamental theorem of distribution' to be reconciled with the idea of Ricardo's small interest in the analysis of the system's tendency towards the *stationary state*?[55] Whence would arise the changes in money wages (or in the labour content of wage goods included, in given quantities, in the 'basket')? How could these changes be explained?[56]

In other words, the idea that in Ricardo 'the particular question of the fall in the rate of profit' does not occupy the centre of the stage would seem to imply that the problem of distribution with a *given technology* is to be found there. But this question can be discussed only in terms of alternative levels of real commodity wages, which, though plausible in principle, are outside the main line of Ricardo's analysis.[57]

It can thus be said that, if the 'fundamental theorem' is correctly defined, it is not easily reconciled with Hollander's view of the little importance that Ricardo held for the problem of growth (the tendency towards the stationary state); reconciliation with this view (which is in any case unacceptable) requires that the theorem be defined in terms that seem largely irrelevant to Ricardian analysis.

Hollander's comparison of Sraffa and Ricardo is obviously based on the re-interpretation of the latter in supply and demand terms. According to Hollander, return to an equilibrium situation in relative prices after a change in the wage rate involves, for Ricardo, production changes such as to make supply and demand again equal for every commodity. In fact, continues Hollander, the idea that Ricardo hypothesized a constant level of production in each sector when studying the effects of a change in wages is unfounded, as is that which attributes to him the refusal of supply and demand analysis. Hollander puts the difference between Ricardo and Sraffa as follows:

> In Sraffa's model there is no process analysis. Re-establishment of equilibrium following a disturbance requires that the condition of profit

[55] See Hollander (1979, for example p. 12): 'It will be a main theme of the present work that to single out the theorem relating to a declining rate of return on capital is to exaggerate the import of a particular application of the basic theory. I shall show that Ricardo paid more careful attention to the general principle of the inverse profit–wage relationship than to the particular issue of a falling profit rate. More important, the empirical relevance of the notion of a barrier to economic progress was not considered by Ricardo to be very serious.'

[56] A reply could at first sight be sought in Ricardo's reflections on taxes: a tax on wages, given the *real* wage and the 'state' of technology, could for example be connected with a lower level of the rate of profit. Such a reply would not solve the question raised above in the text, because the hypothesis would imply changes in one of the parameters of the 'basic model' (in the example, from a zero coefficient to a positive one of tax-take on wages) for the examination of a particular economic problem, and would therefore be equivalent, in terms of the same 'basic model', to a change in the 'state' of technology.

[57] As has been pointed out above, the question of alternative price levels, given the technology and the real commodity wage, cannot even be posed in the context of Ricardo's natural equilibrium analysis.

rate equality be satisfied, but nothing is said about the mechanism of adjustment. The condition is, as it were, simply a mathematical prerequisite. Ricardo, for his part, nowhere turned his back on Smithian process analysis; re-establishment of equilibrium entails, accordingly, reactions by capitalists to profit rate differentials which manifest themselves in expansions or contractions of the various industries. It is an historical anachronism to attribute the Sraffian procedure to Ricardo.

Sraffa moreover does not provide a theory of distribution; one of the distributive variables must be given exogenously .... This problem does not arise in Ricardian theory. Neither the profit rate nor the wage rate appear as data of the analysis; the wage rate is a variable determined by the general system of demand and supply relationships in the labour market while the profit rate is merely a *formal* residual, there being a mutual dependency of the one upon the other. (Hollander, 1981, pp. 32–3)

The undoubted and profound differences between Ricardo and Sraffa, as has been said elsewhere,[58] concern mainly the context of the analysis—certainly not the central importance, accepted by both, of the concept of natural prices. Sraffa's 'procedure', which only studies production prices, is essentially no different from that of Ricardo, which assumes Smithian mechanisms for the adjustment of market prices on natural prices and concentrates his analysis on the latter.

To shift attention, as Hollander does, on to the adjustment mechanisms and to consider them the main object of Ricardo's analysis is to disregard its basic theme. The idea that no theory of distribution is present in Sraffa would seem to suggest that a distribution theory is either neoclassic or nothing. Basically, the argument still turns on the view that the wage is not an external datum arising from historical and social conditions, but is determined within the model in response to supply and demand. This confirms, if there were any need to do so, the methodological and analytical relevance of the hypothesis of the given real wage as dividing classical and neoclassical approaches to economic theory.

Hollander's basic thesis is that there is a profound continuity of methods and frames of reference between Ricardo and the neoclassical school, particularly Marshall and Walras, and that the differences between them boil down to the stress laid on various problems by individual economists. Without repeating what has been said above, it is enough to recall that Hollander's arguments (1) unjustifiably emphasize the allocative mechanisms in Ricardo; (2) neglect the part played by the social structure; and (3) err in

---

[58] See Caravale and Tosato (1980), ch. 3.

considering wages as an endogenous variable. The circumstance that Ricardo, Marshall and Walras all postulate uniform rates of profit in the various economic sectors is too slight to support such a grave thesis.

The 'cultural operation', as one might perhaps call it, of the 'New View', and of Hollander's book in particular, designed to integrate Ricardo in the tradition of neoclassical general equilibrium theories, should therefore be rejected, as should any other attempt to alter the specific features of Ricardo's 'legacy' in the light of any theoretical model chosen in advance.

REFERENCES

Bailey, S. (1967). *A Critical Dissertation on the Nature, Measures and Causes of Value.* London: F. Cass (first published in 1825).

Bharadwaj, K. (1978). *Classical Political Economy and Rise to Dominance of Supply and Demand Theories.* New Delhi: University of New Dehli Press.

Campanelli, G. (1980). 'La Prima Formulazione Matematica del Capitale Fisso nel Sistema di Ricardo'. *Annali della Fondazione Einaudi*, 14, 241–80.

Caravale, G. A. and Tosato, D. A. (1980). *Ricardo and the Theory of Value, Distribution and Growth.* London: Routledge & Kegan Paul.

Casarosa, C. (1978). 'A New Formulation of the Ricardian System. *Oxford Economic Papers*, 30, 38–63.

Casarosa, C. (1982). 'The New View of the Ricardian Theory of Distribution and Economic Growth'. In M. Baranzini (ed.), *Advances in Economic Theory.* Oxford: Basil Blackwell.

Casarosa, C. (1983). 'Equilibrio di Mercato, Equilibrio Naturale ed Equilibrio Dinamico in Ricardo: Interpretazioni Recenti'. *Quaderni di Storia dell' Economia Politica*, 1, 91–120.

Eatwell, J. (1977). 'The Irrelevance of Returns to Scale in Sraffa's Analysis'. *Journal of Economic Literature*, 15, 61–8.

Eatwell, J. (1977–8). 'Theories of Value, Output and Employment'. *Annali della Facoltà di Economia e Commercio*, 5, 29–86. Perugia: University of Perugia.

Eltis, W. A. (1984). *The Classical Theory of Economic Growth.* London: Macmillan.

Findlay, R. (1974). 'Relative Prices, Growth and Trade in a Simple Ricardian System'. *Economica*, 41, 1–13.

Garegnani, P. (1981). *Marx e gli economisti classici.* Turin: Einaudi.

Garegnani, P. (1983). 'The Classical Theory of Wages and the Role of Demand Schedules in the Determination of Relative Prices', *American Economic Review*, Papers and Proceedings, 63, 309–13.

Hicks, J. (1979). 'The Ricardian System: A Comment'. *Oxford Economic Papers*, 31, 133–4.

Hicks, J. and Hollander, S. (1977). 'Mr. Ricardo and the Moderns'. *Quarterly Journal of Economics*, 91, 351–69.

Hollander, S. (1973). 'Ricardo's Analysis of the Profit Rate'. *Economica*, 40, 260–82.

Hollander, S. (1975). 'Ricardo and the Corn Profit Model: Reply to Eatwell'. *Economica*, 42, 188–202.

Hollander, S. (1979). *The Economics of David Ricardo*. London: Heinemann.

Hollander, S. (1981). 'On the Substantive Identity Between the Ricardian (Classical) and Neo-Classical Conceptions of Economic Organization'. Paper presented at the Perugia Workshop on Ricardo (unpublished).

Hollander, S. (1982). '"Dynamic Equilibrium" with Constant Wages: J. S. Mill Analysis of the Secular Wages Path, or Mill as "Cambridge" Economist'. Unpublished paper.

Hollander, S. (1983). 'On the Interpretation of Ricardian Economics: The Assumption Regarding Wages'. *American Economic Review*, Papers and Proceedings, 73, 314–18.

Kahn, R. (1979). 'The Development of Theories of Employment and Prices'. Unpublished paper.

Little, L. M. D. (1957). 'Classical Growth'. *Oxford Economic Papers*, 9, 152–77.

Lunghini, G. (1977). *La crisi dell'economia politica e la teoria del valore*. Milan: Feltrinelli.

Marshall, A. (1920). *Principles of Economics* (8th edn). London: Macmillan. Reprinted 1966.

Marshall, Alfred and Marshall, Mary Paley (1879). *The Economics of Industry*. London: Macmillan.

Marx, K. (1969). *Theories of Surplus Value*. London: Lawrence and Wishart.

Marx, K. (1977). *Grundisse*. Harmondsworth: Penguin.

Marx, K. (1979). *Capital* (3 vols). Harmondsworth: Penguin.

McCulloch, J. R. (1818). 'Review of *Principles of Political Economy and Taxation* by D. Ricardo'. *Edinburgh Review*, 16, 58–87.

Napoleoni, C. (1977). 'Sull'interpretazione sraffiana di Ricardo', *Il Veltro*, 21, 251–63.

Nazzani, E. (1883). 'Due parole sulle prime cinque sezioni del capitolo "On Value" di Ricardo'. *Rendiconti del Reale Istituto Lombardo di Scienze e Lettere*; reprinted in A. Quadrio Curzio and R. Scazzieri (eds), *Protagonisti del pensiero economico— Struttura produttiva, scambio e mercati, 1848–1872*, Il Mulino Bologna.

O'Brien, D. P. (1981). 'Ricardian Economics and the Economics of David Ricardo'. *Oxford Economic Papers*, 33, 352–85.

Pasinetti, L. (1960). 'A Mathematical Formulation of the Ricardian System'. *Review of Economic Studies*, 27, 78–98.

Pasinetti, L. (1982). 'A Comment on the "New View" of the Ricardian System'. In M. Baranzini (ed.), *Advances in Economic Theory*. Oxford: Basil Blackwell.

Picchio del Mercato, A. (1981). 'Il salario cime prezzo naturale del lavoro nell' economia politica classica'. *Ricerche Economiche*, 35, 84–116.

Ricardo, D. (1951–73). *The Works and Correspondence* (11 vols), ed. P. Sraffa with the collaboration of M. H. Dobb. London: CUP.

Robinson, J. (1972). *Economic Heresies*. London: Macmillan.

Roncaglia, A. (1978). *Sraffa and the Theory of Prices*. Chichester: John Wiley.

Samuelson, P. (1978). 'The Canonical Classical Model of Political Economy'. *Journal of Economic Literature*, 16, 1415–34.

Say, J. B. (1819). *Traité d'Economie Politique* (4th edn). Paris: Deterville.

Shibata, K. (1939). 'On the General Profit Rate'. *Kyoto University Economic Review*, 14, 40–66.

Smith, A. (1954). *An Inquiry into the Nature and Causes of the Wealth of Nations*. Reprint, London: Dent (first published in 1776).

Sraffa, P. (1925). 'Sulle relazioni fra costo e quantità prodotta'. *Annali di economia*, 2, 277–328.

Sraffa, P. (1926). 'The Laws of Returns under Competitive Conditions'. *Economic Journal*, 36, 535–50.

Sraffa, P. (1928–9). '16 Lectures on Advanced Theory of Value'. Unpublished.

Sraffa, P. (1951). Introduction to *The Works and Correspondence of David Ricardo*, vol. I. London: CUP.

Sraffa, P. (1960). *Production of Commodities by Means of Commodities*. Cambridge: CUP.

Steedman, I. (1977). *Marx After Sraffa*. London: New Left Books.

Steedman, I. (1981). 'Ricardo, Marx, Sraffa'. In I. Steedman and others, *The Value Controversy*. London: Verso Editions and New Left Books.

Steedman, I. (1982). 'Marx on Ricardo'. In I. Bradley and M. Howard (eds), *Classical and Marxian Political Economy, Essays in Honour of R. L. Meek*. London: Macmillan.

Stigler, G. J. (1965). 'Textual Exegisis as a Scientific Problem'. *Economica*, 32, 447–50.

Whewell, W. (1831). 'Mathematical Exposition of some of the Leading Doctrines in Mr. Ricardo's *Principles of Political Economy and Taxation*'. *Transactions of the Cambridge Philosophical Society*.

8

A Reconsideration of Sraffa's Interpretation of Ricardo on Value and Distribution

DOMENICO TOSATO

1 INTRODUCTION

Sraffa's edition of *The Works and Correspondence of David Ricardo* marks a turning point in the interpretation of Ricardo's thought, not only on account of the newly found papers and letters first published on that occasion, but also, and above all, because of the editor's truly remarkable 'Introduction' (Sraffa, 1951). The dominant position of economics on the key issues of the Ricardian theory of value and distribution has been deeply influenced by Sraffa's ideas ever since.

The connection between Ricardo's work and Sraffa's interpretation was further strengthened by the appearance, some ten years later, of Sraffa's *Production of Commodities by Means of Commodities*. As he himself mentions in the 'Preface', his standpoint 'is that of the old classical economists from Adam Smith to Ricardo' (Sraffa, 1960, p. v); and in the appendix ('References to the Literature'), specific points of contact with Ricardo's approach are indicated. In fact, problems in the theory of value long tackled by Ricardo are here to be found again, and the solution offered in *Production of Commodities* has come to be considered by many people the fitting conclusion to Ricardo's line of research.

On this basis, Garegnani (1976, 1981, 1983), Eatwell (1977), Roncaglia (1978) and Bharadwaj (1978) have advanced the idea of a logical and analytical separation, in classical as opposed to neoclassical economics, between the theory of value and distribution, on one hand, and the theory of the determination of commodity outputs and the accumulation of capital, on the other. In their view, the theoretical core of classical economics, including Ricardo, consists of the definition of prices and the rate of profit, *given* the state of the economy, as represented by the size and composition of output, the technique of production in use and the wage rate of labour.

I am grateful to G. Caravale and W. Eltis for helpful comments.

Sraffa's interpretation of the Ricardian theory of value and distribution, and, more generally, the relation between Ricardo's analysis and Sraffa's own contribution, is reconsidered in this paper, in the context of a theory of natural prices. The idea of a substantial identity of issues addressed by Ricardo and Sraffa is refuted, as well as the related notion of a separation in Ricardo between price and quantity determination.

The first part of the paper examines the arguments that lend support to the claim of a substantial identity of objectives in Ricardo's and Sraffa's theories of value and distribution. The fundamental steps of Ricardo's analysis, as they emerge from Sraffa's interpretation, are thus reviewed. The logical sequence which results from that interpretation leads to the conclusion that, in the unsuccessful attempt to overcome the limitations of his theory of profits, Ricardo would have shifted considerably the central theme of his investigation on value. He would have thus abandoned the primitive objective of giving general validity to his fundamental theorem on distribution, that is to the dynamic relation between the rate of profit, diminishing returns, the rising cost of agricultural wage goods and money wages. Apparently satisfied with the only approximate solution of this problem he could reach on the basis of the labour theory of value, Ricardo would have then concentrated his attention—and this is the key point of Sraffa's interpretation in his 'Introduction' to Ricardo's *Works*—on the static problem of determining the relation between the rate of profit and alternative levels of the real wage, given the margin of cultivation on land. The difficulties met in eliminating the effect of changes in wages on the measurement of the social aggregates involved in the determination of profits and the rate of profit would represent the analytical motivation explaining the change that would have taken place in the main objective of Ricardo's theory.

A smooth transition from Ricardo's to Sraffa's theory of value and distribution is thereby effected. Sraffa's inverse profit–wage relation of *Production of Commodities* is identified with Ricardo's fundamental theorem on distribution. The result that Sraffa achieves through measurement in terms of the standard commodity is viewed as the solution that Ricardo was vainly seeking to reach with the help of his invariable measure of value.

A critique of this line of interpretation is presented in the second part of the paper. Ricardo's position on two issues, crucial for that interpretation, is re-examined: the notion of the 'rise or fall of wages' and the role of the invariable measure in the theory of value. The outcome of this re-examination is that, contrary to Sraffa's suggestion, Ricardo's interest in the distributive problems arising from capital accumulation never waned. His attempts to deal with the problems of value theory arising from different proportions between capital and labour in the various branches of the economy were clearly directed at determining the rate of profit in a dynamic, and not in a static, context of analysis. The problem of the determination of the rate of profit when money wages increase as a consequence of the extension of cultivation to land of inferior quality thus re-emerges as the central issue of the theory.

Caravale and Tosato (1980, pp. 46–50) have shown that this problem admits of a solution, and that an inverse relation between the rate of profit and the labour input in agriculture can be established for a class of quite general models of production. It could, nevertheless, be argued that the simultaneous equations approach used to that end represents a break with respect to the line of research followed by Ricardo, who did not possess the modern tools of linear algebra, and that it risks missing the goal of *clarity* in the explanation of profits that Ricardo was seeking. In effect, Ricardo's investigation aimed at reproducing, for the general case, the clear result that holds when the labour theory of value is valid—namely, the possibility of determining profits as a residual, which is obtained by subtracting a changing money wage from the constant value of the output net of rent of each labourer.[1] The difficulties encountered by Ricardo can in fact be overcome, building on Ricardo's own indications—contained especially in his final paper, 'Absolute Value and Exchangeable Value'—and with a specific, though restrictive assumption about the property of the invariable standard of value. The dynamic relation between the rate of profit and changes in money wages arising from changes in the difficulty of production of corn can thereby be shown as neatly as for the case in which the labour theory of value is valid.

2 THE RICARDIAN THEORY OF PROFITS IN SRAFFA'S INTERPRETATION

The Theory of Profits in the Essay on Profits

In the *Essay on Profits* Ricardo's attention is centred on the dynamic behaviour of the rate of profit in agriculture. He clearly states from the very beginning the assumptions on which his model is based: 'That no improvements take place in agriculture, and that capital and population advance in the proper proportion, so that the *real wages of labour ... continue uniformly the same*' (*Works*, vol. IV, p. 12; italics added). The scope of the analysis is then described as consisting in the determination of the 'peculiar effects [that] are to be ascribed to the growth of capital, the increase of population, and the

---

[1] The qualification of Ricardo's theory of profits as a 'residual' theory must then be intended in the sense used by Kaldor (1956) and not in that used by Garegnani (1981). For the latter does not consider, as Ricardo instead does, the question of the extension of the margin of cultivation and the subsequent change in the cost of production of a given wage basket, but focuses his attention, on the contrary, on the problem (of Marxian derivation) of the determination of profits as what remains after subtracting from an output of given size and composition alternative values of an institutionally fixed real wage.

extension of cultivation, to the more remote, and less fertile land' (p. 12). There is thus no question that the problem tackled by Ricardo is a typically dynamic one. It is the problem of ascertaining the response of the rate of profit to decreasing returns in agriculture, when the real wage rate is taken as given. Ricardo's answer is straightforward—the rate of profit is regulated by the conditions of production of corn on the marginal land. 'Profits of stock fall because land equally fertile cannot be obtained, and through the whole progress of society, profits are regulated by the difficulty or facility of procuring food' (vol. IV, p. 13n.).[2]

The problem of value receives only minor attention at this early stage of Ricardo's theoretical elaboration. The idea that relative prices are regulated by difficulty of production is, none the less, already there (vol. IV, pp. 19–20), though difficulty of production is related at times to the quantity of embodied labour, and at other times to the cost of production.[3]

As is well known, Sraffa suggests the idea of the 'corn model' as a rational foundation for Ricardo's theory of profit. Measurement of the net product and of capital in terms of corn in the famous Table of the *Essay* would reflect Ricardo's assumption of physical homogeneity of input and output in agricultural production, realized under the restrictive hypotheses that capital consists only of advances to labourers and that wages in turn consist only of corn.[4]

With these assumptions, the residual nature of profits, which can be determined prior to prices, stands out in full evidence: profit is what remains after subtracting a *given corn wage* from a varying agricultural output per unit of labour. Note that, in theory, nothing forbids us to think of profit as that which remains after subtracting a *varying corn wage* from a given output per labourer, assuming an unchanged margin of cultivation. But this latter idea is clearly far removed from Ricardo's aim in the *Essay*, and is probably equally distant from a correct understanding of the spirit that prompted Sraffa to suggest the corn model as a rational foundation for Ricardo's central proposition: the dynamic relation between the rate of profit and the conditions of production in agriculture.

The Labour Theory of Value and the Profit–Wage Relation

The point of view adopted by Ricardo in the *Principles* is more general. Under strong criticism from Malthus, he abandons (according to the corn

---

[2] The same ideas are stated in Ricardo's letter to Malthus of 18 December 1814 (vol. VI, p. 162).

[3] Ricardo's position on value at the time of the *Essay* and in the immediately subsequent defence of the Table from Malthus's repeated criticism is analysed by Hollander (1979, pp. 154–63).

[4] Garegnani's paper in this volume offers strong support to Sraffa's interpretation of Ricardo's early theory of profit, which has been challenged by Hollander (1973). The fundamental issue in the debate, namely Ricardo's assumption about the composition of wages, is taken up also by Rankin (1984).

model interpretation) the assumption of physical homogeneity between input and output in one special branch of production; or (according to the alternative view) he recognizes the limitations of his corn calculations in the *Essay*, when there are heterogeneous inputs in agricultural production. In either case, Ricardo is forced to face up to the problems of value, and his analysis of distribution now centres on the inverse relation between the rate of profit and the money wage.

Assume that: (1) commodities are produced with the employment of direct labour only, with advances for one year; (2) the real (or commodity) wage of labour consists of a given basket of wage goods; and (3) the quantity of *gold* produced by one labourer in one year is used as numeraire of the system, gold being, by assumption, a commodity produced at all times and places by the same quantity of labour. Ricardo's theory of natural prices is then defined by the following system of equations:

$$p_j = n_j w(1 + r) \quad (j = 1, \ldots, m) \tag{1}$$

$$w = \Sigma p_j \bar{x}_j \tag{2}$$

$$p_g / n_g = 1 \tag{3}$$

where p_j and n_j are respectively the price and quantity of labour embodied in commodity j; p_g and n_g are the corresponding variables for the commodity gold; $\bar{x}_j$ is the quantity of commodity j in the wage basket (if commodity j is not a wage good, then $\bar{x}_j = 0$); w, defined as the value of the given wage basket, is the money wage rate; and r is the general rate of profit.

As can be immediately seen, the solution of the system of equations (1)–(3) is:

$$\frac{p_j}{p_g / n_g} = n_j \tag{4}$$

$$r = \frac{1 - w}{w} \tag{5}$$

$$\frac{w}{p_g / n_g} = \Sigma n_j \bar{x}_j. \tag{6}$$

In words, absolute prices (i.e., prices measured in terms of the standard of value) are equal to the quantity of labour embodied in the different commodities. The rate of profit varies inversely with the money wage, which, in turn, is equal to the quantity of labour embodied in the wage basket.

The very simple assumption made about the productive technology confers peculiar properties on the solution (see Caravale and Tosato, 1978; 1980, esp. pp. 39–40). As opposed to the corn model, relative prices are now determined prior to the rate of profit. From equations (3) and (4),

$$\frac{p_j}{n_j} = 1 \tag{7}$$

follows, showing that the value of the output of the last unit of labour everywhere employed in the economy is constant and thus independent of wages. This implies that the profit–wage relation (5) is verified simultaneously in all branches of production and emerges as a direct generalization of the same sectoral approach of the *Essay*, where Ricardo in fact already hints at that relation as a general explanation of profits.[5] Heterogeneity of input and output, whatever sector of the economy is considered, does not therefore reduce in the least the possibility of a clear understanding of the determination of profits and of the rate of profits.

Note that both a static and a dynamic application of equation (5) are, in theory, possible, depending on whether changes in money wages are supposed to originate in a variation in the real wage (given the margin of cultivation) or in the difficulty of production of agricultural wage goods (given the real wage).[6] Note furthermore that, as a consequence of equation (7), w measures at the same time the money wage rate and the share of wages in the value of output of each labourer. The identity between a 'greater value' and a 'greater proportion' of wages, on which Ricardo insists so strongly,[7] is thereby apparent. The inverse profit–wage relation can thus be viewed equivalently as a relation between the rate of profit and the money wage rate or the share of wages.

Ricardo's analysis in the chapter 'On Profits' neatly falls within this theoretical scheme. The rate of profit is determined at a sectoral level; it is shown to depend on the difference between a constant value (to be distributed as wages and profits) and a varying money wage rate, and to be necessarily equal in the production of all commodities.

Contrary to this reconstruction, Sraffa's interpretation of Ricardo's theory of profit in the *Principles* follows a different course. Building on Ricardo's statement, at the end of the chapter 'On Value', that the rate of profit depends upon the 'proportion of the annual labour of the country which is devoted to the support of the labourers' (vol. I, p. 49), Sraffa suggests that, with the

---

[5] See, in particular, Ricardo (vol. IV, pp. 26n., 35–6, 37); see also the correspondence with Malthus subsequent to the publication of the *Essay*. Extensive discussion of this issue is offered by Hollander (1973; 1975; 1979, pp. 175–83).

[6] Ricardo's position on this issue will be considered in section 3 below.

[7] See, for instance, Ricardo (vol. II, pp. 61–2, 252–3); see also Sraffa (1951, p. lii) and Hollander (1979, pp. 201–2).

adoption of a general theory of value, Ricardo's method of analysis would have changed from the *micro-* or *sectoral* approach of the *Essay* to the *macro-* or *aggregative* approach[8] of the *Principles*: 'it became possible for Ricardo to demonstrate the determination of the rate of profit in *society as a whole* instead of through the *microcosm of one special branch of production*' (Sraffa, 1951, p. xxxii; italics added). Sraffa is thus led to the well-known conclusion that:

the rate of profit was no longer determined by the ratio of the corn produced to the corn used up in agricultural production, but, instead, by the ratio of the total labour of the country to the labour required to produce the necessaries for that labour. (Sraffa, 1951, p. xxxii)

Let X_j be the output of commodity j and L be the total quantity of labour; then the rate of profit—as a ratio of the value of the aggregate surplus to the value of the aggregate wage capital—is defined as

$$r = \frac{\Sigma p_j X_j - L\Sigma p_j \bar{x}_j}{L\Sigma p_j \bar{x}_j}. \tag{8}$$

With the labour theory of value, (8) becomes

$$r = \frac{\Sigma n_j X_j - L\Sigma n_j \bar{x}_j}{L\Sigma n_j \bar{x}_j}. \tag{9}$$

Observing now that $\Sigma n_j X_j$ is the quantity of labour embodied in total output, i.e. total labour, and letting

$$L_w = L\Sigma n_j \bar{x}_j \tag{10}$$

be the quantity of labour embodied in the aggregate wage capital (necessary social consumption), the rate of profit can be finally written as

$$r = \frac{L - L_w}{L_w} \tag{11}$$

or, alternatively, as

---

[8] This terminology does not coincide with the distinction between the 'simultaneous' and the 'aggregative' or 'surplus' approach of Eatwell (1975) and Garegnani (1981). While the classification used here focuses on the level of the analysis, their distinction centres on the issue of 'clarity'—Garegnani uses the term of 'transparency'—in the determination of the rate of profit. This question is considered in further detail below.

$$r = \frac{1 - L_w/L}{L_w/L} \qquad (12)$$

which is similar to the previous definition (5), but emphasizes instead the dependence of the rate of profit on the share of wages, rather than on the wage rate.

Obviously, no uncertainty arises in passing from one to the other concept of wages if the assumption is made that a change in the money wage reflects a corresponding change in the real wage, for instance 'from the circumstance of the labourer being more liberally rewarded' (vol. I, p. 48). The ratio of necessary labour to total labour in equation (12) would clearly vary in this case in the same direction as the money wage rate.

If, on the other hand, the assumption is made of a change in the money wage in consequence of a change in the price of corn, the conclusion is not equally obvious. Suppose that such a change is independent of capital accumulation, as could happen in the case of improvements in the production of corn or a reduction of import duties: total labour would then remain unchanged, while necessary labour would diminish. We could again conclude unambiguously that the share of wages moves in the same direction as the wage rate. Suppose instead that the change in money wages is caused by the accumulation of capital, the growth of population, the extension of production to the less fertile land and the subsequent rise in the price of corn; suppose, in other words, that our problem is exactly the same as the problem Ricardo considered in the *Essay*: in this case, the consequence on the share of wages would not be quite as evident; for necessary labour and total labour would both change in the same direction, and it would not be immediately apparent what the resulting change in their ratio would be.[9]

Eatwell (1975) and Garegnani (1981, pp. 36–8) assign considerable relevance to the possibility of showing with 'clarity' the inverse relation between profits and wages, and attribute this property to the theoretical constructions which succeed in eliminating the 'disturbing' presence of prices from the formula used to determine the rate of profit. It is clear that, with the labour theory of value, both the micro- and the macro-approach possess this property, as equations (5) and (12) show.[10] Thus, while from this particular point of view no difference can be perceived between the two approaches under considera-

---

[9] Definition (11) of the rate of profit shows the same problem from a different point of view: the possibility of making unambiguous statements about the behaviour of the profit rate as a result of a change in money wages depends on total labour being constant, i.e. on the fact that the envisaged changes in money wages originate exclusively in changes in real wages.

[10] According to Eatwell and Garegnani, the corn model and Sraffa's standard commodity share with the labour theory of value this property of clarity in showing the relation between profits and wages, and therefore represent, in their terminology, the 'surplus' approach to the determination of the rate of profit.

tion, it appears that the macroeconomic approach tends to turn the attention away from a dynamic analysis and to direct it, instead, towards a static theory of profit rate determination. In fact, the above-mentioned difficulty of unambiguously associating changes in the share of wages with capital accumulation easily leads to an almost exclusive consideration of changes in the rate of profit arising from changes in the real wage. The problem of the connection between diminishing returns and the rate of profit tends therefore to be set aside, while that of the distribution of a given output between labourers and capitalists tends to become the central objective of the analysis. This tendency to shift the main axis of the investigation from a dynamic to a static issue is greatly strengthened by the consideration of the difficulties to be faced when a more general assumption about the structure of production is adopted.

The Rate of Profit and the Role of the Invariable Measure

Assume that commodities are produced by means of commodities and labour[11] according to the production scheme used by Sraffa. Natural prices are then defined by

$$p_j = \Sigma p_i a_{ij}(1+r) + n_j w(1+r) \tag{13}$$

where a_{ij} is a technical coefficient indicating the quantity of commodity i required to produce a unit of commodity j.

The neat properties of a direct labour technology are generally lost. As Ricardo clearly states, the difficulty is connected not with the presence of capital as such, but with the existence of different proportions between capital and labour in the various branches of production; see, for instance, Ricardo's famous letter to Mill of 28 December 1818 (vol. VII, p. 377). Relative prices are

$$\frac{p_j}{p_k} = \frac{n_j}{n_k} \cdot \frac{(\Sigma p_i a_{ij}/n_j) + w}{(\Sigma p_i a_{ik}/n_k) + w} \tag{14}$$

and they cease, therefore, to coincide with relative labour quantities, since changes in wages, as Ricardo says, represent now a second cause of variation in relative prices, which certainly operates as a consequence of changes in difficulty or facility of production, but may also work independently of such changes. As a consequence, it seems impossible to arrive at a relation between

---

[11] The absence of fixed capital still does not make the production model under consideration a truly general one.

the rate of profit and the money wage that does not contain prices. For suppose that value added of gold per unit of labour is now chosen as the unit of measurement:[12]

$$\frac{p_g - \Sigma p_i a_{ig}}{n_g} = 1. \tag{15}$$

The rate of profit in gold production is then

$$r = \frac{1-w}{w + (\Sigma p_i a_{ig}/n_g)} \tag{16}$$

namely, the ratio of profits per unit of labour to total capital (advances and means of production) per unit of labour.

As equation (16) shows, dependence of r on prices obviously occurs through the component of total capital represented by the means of production. However, a second source of dependence of r on prices is represented by money wages, if the idea is maintained that real wages consist of a given basket of commodities. Departure of relative prices from relative labour values implies that money wages can no longer be reduced to the quantity of labour embodied in the given wage basket, and that it may even be hard to predict the effect of a change in the difficulty of production of corn on money wages, because the values of the corn and non-corn components of wages may change in opposite directions. These circumstances represent an obvious and major obstacle to the determination of profits and of the rate of profit in the model of production under consideration, notwithstanding the fact that the value of the output to be shared remains, by definition of the standard of value, constant through time.[13]

Ricardo tries to deal with the obstacle to the determination of the rate of profit arising from different proportions between means of production and labour by searching for a suitable unit of measurement. In the first edition of the *Principles* he thinks that a satisfactory measure of value ought to fulfil the sole requisite that the same quantity of labour should at all times and all places be required for its production. Gold is supposed to be such a commodity, and Ricardo refers to it as being an *invariable* standard. But in

[12] Note that the choice of the value of the net output, instead of the value added, per unit of labour as standard of value would have the inconvenience of involving quantities produced of the various commodities. Such a standard would then vary as the composition of output changes and would consequently not qualify as an invariable unit of measurement.

[13] Note that value added per unit of labour is constant and independent of distribution also for those commodities that require the same proportion between means of production and labour as the commodity chosen as a standard of value.

the third edition of the *Principles* he draws attention to a second requisite. The relation between this new requisite and the effects on relative prices of a rise or fall of wages is obvious. Thus, considering the case of a commodity, the price of which has changed only on account of a variation in wages, it would be highly convenient to have a measure of value capable of eliminating this 'disturbance'. It is with reference to such a situation that Ricardo writes, in 'Absolute Value and Exchangeable Value': 'If the measure was perfect ... it [the value of the commodity being measured] ought not to vary at all' (vol. IV, p. 373). Therefore the second requisite that a perfect measure of value should fulfil can be formulated as the condition that commodity prices should be independent of distribution, when measured in terms of such a standard.

Sraffa suggests that the modification introduced by Ricardo in the requisites for the definition of the standard measure of value implies a change in its analytical role. In the first edition of the *Principles*, the invariable measure of value has the role of identifying unambiguously variations in the 'difficulty or facility of production'. In the third edition, it is brought to bear on the problem of distinguishing between two concurrent causes of alteration in relative values: changes in quantities of labour and changes in wages. But this question does not admit of a solution, as it calls for a contradictory definition of the concept of absolute value, which Ricardo 'never completely succeeded in resolving'. He would thus have ended, according to Sraffa, by concentrating his attention on the problems arising from changes in wages, thereby assigning only minor relevance to the problems originating from variations in the conditions of production of wage goods.

Such a modification in the scope of the analysis would have been justified by the difficulties Ricardo was finding in trying to attain a satisfactory solution to the key issue of determining the rate of profit. Sraffa suggests that Ricardo would have been increasingly concerned by the fact that apparent changes in the magnitude of the aggregates, arising from variations in wages only, might preclude the possibility of making unambiguous inferences about the rate of profit. Ambiguities could arise even 'in the extreme case where the aggregate is composed of the same commodities in the same quantities', because 'measurement is in terms of value and relative values have been altered as a result of a change in the division between wages and profits' (Sraffa, 1951, p. xlviii). Sraffa is accordingly led to conclude that:

> Ricardo was not interested for its own sake in the problem of why two commodities produced by the same quantities of labour are not of the same exchangeable value. He was concerned with it only in so far as thereby relative values are affected by *changes in wages* .... *The search for an invariable measure of value,* which is so much at the center of Ricardo's system, *arises exclusively from the second* [point of view].
> (Sraffa, 1951, p. xlix; italics added)

The Ricardo–Sraffa Theory of Profits

Suppose, with Sraffa, that Ricardo's choice of the unit of measurement corresponds to the aim of making the social aggregate to be distributed as wages and profits invariant to changes in wages. In the model of production of commodities by means of commodities and labour considered in the previous section, this aim can be reached if the value added per unit of labour in the production of the commodity selected as a standard of value is a weighted average for the system as a whole. Gold should therefore have the property

$$\frac{p_g - \Sigma p_i a_{ig}}{n_g} = \Sigma \frac{p_j - \Sigma p_i a_{ij}}{n_j} \lambda_j \tag{17}$$

with weights

$$\lambda_j = \frac{n_j X_j}{L} \tag{18}$$

equal to the quantity of labour employed in sector j as a percentage of total labour. Taking account of definitions (15) and (18), it follows from (17) that measurement in terms of gold implies that the total value added—which is identical to the value of the social net output—is equal to total labour:

$$\Sigma(p_j - \Sigma p_i a_{ij}) X_j = L. \tag{19}$$

Following Sraffa's aggregative approach, and letting L'_w stand for the value of total wages, the rate of profit is then defined as

$$r = \frac{L - L'_w}{L'_w + \Sigma p_i a_{ij} X_j} \tag{20}$$

which generalizes the result previously obtained with equation (11).

Note that exactly the same difficulties encountered by the micro-approach to the profit rate determination are now encountered by the aggregative approach. In particular, the possibility of eliminating the disturbing presence of prices again fails, because of the difficulty of determining the effect of capital accumulation, given the real wages of labour, on the difference between total labour and the value of total wages (which can no longer be identified with necessary labour). It is clear that this specific difficulty can be avoided if total labour is assumed to be given and changes in money wages are accordingly supposed to reflect corresponding changes in real wages only.

This then would be the basic analytical motivation for Ricardo's decision to confine his investigation to the problem of determining the rate of profit under the assumption of given commodity outputs and technology.

Dividing the right-hand side of (20) by L, we obtain

$$r = \frac{1-(L'_w/L)}{(L'_w/L)+(\Sigma p_i a_{ij} X_j/L)} \tag{21}$$

which generalizes the preceding definition (12). Comparing equations (16) and (21), which define the rate of profit according to the micro- and the macro-approaches respectively, an interesting result emerges when, taking account of the definition of L'_w, the identity between the share and the rate of wages is acknowledged. The standard of measurement defined as a commodity yielding an average value added per unit of labour also has the property of being 'produced with such proportions of the two kinds of capital [advances to labour and means of production] as approach nearest to the average quantity employed in the production of most commodities' (*Works*, vol. I, p. 45).

Notwithstanding this notable property, Ricardo's standard does not solve the problem of providing a clear definition of the *rate* of profit even if, with the assumption of given total labour, total profits can be unambiguously defined. Equation (21), however, offers a clear hint of the direction of possible research for a medium of value that might do the trick. Let total labour—and thus also total net output—be equal to 1, and call R the ratio of the net output of the economy to the value of the total capital necessary for its production. Equation (21) can then be rewritten as

$$r = R\left(1 - \frac{L'_w}{L}\right) \tag{22}$$

which has a very familiar look and shows the two steps that must be taken in order to make the determination of the rate of profit independent of prices.

The first step is to make R a constant. Obviously, no acceptable measure of value can eliminate the influence of prices—and, through prices, of distribution—on the valuation of the means of production. But equation (22) shows that there is no need for a measure of capital independent of distribution; what should be aimed at instead is to make the ratio of the value of net output to the value of capital independent of prices: this is what Sraffa's truly ingenious standard commodity accomplishes.

The definition of this standard of measurement, however, requires the assumption of given outputs (or of constant returns to scale in all sectors of the economy). This circumstance has relevant implications for the notion of wages consistent with the rest of the analysis. Not only must changes in money wages or in the share of wages now reflect corresponding changes in the real wages of labour, but also, and more fundamentally, the very idea of money wages as the value of a given basket of commodities must be given up and be replaced by a notion of wages as generic purchasing power over commodities in general. In fact, if different real wages were conceived of in terms of alternative baskets of wage goods, the determination of money wages would require the previous knowledge of prices; a clear definition of total profit and of the rate of profit would then continue to be precluded. It is, therefore, vital that wages be thought of directly in value terms, as a portion of the value of the net output of the standard system. This is precisely the second step that is involved in Sraffa's approach.

By a simple manipulation of the expression embodying Sraffa's interpretation of the Ricardian system in the 'Introduction', we are naturally and easily led to a result formally similar to one of the central propositions of *Production of Commodities*: the linear relation between profit and wages, when the standard commodity is used as numeraire. If it is considered that in Sraffa's system the wage rate coincides with the share of wages, the similarity of the formulae would turn into an identity were it not for a crucial difference in the properties of the two 'standard' ratios. While in the Ricardian system the 'standard' ratio depends on money wages and thereby on changes in the conditions of production of corn, in the Sraffian system it is a technological parameter independent of distribution, and changes in the coefficients of production are, by assumption, ruled out.

The meaning of the analytical operation carried out by Sraffa in *Production of Commodities* may now appear particularly clear. When the assumption of wage capital only is dropped, and when it is admitted that the ratio of labour to means of production may differ in the various branches of the economy, the simplicity of the Ricardian relation between the rate of profit and the share of wages is lost. This simplicity is restored in the Sraffian system. Continuity between Sraffa's interpretation of Ricardo's theory and his own analytical construction in *Production of Commodities* is thus claimed to be twofold. First, there is continuity with Ricardo's corn model, namely with the idea of physical homogeneity which is now realized through the standard system. Second, there is formal continuity with Ricardo's labour values model, in the sense that Sraffa's linear relation appears to be a straightforward generalization of a result which in the Ricardian system apparently can be obtained only with the labour theory of value.

It is now clear that the role that Sraffa envisages for the invariable measure of value in the Ricardian system is identical to the role the standard commodity performs in his system. A position such as that of Pasinetti, who writes 'After a century and a half, Sraffa's standard commodity has ... fulfilled Ricardo's dream of an "invariable measure" of value' (1977, p. 120), is in line with this conclusion.

The cost of restoring the simplicity of the relation between profits and wages should not, however, be disregarded, or minimized. Sraffa is compelled to assume outputs as given; he is thus confined to a static framework of analysis, in which the possibility of changes in the techniques of production is excluded. The only magnitude free to vary is the wage rate or, what is the same in his system, the share of wages. But in this situation changes in wages must be thought of independently of changes in the difficulty of producing wage goods.

The outcome of Sraffa's own research on the determination of the rate of profit thus appears to be but the last stage of his reconstruction of Ricardo's thought; or perhaps—bearing in mind that several of the main results of *Production of Commodities* were reached in the early 1930s—it is the reverse, namely, the reconstruction of Ricardo's thought which appears to be but the final step of Sraffa's own research.

3 A CRITIQUE OF SRAFFA'S INTERPRETATION

The Notion of 'Rise or Fall of Wages'

Assuming money to be of an unvarying value, Ricardo considers in the *Principles* (vol. I, p. 97) two separate causes for a rise or fall of wages: a change in the price of the commodities on which the wages of labour are expended, and a variation in the conditions of demand and supply of labour.

The first cause identifies the origin of changes in the natural price of labour, which is said to depend on: 'the price of the food, necessaries and conveniences required for the support of the labourer and his family. With a rise in the price of food and necessaries, the natural price of labour will rise; with the fall in their price, the natural price of labour will fall' (vol. I, p. 93).

As this passage clearly shows, Ricardo distinguishes here between a *real* or *commodity wage* and a *natural price of labour*. The first is a given basket of commodities, defined by the condition that the labourers should be in a position 'to subsist and to perpetuate their race, without either increase or diminution'; the second is the value of that basket. While Ricardo says very little about the level of 'subsistence' (commodity wage), apart from observing that 'it essentially depends on the habits and customs of the people' and may therefore vary in time and space, he establishes instead a general rule for the behaviour of the natural price: 'With the progress of society the natural price of labour has always a tendency to rise, because one of the principal commodities by which its natural price is regulated, has a tendency to become dearer, from the greater difficulty of producing it' (vol. I, p. 93).

The second cause of a rise or fall of wages identifies instead the origin of changes in the market price of labour, namely 'the price which is really paid for it, from the natural operation of the proportion of the supply to the demand'. As a consequence, 'labour is dear when it is scarce, and cheap when it is plentiful' (vol. I, p. 94). In this case the basket of commodities bought by the labourer can be determined only after prices are known. A difference in the elasticities of consumption as between necessaries and conveniences will of course play a role at this stage.

Thus, with the first cause of a rise or fall of wages Ricardo refers to changes in money wages arising exclusively from changes in the price of wage goods, assuming an unvarying commodity wage; and with the second he refers instead to changes in money wages arising from the working of demand and supply in the labour market and therefore involving changes in the level of subsistence.[14] In other words, a rise or fall of wages owing to the first cause is synonymous with a change in the natural price of labour, while a rise or fall owing to the second cause is synonymous with a change in the market price.

In the chapter 'On Value' in the *Principles*, Ricardo generally refers to a rise or fall of wages without further specification. Only at the end of the chapter, in section VII, where he distinguishes the effects on prices and on profits of changes in money wages arising from an alteration in the value of money from those originating from other causes, does he write:

> a rise of wages, *from the circumstance of the labourer being more liberally rewarded, or from a difficulty in procuring the necessaries on which wages are expended*, does not, except in some instances, produce the effect of rising prices, but has a great effect in lowering profits. In this case, a greater proportion of the annual labour of the country is devoted to the support of the labourers. (vol. I, pp. 48–9; italics added)

If 'the circumstance of the labourer being more liberally rewarded' is meant to refer to different levels and compositions of the commodity wage—which, as already mentioned, cannot be considered absolutely fixed in time and space—then Ricardo is here merely saying that profits depend on the natural price of labour, which may vary for two logically distinguishable reasons: a change in the level of subsistence and a change in the cost of wage goods.[15] If, on the other hand, 'the circumstance of the labourer being more liberally rewarded' is meant to refer to the level of real wages determined by the operation of the principle of demand and supply, Ricardo seems here to consider on the same plane, as regards the effects on profits, the two causes of a rise or fall of wages more fully identified in the subsequent chapter 'On Wages'.

It is clear that these two interpretations have radically different implications.

[14] The term 'subsistence' is here used simply in the sense of real wages, without any implication for a specific rate of population growth.

[15] In terms of the symbols used in equation (3), the level of subsistence is represented by the vector of quantities $\bar{x}_j$; and the cost of the wage goods by the natural prices p_j.

In one case, profits and the rate of profit are made to depend exclusively on the natural price of labour, while the influence of demand and supply is limited to the determination of market prices, for commodities as well as for labour. This means that the market wage falls in the same logical category as the market price of commodities: it is envisaged as a temporary deviation from the corresponding natural value.[16] No general proposition can therefore be established, within the system of market prices, between the rate of profit and the wage rate.[17] In the other case, profits and the rate of profit are made to depend not only on the behaviour of the natural price of wage goods, but also on demand and supply in the labour market, since the level of subsistence is now determined, given the price of wage goods, by 'the proportion of the supply to the demand'. This means that a role is attributed to the working of demand and supply in the labour market that is quite different from that assigned to the same principle in the commodity markets. In other words, deviations of market price from natural price in the labour market are supposed to have a systematic—and not only a temporary and accidental—nature.[18] A system of natural prices and profits is thus envisaged to exist even when the market price of labour has not adjusted to the natural price.[19]

Notes on Malthus seems to support the second interpretation.[20] Malthus criticizes Ricardo for having confined his attention exclusively to changes in wages arising from changes in the price of necessaries.

> We can know little of the laws which determine profits, unless, in addition to the causes which increase the price of necessaries, we explain the causes which award a larger or a smaller share of these necessaries to each labourer. And here it is obvious that we must have recourse to the great principles of demand and supply, or to that very principle of competition brought forward by Adam Smith, which Mr Ricardo expressly rejects, or at least considers as of so temporary a nature as not to require attention in a general theory of profits. (vol. II, p. 269)

Ricardo dismisses this criticism, observing that Malthus's remark can at most be levelled against the fact that he has attributed an insufficient weight to the

---

[16] 'However much the market price of labour may deviate from its natural price, it has, like commodities, a tendency to conform to it' (vol. I, p. 94).

[17] Note that, when commodity prices diverge from their natural prices, there will not be a uniform profit rate throughout the economy.

[18] See the passage (vol. I, pp. 94–5) cited on p. 207 below.

[19] Eltis (1984, p. 205) clearly points out the implication of this second line of interpretation as regards the difference between commodities and labour in the adjustment of market prices to natural values.

[20] See also, in the same sense, 'Absolute Value and Exchangeable Value' (vol. IV, pp. 366–7).

role of demand and supply in the determination of the real wage, and certainly not against the fact that he has omitted to consider this cause. He indicates passages of the *Principles* where the two causes of a rise or fall of wages are explicitly mentioned[21] and suggests that misunderstanding might be due to his habit of classifying both causes 'under the name of high or low wages' and of reckoning wages by proportions (see vol. II, pp. 252, 264–8).

Ricardo, however, does not seem to answer the real issue raised by Malthus, concerning the permanent as opposed to temporary role of demand and supply in the determination of the price of labour. In Malthus's theoretical system natural prices are long-run market prices. There is consequently no reason for ignoring the effects on profits of changes in the long-run market price of labour. In Ricardo's analytical framework, on the contrary, natural prices reflect the cost of production; it is, therefore, difficult to envisage a role for the principle of demand and supply, even if limited to a particular market. In fact, a consistent line of argument in Ricardo, beginning from the pre-*Essay* period, excludes any *systematic* influence of demand and supply on the price of labour. A unique, permanent cause for a rise or fall of money wages is repeatedly stated: the change in the cost of production of wage goods, given the commodity wage.[22] The fact that changes in the level and composition of the commodity wage itself have lasting effects on the rate of profit raises no problem in this context. Since no general law can be established for such changes, they do not represent a *permanent* cause of a rise or fall of money wages and may therefore be disregarded by the theory.

A widely accepted line of interpretation[23] of Ricardo's theory of profit is based on this idea that changes in money wages reflect exclusively changes in the natural price of labour, and on the related idea that diminishing returns in agriculture are the only systematic cause of change in the cost of labour. Accordingly, the profit–wage relation represents a typically dynamic tool of analysis of the effects of capital accumulation on the rate of profit via the induced change in the natural price of labour.

As Ricardo never ceases to remind his reader, the effect of diminishing returns may be checked by improvements in the production of wage goods and by importation of cheap corn from abroad. A comparative static application of the profit–wage relation may thereby be envisaged and may be considered implicit in Ricardo's own stand on the corn laws. In these

---

[21] Though it is hard to think that Ricardo meant his footnote to represent an extensive reference to the *Principles*, it is none the less worth noting that the passages mentioned are from the chapter 'On Wages' and the subsequent chapter, 'Taxes on Wages'. No mention is made of the passage in the chapter 'On Value' previously cited in the text.

[22] See, for instance, letter to Malthus of 26 June 1814 (vol. VI, p. 108), *Essay on Profits* (vol. IV, pp. 22–3), letter to Malthus of 11 October 1816 (vol. VII, p. 78), *Principles* (vol. I, pp. 125–6, 289–90, 292), letter to McCulloch of 13 June 1820 (vol. VIII, p. 193).

[23] See for instance, Stigler (1952), Blaug (1958; 1978, pp. 91–152), Pasinetti (1960).

instances, however, alternative values of the money wage originate from the consideration of alternative prices of wage goods, and not from alternative levels of the basket of commodities representing the real wage of labour. Static applications of this kind of the profit–wage relation are thus perfectly consistent with the stated notion of money wages.

The above-mentioned line of interpretation of Ricardo's theory has been recently challenged by Hicks and Hollander (1977), Casarosa (1978), Hollander (1979, 1983) and Eltis (1984) (see also the papers by Casarosa and Hollander in this volume). These authors refer to Ricardo's statement in the *Principles* that

> Notwithstanding the tendency of wages to conform to their natural rate, their market rate may, in an improving society, for an indefinite period, be constantly above it; for no sooner may the impulse which an increased capital gives to a new demand for labour be obeyed, than another increase of capital may produce the same effect; and thus, if the increase of capital be gradual and constant, the demand for labour may give a continued stimulus to an increase of people. (vol. I, pp. 94–5)

According to their view, the dynamic process described by Ricardo's growth model is thus characterized, at least after a certain stage in the accumulation of capital has been reached, by a constantly falling real wage of labour. This circumstance operates in the sense of reducing the increase in money wages attributable to the working of the law of diminishing returns, without superseding it. A role is thereby attributed to the principle of demand and supply in the labour market, and the rate of profit is made to depend on the behaviour of the market wage. Hollander claims that this is the truly general application of Ricardo's fundamental theorem on profits, because the assumption of a given commodity wage should be simply considered a 'strong case', not Ricardo's full theory (see Hollander, 1979, pp. 11–13, 395–404).

It is clear that neither of these interpretations of the notion of money wages in Ricardo can offer valid support for Sraffa's emphasis on the static aspects of Ricardo's theory of profit. Under the first interpretation, there is no purpose for a relation between the rate of profit and the money wage rate, when the latter is taken to represent alternative levels of the subsistence of the labourers. On the other hand, the second interpretation—with its emphasis on the role of the market and of the market price of labour—seems very far from the overall stand taken by Sraffa on wages, which, classically, are considered as exogenously given rather than market-determined.

Note that a consistent application of the approach to profit rate determination based on the market price of labour should anyway yield a dynamic interpretation of the profit–wage relation similar to that obtained by the approach based on the natural price of labour. Hollander (1979, p. 12), however, criticizes the tendency to single out the dynamic aspect of the profit–wage relation and maintains that 'Ricardo paid more careful attention to the general principle of the inverse profit–wage relation than to the particular issue of a falling profit rate.' This implies, however, either the abstract consideration, already rejected, of alternative levels exogenously given of the real wage, or the acknowledgement of a role to the short-run fluctuations of the wage rate owing to occasional changes in demand and supply of labour. But to base the main application of the inverse profit–wage relation on such a notion of short-run market price would really seem to push Ricardo's interpretation too much in a Marshallian direction.

Finally, as regards the two interpretations considered, large and consistent textual evidence as well as reasons of internal coherence with the overall analytical system developed by Ricardo are in favour of an interpretation of the term 'money wage' as being equivalent to the notion of the natural price of labour rather than to that of the market price of labour, even when the latter is taken in the limited sense of a well defined path through time excluding all temporary fluctuations.[24]

Requisites and Role of the Invariable Measure of Value

As already mentioned, in the third edition of the *Principles* Ricardo believed that the unique requisite of constant conditions of production was no longer sufficient to define a perfect measure of value, which ought also to satisfy the condition that commodity prices be independent of distribution. However, such a perfect measure of value cannot be found; for, even if the chosen unit of measurement were to satisfy the first requisite, 'it would be subject to relative variations from a rise or fall of wages, on account of the different proportions of fixed capital [to labour] which might be necessary to produce it, and to produce those other commodities whose alteration of value we wished to ascertain' (vol. I, p. 44).

A commodity always produced with the same quantity of labour would then be a perfect measure of value only of those commodities whose production requires the same proportion of fixed capital to labour. In this event, a change in value could be unambiguously attributed to a change in difficulty or facility of production of the commodity being measured. When, instead, the proportion of fixed capital to labour is different in the commodity being measured compared with the commodity chosen as unit of measurement, variations in value may originate either from changes in the conditions of production, or from a rise or fall of wages, or from both. In this case,

[24] This issue is extensively discussed in Caravale's paper in this volume. Caravale and Tosato (1980, ch. 1) stress the reasons of internal coherence that lead to the interpretation of Ricardo's theory in terms of a natural equilibrium growth model.

measurement in terms of the chosen standard does not succeed in eliminating the effect of a change in wages; it is, therefore, impossible to isolate the sole variations in the underlying conditions of production.

According to Sraffa, Ricardo's preoccupation with the effect of changes in wages on relative prices and on the aggregate to be distributed explains the 'considerable alterations that were made in connection with the choice of the invariable standard of value' (Sraffa, 1951, p. xl). As we saw, the consideration of these alterations is at the root of Sraffa's two basic ideas in the reconstruction of Ricardo's theoretical approach: (1) to envisage variations in wages independently of changes in difficulty of production; and (2) to attribute to the invariable measure of value the role of measuring net output independently of prices and of distribution, so that the true nature of profits could emerge clearly, thus refuting Adam Smith's idea that prices result from the 'adding up' of *independently determined* cost components, as neatly as the construction of the *Essay* (especially in the corn model version) and the subsequent labour theory of value had succeeded in doing.

To the considerable alterations made by Ricardo in connection with the choice of the invariable measure of value, Sraffa opposes the idea that 'no essential change was made in successive editions about the rule which determines value' (1951, p. xl) and rejects the previously accepted notion of a weakening of Ricardo's stand on the labour theory of value. The textual evidence and the reasoning on which this idea is based have been competently criticized by Napoleoni (1977) and will not be reviewed in this context. The point made here is that Sraffa's position appears to be contradictory.

Faced with the failure, at a theoretical level, of his impossible attempt to eliminate the effect of variations in money wages on relative prices, Ricardo is compelled to accept, at a practical level, an approximate solution of his problem of choice of the standard.

> Neither gold, then, nor any other commodity, can ever be a perfect measure of value for all things; but I have already remarked, that the effect on the relative prices of things, from a variation in profits, is comparatively slight; that by far the most important effects are produced by the varying quantities of labour required for production; and therefore, if we suppose this important cause of variation removed from the production of gold, we shall probably possess as near an approximation to a standard measure of value as can be theoretically conceived. (vol. I, p. 45)

Ricardo appears, therefore, to be satisfied with a measure of value by assumption *invariable*, but theoretically *imperfect* (see also Hollander, 1979, p. 219): invariable as regards the quantity of labour required for its production, imperfect as 'it would be subject to relative variations from a rise or fall of wages'. Thus 'the exceptions he [Ricardo] had discovered in the fundamental rule determining value', Sraffa comments, 'cropped up again in attempting to define the qualities of an invariable standard' (1951, p. xli). The implications of the tight connection between labour values and invariable standard that Sraffa underlines are far-reaching. Since the measure of value has been found imperfect from a theoretical point of view, it follows that the notion that exchangeable values are regulated by relative labour quantities is also imperfect from the same theoretical point of view. Ricardo's insistence on the problem of defining a perfect measure of value is evidence of his awareness of the limitations of the labour theory of value, as a theory.[25] Sraffa's idea that no change took place on the issue of value between successive editions of the *Principles*[26] appears, therefore, in direct contradiction with the 'considerable alterations' made with reference to the choice of the standard and with Ricardo's admission of the failure to produce a perfect measure of value.[27]

Furthermore, the tight connection between labour values and invariable standard reveals that, contrary to Sraffa's interpretation, the role of the standard has not changed in the third edition of the *Principles*. It remains the same as that stated in the first edition: it is the role, intimately related to the process of capital accumulation, of measuring changes in difficulty of production, and not the role of making the value of net output independent of distribution (and of prices) in a context of given commodity outputs and exogenous wage variations.

As was shown in section 2, the standard of measurement in a model of production of commodities by means of commodities and labour has the property of being produced with an average ratio of means of production to labour and leads to the conclusion that the value of the net output of the economy is indeed independent of distribution. This circumstance would seem to lend support to Sraffa's interpretation of the analytical role of the invariable measure. In reality, independence of the value of the net output from distribution is not the purpose pursued by Ricardo, whose motivation for the choice of an average commodity is different.

The attempt to eliminate the disturbance caused by changes in wages on the determination of the rate of profit can be carried out at both the aggregative and the micro-level of analysis, distinguished earlier. When the

---

[25] See also Stigler's (1958) distinction in Ricardo between an analytical and an empirical labour theory of value.

[26] Hollander (1979, p. 217) agrees with Sraffa on this point, but moving from the opposite stand that Ricardo never had an analytical labour theory of value.

[27] See Ricardo's penultimate letter to Malthus of 15 August 1823 (vol. IX, p. 352), where he writes: 'My complaint against you is that you claim to have given us an accurate measure of value, and I object to your claim, not that I have succeeded and you have failed, but that we have both failed.'

aggregative approach is adopted, it is obvious that the standard of measurement should aim at making the value of the net output of the economy independent of wages. If, then, the labour theory of value holds, any commodity can satisfactorily achieve the aim; if, however, the labour theory of value does not hold, only an average commodity can do so. This explains Sraffa's interpretation of the role of the standard commodity in the third edition of the *Principles*, where, as was just maintained, Ricardo perceives more clearly the nature of the limits of the labour theory of value.

On the other hand, when the micro-approach is considered, the role of the standard of value—as the definition of the rate of profit in equation (16) immediately suggests—is to make prices independent of distribution, precisely as Ricardo attempts to do. It is clear that, if this objective could be attained (as it is attained whenever the labour theory of value is valid), it would also follow that the value of the aggregate net output would be independent of distribution. This, however, would be a derived consequence and not the primary aim of the choice made.

Aware of the fact that the objective he was pursuing could not be reached, Ricardo chose to be content with the same type of approximation to absolute prices as he had accepted for relative prices. The motivation for Ricardo's choice of a commodity produced under average conditions is thus not to obtain a measure of the value of the social net output independent of distribution, but rather to make labour quantities as good an approximation as possible to true prices for the largest mass of commodities.[28] This motivation is fully brought out in the final paper, 'Absolute Value and Exchangeable Value',[29] where Ricardo writes:

> in chusing amongst measures which are all acknowledged to be imperfect which shall we select ... ?
>
> To me it appears most clear that we should chuse a measure produced by labour employed for a certain period .... a commodity produced by labour employed for a year is a mean between the extremes of commodities produced on one side by labour and advances for much more than a year, and on the other by labour employed for a day without any advances, and *the mean will in most cases give a much less deviation from truth than if either of the extremes were used as a measure.* (vol. IV, p. 405; italics added)

---

[28] Equation (14) intuitively shows that the maximum and the average errors of the relative labour quantities n_j/n_g, used as an approximation of the true price ratios p_j/p_g, are reduced to a minimum if gold is a mean commodity and if the largest mass of commodities clusters around the mean as regards the conditions of production.

[29] The same idea is to be found in a letter to McCulloch of 13 June 1820 (vol. VIII, p. 193). Hollander's (1979, p. 238) interpretation of Ricardo's passage reproduced in the text is similar to that given here.

The fact that Ricardo, confronted with the problems of the labour theory of value, did not try the aggregative route to profit rate determination, but on the contrary tried to restore general validity to the labour theory of value,[30] strongly suggests that measurement of change in difficulty or facility of production remains, in the third edition of the *Principles*, as in the first, the vital issue of Ricardo's theory of value and distribution.

Ricardo's Theory of Profit: An Invariable Measure of Changes in Money Wages

Ricardo's use of an average commodity as an invariable standard of value faces two possible objections. First, given Ricardo's assumptions of diminishing returns in agriculture and of a fixed wage basket, the average changes whenever a change occurs in difficulty or facility of production, if there are different ratios of means of production to labour in the various sectors of the economy. This means that an average commodity cannot meet the requirement of being invariant.[31] The second objection is that it does not help to solve the problem of profit rate determination in a dynamic perspective with the desired clarity. Building on Sraffa's general solution to the question of the definition of natural prices, the existence of an inverse relation between the rate of profit and the labour coefficient of any specific sector of the economy can be proved. But, as already mentioned, it can be argued that this result does not possess the weight of the immediate evidence. It may be further maintained that it bypasses altogether the notion of a profit–wage connection, since the problem of determining the behaviour of money wages, given the real wage, remains unresolved.

The question may then be asked if it is possible to find a unit of measurement free of these shortcomings. Ricardo's last letter to Mill, of 5 September 1823 (vol. IX, p. 387), contains a general negative conclusion of his line of research: 'strictly speaking there is not in nature any correct measure of value, nor can ingenuity suggest one, for what constitutes a correct measure for some things is a reason why it cannot be a correct one for others.' It is, therefore, certainly not in the direction, vainly sought for by Ricardo, of making relative prices independent of distribution that one should look, but rather, as suggested by Sraffa, in the direction of a composite commodity with the required properties. The indications offered by Ricardo at this purpose in 'Absolute Value and Exchangeable Value' make the task a relatively easy one.

Equation (16) shows that two difficulties are met when a more general model of production is considered. In this case the rate of profit depends on prices for two reasons: (1) because the value of the means of production

---

[30] See, on this specific point, Caravale and Tosato (1980, pp. 54–8, 82–5).
[31] This is the reason for Caravale and Tosato's (1978; 1980, p. 85) conclusion that Sraffa's standard commodity is not a useful tool of analysis in the Ricardian system.

required to produce the commodity used as a standard depends on prices, and (2) because money wages equally depend on prices in a complex way.

To overcome these difficulties, consider first the so-called 'labour approach' to prices as opposed to the 'commodity approach'. Sraffa's commodity approach is in fact better suited to represent the Marxian approach to the theory of value in terms of constant and variable capital than is that of Ricardo, who suggests that all exceptions to the general rule of value can be reduced to 'one of time', namely, to labour employed for a longer or a shorter period (see Ricardo's letter to McCulloch of 13 June 1820: vol. VIII, p. 193). The definition of the standard of value in 'Absolute Value and Exchangeable Value'—where a commodity produced by labour employed for a year is considered a mean (see the passage quoted on p. 211 above)—confirms that this is the structure of production Ricardo envisages.

Transforming the commodity approach into the 'dated labour approach', as shown by Sraffa, natural prices defined by equation (13) can therefore be expressed as

$$p_j = w(1+r)\{n_j^{(0)} + (1+r)n_j^{(1)} + (1+r)^2 n_j^{(2)} + \ldots\}. \tag{23}$$

where $n_j^{(0)} = n_j$ is the quantity of direct labour required for the production of a unit of commodity j and $n_j^{(t)}$ is the quantity of indirect labour required to produce a unit of the same commodity j at the tth stage of the reduction process. Now let N_j be the total (direct and indirect) labour employed in the production of commodity j, and let t_j, defined by the relation

$$(1+r)^{t_j} = (1+r)\Sigma(1+r)^t \frac{n_j^{(t)}}{N_j}, \tag{24}$$

be the average period of employment of labour in the production of commodity j. Natural prices can therefore be rewritten as

$$p_j = N_j w(1+r)^{t_j}. \tag{25}$$

As regards the unit of measurement, assume, in line with Ricardo's position in his final paper, (1) that gold is produced with labour employed for a year; and (2) that a year is the period of production also of 'corn and most other vegetable food which forms by far the most valuable article of daily consumption' (vol. IV, p. 406), implying that, by definition, gold is a perfect measure of the commodity subject to being produced under diminishing returns. Assume, furthermore (departing here from Ricardo), (3) that gold is not a social average, but represents a *mean commodity with respect to the given size and composition of the wage basket*. In formal terms, indicating the commodity corn with the index c and letting the index k represent all other wage goods, these properties respectively imply the following relations:

$$p_g = N_g w(1+r) \tag{26}$$

$$\frac{p_c}{p_g/N_g} = N_c \tag{27}$$

and

$$(1+r) = \sum \frac{N_k \bar{x}_k}{N_{nc}} (1+r)^{t_k} \quad (k = 1,\ldots,m-1) \tag{28}$$

where the total, direct and indirect, quantity of labour required to produce the non-corn component of the wage basket is denoted by

$$N_{nc} = \Sigma N_k \bar{x}_k. \tag{29}$$

Note that since, by assumption, corn is produced in the same length of time as is gold, condition (28) is sufficient to establish the desired property that labour employed for a year is a weighted average of the conditions of production of all wage goods.[32]

Generalizing the initial choice of numeraire (3), consider now as unit of measurement the value of the output of gold obtained by one unit of total labour:

$$\frac{p_g}{N_g} = 1. \tag{30}$$

With such a unit of measurement, the rate of profit in gold production turns out to be formally identical with the rate of profit defined, for a technology of production using only direct labour, by equation (5), here repeated:

$$r = \frac{1-w}{w}. \tag{31}$$

Money wages measured in terms of the chosen standard are equal to

$$w = N_c \bar{x}_c + N_{nc} \tag{32}$$

namely to the sum of the quantity of direct and indirect labour needed to produce the quantity of corn plus the quantity of direct and indirect labour required to produce all the óther commodities included in the given wage basket. If we assume, therefore, that wage goods different from corn are produced under conditions of constant returns to scale, then changes in the

---

[32] This mean would coincide with the social average only if the composition of the given commodity wage were the same as that of the aggregate net output.

difficulty of production of corn have an immediately predictable effect on money wages and thereby on profit and the rate of profit.

Following Ricardo's hypotheses about the productive structure of the economy and about the properties of the unit of measurement of value, and adding the further (restrictive) condition that the chosen standard must be an average commodity with reference to the conditions of production of wage goods only, a clear connection between the rate of profit and capital accumulation is thus obtained even in a situation in which the labour theory of value does not hold. The adoption of the micro- as opposed to the aggregative approach to profit rate determination is decisive at this regard, for only in the context of the sectoral approach can the assumption be made that the value to be shared as wages and profits is constant through time.

The conclusion reached suggests a final consideration. From the assumption, made by Ricardo, that the period of production in agriculture is identical with that of the invariable measure, it follows that equation (31) defines the rate of profit not only in the production of gold, but also in the agricultural sector. It is maintained that this essentially implies a return to the position Ricardo had taken in the *Essay*—a return to the corn model assumption and to the related idea that the rate of profit in agriculture determines the general rate of profit (see Blaug, 1958, esp. pp. 11 and 24). This circumstance is considered as a sort of implicit admission, which Ricardo himself makes, of the failure of his repeated attempts to generalize or to substantiate his initial stand on profits. Hollander (1979, p. 256) further remarks that: 'In strict logic this line of reasoning is incomplete unless we also assert that wages are fixed in terms of corn and devoted entirely to corn.'

The preceding analysis shows that the validity of Ricardo's belief in the fundamental role of the rate of profit in agriculture can be extended to the mixed wage basket case, provided that the standard of value is appropriately defined. The result obtained therefore seems to represent, independently of the outcome of the debate on the corn model, a generalization of Ricardo's position in the *Essay* more in line with the overall purpose of his theoretical construction than Sraffa's linear profit–wage relation appears to be.

REFERENCES

Bharadwaj, K. (1978). 'Maurice Dobb's Critique of Theories of Value and Distribution'. *Cambridge Journal of Economics*, 2, 153–74.
Blaug, M. (1958). *Ricardian Economics*. New Haven: Yale University Press.
Blaug, M. (1978). *Economic Theory in Retrospect* (3rd edn). Cambridge: CUP.
Caravale, G. A. and Tosato, D. A. (1978). 'Saggio di profitto e merce tipo nella teoria di Ricardo'. *Rivista di politica economica*, 68, 3–70.
Caravale, G. A. and Tosato, D. A. (1980). *Ricardo and the Theory of Value, Distribution and Growth*. London: Routledge & Kegan Paul.

Casarosa, C. (1978). 'A New Formulation of the Ricardian System'. *Oxford Economic Papers*, 30, 38–63.

Eatwell, J. (1975). 'Mr Sraffa's Standard Commodity and the Rate of Exploitation'. *Quarterly Journal of Economics*, 89, 543–55.

Eatwell, J. (1977). 'The Irrelevance of Returns to Scale in Sraffa's Analysis'. *Journal of Economic Literature*, 15, 61–7.

Eltis, W. (1984). *The Classical Theory of Economic Growth*. London: Macmillan.

Garegnani, P. (1976). 'On a Change in the Notion of Equilibrium in Recent Work on Value and Distribution: A Comment on Samuelson'. In M. Brown, K. Sato and P. Zarembka (eds), *Essays in Modern Capital Theory*. Amsterdam: North Holland.

Garegnani, P. (1981). 'Valore e distribuzione in Marx e negli economisti classici'. In P. Garegnani, *Marx e gli economisti classici*. Turin: Einaudi.

Garegnani, P. (1983). 'The Classical Theory of Wages and the Role of Demand Schedules in the Determination of Relative Prices'. *American Economic Review*, 73, 309–13.

Hicks, J. and Hollander, S. (1977). 'Mr Ricardo and the Moderns'. *Quarterly Journal of Economics*, 91, 351–69.

Hollander, S. (1973). 'Ricardo's Analysis of the Profit Rate, 1814–15'. *Economica*, 40, 260–82.

Hollander, S. (1975). 'Ricardo and the Corn Profit Model'. *Economica*, 42, 188–202.

Hollander, S. (1979). *The Economics of David Ricardo*. Toronto: University Press.

Hollander, S. (1983). 'On the Interpretation of Ricardian Economics: The Assumption Regarding Wages'. *American Economic Review*, 73, 314–18.

Kaldor, N. (1956). 'Alternative Theories of Distribution'. *Review of Economic Studies*, 23, 83–100.

Napoleoni, C. (1977). 'Sull'interpretazione sraffiana di Ricardo', *Il Veltro*, 21, 251–63; reprinted in R. Marchionatti, *Rilevanza e limiti del neoricardismo*. Milan: Feltrinelli, 1981.

Passinetti, L. L. (1960). 'A Mathematical Formulation of the Ricardian System'. *Review of Economic Studies*, 27, 78–98.

Passinetti, L. L. (1977). *Lectures on the Theory of Production*. London: Macmillan.

Rankin, S. (1984). 'The Wage Basket in Ricardo's *Essay on Profits*'. *Cambridge Journal of Economics*, 8, 83–6.

Ricardo, D. (1951–73). *The Works and Correspondence of David Ricardo* (11 vols), ed. P. Sraffa, Cambridge: CUP. (Reference in text is simply to volume and page number.)

Roncaglia, A. (1978). *Sraffa and the Theory of Prices*. New York: John Wiley.

Sraffa, P. (1951). 'Introduction'. In Ricardo (1951), *Works and Correspondence*, vol. I, pp. xiii–lxii.

Sraffa, P. (1960). *Production of Commodities by Means of Commodities*. Cambridge: CUP.

Stigler, G. J. (1952). 'The Ricardian Theory of Value and Distribution'. *Journal of Political Economy*, 60, 187–207; reprinted in G. J. Stigler, *Essays in the History of Economics*, Chicago: University Press, 1965, pp. 156–97.

Stigler, G. J. (1958). 'Ricardo and the 93 per cent Labour Theory of Value'. *American Economic Review*, 48, 358–67; reprinted in G. J. Stigler, *Essays in the History of Economics*, Chicago: University Press, 1965, pp. 326–42.

9

The Debate on Ricardo: Old Results in New Frameworks

PIER LUIGI PORTA

1 THE RICARDO PROBLEM

Lesson 40 of Léon Walras's *Eléments* (Walras, 1954) contains a famous critique of the theory of price determination in the English classical school.[1] It is the purpose of this paper to discuss the drift and significance of that critique, particularly in the light of more recent literature, in which the problem is reconsidered with special reference to the interpretation of the Ricardian system.

In Walras's own words, 'let P be the aggregate price received for the products of an enterprise; let S, I and F be respectively the wages, interest charges and rent laid out by the entrepreneurs, in the course of production, to pay for the services of personal faculties, capital and land.' Price being made equal to cost of production, Walras writes:

$$P = S + I + F.$$

Now, F is eliminated by the English school, through Ricardo's theory of rent, and S is determined directly by the theory of wages. However, I is not determined independently of price. In the equation

$$I = P - S$$

an attempt is in fact made to solve for two unknowns with one equation. 'It is clear now,' Walras comments, 'that the English economists are completely

Thanks are due to Professor Giovanni Caravale for sympathetic comments. The interpretative line advanced in this paper is developed in the author's 'Introduzione' to the Italian variorum edition of Ricardo's *Principles*, drafts of which were circulated from the summer of 1979 (see Porta, 1979 and Ricardo, 1983).

[1] Walras's criticism was not indeed isolated: in Marshall's judgement (1961, vol. I, p. 821), it paralleled 'much both of the form and substance' of a line of attack stemming from Macleod and running through Jevons, Menger, Böhm-Bawerk and Wieser.

baffled by the problem of price determination; for it is impossible for I to determine P at the same time that P determines I.'[2]

2 RICARDO'S DEFENDERS

According to V. K. Dmitriev (1974), Adam Smith's cost of production theory of price fully merits the reproach of circularity so often levelled against the theory of production costs in general, namely that it defines price from prices and determines one unknown from other unknowns. However, in his view, with Ricardo the theory of production costs is completed and is no longer subject to the criticism of underdeterminacy.

In Dmitriev's notation, the cost of production of commodity A, Y_A, can be written as:

$$Y_A = ax_a \cdot f_A(r)$$

where a is the quantity of a staple food (wage good) per worker per unit of time (commodity wage rate), x_a is the price of the wage good and $f_A(r)$ is a function of the profit rate.

In a system with n commodities, Dmitriev argues, we should have n commodity prices as unknowns in addition to x_a and r: altogether $(n+2)$ unknowns. If we now put one of the prices equal to unity, e.g. if in the nth equation we put $Y_N = 1$, the system of n equations can determine the set of relative prices, Y_A, Y_B, ... and x_a (n unknowns altogether), for a given profit rate, but it cannot determine both the profit rate *and* the set of relative prices at the same time; again, no single equation can serve to determine two unknowns. However, *among* the commodities to be considered in the system, there must appear the wage good itself; the corresponding equation is

$$x_a = ax_a \cdot f_a(r)$$

which reduces to

$$f_a(r) = 1/a.$$

Now it is easy to see that this equation determines the rate of profit directly; knowing the rate of profit, the remaining $(n-1)$ equations may determine without difficulty the $(n-1)$ relative prices.

---

[2] 'En bonne mathématique, on ne peut faire servir une seule équation à déterminer deux inconnues.' Nothing can prevent 'the theory of the determination of prices under free competition from becoming a mathematical theory', Walras further observed in the Preface to his fourth edition. 'The illustrious authors of the theories cited in Lesson 40 allow themselves sometimes ... to use a single equation to solve for two ... unknowns. It is very unlikely, at least so I hope, that such procedures will continue indefinitely to stand in the way of a method which promises to convert pure economics into an exact science' (Walras, 1954, pp. 47 and 425).

According to Dmitriev, in the simple observation that the wage good is one of the goods produced in the system lies Ricardo's great merit of having rescued the cost of production theory of price from the charge of under-determinacy; for Ricardo's device solves the problem of price determination *within* the production system. Any solution based on conditions external to the sphere of production (e.g. on demand and supply conditions) would in fact imply avowal of the untenability of the cost of production theory itself.

It seems appropriate at this point to recall Alfred Marshall's warning, that too much should not be made of Ricardo's 'unguarded language' in speaking of a wage good and of a commodity wage rate as a fixed quantity of it.

> The English classical economists frequently spoke of the minimum of wages as depending on the price of corn. But the term 'corn' was used by them as short for agricultural produce in general, somewhat as Petty (*Taxes and Contributions*, ch. XIV) speaks of 'the Husbandry of Corn, which we will suppose to contain all necessaries of life, as in the Lord's Prayer we suppose the word Bread doth'. (cf. Marshall, 1961, vol. I, p. 509, n. 2)

There is ample evidence, according to Marshall, that, in the first place, Ricardo did not mean to speak of a wage good as a specific commodity (even, of course, a composite commodity) and, further, that his assumption of a definite commodity wage rate, fixed at the natural level, should not be taken too seriously. We may well argue that considerable simplifications (such as his 'one-commodity model') were, almost of necessity, induced by Ricardo's habit of illustrating a principle by means of numerical tables: in such cases a practical, rather than a theoretical, necessity was involved.

Consequently Marshall, who would argue about the 'important place' of 'Ricardo's theory of cost of production in relation to value', came to Ricardo's defence on that matter along lines very different from the above considered ones. Dealing in particular with Jevons's attack on Ricardo's theory of value, Marshall wrote: 'His criticism on Ricardo achieved some apparently unfair dialectical triumphs, by assuming that Ricardo thought of value as governed by cost of production without reference to demand.'[3]

This is obviously a 'misconception' that Jevons shares with Walras on the issue. Ricardo, in his *Notes on Malthus*, believed that 'the cost of production regulates the supply, and therefore regulates the price', as 'whatever regulates

---

[3] 'The foundations of the theory [of value] as they were left by Ricardo remain intact', Marshall wrote (1961, vol. I, p. 503). On the theory of wages in the English classical economists, new evidence to support Marshall's argument came to light after his death, particularly in Ricardo's elaborate *Notes on Malthus*. 'Wages—Ricardo summarized at one point—mainly depend on the price of corn. After the observations of Mr. Malthus on the other causes which may affect labour, I must guard myself against being supposed to deny the effect of those other causes on wages' (*Works*, vol. II, Note 187, p. 291; cf. also *ibid.*, Note 171, pp. 264ff.).

the supply regulates the price' (*Works*, vol. II, p. 49 Note 20, p. 225 Note 143); and he would insist that 'in the usual and ordinary course of things, the demand for all commodities precedes their supply' (vol. I, p. 409). His analysis on the influence of demand and supply on price, under different circumstances, appears to substantiate much of what Marshall has to say on the 'all-ruling law of supply and demand' (Marshall, 1961, vol. I, pp. 348–50, 819–20).[4] Demand (and indeed utility) is consistently implied in Ricardo's guiding principle on supply analysis: 'We do not say,' he argues, 'the commodities will under all circumstances be produced, but if they are produced we contend that there will always be some who will have the will and power to consume them' (*Works*, vol. II, p. 314 Note 203). Ricardo regarded 'the natural laws of variation of utility as too obvious to require detailed explanation'; he admitted that 'cost of production could have no effect upon exchange value if it could have none upon the amount which producers brought forward for sale.' His doctrines 'imply that what is true of supply, is true *mutatis mutandis* of demand, and that the utility of a commodity could have no effect upon its exchange value if it could have none on the amount which purchasers took off the market' (Marshall, 1961, vol. I, p. 817).[5]

Some recent debates on the Ricardian system do bear obvious similarities with the above outlined interpretations. Perhaps the more recent treatment differs from the old in casting some essential features of the respective arguments in a more extreme form; if pushed too far, there is an impending danger of sterility in this tendency. This will become apparent from the next sections.[6]

3 RICARDO'S MODERN INTERPRETERS

In Piero Sraffa's standard system,[7] the net output vector, **Y**, and the gross output vector, **X**, are made up of the same commodities, bearing the same

[4] 'The "cost of production principle" and the "final utility" principle are undoubtedly component parts of the one all-ruling law of supply and demand; each may be compared to one blade of a pair of scissors. When one blade is held still, and the cutting is effected by moving the other, we may say with careless brevity that the cutting is done by the second; but the statement is not one to be made formally, and defended deliberately' (Marshall, 1961, vol. 1, p. 820).

[5] Professor Rankin suggested that, contrary to today's common parlance, the term 'supply and demand' was applied to the short run in the language of classical political economy and to monopolized commodities, i.e. to the cases in which price may differ from marginal cost of production. In his view, this can provide a clue to Ricardo's 'strictures on "supply and demand"' theories on one side, and his 'evident recognition of the influence of demand on relative prices in the long run' on the other (cf. Rankin, 1980, p. 251).

[6] See also Professor O'Brien's observations leading to a 'via media' through the flames of recent debates (O'Brien, 1981) and Professor Blaug's recent contribution to the Sassari Conference (Blaug, 1983, esp. pp. 914–17).

[7] 'It can be said that in any actual economic system there is embedded a miniature Standard system .... there is always a way, and never more than one way, of transforming a given economic system into a Standard system' (Sraffa, 1960, pp. 20, 26).

proportions one with another. The ratio of the value of the net output of the standard system to the value of the gross output is consequently independent of the price vector. Of course, the same properties must hold for the net output vector, **Y**, and the vector of the means of production, **X** − **Y**, as for the ratio, R, between the values of those two sets of magnitudes.

The latter ratio[8] also indicates the *maximum* rate of profit for the system (i.e. the rate of profit that would emerge if the whole net product went to profit) and is given by

$$R = \frac{\mathbf{p}\mathbf{Y}}{\mathbf{p}(\mathbf{X} - \mathbf{Y})}. \tag{1}$$

Under the above stated proportionality condition, it is clear that any change in the price vector, **p**, though it will influence the two values appearing in (1), will leave their ratio unaffected, i.e. equal to the maximum rate of profit of the system. If both the total labour force and the value of the net product are now made equal to unity (so that the wage rate coincides with the share of wages in the net product), we have

$$r = (1 - w)R \tag{2}$$

where r is the profit rate and w the wage rate. This is the well-known linear factor-price frontier; in this case a change of r does affect **p**, though it does not affect R.

The essence of Sraffa's exposition was here to observe that relation (2) does not hold in the standard system only, but is of general validity;[9] whenever the wage rate is *measured* in terms of the net product of the standard system that can be associated with the system actually given, whatever it may be, the relation between the distributive variables will be linear and independent of the relative prices of commodities.

No restriction is laid upon the actual commodity composition of the wage:

[8] 'The possibility of speaking of a ratio between two collections of miscellaneous commodities without need of reducing them to the common measure of price arises of course from the circumstance that both collections are made up in the same proportions—from their being in fact quantities of the same composite commodity' (Sraffa, 1960, p. 21).

[9] The question is 'whether the decisive role which the Standard commodity plays in this connection lies in its being the constituent material of the national income and of the means of production ... or in its supplying the medium in which wages are estimated. For the latter is a function which the appropriate Standard commodity can fulfil in any case, whether the system is in the Standard proportions or not.' It is necessary to observe that 'the actual system consists of the same basic equations as the Standard, only in different proportions; so that, once the wage is given, the rate of profits is determined for both systems regardless of the proportions of the equations in either of them. Particular proportions, such as the Standard ones, may give transparency to a system and render visible what was hidden, but they cannot alter its mathematical properties' (Sraffa, 1960, pp. 22–3).

that a *macro*economic relation, such as the one between the wage and profit rate, appears to emerge, undisturbed by the price vector, is a matter of sheer measurement in terms of a special kind of composite commodity.

This very property has been recently exploited by Professor Hollander (1979, ch. 6, esp. pp. 304–5), in order to show that, even in a Sraffian system, from the standpoint of *process analysis*, in no sense are income distribution and relative prices independent. Nothing can conceal the fundamental fact that the distributive variables and prices are aspects and outcomes of a unique general equilibrium process. Whenever the wage rate is changed, if factor proportions are different, the corresponding change to a new equilibrium profit rate is brought about through variations in the system of relative prices and accompanying reallocation of resources.

'Assuming a general wage increase,' Hollander explains,

> then at *given prices* the profit rate must decline across the board; the decline will evidently be sharper in 'labour-intensive' than in 'capital-intensive' industries, and, accordingly, reallocation of resources between sectors will be set in motion to assure equalization of the return on capital. In the new equilibrium the prices of commodities produced by labour-intensive processes will have risen relatively to those produced by capital-intensive processes and the profit rate will again be equalized everywhere, but at a lower level than in the initial equilibrium. (Hollander, 1979, p. 303)

What this seems to imply is that, with fixed coefficients of production at the industry level, the fundamental relationship between labour and means of production still remains one of substitution, operating through output composition effects, in the system as a whole. The same argument also leads Professor Hollander to emphasize the result that—except for the case of uniform factor proportions—there is 'no way of avoiding the logical conclusion that a change in the pattern of demand may affect the wage rate' (Hollander, 1979, p. 300), and that 'a general wage change will generate differential effects on costs, thus disturbing the profit structure at going prices and setting in motion a corrective process, the outcome of which is a new price structure and a new general level of profits' (pp. 302–3). The function of a perfect measure of value can only be to make a correct 'prediction' easier on the distributive variables and the relative price system, by cutting through, as it were, the complicated interrelations of prices and factor rates; but this can in no way alter the 'actual adjustment process' (p. 304):[10] indeed, it has nothing to do with the latter.

---

[10] 'Ricardo could not possibly have believed that the matter of distribution is somehow solved prior to that of relative price, as modern interpreters suggest, in the light of his own insistence upon the operational significance of profit rate differentials' (Hollander, 1979, p. 304).

Let us recall at once that there is an obvious link between Sraffa's standard system and Dmitriev's defence of the Ricardian system. Both share the feature of exhibiting the rate of profit as a ratio of *physical* quantities of a commodity, this being a staple food for Dmitriev and a composite commodity of a peculiar kind for Sraffa. The difference between the two authors is that, while for Dmitriev the commodity composition of the wage is given, no such restriction applies to Sraffa, who makes use of the standard commodity only as a measuring device and introduces the standard system merely as an auxiliary construction.

Further, it should be noted that Sraffa's standard system is complementary to his own peculiar interpretation of the development of Ricardo's analytical framework.[11] The discussion of the properties of the standard system seems to suggest itself as the natural development of Ricardo's preoccupation with the problem of determining a rate of surplus undisturbed by variations in relative prices. This separation between distribution and pricing is, according to Sraffa, the theoretical aim that inspired Ricardo, from his early numerical tables (his 'corn model') to his recourse and continuous adherence to the labour theory of value and down to his well-known extensive changes in the chapter 'On Value' in the *Principles*. I shall presently argue that, as a positive contribution to Ricardo's scholarship, this interpretation has derived its force from two circumstances: first, that it provided ground for justifiable opposition to a traditional—largely Marshallian—reconstruction on the meaning and significance of Ricardo's theory of value; second, that Sraffa's construction faces the Marxian surplus problem. Marx expressed admiration for the beautiful simplicity of the surplus approach in Quesnay,[12] and one is tempted to suppose that he would not have refrained from enthusiasm before Sraffa's more ingenious system. There is a sense in which such a system offers a picture of Ricardo that Marx might have found more attractive than Ricardo himself.[13]

If Marshall may have failed to do full justice to Ricardo (perhaps running into an excess of the generosity he had himself recommended in reading Ricardo—cf. 1961, vol. I, p. 813), subsequent commentators would seem to have experienced even greater difficulties in facing their task. Professor Hollander's recent case appears to be no exception in this respect. He insists on a Marshallian interrelation of demand, supply and pricing, where income distribution is an *aspect* of the pricing process; a relevant aspect indeed, on

---

[11] Expounded at length in his Introduction to Ricardo's *Principles* (see Ricardo, *Works*, vol. I, pp. xxx–xlix).

[12] Marx (1965–8); cf. also Sraffa (1960, p. 93), quoted below.

[13] The Marxian connection explains the stout defence made by some neo-Ricardians of the Sraffian interpretation on the development of Ricardo's thought. Cf. Garegnani (1982), Bharadwaj (1983). On the weakness of that interpretation, see Hollander (1979). My article (Porta, 1982) on the Ricardian foundations of Marxism discusses the issue at greater length.

which Ricardo would wish to focus particularly. Ricardo's fundamental theorem on distribution emerges as an inseparable part of the *general equilibrium* setup of his system. However, it has always proved difficult to trace Ricardo's own words an *analytical* general equilibrium system. We shall presently see some special difficulties that seem to be encountered by Professor Hollander in his recent re-interpretation of Ricardo.

4 DAVID RICARDO AND THE CLOSE OF HIS SYSTEM

It is here conjectured that Ricardo may soon cease to be all things to all men. Ricardo has long enjoyed a special position in the history of economic theory, as a result of a method of analysis that gave overwhelming importance to developing the supposed 'rationale' of his system, so confining the textual basis (however accurate and sophisticated) of the analysis to a subsidiary role (cf., e.g., *Works*, vol. I, p. xxxi, and Hollander, 1979, p. 679).

In what follows we shall attempt to discover where recent interpreters may have gone off the track in this respect; I shall consequently restate the analytical core of the Ricardian system and see whether we can still be satisfied that the system is determinate.

Piero Sraffa bases his own positive contribution to the interpretation of Ricardo on the so-called 'corn-ratio theory of profits' (*Works*, vol. XI, p. 20). This was 'never explicitly stated by Ricardo', says Sraffa (vol. I, p. xxxi), but it outlines 'the problem of value which interested Ricardo', i.e. 'how to find a measure of value which would be invariant to changes in the division of the product' (vol. I, p. xlviii). 'If a rise or fall of wages by itself brought about a change in the magnitude of the social product, it would be hard to determine accurately the effect on profits.' 'This was of course,' Sraffa adds, 'the same problem as has been mentioned earlier in connection with Ricardo's corn-ratio theory of profits' (vol. I, p. xlviii).

In this way an analogy can be established between Ricardo's one-commodity model (the so-called 'corn model') and Sraffa's standard system: the analogy, however, conceals the fact that in the latter the technology of the system is given, contrary to the former, where attention is focused (although the case of a 'corn model' admittedly is a very special one) on the principle of diminishing returns in agriculture. It is to be recalled that it would be '*impossible*'—as is rightly emphasized by Professor Caravale (1982, section 4; italics added)—to distinguish, in Ricardo, the problem of alternative distributive setups from that of changes in technology. Ricardo found it convenient to describe the principle of diminishing returns by means of numerical examples in pure quantity terms. However, his correspondence and published writings show that he was uninterested in a full discussion of the particular assumptions underlying such special examples, as these particular assumptions were of no theoretical interest in themselves; rather, he would be led to appreciate and discuss the significance of the embodied labour principle as a measure of value, which enabled him to take full advantage of his newly discovered theory of rent. Ricardo's 'agricultural' language is suggested quite simply by the need to emphasize the diminishing-returns principle in the production of wage goods,[14] the significance of which extends beyond a single industry to the system as a whole and provides the basis for the inverse relationship between the money-wage rate and the profit rate.

What seems important to appreciate is that Ricardo's agricultural language *and* the introduction of the labour theory of value, on one side, and his discussion on the limits of the labour theory of value, on the other, belong to two separate contexts. The first group of elements comes into the picture in order to establish Ricardo's theoretical model based on diminishing returns; the second belongs to his effort to eliminate the possibility that value be dependent on wages. (Ricardo's effort to eliminate such a possibility was justified by the fact that *this* was the very criticism he directed against Adam Smith's theory of value, and from which he would have liked his own theory to be free.)[15] Sraffa's interpretation makes a peculiar mixture of the two elements; and, drawing on the particular cases built by Ricardo in order to explore the impact of the exceptions to his theory of value, he infers that we should conceive Ricardo to have been exclusively concerned from his early works with the problem of separating distribution from pricing. The fact that this interpretation confines to the background what looms so large in the texts and appeared as most strikingly novel to Ricardo's contemporaries, namely his application of the principle of diminishing returns, seems to provide sufficient ground to cast doubts on its validity (see Porta, 1978). On the other hand, I should emphasize that there are strong *theoretical* reasons to justify Sraffa's analysis. In the first place, it shows that, contrary to a traditional (e.g. Marshallian) interpretation, Ricardo's reformulations of the chapter 'On Value' in his *Principles* have nothing to do with the problem of the sources of value, but concern only a measurement problem; second, it applies to some mathematical properties of non-negative matrices income distribution analysis. In Sraffa's own account, 'it was only when the Standard system ... had emerged ... that the above interpretation [i.e. the corn-ratio theory of profits] of Ricardo's theory suggested itself as a natural conse-

---

[14] The expression 'wage goods', in this context, is not meant to imply that the wage rate is made up of a composite commodity in a definite quantity; it is only used in the looser sense that commodities subject to diminishing returns in production must appear in the consumption basket of the worker.

[15] The fundamental problem of value that interested Ricardo was to free his own theory from the *petitio principii* affecting Smith's theory. It is perhaps significant to note, in particular, that the *petitio principii* argument also provides Ricardo's starting point to his much quoted discussion of value at the very end of his life (see Ricardo, 1979).

quence', which perhaps gives a rather obvious clue to the un-Ricardian character of the interpretation itself. Un-Ricardianism is particularly evident for Sraffa's standard commodity, which, being defined for a given technology, 'represents an analytical tool lying outside Ricardo's main scheme of reference': in fact, any 'attempt to use the standard commodity in the Ricardian framework does not appear to be fruitful' (Caravale and Tosato, 1980, esp. pp. 83, 85).

Professor Hollander, on the other hand (1979, p. 304), offers an explanation of actual adjustment processes and of the 'causal mechanisms' through which they are supposed to operate. The process is supposed to work, as Ricardo himself envisaged, in a case in which profits are disturbed and rendered unequal in different trades by taxation, through capital being removed from one employment to another and relative prices being altered (Hollander, 1979, p. 273). Ricardo, in 'Taxes on Profits' (*Works*, vol. 1, pp. 207–10), argues that, in the case of different factor proportions from industry to industry, a tax on income will alter relative prices. He goes on to consider that, in the absence of taxation, an abundance of money will raise the prices of all commodities in the same proportion. 'But,' he adds,

> this is no longer true when any of these commodities is taxed; if in that case they should all rise in proportion to the fall in the value of money, profits would be rendered unequal; in the case of the commodity taxed, profits would be raised above the general level, and capital would be removed from one employment to another, till an equilibrium of profits was restored, which could only be, after the relative prices were altered.

'The extension to the problem of a wage change would have been very simple,' Hollander comments (1979, p. 303).

However, there is no evidence that Ricardo wished to pursue this line of analysis. That the extension would be 'very simple' is a statement relevant to present-day general equilibrium analysis, having little to do with the discussion of the essential architecture of the Ricardian system. (This point is further discussed in the appendix to this paper.) Like Smith, from whom he took the idea of resource allocation in a general competitive equilibrium, Ricardo simply did not work out in detail the full analysis of equilibrium for the system as a whole, and it is no wonder that it should prove almost impossible to go beyond rather general—though suggestive—statements of his on that matter. It might be more fruitful—and perhaps not too far even from Hollander's own perspective—to see to what extent *Sraffa's* analysis, as a piece of general equilibrium theory, can be brought beyond comparative statics and supplemented with what Hollander likes to call 'process analysis'.

Hollander's illustrations of 'process analysis' are taken from a number of cases. Some of them involve a change in technology while others do not; it would seem more appropriate, however, to distinguish the cases where the cost conditions of a particular industry are subject to change from those in which there is a temporary divergence between price and marginal costs. As we shall see in dealing with the case of the labour market and the fix-wage model, on the second type of cases Ricardo contributes a clear piece of market equilibrium analysis, while for cases of the first type Ricardo's growth model, exhibiting convergence to the stationary state, is his outstanding analytical contribution. Both of these instances are curiously underrated by Professor Hollander, evidently absorbed in the discussion of other more difficult points, such as the analysis of equilibrating mechanisms in a multi-market framework.

It would be wrong to underestimate the role of demand in Ricardo's theory; but the Marshallian defence of Ricardo must operate basically through the simple working of the principle of diminishing returns, rather than through Professor Hollander's more complex output composition and price effects in a multi-market equilibrium model. In Ricardo's theory the demand for the product of the increasing cost industry determines its price; the interrelations of the different parts of the system are the context in which some transmission mechanisms are discussed. As a suggestion for a general equilibrium theory, Ricardo's analysis proved fruitful and full of interest. Ricardo considered as obvious the relaxation of the particular assumptions on which his own 'strong cases' were built, but was unable to supply the *analysis* required for full generalization. There is the danger that, in tracing the seeds of subsequent developments to all their implications, we lose sight of precisely the new elements of an analytical system, such as they emerged historically. In the case at hand, this would condemn to growing sterility any subsequent stage of the debate on the Ricardo problem, in sharp contrast to the increasingly extended use of highly sophisticated scholarship.[16]

5 THE FIX-WAGE MODEL

Walras said that the classical economists in their theory determined the wage directly. Professor Hollander's recent reappraisal of Ricardo's economics insists at length that Ricardo did not have what he calls a fix-wage model, i.e. one 'in which *w* (the *real* wage) is given' (cf. Hicks, 1973, p. 48).

The importance that Professor Hollander attaches to this point is connected with his notion of the role of the forces of demand and supply in the determination of wages: 'It is clear that wages are treated as a (variable) price

[16] Some recent contributions to the debate seem to offer evidence in that sense and induce to suspect that a prophecy of this kind may come close to the truth: cf. Garegnani (1982), Bharadwaj (1983) and the exchanges between Garegnani and Hollander in the *Cambridge Journal of Economics* (1983) and between Roncaglia and Hollander in the *Journal of Post-Keynesian Economics* (1982).

determined by demand–supply relations; it is not the case that Ricardian theory is of the fix-wage variety' (Hollander, 1979, p. 679).

However, one finds little justification for this view, and it is not difficult to demonstrate that the so-called fix-wage model is not based upon an exogenous determination of the wage more than the model proposed by other commentators. The strong defence of the latter made by Professor Hollander and other self-styled supporters of the 'New View' on Ricardo appears to be directed at a relatively minor point. That Ricardo himself appeared quite prepared to admit both views, coupled with his frequent switch from the fix-wage model to the 'New View', would seem to offer no interpretative puzzle (*Works*, vol. II, p. 268, Note 171). Both models entail the application of a supply and demand equilibrium analysis; in Ricardo's explanation the natural wage is in any case the outcome of an equilibrating process.[17]

As the demand for people increases with the accumulation of capital, the commodity market wage rate increases: the only interpretative difference between the two approaches lies in the speed of the supply response. The fix-wage model provides an example of pure market equilibrium analysis and of its stability, taking place under a given cost structure of production (see Pasinetti, 1974, p. 13 and appendix; also Samuelson, 1978); in the alternative model the cost structure of production may change while the system works out its solution of natural values. So the fix-wage model really provides the foundation of Ricardo's theory of market equilibrium; although evidently Ricardo admitted that a change in the cost structure of production may interfere with that process. The two demand and supply equilibrium processes are then no longer separable, and natural values are attained only at the stationary state. A closely similar argument is consistently implied by Ricardo on the natural and market price of commodities: when supply can and is allowed sufficient time to adjust, given the state of demand, natural price sinks to a level with (marginal) cost of production.[18] This strict analogy is emphasized in one of Ricardo's *Notes on Malthus*: 'The natural price of corn is the price at which it can be supplied affording the usual profits. With every demand for an increased quantity it will rise above this price therefore if capital and population regularly increase the market price may for years exceed its natural price' (*Works*, vol. II, pp. 227–8, Note 145).

6 THE CORN MODEL

It is among Hollander's merits to have drawn attention to the absence of a 'corn model' in Ricardo (Hollander, 1973). Despite the strenuous defence

---

[17] Recent literature on the issue includes Casarosa (1978), Hicks and Hollander (1977). See also Casarosa's more recent paper in this volume and Pasinetti's *Comment* in Baranzini (1982).

[18] *Principles*, ch. XXX (*see Works*, vol. 1, pp. 382ff); also *Notes on Malthus*, Note 9 (*Works*, vol. II, pp. 24–5).

made by some authors (Garegnani, 1982; Bharadwaj, 1983), it would be extremely difficult to deny the poor textual basis of the so-called 'corn ratio theory of profits'. Dr Bharadwaj in particular (1983) recalls a number of cases in which Ricardo's main correspondent, Robert Malthus, speaks of a material rate of produce (p. 19, n. 2). A few paragraphs later (p. 21) she adds: 'That Ricardo himself must have continued to found his theory on the "material rate of produce" proposition is evident when Malthus in his letter of 5 August protests: "In no case of production is the produce exactly of the same nature of capital advanced. Consequently we can never properly refer to a material rate of produce, independent of demand, and of the abundance of capital."' The last nine words are emphasized by Dr Bharadwaj, who adds: this 'confirms that Ricardo maintained such an independence'. The statement appears to imply Sraffa's conjecture that Malthus's expressions are an echo of Ricardo's own formulations, not to be found in any of Ricardo's extant papers, and probably made use of by him in conversation.

However, there is little basis for this conjecture: in view of the simplicity of the statement involved and of the elaborate treatment of the subject by Ricardo in writing, it is difficult to resist the idea that Ricardo would have said so directly, if only he had wished to. It may well be closer to the truth to suppose that Malthus makes use of the case of the 'corn model' only to show the *extreme* and *particular* case, which Ricardo would be in *constant* need to resort to (in Malthus's view),[19] in order to maintain his proposition of an inverse wage–profit relationship, which was the real question behind the current discussion of the two authors on trade restrictions. On the other hand, Malthus's last nine words merely reflect and repeat *his own* theoretical emphasis, not Ricardo's. Note moreover that, when Ricardo actually resorts to an agricultural form of his theory, he does so either to summarize the contrast of his position with Malthus's opinion (cf. his letter to Trower of 8 March 1814) or to enable him to present his argument in a particularly forceful fashion (cf. his table in the *Essay* and his argument against the lead taken by the profits of commerce) (Porta, 1978, pp. 457–9). How and why should he deem natural to hold a material theory of profit (as a more general foundation of particular statements) has never been explained.

As a matter of fact, throughout the extensive 1814 correspondence, Ricardo's reasoning lends no support to his supposed attachment to the precious little idea of a corn model as his 'guiding principle'. It is simply no more than a useful example.

Let us recall first of all that Malthus's phrase 'rate of produce' came from an attempt to interpret Ricardo's assertion that 'the rate of profit and of

---

[19] 'But *you must mean* [my emphasis] that it is the *rate* of production, not the absolute quantity of produce, which determines profits', Malthus writes in his first extant statement on the matter (6 July 1814, *Works*, vol. VI, p. 111). See below.

interest must depend on the proportion of production to the consumption necessary to such production' (*Works*, vol. VI, p. 108): 'But you must mean,' Malthus replied, 'that it is the *rate* of production, not the absolute quantity of produce which determines profits.' Malthus, however, who held the view that Ricardo's assertion did not solve the controversy, pressed for further clarification and wrote: 'It is not the *quantity* of produce compared with the expence of production that determines profits (which I think is your proposition), but the exchangeable value or money price of that produce, compared with the money expence of production.' Ricardo in his reply (vol. VI, p. 144) *denies* the former statement ('that it is the *quantity* of produce compared with the expence of production, that determines profits') to reflect his own opinion correctly. Ricardo's statement, that whatever 'augments production compared with the means necessary to that production' will increase profits, thus fits squarely with his future statements on the dependence of profits on wages.[20]

'A rise in the price of raw produce,' Ricardo says,

> may be occasioned by a gradual accumulation of capital which by creating new demands for labour may give a stimulus to population and consequently promote the cultivation or improvement of inferior lands,—but this will not cause profits to rise but to fall, because not only will the rate of wages rise, but more labourers will be employed without affording a proportional return of raw produce. The whole value of the wages paid will be greater compared with the whole value of the raw produce obtained. (*Works*, vol. VI, p. 146; cf. Hollander, 1979, p. 130)

Of course, Ricardo does not make use of the labour theory of value explicitly. But, on the other hand, he never finds it natural to reason *without* 'value'. This is not mere money value: following the discovery of the principle of diminishing returns, one should suggest that the (Smithian) idea creeps into his analysis of a value in terms of labour effort which can be fruitfully combined with that principle. It is clear that Ricardo attempts to explain the link between the price of produce and the profit rate through the direct application of the principle of diminishing returns, and contrasts the effects of the principle with those produced by other causes (bad seasons, fall in the value of money). At the same time, we may note that the reason Ricardo so often talks of agriculture is that in agriculture the operation of the principle of diminishing returns is visible; so Ricardo's habit has nothing to do with his supposed propensity to a surplus approach in pure quantity terms. Of the

---

[20] The significance of these and similar statements in the Ricardo–Malthus correspondence is also emphasized in Ricardo (1983, p. 22, n. 1).

latter, Marx (1965–8, vol. I) actually speaks, in his well-known interpretation of the Physiocrats in *Theorien über den Mehrwert* (see Porta, 1982).

One cannot be sure whether Professor Hollander's extensive reconstruction of the Ricardian system is in every detail fair to Ricardo: but Dr Bharadwaj's treatment is certainly misleading in the picture it gives of Ricardo's attitude as a profit theorist. Such a picture, as is well known, derives from a work by Dmitriev, who, as Bortkiewicz (1906–7) noted, attempted to read Ricardo in that way. But such a reading, Bortkiewicz went on to say, really reflects a *Marxian* problem. Now the question is this: does the latter problem have much bearing on the interpretation of the whole Ricardian system? The answer is that it is not clear why it should. What are the reasons here for giving up the ordinary custom of calling things by their proper names? The knowledge of Marx among economists today seems so improved compared with 30 years ago that there is hardly any reason to disguise Marx in a Ricardian dress.

7 THE ADDING-UP THEORY OF PRICE

A final instance of an inappropriate attribution to Ricardo, first advanced by Sraffa and apparently accepted by Hollander, concerns the so-called 'adding up' of the components theory of price, i.e. the theory whereby wages and profits are conceived as coordinate quantities, which can be regarded as acting upon the value of the product in the same way (see *Works*, vol. I, p. xxxv).

The notion that Smith had opened the way to make wages, profits and rent the sources of value comes from Marx's *Theorien über den Mehrwert* (Marx, 1965–8, vol. II, section X.B.1). As Marx makes clear, the merit of Ricardo's strong insistence on the importance of the labour theory of value is that the latter theory *starts* with value, i.e. makes value prior to distribution.[21] Smith, on the contrary, confines himself to the surface, the mere appearance of things, and simply supposes himself behind the individual capitalist in fixing the cost-price of his own commodity: hence Smith's essential difference from Ricardo on natural price, Marx concludes. Smith's analysis is based upon the erroneous presupposition that wages, profit and rent determine autonomously the value of the commodity. This problem—of the *causes* of value, as it were—is of obvious interest to Marx, who interprets the labour theory of value as a proposition on the source of value.[22] That capital is *productive*

---

[21] Hence, in Marx's view, is the great historical significance of Ricardo for the economic science (1965–8, vol. II, ch. X.A.2).

[22] It is due to Sraffa's 'Introduction' to Ricardo's *Principles* that nowadays nobody any longer doubts that Ricardo's case is different in this respect, as we shall see presently.

of interest is, to Marx, the most complete fetish of the vulgar economy.[23]
Is Smith a vulgar economist? Sraffa's attribution to him of the adding-up
approach obviously leads to the affirmative answer. Marx, on the contrary,
raises the problem, but (as we have recalled above) grants Smith the benefit
of doubt: Smith, he says, is contradictory, and after treating and discovering
the nature of value and surplus value, he comes to represent capital and land
as independent sources of value, which in fact *is* the vulgar approach (Marx,
1965–8, vol. I). The real truth, to Marx, is that capital is productive of value
only as a social relationship, as a violent force against waged labourers, a
force compelling them to do surplus work. But, Marx goes on to argue,
as usually conceived by economists, as accumulated labour in money or
commodities, capital can never be a source of value of commodities, since
labour is *the* source of their value.[24]

Piero Sraffa, in his early years, would emphasize Marshall's theory of real
cost as an adding-up theory of price. Marshall's theory was described by him
in the tradition of the 'vulgar economy':

> Marshall regards the 'real cost of production' of a commodity as the sum of
> 'efforts and sacrifices' involved in the abstinences or waitings and in the
> labour of all kinds that is directly or indirectly required for the
> production of a commodity ... . For Marshall, wages, interest and
> profits, are ... coordinate quantities, that can be regarded as acting
> upon the value of the product in the same way. Both are the inducement
> required to call forth certain sacrifices, which are equally necessary for
> production.[25]

Sraffa evidently appears to have been influenced by Marshall's conviction
that the analysis of the concept of real cost of production as a long-run theory

---

[23] Marx, 1965–8, vol. III, appendix on 'Revenue and its Sources'. For a similar forceful remark
on the error of adding up the component parts to obtain value see Marx's popular lecture on
Value, Price and Profit, section 9.

[24] This outlines Marx's basic dogma. Professor Steindl finds it 'regrettable that most of the
renaissance of Marx ... concentrated on the theory of value', thus giving rise to a static theory
of the general equilibrium kind. Nothing of what is being said in this paper on the Marxian
inspiration of Sraffa should be interpreted as a judgement on whether Sraffa's analysis does cover
all the aspects of Marx's theory in an exhaustive way. Surely Marx's legacy is much richer and
more complex. That Sraffa is not—in style and content—fully a Marxian in modern dress seems
sufficiently obvious: cf. 'Reflections on the Present State of Economics', *Banca Nazionale del
Lavoro Quarterly Review*, March 1984, pp. 12–13. Further discussion of the adding-up theory
in Marx can be found in the last section ('Revenue and its sources') of *Das Kapital*, vol. III
(a section including ch. 48 on the trinitarian formula, chs. 49–50 on the process of production and
on competition). Their discussion is deliberately omitted here for the sake of brevity; but any
scholar of the adding-up approach must of course take notice of them.

[25] P. Sraffa, 'Lectures on the Advanced Theory of Value', 1928–9; quoted from MS by courtesy
of the late Professor Sraffa.

of price should be traced to the classical economists; while Marshall insisted on Ricardo as the source of the theory, Sraffa, on the contrary, reads the theory itself in Smith and describes Ricardo as a critic of Smith on the issue.

In this particular case, Marshall was certainly unjustified in attributing to Ricardo an adding-up conception (in Sraffa's sense) of the cost of production theory that was, in fact, too close to his own. But here again we have a case of overreaction, when Sraffa reads in Ricardo a *criticism* of the adding-up approach (*Works*, vol. I, p. xxxv). An adding-up theory makes its appearance largely as an alternative to the Marxian approach to value, and historically can bear no relationship with the Ricardian system.[26] Moreover, we should note that it is among Sraffa's merits to have shown that Ricardo neither conceived labour to be the sole source of value, nor maintained any adding-up theory of price. So it is surprising that, in his argument, Sraffa goes so far as to depict Ricardo as a positive opponent of an adding-up theory, i.e. of Marshall's theory![27] This particular argument in fact conflicts with Sraffa's main thesis that Ricardo was not concerned with finding the source of value, which is a typical Marxian problem and one that we may safely assume not to have unduly troubled the English classical economists' minds. More extraordinary perhaps is the fact that the point should have passed without discussion into Professor Hollander's book (see Hollander, 1979, pp. 284, 675).

It seems clear that at no time did Ricardo intend to affirm that prices reflect the labour input alone; nor, on the other hand, did he analyse the effects on output of different production periods. Böhm-Bawerk's remark still seems to apply, that with Ricardo and Adam Smith the theory of interest is in its primitive state (see Böhm-Bawerk, 1959, vol. I, pp. 49, 59). We can again observe that it does contain the raw seeds of opposite theories, though still undeveloped, and that it would be inappropriate to read subsequent theoretical formulations in their work (see also Ricardo, 1984, p. 12).

8 CONCLUDING REMARKS

The necessary determinants of equilibrium are analysed in the Ricardian system and it is easy to see the importance of demand and supply analysis in

[26] Marx devoted much effort of his positivistic mind to the attempt to provide a sound scientific basis to the concept of 'exploitation'. Unfortunately, he did so on the basis of the labour theory of value. To modern Marxian economics it is still an open question whether there is any other way to achieve that result.

[27] Curiously, quite a number of commentators share this view. See for instance K. Bharadwaj (1978), who writes (correctly) that Ricardo's inclusion of profits in the cost of production is a matter of 'definition, not a *theory* of the determination of value' (p. 257); a few pages later, however, she adds that 'Ricardo was aware of the difference in approach' of 'treating labour and time as two independent causes of value' (p. 270), thus implying Ricardo's positive rejection of the Marshallian approach.

that system. However, this does not mean that Ricardo developed a multi-market equilibrium analytical model. Such a model was developed later in history. Again, the fact that general equilibrium allocative analysis is not at variance with the Ricardian (and Smithian) system does not imply that it was actually developed by Ricardo; in particular, on multi-market equilibrium we may assume that Ricardo did not proceed much beyond Adam Smith's analysis.

APPENDIX

This appendix briefly develops the point made above (p. 226) that Hollander's picture of Ricardian general equilibrium analysis receives so little support from the texts that it should, perhaps more correctly, be viewed as a proposition of present-day general equilibrium analysis. As a statement of general equilibrium analysis, however, Hollander's suggestion is far from complete. So his statement remains suspended halfway, as it were, between the reconstruction of the Ricardian system and the contribution to contemporary analysis, without (as sometimes happens) being entirely consistent with either context.

The link between the principle of profit rate equalization through supply variations and the assumption of different factor proportions should be further specified in order to bring out the mechanism through which output variations and price movements are supposed to operate. Not every general equilibrium system would exhibit such features as are presumably desirable in Hollander's view. A linear general equilibrium system will provide an easy counter-example to Hollander's sweeping statement.

Consider the following system

$$\frac{1}{1+\pi}\mathbf{p} = \mathbf{p}\mathbf{A}$$

where $\mathbf{p}$ is the price vector, $\mathbf{A} \geqslant 0$ the (indecomposable) matrix of technical coefficients. There exists a unique $\lambda = 1/(1+\pi) > 0$ real, such that

$$\mathbf{p}^*\mathbf{A} = \lambda\mathbf{p}^*. \quad (\mathbf{p}^* > 0) \tag{A1}$$

If $\lambda < 1$ the system is viable $(\pi > 0)$.

Consider the following dynamic process of price formation through time:

$$\mathbf{p}(t+1) = \mathbf{p}(t)\frac{\mathbf{A}}{\lambda}. \tag{A2}$$

The solution of (A1) is

$$\mathbf{p}(t) = \mathbf{p}(0)\frac{\mathbf{A}^t}{\lambda^t}$$

which converges to $\mathbf{p}^*$ (see also, e.g. Morishima, 1964, ch. VI). In this instance, without mentioning the quantity system, result (A1) is achieved (to the limit), starting with any vector $\mathbf{p}(0)$ with economic meaning, thus demonstrating the stability of the given system.

Consider further the following Sraffian system:

$$\mathbf{p} = \mathbf{p}\mathbf{A}(1+\pi) + \mathbf{a}_n w \qquad (A3)$$

where $\mathbf{p}$ is the price vector, $\mathbf{A} \geqslant 0$ the matrix of technical coefficients, $\mathbf{a}_n \geqslant 0$ the vector of labour inputs; $\pi \geqq 0$, $w \geqq 0$ are the wage rate (posticipated) and profit rate respectively, to be considered as parameters of the system. Suppose in particular $\pi > 0$, $w > 0$.

The solution of system (A3) is as follows:

$$\mathbf{p} = \mathbf{a}_n w\{\mathbf{I} - (1+\pi)\mathbf{A}\}^{-1}. \qquad (A4)$$

The conditions of existence of $\{\mathbf{I} - (1+\pi)\mathbf{A}\}^{-1} \geqq 0$ (granting that the solution itself is economically meaningful) are the well-known viability conditions of system (A3). Observe that:

$$\{\mathbf{I} - (1+\pi)\mathbf{A}\}^{-1} = [(1+\pi)\{(1+\pi)^{-1}\mathbf{I} - \mathbf{A}\}]^{-1}$$
$$= [\hat{\mathbf{R}}\{(1+\pi)^{-1}\mathbf{I} - \mathbf{A}\}]^{-1} = \{(1+\pi)^{-1}\mathbf{I} - \mathbf{A}\}^{-1}\hat{\mathbf{R}}^{-1}$$

where $\hat{\mathbf{R}}$ is the diagonal matrix with elements $(1+\pi)\delta_{ij}$ (δ_{ij} is Kronecker's delta).

Finally:

$$\{\mathbf{I} - (1+\pi)\mathbf{A}\}^{-1} = (1+\pi)^{-1}\{(1+\pi)^{-1}\mathbf{I} - \mathbf{A}\}^{-1}.$$

The subset of real numbers $(1+\pi)^{-1}$ for which $\{(1+\pi)^{-1}\mathbf{I} - \mathbf{A}\}^{-1} \geqq 0$ is known to be the semi-interval $\{\lambda(\mathbf{A}), +\infty\}$, where $\lambda(\mathbf{A}) \geqslant 0$ is the maximum eigenvalue of $\mathbf{A}$. Therefore the relevant viability condition is

$$(1+\pi)^{-1} > \lambda(\mathbf{A})$$

and, if $\lambda(\mathbf{A}) > 0$, we obtain

$$-1 < \pi < \frac{1-\lambda}{\lambda}.$$

Suppose now the wage rate to change from w_0 to w_1. Divide time into periods: $T = \{1, 2, \ldots, t, \ldots\}$ and imagine prices at time $(t+1)$ to reflect costs in each sector at time t. The following system would reflect a stationary equilibrium:

$$\mathbf{p}_{t+1}' = \mathbf{p}_t = \mathbf{p}_t \mathbf{A}(1+\pi) + \mathbf{a}_n w_0$$

When, at time $\dot{t}$, the wage rate changes from w_0 to w_1, we have:

$$\mathbf{p}_{\dot{t}+1} = \mathbf{p}_{\dot{t}} \mathbf{A}(1+\pi) + \mathbf{a}_n w_1.$$

$$\begin{aligned}
\mathbf{p}_{\dot{t}+2} &= \mathbf{p}_{\dot{t}+1} \mathbf{A}(1+\pi) + \mathbf{a}_n w_1 \\
&= \{\mathbf{p}_{\dot{t}} \mathbf{A}(1+\pi) + \mathbf{a}_n w_1\} \mathbf{A}(1+\pi) + \mathbf{a}_n w_1 \\
&= \mathbf{p}_{\dot{t}} \mathbf{A}^2 (1+\pi)^2 + \mathbf{a}_n w_1 \mathbf{A}(1+\pi) + \mathbf{a}_n w_1.
\end{aligned}$$

$$\begin{aligned}
\mathbf{p}_{\dot{t}+s} &= \mathbf{p}_{\dot{t}} \mathbf{A}^s (1+\pi)^s + \mathbf{a}_n w_1 \mathbf{A}^{s-1} (1+\pi)^{s-1} + \ldots \\
&\quad + \mathbf{a}_n w_1 \mathbf{A}(1+\pi) + \mathbf{a}_n w_1 \mathbf{A}^0 (1+\pi)^0 \\
&= \mathbf{p}_{\dot{t}} \mathbf{A}^s (1+\pi)^s + \mathbf{a}_n w_1 \left\{ \sum_{k=0}^{s-1} (1+\pi)^k \mathbf{A}^k \right\}.
\end{aligned}$$

Passing to the limit, and recalling that

$$\mathbf{A}^s (1+\pi)^s \to 0$$

and that

$$\sum_{k=0}^{s-1} (1+\pi)^k \mathbf{A}^k = \{\mathbf{I} - (1+\pi)\mathbf{A}\}^{-1}$$

we obtain

$$\mathbf{p} = \lim \mathbf{p}_{\dot{t}+s} = \mathbf{a}_n w_1 \{\mathbf{I} - (1+\pi)\mathbf{A}\}^{-1}.$$

So the solution of our Sraffian system is shown to be stable independently of the level attained by each activity. Given the technique, there is no definite correspondence between changes in the gross output vector and changes in the wage rate. What Hollander seems to have in mind (see above pp. 222 and 226) is to show that *Sraffa's* results on relative prices (when distribution changes) are in any case to be read as the outcome of an equilibrating process through resource allocation, as is customary (though by no means necessary) in general equilibrium analysis. This specific point, however, cannot be directly established with the aid of Ricardo's texts and furthermore cannot be proved for the general equilibrium system of the Sraffian description, as

Hollander appears to expect. Finally, the outlined argument shows the impassable obstacles that are encountered when attempting to attribute directly to Ricardo a system in general equilibrium analysis.

REFERENCES

Baranzini, M. (ed.) (1982). *Advances in Economic Theory*. Oxford: Basil Blackwell.

Bharadwaj, K. (1978). 'The Subversion of Classical Analysis: Alfred Marshall's Early Writing on Value'. *Cambridge Journal of Economics*, 2, 253–71.

Bharadwaj, K. (1983). 'On a Controversy over Ricardo's Theory of Distribution'. *Cambridge Journal of Economics*, 7, 11–36.

Blaug, M. (1983). 'Ricardo e il problema della politica economica'. *Rivista di politica economica*, 73, n.s., 899–917.

Böhm-Bawerk, E. von (1959). *Capital and Interest* (3 vols) (translation of *Kapital und Kapitalzins*, fourth edn, Jena, G. Fisher, 1921). South Holland: Libertarian Press.

Bortkiewicz, L. von (1906–7). 'Wertrechnung und Preisrechnung im Marxschen System'. *Archiv für Sozialwissenschaft und Sozialpolitik*, vol. 23, 1–50; vol. 25, 10–51 and 445–88.

Caravale, G. (1981). 'Notes on Ricardo's Problem of Value, Distribution and Growth'. Unpublished paper.

Caravale, G. (1982). 'Note sulla teoria ricardiana del valore, della distribuzione e dello sviluppo'. *Giornale degli economisti e annali di economia*, 41, n.s., 141–83.

Caravale, G. and Tosato, D. (1980). *Ricardo and the Theory of Value, Distribution and Growth*. London: Routledge & Kegan Paul.

Casarosa, C. (1978). 'A New Formulation of the Ricardian System'. *Oxford Economic Papers*, 30, 38–63.

Casarosa, C. (1982). 'The New View of Ricardian Theory', in Baranzini (1982).

Dmitriev, V. K. (1974). *Economic Essays*, ed. D. M. Nuti (first published in 1904). Cambridge: CUP.

Garegnani, P. (1982). 'On Hollander's Interpretation of Ricardo's Early Theory of Profits'. *Cambridge Journal of Economics*, 6, 65–77.

Hicks, J. R. (1973). *Capital and Time*. Oxford: Clarendon Press.

Hicks, J. R. and Hollander, S. (1977). 'Mr Ricardo and the Moderns'. *Quarterly Journal of Economics*, 91, 351–69.

Hollander, S. (1973). 'Ricardo's Analysis of the Profit Rate'. *Economica*, 40, n.s., 260–82.

Hollander, S. (1979). *The Economics of David Ricardo*. London: Heinemann.

Marshall, A. (1961). *Principles of Economics* (9th (variorum) edn), ed. C. W. Guillebaud (2 vols). London: Macmillan.

Marx, K. (1965–8). *Theorien über den Mehrwert* (Vierter Band des 'Kapitals'). In *Karl Marx–Friedrich Engels Werke*, vol. XXVI, Berlin: Dietz Verlag.

Morishima, M. (1964). *Equilibrium, Stability and Growth*. London: Oxford University Press.

O'Brien, D. P. (1981). 'Ricardian Economics and the Economics of David Ricardo'. *Oxford Economic Papers*, 33, 352–86.

Pasinetti, L. L. (1974). *Growth and Income Distribution.* Cambridge: CUP.

Pasinetti, L. L. (1982). 'A Comment on the "New View" of the Ricardian Theory', in Baranzini (1982).

Porta, P. L. (1978). 'Il dibattito tra Ricardo e Malthus: aspetti di teoria del valore e della distribuzione'. *Giornale degli economisti e annali di economia,* 37, n.s., 317–44 and 453–68.

Porta, P. L. (1979). 'Ricardo'. Unpublished paper.

Porta, P. L. (1982). 'I fondamenti ricardiani del marxismo'. *Giornale degli economisti e annali di economia,* 41, n.s., 721–40.

Rankin, S. C. (1980). 'Supply and Demand in Ricardian Price Theory: a Reinterpretation. *Oxford Economic Papers,* 32, n.s., 241–62.

Ricardo, D. (1951–73). *Works and Correspondence* (11 vols), ed. P. Sraffa. Cambridge: CUP.

Ricardo, D. (1979). 'Notes on Malthus's *Measure of Value'.* Edited from MS by P. L. Porta. *Rivista internazionale di scienze economiche e commerciali,* 26, 7–35.

Ricardo, D. (1983). *Principi di economia politica e dell' imposta.* Introduzione di Pier Luigi Porta 'Classici dell' economia', collana diretta da G. Di Nardi. Torino: Unione Tipografico-Editrice.

Ricardo, D. (1984). *Note a Malthus e saggi.* Introduzione di Pier Luigi Porta 'Classici dell' economia', collana diretta da G. Di Nardi. Torino: Unione Tipografico-Editrice.

Robertson, H. M. (1957). 'The Ricardo Problem'. *South African Journal of Economics,* 25, 171–86.

Roncaglia, A. (1982). 'Hollander's Ricardo'. *Journal of Post-Keynesian Economics,* 4, 339–59.

Samuelson, P. A. (1978). 'The Canonical Classical Model of Political Economy'. *Journal of Economic Literature,* 16, 1415–34.

Sraffa, P. (1960). *Production of Commodities by Means of Commodities.* Cambridge: CUP.

Walras, L. (1954). *Elements of Pure Economics.* London: Allen & Unwin.

10

The Theory of the Natural Wage

ANNALISA ROSSELLI

Your suggestion of a copious chapter of clear and concise definitions would be of great use, but it requires a degree of precision and accuracy beyond what I could furnish. (Ricardo to Trower, 22 March 1818)

One of the most controversial points in the interpretation of Ricardo concerns his wage theory, and the concept of the 'natural wage' on which that theory is based. Numerous differences of opinion have arisen over the natural wage and its role in Ricardo's analysis, and these divergences have extended to the characteristics of his whole theory of distribution. Thus, the meaning given to the natural wage has become the touchstone for discriminating between the various interpretations.

The controversy goes back to Ricardo's time, but more recently it has developed through a series of mathematical models of growth, each involving a definition of the natural wage that is proposed as the best expression of Ricardo's thought.

The aim of the present study is to contribute to this debate by seeking to clarify the origins of the problem. In this connection the following questions must be considered:

(1) What were the problems in connection with which Ricardo introduced the idea of the natural wage, and what thesis did he aim to prove?
(2) What did Ricardo see as the key aspects distinguishing his theory from others?
(3) What definitions did Ricardo himself propose for the natural wage?

After discussing these points I shall conclude with a few comments on recently proposed Ricardian models.

This paper went through various drafts. I wish to thank C. Benetti, S. Hollander, A. Roncaglia and F. Vianello for their comments on earlier drafts, and G. Caravale and A. Simonazzi for their comments on the present version. The paper greatly benefited from many discussions with M. C. Marcuzzo during long periods of joint working on Ricardian economics.

239

1 THE ORIGIN OF THE THEORY OF WAGES

Ricardo developed his theory of wages within the analysis of the accumulation process and its effects on the rate of profit.

While a wage theory is required for other problems dealt with by Ricardo (taxation of raw produce, taxation of wages), the origins of his wage theory can be found in his demonstration of the falling rate of profit. His thesis is well known: with the process of accumulation, the rate of profit decreases, not because there are fewer opportunities for the employment of capital—as the theory derived from Smith maintained—but because agricultural production becomes more difficult when less fertile lands are brought under cultivation to meet the needs of a growing population.

According to Sraffa's interpretation (1951, pp. xxxi–xxxiii), Ricardo's proof of this thesis was worked out in two distinct phases.[1] These phases are reflected in two different formulations of the argument. The first version appears in the 1814–15 correspondence and in the *Essay on Profits* (February 1815);[2] the second version took shape during the preparation of the first edition of the *Principles* (1817), where it is fully set out. It may be worth mentioning that Ricardo's theory of wages changes concurrently with this development.

The pivot of the analysis is the rate of profit in agriculture, but its role differs in the two versions. In the first line of reasoning the rate of profit in agriculture determines the general rate of profit to which all other sectors must conform. In the second, the rate of profit in agriculture does not play a determining role, although, as the general rate of profit is uniform throughout the system, the rate of profit in agriculture coincides with the general rate.

If we look at Ricardo's system, the rate of profit in agriculture, π, is given by

$$\pi = \frac{p - wL}{wL} \tag{1}$$

where
p = money price of one unit of 'corn'
w = money price of one unit of labour
L = units of labour necessary to produce one unit of corn.
Simplifying Ricardo's argument further, we may assume that there is no fixed capital and that the circulating capital is equal to the wage bill.

[1] This interpretation has been recently disputed. See Hollander (1979, 1983); Garegnani (1982, 1983) and Langer (1982). Much of what will be said about Ricardo's theory of profit in this section is taken from Vianello (1983).

[2] More precisely, the first hints of Ricardo's theory of profits can be found in the letters to Malthus, 10 and 17 August 1813, in Ricardo, *Works* (vol. VI, pp. 92–5).

The money price of corn, the wage rate and the quantity of labour necessary to produce one unit of corn vary with the accumulation process. If we define

α = rate of change for p

β = rate of change for w

γ = rate of change for L

the rate of change of the profit rate, δ, is given by

$$\delta = \alpha - (\beta + \gamma). \tag{2}$$

To prove that the rate of profit falls with the accumulation, it is therefore necessary to prove that $\alpha < \beta + \gamma$, or in other words that the increase in the money price of corn is not large enough to offset the increase in the circulating capital that is necessary to produce corn[3] (see Ricardo's *Works*, vol. IV, p. 13 and the table in vol. IV, p. 17). The money price of corn and the money wage rate may increase at the same rate ($\alpha = \beta$; see vol. IV, p. 36) or the corn wage may even decrease ($\beta < \alpha$): 'The whole amount of wages paid will be greater, but the portion paid to each man, will in all probability, be somewhat diminished' (Ricardo to Malthus, 18 December 1814; vol. VI, p. 163). But the increase in the quantity of labour necessary to production ($\gamma > 0$) will always be such that, even if $\beta < \alpha$, the total increase in circulating capital will be higher than the increase in the price of corn.

In the *Principles*—on the basis of the labour theory of value—Ricardo's argument is refined. The chain of causes and effects supporting the hypothesis is modified. Now the price of corn is determined by the conditions of its production ($\alpha = \gamma$). When there is an increase in the money wage rate, $\beta > 0$, the rate of profit necessarily falls.

The second stage of the argument gives Ricardo's thesis a more general character. What is true for the rate of profit in agriculture is true for the rate of profit in every sector of the economy. The effects of accumulation on the rate of profit become only a particular case. Anything causing an increase in the money wage will have the same effect on the rate of profit: 'if labour rises, no matter from what cause, profits will fall' (vol. VII, p. 57). Hence in order to show that, in the presence of laws restricting imports of low-cost corn, accumulation leads to a decrease in the profit rate, Ricardo had to demonstrate that if the price of corn rises money wages must also rise.

---

[3] Profits and capital are measured in corn

$$\pi = \frac{p - wL}{wL} = \frac{1 - (w/p)L}{(w/p)L}.$$

This does not mean that they are made up of corn, although the circulating capital may be mainly constituted by corn.

Malthus's response is to deny any link between the price of corn and the price of labour. Just as earlier he had opposed Ricardo's thesis on the falling rate of profit by arguing that the price of corn, sustained by favourable demand conditions, could rise more than the costs, he now tried to break the link between the price of labour and the cost of its production—that is, between the price of labour and the price of the agricultural products that constitute most of the wage basket. Allowing for a decrease in the money wage while the price of corn and the labour necessary to its production increase, Malthus wants to prove that the rate of profit does not necessarily fall (i.e., if $\beta < 0$ and $\alpha = \gamma$, then $\alpha > \beta + \gamma$). According to Malthus, the price of corn and the price of labour are determined independently in each market by the conditions ('proportion') of supply and demand. Ricardo notes: 'You appear to me to think ... that money wages may as often rise with facility of production as fall' (Ricardo to Malthus, 14 October 1816; vol. VII, p. 81).

Malthus's attack develops along two complementary lines. On the one hand, an increase in the price of wage goods may or may not bring with it an increase in the money wage rate. The money wage may remain stationary or even decrease (in which case the real wage[4] decreases) as the demand for labour falls short or remains equal to the available supply: 'it appears to me that the money price of corn will rise, ... the money price of labour remain stationary nearly ...' (Malthus to Ricardo, 8 January 1816; vol. VII, p. 9; see also vol. VI, p. 111).

On the other hand, a fall in the price of wage goods may leave the money price of labour unaffected, or may even lead to an increase in the money wage (and therefore an increase in the real wage), if the supply of labour falls short of the demand (see Malthus's letter to Ricardo, 8 September 1816; vol. VII, p. 69; see also vol. VI, p. 225).

Ricardo's answers are always quite firm, though they are not always supported by detailed explanations. He simply states that higher money wages in the presence of a lower price of the wage goods are a 'very peculiar' situation which may be conceivable only if wages are in an 'unusual state' (vol. VII, p. 78). Or, conversely, 'it is impossible to conceive that the money price of wages should fall, or remain stationary with a gradually increasing price of necessaries' (vol. I, p. 118).

Ricardo's point, though scarcely explained, is quite clear. What he tries to do is to set up a scale against which different causes affecting the money wage can be weighed. In no circumstances may imbalances between supply and demand in the labour market offset the effects of changes in the price of wage goods. On the contrary, the money wage rate increases when there is an

---

[4] Throughout this paper 'real wage' means the purchasing power of the money wage. This follows Malthus's usage and not Ricardo's, for whom real wage meant the wage share in the produce of the marginal land.

increase in the price of wage goods, even if there is a fall in the demand
for labour:

> I say that, under these circumstances [i.e. diminishing demand for
> labour], wages would fall, if they were regulated only by the supply
> and demand of labourers; but we must not forget, that wages are
> also regulated by the prices of the commodities on which they are
> expended ... . Instead, therefore, of the money wages of labour falling,
> they would rise ... . (*Works*, vol. I, p. 101)

The fall in the rate of profit is never explained by what happens in the
labour market. This was clearly stated in the *Essay*; but, as we have seen, the
argument provided at that stage relies crucially on an increase in the quantity
of labour necessary to the production of corn, rather than on an increase in
the money wage rate. As demand and supply

> alternately take the lead and wages in consequence are liberal or scanty,
> nothing can be positively laid down, respecting profits, as far as wages
> are concerned.
>   But I think it may be most satisfactorily proved, that in every society
> advancing in wealth and population, independently of the effect pro-
> duced by liberal or scanty wages, general profits must fall ... . (*Works*,
> vol. IV, p. 23)

There is an asymmetry: both causes (the proportion between demand and
supply of labour and the prices of wage goods) affect the wage rate, but only
one of these can counteract the other.

This asymmetry in Ricardo's argument is obscured by his habit of referring
to 'permanent' and 'temporary' causes.[5] It is easy to misunderstand their
meaning as having something to do with time only. And Ricardo has to
defend himself against the charge of overlooking variations in supply and
demand of labour as if they had no effect on wages, or dismissing these as
short-term phenomena.[6]

It is the change in the money price of wage goods that is the sufficient
(but not necessary) condition for a change in money wages. At the beginning
of their correspondence on wages, Ricardo tried to make himself clear to
Malthus:

---

[5] 'the only adequate and permanent cause for the rise of wages is the increasing difficulty of
providing food and necessaries' (vol. I, p. 296); 'there can be no permanent fall of wages but in
consequence of a fall of the necessaries on which wages are expended' (vol. I, p. 132).

[6] 'After the observations of Mr Malthus on the other causes which may affect labour, I must
guard myself against being supposed to deny the effect of those other causes on wages' (vol. II,
p. 291; see also vol. II, pp. 264–5).

Two opposite causes are influencing the price of labour, one the enhanced price of some of the things on which wages are expended,— the other the fewer enjoyments which the labourer will have the power to command,—you think these may balance each other, or rather that the latter will prevail, I on the contrary think the former the most powerful in its effect. I must write a book to convince you. (Ricardo to Malthus, 10 January 1816; vol. VII, p. 10)

However, even the book failed to convince Malthus, who never abandoned the idea of a rigidity in the money wage rate. But this debate, during the months when he was writing the *Principles*, may have induced Ricardo to give a more rigorous form to his ideas, working out a theoretical argument designed to rule out possibilities suggested by Malthus.

2 THE ROLE OF THE NATURAL WAGE

The thesis that Ricardo wished to prove required a wage theory meeting certain important conditions. It will be useful to list these here.

(1) The prevailing wage rate of a system must be determined in real terms, and must be constant over time, so as to provide a clear-cut solution to the question of an increase in money wages, following an increase in the price of wage goods.
(2) The wage rate must be *kept* at that constant level by market forces. Supply and demand must not be brought in to determine the level of wages, but simply to correct deviations from it.[7] In fact, any link between the value of labour and its scarcity in relation to the demands of accumulation is foreign to Ricardo's analysis: 'no point is better established, than the supply of labourers will always ultimately be in proportion to the means of supporting them' (vol. I, p. 292).
(3) The wage rate is the independent variable in the distribution and the profit rate is determined by it. The wage rate and the profit rate are not determined simultaneously (Malthus) or independently (Smith).

Hence, according to Ricardo, for any economic system there is a wage rate which is defined in real terms, and which should meet the above requirements. This is the natural wage. The Malthusian law of population provides the law for the market adjustment. The rate of increase of population may be high or

---

[7] Torrens, in *Essay on the Corn Trade* (1815), from which Ricardo derives the opening sentences of his chapter on 'Wages', is very clear on this point: 'the market price of labour is regulated by the proportion ... between the demand and supply, its natural price is governed by other laws' (p. 62).

low, positive or negative, according to the standard of living of the workers. For a given level of the demand for labour, if the market wage is higher than the natural wage, then there will be an excess of supply in the labour market. This, in turn (according to a law that Ricardo does not care to specify), lowers the wage rate. The same mechanism works in the opposite case.

There is a clear parallel between the theory of the natural prices and the theory of the natural wage. Ricardo himself claims that the word 'natural' is used 'so that we may have one common language to apply to all cases which are similar' (vol. II, p. 227). In the *Principles*, at the proof stage the sections on the natural and market prices and on wages were in the same chapter (see Sraffa, 1951, p. xxvi).[8]

The natural price of a product reflects the technical conditions of its production; thus the natural wage is determined by the conditions of production of human beings, by the input–output relationship between the standard of living of workers and variations in population. Just as production techniques are relatively constant over time, the habits of workers change very slowly.

In the case of reproducible goods, value derives from the difficulty of production and not from scarcity. Their supply can never fall short of demand, because producers will always engage in production when it is profitable to do so. Labour is also a reproducible commodity and, in Ricardo's own words, 'the tendency of the population to increase is, in our state of society, more than equal to that of the capital to increase' (Ricardo to Malthus, 5 October 1816; vol. VII, p. 72).[9] This happens because it is in the workers' nature, if not in their interest, to enjoy those 'delights of domestic society' (vol. I, p. 407) that produce abundant progeny as soon as the conditions of life allow it. And while demographic control might, in Ricardo's view, be used to check a fall in the standard of living when the population increases too rapidly, Ricardo certainly did not see such control as a practical and effective means of increasing the price of labour.

The similarities between the theory of the natural prices of commodities and the theory of the natural price of labour are therefore manifold. Both arise from the behaviour (which we could call 'natural') of individual economic agents; the corresponding market values function as signals guiding the behaviour of the economic agents. The supply of both goods and labour conforms to an existing effective demand: in the first case this is the need for a certain quantity of goods (the 'will') together with the 'power' to pay its natural price; in the second case the effective demand takes the form

---

[8] The link between natural wage and natural prices was soon noticed in the literature: 'Mr Ricardo seems evidently to have felt that he was driven by his theory, that the actual price of every commodity is regulated by its cost of production or natural price, to give a natural price of labour' (West, 1826, p. 63).

[9] 'Our state of society' is elsewhere called 'natural state of society' (vol. I, 101).

of capital earmarked for acquiring productive labour. But Ricardo's concern is to assert the existence of a mechanism by which supply is adjusted to demand, not to give a definite rule:

> Some, indeed, have attempted to estimate the fall of price which would take place, under the supposition of the surplus bearing different proportions to the average quantity. Such calculations, however, must be very deceptious, as no general rule can be laid down for the variations of price in proportion to quantity. (*Works*, vol. IV, p. 220)

So far we have tried to reconstruct what Ricardo would have liked to include in his theory of wages. We turn now to the question of what he was actually able to achieve.

3 DEFINITIONS

The natural wage is defined (*Principles*, ch. 5) as that price of labour 'which is necessary to enable the labourers, one with another, to persist and to perpetuate their race, without either increase or diminution' (vol. I, p. 93). It is that rate of wage at which the level of population, whatever it may be, is kept constant. We do not need to know what is the rate of growth of population for any given wage rate; it is enough to know the level of wage at which the rate of population growth is zero.

The process of accumulation that underlies this definition of natural wage is depicted as a series of steps, whereby each increase in capital and in the demand for labour[10] is followed by a time interval long enough to allow the supply of labour to adjust itself to the demand. This adjustment mechanism is very carefully specified and can be followed almost step by step.

(1) An increase in the demand for labour (arising from an increase in capital) faces a shortage in the supply of labour.
(2) Competition among capitalists raises money wages.
(3) With constant commodity prices, an increase in the money wage improves the standard of living of the labourers and therefore their number is increased.
(4) The growth of population generates an increase in the demand for corn. The increase in money wages will now be spent on 'necessaries' rather than on 'conveniences'.

---

[10] In this paper it has been assumed for the sake of simplicity that there is a constant proportionality among the rate of profit, the rate of accumulation and the rate of growth in the demand for labour.

(5) The market price of corn increases, while the market price of conveniences falls. Profits in agriculture rise above the general level.

(6) Capital is attracted into the agricultural sector and corn production increases.

(7) As lands of inferior quality are brought under cultivation, the cost of production of corn increases, and therefore its price cannot go back to the former level.

(8) The initial increase in money wages is entirely absorbed by the increase in expenditure on agricultural products.

(9) The real wage returns to the level of the natural wage, because of the increase in the money price of wage goods, and because of the increased supply of labour—if such is the case—which lowers the money wage.

(10) In the end, the growth of population is checked and the process ceases, to recommence with the next increase of capital.

This process is here reconstructed in some detail to show how every step results from the action of economic agents in response to market signals. Conclusions are not drawn from the mechanical application of models. Ricardo was interested in descriptions: he dealt with actual as opposed to a priori market mechanisms[11] (though at times he misunderstood these or overestimated their effects). Some interpretations tend to neglect this feature of Ricardo's theory, and this leads to oversimplifications, like the idea that Ricardo assumed that wages were paid in corn, neglecting the role played by changes in the corn price in the adjustment mechanism. One commentator, attempting to explain the rise in money wages, attributes to Ricardo a strange mechanism of short-term indexation, whereby wages are linked to the price of agricultural goods but not manufactured goods (see Gootzeit, 1973, pp. 58–9).

But the accumulation process can hardly be represented as a step function, because the propensity to save by capitalists, which regulates their investment decisions and therefore the pace of accumulation, does not change so abruptly. Nor can the supply of labour be assumed to adjust instantaneously to the demand for it. Thus, while the above definition of natural wage may well have served the purpose that Ricardo had in mind, it implies a very implausible description of the accumulation process, so that it is useless outside the stationary state, when the rate of accumulation is zero and the demand for labour no longer grows. Malthus (like many others after him)[12] was quick to notice that: 'This price I should really be disposed to call a most unnatural price; because in a natural state of things ... such a price could not generally occur for hundreds of years' (vol. II, pp. 227–8).

[11] On this point, see Marcuzzo and Rosselli (1983).

[12] More recently, the difficulties in the definition of natural wage in the *Principles* have been brought to light by Caravale and Tosato (1974, 1980); in particular, see their 1980 chapter 4.

In a few passages Ricardo himself seems to have suggested another definition (vol. IV, p. 12). The role of the natural wage rate was not to adjust the *level* of the labour supply to that of the demand, but to make the *rate* of growth of the supply of labour conform to the rate of growth of the demand. The wage rate is still assumed to be constant in real terms, but the rate of change, and not the level of the labour supply, is the adjusting variable.

But even this new definition presents certain difficulties. The rate of growth of the demand for labour cannot be assumed to be constant, as it is a function of the rate of profit; and as the accumulation proceeds, the rate of profit falls. Consequently, the wage level that keeps the rate of growth of population in step with the decreasing demand for labour cannot remain constant.

Malthus again was scoring a point:

> if from the first he [the labourer] had no more than sufficient to keep up the actual population, the labouring classes could not increase .... . On the other hand, if the real wages of labour were such as to admit of and encourage an increase of population, and yet were always to remain the same, it would involve the contradiction of a continued increase of population after the accumulation of capital, and the means of supporting such an increase had entirely ceased. We cannot then make the supposition of a *natural* and *constant* price of labour .... . (vol. II, p. 255)

Malthus's suggestion was to define the natural wage as that wage which makes the average supply of labour equal to the average demand (vol. II, pp. 227–8). Ricardo did not follow his advice. At one stage (vol. II, p. 228) he was on the point of giving in,[13] but in the end he reverted to his own idea.

Ricardo could easily have confuted Malthus by simply stating that, as far as his theory of value and distribution goes, the level of wage was to be assumed as given, and by not specifying the market mechanism that keeps the wage at its constant level. But he did not wish to take that step. He only sought, as far as possible, to avoid using Malthusian mechanisms to prove his own theses, and to advise against the too literal application of Malthus's population theories.

In the two other cases where Ricardo had to explain why money wages rise following an increase in the cost of production of labour, he resorted to strong *ad hoc* hypotheses. A tax on wages will increase the money wage because of competition over the available supply of labour between capitalists and the government, which uses the tax revenue to finance public works (see vol. VIII, pp. 169–70). A tax on wage goods implies that there has already

---

[13] This idea was rejected at an earlier stage; see Ricardo to Malthus, 30 January 1818; vol. VII, pp. 250–1.

been an increase in money wages; otherwise the wage goods could not be bought at the higher prices (vol. VIII, pp. 255–8).

When McCulloch, taking Ricardo's argument too literally, used a decrease in population to explain why money wages rise if the state taxes wages and spends the revenue abroad, Ricardo commented:

> the question between us comes to this. Will the population be in the first instance very much depressed, and then afterwards violently stimulated, or will it continue in that course which the circumstances of the capital and the demand of labour originally required it to be? The value of things I believe to be influenced, not by immediate supply and demand only, but also by contingent supply and demand. (*Works*, vol. VIII, p. 196)

Mitchell (1967, pp. 365–6)[14] suggested that Ricardo did not abandon the Malthusian market mechanism because he had an ideological bias which led him to consider the workers as the only ones responsible for their standard of living. Or perhaps he held to his theory of the adjustment of market wages to the natural wage because he hesitated to present a solution that eliminated, rather than solved, a serious analytical problem.

4 RICARDIAN MODELS

Since the time of Malthus there has been a long tradition of criticism centred on Ricardo's wage theory and its contradictions. E. Cannan, for example, wrote: 'After having taken the trouble to define and explain "market" wages and "natural" wages, Ricardo makes no use of the distinction. He finds the unqualified term "wages" ... sufficient for all his purposes' (Cannan, 1917, p. 250). G. Stigler praises the 'correct views' on the actual behaviour of wages— which, however, 'Ricardo did not know how to incorporate into his theoretical system' (Stigler, 1965a, p. 172). Similar comments can be found in many of the main commentators on Ricardo (e.g. Mitchell, 1967, pp. 319–22; St Clair, 1965, pp. 118–19).

Recently there has been a new interest in Ricardo's theory of wages, based on several attempts to construct a mathematical model of his system. In what can be considered as an archetypal model (Pasinetti, 1960), the natural wage is given exogenously in real terms. Once the wage rate is given, the other two distributive variables can be determined, and the variation of these is studied in relation to the variation of capital. But the market mechanism that brings

[14] And also 'their happiness or misery depends mainly on their number compared with the demand for their labour, and therefore on themselves' (vol. IX, p. 62).

wages to their natural level is analysed separately, and capital is assumed to be constant throughout the adjustment process—as if the adjustment of wages to the natural level, through changes in population, took place instantaneously; or as if Ricardo had such confidence in this adjustment that he felt it could be treated as instantaneous (Pasinetti, 1960, p. 81).

By introducing a given wage rate and assuming that the supply of labour is always adequate to capital, Pasinetti was able to formalize the idea of an infinitely elastic supply of labour at the given wage rate, an idea that had often been presented in the literature (see, e.g., Kaldor, 1956, p. 85; Blaug, 1958, pp. 120–1).

The difficulties of accepting such a picture of the accumulation process have already been noted (see p. 247 above). The next strategy has been to set up a dynamic model in which capital is continuously increased at a rate equal to the profit rate or to a fixed proportion of it. I believe that the attempts to incorporate the natural wage into these models failed to capture what Ricardo wanted to do with his natural wage theory—at least, according to the reconstruction of the origin of the theory that I have presented here.

Two approaches have been used in trying to incorporate the concept of the natural wage into a dynamic model. The first is that followed by Hicks and Hollander (Hicks and Hollander, 1977; Hicks, 1979; Hollander, 1979; Hollander, 1984) and extended by others (e.g. Gordon, 1983). In these models, the natural wage is the minimum subsistence wage. Below that wage level the population decreases. But during the accumulation process the population must always be increasing, and therefore the actual wage is always above it. If it drops to the natural level, it is immediately pushed up again by the increasing demand for labour.

So the natural wage, with which Ricardo opens his chapter on wages in the *Principles*—the wage belonging to that family of 'natural' variables on which he proposes to base his analysis (vol. I, p. 92)—turns out to play a very minor role. It is relegated, in fact, to that stationary state which, as Hicks and Hollander recognized (1977, p. 367), Ricardo did not consider very important.

The wage rate discussed in the model is therefore a short-run market wage which is determined by the proportion between circulating capital and the supply of labour, according to strict wage fund theory. This wage is allowed to vary within a limited range bounded from below by the natural wage and from above by that level of wage at which the rate of profit, and therefore the rate of accumulation, is zero. And, since, in a one-sector model, this maximum level is given by the marginal productivity of labour and is of course decreasing, it follows that the market wage too, 'sooner or later', will decrease, until the system reaches the stationary state, in which everything (minimum and maximum wage rate, market rate and natural rate) becomes equal.

One is led to conclude, as Cannan did, that there is no real distinction between the market wage and the natural wage. It is impossible to distinguish between changes in wages arising from imbalances in the labour market and changes in wages arising from changed techniques of production of the wage goods or of labour. There is no way of ranking the different influences according to their importance.

Even that carefully delineated sequence of causes and effects used by Ricardo to explain the changes in money wages is wiped out: 'Money wages are rising and real wages are falling. Why? It cannot be claimed that Ricardo gives a clear answer. He is just reading off these results from the model that is in his mind' (Hicks and Hollander, 1977, p. 366).

Another type of dynamic model (e.g. Levy, 1976; Casarosa, 1978) goes back to Ricardo's alternative definition of natural wage. The aim of this model is to determine the wage level that will allow the supply and demand for labour to grow at the same rate, whatever that rate may be.

This kind of model avails itself of two basic functions of the wage rate. The rate of growth of the demand for labour is a function of the rate of profit, which is a function of the wage rate. The rate of growth of the supply of labour is made dependent on the wage rate, by assigning to each level of the real wage a corresponding rate of growth of the population.

Taking N^s as the supply of labour and N^d as the demand for labour, we have

$$\dot{N}^s/N^s = f(w, p) \quad f_w > 0, f_p < 0$$

where p = price of corn, or price of a wage bundle, and w = money wage, and

$$\dot{N}^d/N^d = g(w) \quad g' < 0.$$

For any given p, the model finds the value for $w = w(p)$ given by

$$f(w, p) = g(w). \tag{3}$$

Let $w_0 = w(p_0)$ such that:

$$f(w_0, p_0) = g(w_0) = 0.$$

w_0/p_0 is called the 'natural wage'; when $f(w, p) = g(w) \neq 0$, $w(p)/p$ is called by Casarosa (1978) the dynamic equilibrium wage. So the natural wage is only a special case of the dynamic equilibrium wage. But the dynamic equilibrium wage is a special case of the market wage.

It is claimed that Ricardo explains the behaviour of the distributive variables in terms of dynamic equilibrium. But the implications of a dynamic equilibrium wage are not of minor importance:

(1) The wage rate is not constant in real terms, but is decreasing. The solution to (3) is such that w/p is constant only under very special assumptions about the supply of labour function.[15] In general, the equilibrium real wage changes as the price of corn and the productivity in agriculture change.

(2) The price of corn must be taken as constant throughout the entire adjustment process; in other words, when population changes, its effect on the labour market must be felt *before* the increase in the demand for corn and the cultivation of inferior lands produce their effect on the price of corn. Otherwise, it must be assumed once again that the supply of labour adjusts instantaneously to the demand.

(3) Last but not least, what causes what in the distribution of the produce cannot be determined. Population adjusts to capital and capital to population; the rate of profit depends on the wage rate and the wage rate depends on the rate of profit. It is the scarcity of capital compared with labour and of labour compared with capital that governs distribution.

(4) Moreover, as is acknowledged by the authors of these models (e.g. Casarosa, 1978, p. 50), the path of the dynamic equilibrium wage is not a steady-state path along which the wage rate actually moves in time. With any change in the price of wage goods, the equilibrium is abandoned. The dynamic equilibrium wage can then be actually reached only if the marginal productivity in agriculture does not change—and cannot be maintained unless productivity in agriculture does not change. But Ricardo's theory of accumulation is based on the hypothesis of diminishing returns in agriculture. So the dynamic equilibrium wage can hardly be presented as an 'attraction point' for wages in a Ricardian system.

It may be useful to conclude with a note on Stigler's rule for choosing among competing interpretations of the same theory: 'the test of an interpretation is its consistency with the main analytical *conclusions* of the system of thought under consideration' (Stigler, 1965b, p. 448; italics added).

If the main analytical conclusion to be drawn from the theory of accumulation in Ricardo is the fall in the rate of profit, then all the models are valid: both fix-wage and flex-wage models are compatible with an increasing money wage and a falling rate of profit.

But perhaps Stigler's rule should be reconsidered. It may be more important to be consistent with the premises than with the conclusions of the system of thought under consideration.

[15] Caravale and Tosato (1974, 1980) follow the strategy of assuming the rate of growth of population as a function not only of the real wage rate, but also of the population level. It is as if the law that regulates variations in population in accord with wages were affected by the population level already attained. It is only by introducing this assumption—which, as they admit, cannot be supported by any textual evidence—that the wage rate can be made constant.

REFERENCES

Blaug, M. (1958). *Ricardian Economics: a Historical Study*. New Haven, Conn.: Yale University Press.

Cannan, E. (1917). *A History of the Theories of Production and Distribution in English Political Economy from 1776 to 1848*. London: T. S. King & Son.

Caravale, G. and Tosato, D. (1974). *Un modello ricardiano di sviluppo economico*. Turin: Boringhieri.

Caravale, G. and Tosato, D. (1980). *Ricardo and the Theory of Value Distribution and Growth*. London: Routledge & Kegan Paul.

Casarosa, C. (1978). 'A New Formulation of the Ricardian System'. *Oxford Economic Papers*, 30, 38–63.

Garegnani, P. (1982). 'On Hollander's Interpretation of Ricardo's Early Theory of Profits'. *Cambridge Journal of Economics*, 6, 65–77.

Garegnani, P. (1983). 'Ricardo's Early Theory of Profits and Its "Rational Foundation": A Reply to Professor Hollander'. *Cambridge Journal of Economics*, 7, 175–8.

Gootzeit, M. (1973). 'The Corn Laws and Wage Adjustment in a Short-run Ricardian Model'. *History of Political Economy*, 5, 50–71.

Gordon, K. (1983). 'Hicks and Hollander on Ricardo: A Mathematical Note'. *Quarterly Journal of Economics*, 98, 721–6.

Hicks, J. (1979). *Causality in Economics*. Oxford: Blackwell.

Hicks, J. and Hollander, S. (1977). 'Mr Ricardo and the Moderns'. *Quarterly Journal of Economics*, 91, 351–69.

Hollander, S. (1979). *The Economics of David Ricardo*. Toronto: University of Toronto Press.

Hollander, S. (1983). 'Professor Garegnani's Defence of Sraffa on the Material Rate of Profit'. *Cambridge Journal of Economics*, 7, 167–74.

Hollander, S. (1984). '"Dynamic Equilibrium with Constant Wages": J. S. Mill's Malthusian Analysis of the Secular Wage Path'. *Kyklos*, 37, 247–65.

Kaldor, N. (1956). 'Alternative Theories of Distribution'. *Review of Economic Studies*, 23, 83–100.

Langer, G. F. (1982). 'Further Evidence for Sraffa's Interpretation of Ricardo'. *Cambridge Journal of Economics*, 6, 397–400.

Levy, D. (1976). 'Ricardo and the Iron Law. A Correction of the Record'. *History of Political Economy*, 8, 235–52.

Marcuzzo, M. C. and Rosselli, A. (1984). 'The Price of Gold: A Reconsideration of Ricardo's Monetary Theory'. *Studi e Ricerche dell' Istituto Economico*.

Mitchell, W. (1967). *Types of Economic Theory*. New York: Augustus M. Kelley.

Pasinetti, L. (1960). 'A Mathematical Formulation of the Ricardian System'. *Review of Economic Studies*, 27, 78–98.

Ricardo, D. (1951–73). *Works and Correspondence* (11 vols), ed. P. Sraffa with the collaboration of M. Dobb. Cambridge: CUP.

St Clair, O. (1965). *A Key to Ricardo*. New York: Augustus M. Kelley.

Sraffa, P. (1951). Introduction. In D. Ricardo, *Works and Correspondence*, vol. I. Cambridge: CUP.

Stigler, G. (1965a). *Essays in the History of Economics*. Chicago: Chicago University Press.

Stigler, G. (1965b). 'Textual Exegesis as a Scientific Problem'. *Economica*, 32, 447–50.

Torrens, R. (1815). *An Essay on the External Corn Trade*. London.

Vianello, F. (1983). 'On Ricardo's Principle that the Profits of the Farmer regulate the Profits of All Other Trades'. *Studi e Ricerche dell' Istituto Economico*.

West, E. (1826). *Price of Corn and Wages of Labour*. London.

PART V

The Machinery Question

11

Ricardo on Machinery and Technological Unemployment

WALTER ELTIS

The statements that Ricardo made in the last two years of his life concerning the tendency of machinery to reduce the demand for labour and to cause technological unemployment are very strong indeed. On 30 May 1823 it is recorded that, in the House of Commons,

> Mr Ricardo said, his proposition was, not that the use of machinery was prejudicial to persons employed in one particular manufacture, but to the working classes generally. It was the means of throwing additional labour into the market, and thus the demand for labour, generally, was diminished. (Ricardo, *Works*, vol. V, p. 303)

In the chapter 'On Machinery', which he added to the third edition of *Principles of Political Economy and Taxation* in 1821, he wrote:

> the same cause [investment in machinery] which may increase the net revenue of the country, may at the same time render the population redundant, and deteriorate the condition of the labourer. (vol. I, p. 388)

While in a letter to McCulloch on 30 June 1821 he wrote:

> If machinery could do all the work that labour now does, there would be no demand for labour. Nobody would be entitled to consume any thing who was not a capitalist, and who could not buy or hire a machine. (vol. VIII, pp. 399–400)

These statements about the possible effects of mechanization on the demand for labour are no less strong than Marx's, although, as will become evident, Ricardo's reasons for arriving at them are different.

The author is a Fellow of Exeter College, Oxford. He is grateful to Alberto Chilosi and to Samuel Hollander for helpful comments on an earlier draft of this paper.

The statements that Ricardo made from 1821 onwards about the influence of machinery contrast very sharply with those that he had made earlier. For instance, in his *Essay on the Influence of a Low Price of Corn on the Profits of Stock* (1815),

> The effects [of a lower price of corn] on the interests of ... [the labouring] class would be nearly the same as the effects of improved machinery, which, it is now no longer questioned, has a decided tendency to raise the real wages of labour. (vol. IV, p. 35)

And in a letter to McCulloch of 29 March 1820:

> The employment of machinery I think never diminishes the demand for labour—it is never a cause of a fall in the price of labour ... (vol. VIII, p. 171)

This was a comment on an 1820 *Edinburgh Review* article on Barton's *Observations on the Conditions of the Labouring Classes*, where McCulloch had written:

> The fixed capital invested in a machine, must always displace a considerably greater quantity of circulating capital,—for otherwise there could be no motive for its erection; and hence its first effect is to sink, rather than increase, the rate of wages. (McCulloch, 1820, p. 171)

McCulloch then went over to what he believed to be Ricardo's position in an article he published in the *Edinburgh Review* in 1821, just 15 months after his previous article:

> It appears, therefore, however much it may be at variance with the common opinions on the subject, that an improvement in machinery is always more advantageous to the labourer than the capitalist. In particular cases, it may reduce the profits of the latter, and destroy a portion of his capital; but it cannot, in any case, diminish the wages of the labourer, while it must raise their value relatively to commodities, and improve his condition. (McCulloch, 1821, p. 116)

The third edition of Ricardo's *Principles* was published in the same month as McCulloch's new article, and McCulloch read with consternation in the new chapter:

> Ever since I first turned my attention to questions of political economy, I have been of opinion, that such an application of machinery to any

branch of production, as should have the effect of saving labour was a general good, accompanied only with that portion of inconvenience which in most cases attends the removal of capital and labour from one employment to another. It appeared to me, that provided the landlords had the same money rents, they would be benefited by the reduction in the prices of some of the commodities on which those rents were expended, and which reduction of price could not fail to be the consequence of the employment of machinery. The capitalist, I thought, was eventually benefited precisely in the same manner. He, indeed, who made the discovery of the machine, or who first usefully applied it, would enjoy an additional advantage, by making great profits for a time; but, in proportion as the machine came into general use, the price of the commodity produced, would, from the effects of competition, sink to its cost of production, when the capitalist would get the same money profits as before, and he would only participate in the general advantage, as a consumer, by being enabled, with the same money revenue, to command an additional quantity of comforts and enjoyments. The class of labourers also, I thought, was equally benefited by the use of machinery, as they would have the means of buying more commodities with the same money wages, and I thought that no reduction of wages would take place, because the capitalist would have the power of demanding and employing the same quantity of labour as before, although he might be under the necessity of employing it in the production of a new, or at any rate of a different commodity ... .

These were my opinions, and they continue unaltered, as far as regards the landlord and the capitalist; but I am convinced, that the substitution of machinery for human labour, is often very injurious to the interests of the class of labourers.

My mistake arose from the supposition, that whenever the net income of a society increased, its gross income would also increase; I now, however, see reason to be satisfied that the one fund, from which landlords and capitalists derive their revenue, may increase, while the other, that upon which the labouring class mainly depend, may diminish ... . (*Works*, vol. I, pp. 386–8)

McCulloch's reaction was to tell Ricardo how appalled he was 'to see an Economist of the highest reputation strenuously defending one set of opinions one day, and unconditionally surrendering them the next' (*Works*, vol. VIII, p. 382).

Ricardo and his contemporaries undoubtedly believed that he had changed his opinion on a major issue of great practical importance. It has been shown that much of the underlying argument that led to Ricardo's new thinking on the influence of machinery on the demand for labour was in fact implicit in the previous editions of the *Principles*.[1] It is at the same time entirely clear that Ricardo began to perceive the full implications of this aspect of his argument only in 1821.

There are also important new elements in the machinery chapter. The most striking of these is Ricardo's arithmetical example, which shows how the construction of machinery may reduce the subsequent demand for labour. This bears a considerable resemblance to the arithmetical example that Barton published in 1817. Sismondi and Malthus published examples of the same kind in 1819 and 1820[2] and John Stuart Mill went on to reproduce the essentials of Ricardo's example in his *Principles of Political Economy* (1848) and to draw conclusions very similar to Ricardo's (Mill, *Works*, vol. II, pp. 93–9).

Barton's book is one of the very few that Ricardo cited and quoted from, and as it includes the first of the four arithmetical examples to be published, he undoubtedly deserves credit for originating an important element of the argument that Ricardo went on to develop. His example to show how the construction of machinery can reduce the demand for labour therefore merits quotation in full:

> It does not seem that every accession of capital necessarily sets in motion an additional quantity of labour. Let us suppose a case.— A manufacturer possesses a capital of £1,000, which he employs in maintaining twenty weavers, paying them £50 per annum each. His capital is suddenly increased to £2,000. With double means he does however hire double the number of workmen, but lays out £1,500 in erecting machinery, by the help of which five men are enabled to perform the same quantity of work as twenty did before. Are there not then fifteen men discharged in consequence of the manufacturer having increased his capital?
>
> But does not the construction and repair of machinery employ a number of hands?—Undoubtedly—As in this case a sum of £1,500 was expended, it may be supposed to have given employment to thirty men for a year, at £50 each. If calculated to last fifteen years, (and machinery seldom wears out sooner) then thirty workmen might always supply fifteen manufacturers, with these machines;—therefore each manufacturer may be said constantly to employ two.—Imagine also that one man is always employed in the necessary repairs. We have then five weavers, and three machine-makers, where there were before twenty weavers.
>
> But the increased revenue of the manufacturer will enable him to

---

[1] See, for instance, Hollander (1971, 1979).

[2] Sismondi (1819, vol. II, pp. 324–6); and Malthus (1820, pp. 261–2; reprinted in Ricardo, *Works*, vol. II, pp. 235–6).

maintain more domestic servants.—Let us see then how many.—His yearly revenue, being supposed equal to ten per cent on his capital, was before £100—now £200. Supposing then that his servants are paid at the same rate as his workmen, he is able to hire just two more. We have then, with a capital of £2,000, and a revenue of £200 per annum,

> 5 weavers,
> 3 machine-makers,
> 2 domestic servants,
> 10 Persons in all, employed.

With half the capital, and half the revenue, just double the number of hands were set in motion.

The demand for labour depends then on the increase of circulating, and not of fixed, capital. Were it true that the proportion between these two sorts of capital is the same at all times, and in all countries, then indeed it follows that the number of labourers employed is in proportion to the wealth of the state. But such a proposition has not the semblance of probability. As arts are cultivated, and civilization is extended, fixed capital bears a larger and larger proportion to circulating capital. The amount of fixed capital employed in the production of a piece of British muslin is at least a hundred, probably a thousand times greater than that employed in the production of a similar piece of Indian muslin.— And the proportion of circulating capital employed is a hundred or a thousand times less. It is easy to conceive that under certain circumstances, the whole of the annual savings of an industrious people might be added to fixed capital, in which case they would have no effect in increasing the demand for labour. (Barton, 1817, pp. 15–17)

Ricardo quoted the last of these four paragraphs in the third edition of his *Principles* and constructed a far sharper example than Barton's to show how the construction of machinery can reduce the demand for labour by cutting the total amount of circulating capital. Wage goods have to be made available to workers in advance of production in all classical models, so a reduction in the stock of consumable commodities, which forms a high fraction of circulating capital, must reduce a classical economy's ability to pay wages and therefore to support labour.[3] Ricardo's example is not cluttered with the presence of maintenance workers and of servants who become newly employed as a result of an increase in profits. Still more important, it does not involve a doubling of the capital stock. Ricardo's analysis of the problem (which naturally ran deeper than Barton's) showed him, for reasons which will become clear, that extra capital will always raise employment. It is only the conversion of part of the existing capital stock

---

[3] See Hicks (1969, p. 151), for an account of the underlying foundations of this line of argument.

from circulating capital to machinery that can reduce employment. His example therefore required an unchanged total capital, and within that total, a change in the composition of capital.

In Ricardo's example, a capitalist has a total capital valued at £20,000, which is initially £13,000 circulating and £7,000 fixed. The profit to the capitalist is £2,000, which is entirely consumed, so his total capital is constant. In a particular year he converts £7,500 of his circulating capital into fixed capital by making use of Barton's assumption that some of the workers are employed to construct a machine instead of to produce provisions. In consequence, in the following year his total capital will still be £20,000, but his fixed capital will be up from £7,000 to £14,500 as a result of the construction of the machine, while his circulating capital will be down from £13,000 to £5,500. Ricardo concludes that in this case, where there is no net accumulation of capital, the capitalist's 'means of employing labour, would be reduced in the proportion of £13,000 to £5,500, and, consequently, all the labour which was before employed by £7,500, would become redundant' (*Works*, vol. I, pp. 388–9). At first sight surprisingly, as he appears to have made use of vital elements in Barton's argument, Ricardo supplements his quotation from him with the qualification:

> It is not easy, I think, to conceive that under any circumstances, an increase of capital should not be followed by an increased demand for labour; the most that can be said is, that the demand will be in a diminishing ratio. (*Works*, vol. I, p. 396)

It will become evident that this qualification can be derived straightforwardly from some of the fundamental propositions of Ricardo's *Principles*, and this has been widely shown.[4]

For an argument concerned primarily with the interrelationship between capital accumulation and employment, when the ratio of fixed to circulating capital is changing, the most convenient unit to work with is clearly a physical commodity unit. Until recently this would have had to be corn, but Hicks (1972) has reminded us that a consumption basket consisting of a variety of goods can be brought into the analysis as a single composite commodity, provided that the individual items in the consumption basket are consumed in relative proportions which remain unaltered. There are many passages where Ricardo explicitly or implicitly assumes that workers consume the food and manufactures which make up their necessary consumption in fixed proportions (see e.g. vol. I, pp. 102–4), so it will not misrepresent him if the unit in which output is measured is the basket of commodities that makes up the natural wage. As Hicks has pointed out, some of the items in the

[4] See, for instance, Blaug (1958, 1978), Hollander (1971, 1979), O'Brien (1975) and Berg (1980).

basket will be produced with diminishing returns and others with constant or increasing returns. However, in a Ricardian model the diminishing returns items in the basket have more effect on the behaviour of costs as output expands, so costs rise as the output of necessities is increased and extra units of the composite good are produced. With Hicks's reformulation, many of the results of the 'corn' model can be extended to a world where, as in the *Principles*, workers consume both food and manufactures.

In the present brief statement of how the model can be used to analyse the influence of the adoption of machinery, k_c will be written for circulating capital per worker, and k_f for fixed capital per worker. If the wage is at the natural level, and if wage goods provided in advance of production are the sole element in circulating capital, k_c will equal 1, since the wage goods that provide the natural wage are the unit of output. k_c will then exceed 1 to the extent that the wage exceeds the natural wage and to the extent that there are further elements in circulating capital. k_f may rise relative to k_c for two reasons. First k_f will rise if there is no change in the physical capital goods with which a labourer works, but the relative prices of these goods rise in relation to the price of the consumption basket. It will also rise, of course, if relative prices are unchanged but there is an increase in the quantity of fixed capital per worker.

If N is written for total employment and K for the total capital stock, then

$$K = (k_c + k_f)N. \tag{1}$$

If F is written for $(k_c + k_f)/k_c$, the ratio of total capital per worker to circulating capital per worker, (1) can be rewritten as:

$$K = k_c F N \tag{2}$$

and from (2) it is evident that

elasticity of N with respect to K

$$\tag{3}$$

$$= \frac{1}{1 + \left(\begin{array}{c}\text{elasticity of } k_c \\ \text{with respect to } N\end{array}\right) + \left(\begin{array}{c}\text{elasticity of } F \\ \text{with respect to } N\end{array}\right)}.$$

With the assumptions that are often made in restatements of Ricardo's argument that the wage does not persistently depart from the natural level, and that wage goods form the whole of circulating capital, the elasticity of k_c with respect to N will be zero. If it is also assumed that the ratio of total capital to circulating capital is constant, F will be constant, and in that event the elasticity of F with respect to N will also be zero. In equation (3) the elasticity of N with respect to K will then be unity: employment will grow in proportion to the capital stock. That is what Ricardo usually says, so he generally discusses the relationship between employment and the capital stock *as if* there is no persistent tendency for the wage to depart from the natural level, and no clear tendency for total capital per worker to grow faster than circulating capital per worker.

There was, however, a line of argument that was actually present in the first two editions of the *Principles* in embrionic form, which could have made Ricardo aware that, in a rigorous version of his model with the assumptions as stated, employment would grow more slowly than the capital stock. In the first chapter of the *Principles* Ricardo explains the determination of the relative prices of machinery and necessities, and measures these in money that is produced by a gold mining industry. In the third edition he assumes that machinery necessities and gold are produced by workers who use the same constant and circulating capital per head, so the marginal output of a year's labour in each industry will be sold for the same sum of money, which will go only to wages and profits since marginal production yields no rent. If a worker in gold mining produces G pieces of money a year, while a worker in necessity output produces Q units of necessities, these Q units must sell for G pieces of gold, so the price of a unit of necessities will be G/Q pieces of gold. As the natural wage is one unit of necessities, this will also be G/Q pieces of gold. As capital accumulation and consequent population growth force the economy on to inferior land, Q, the output of necessities per worker, will fall, with the result that G/Q, the money wage and the money price of a unit of necessities, will rise correspondingly.[5] In contrast, the productivity of the workers who produce machinery will not fall.

Ricardo always writes about the production of machinery and its cost in terms of gold, as if it is produced at constant cost. The constant amount of machinery a worker produces in a year will therefore sell for the G pieces of money that a gold miner produces in the same period. As the capital stock and employment grow, therefore, the price of the machinery a worker produces in a year will stay constant at G pieces of gold, while the wage and the price of necessities, which is G/Q pieces of gold, will rise continuously.

In the first two editions of the *Principles*, Ricardo arrived at the result that a rise in wages would not raise the cost of machinery, and of course made it very clear (after chapter 1) that the real cost of producing necessities, and therefore of employing labour, would tend to rise as capital and population grew. He did not however bring the two lines of argument together and state explicitly that the incentive to employ machinery would increase as the

---

[5] This exposition follows Pasinetti (1960) in the explanation of the prices of 'corn' and 'gold' and their divergence in his mathematical restatement of Ricardo's system.

economy developed. There is merely a general remark in the second edition (but not the first) referring to 'the early stages of society, before much machinery or durable fixed capital is used' (*Works*, vol. I, p. 62), but there is no explanation of the introduction of machinery as a direct consequence of a relative change in the price of machinery and the wage. It is no wonder, since there is no evidence that Ricardo actually inferred that machinery would be increasingly resorted to as labour productivity in necessity production fell, that he did not go on to perceive that, as a consequence of increasing mechanization, employment would grow more slowly than the capital stock.

Ricardo's failure to draw that inference at that stage could have been because, in the early editions of the *Principles*, gold mining did not in fact involve the same capital intensities as machinery and necessity production. Gold was produced without fixed capital, with the result that a rise in wages reduced the prices of both necessities and machinery measured in gold. What happened to the relative prices of machinery and necessities, and to the wage as the economy developed, therefore came out very much less clearly than with the assumptions made in the third edition, on which the argument stated above was based. With the assumption made there that there are equal capital intensities in machinery production, necessity production and gold mining, it becomes crystal clear that, as a population presses on to inferior land, money wages rise while the price of machinery does not, and this may well have led Ricardo to understand the full implications of his argument. It is only with the third edition that he added the footnote to chapter 1:

> We here see why it is that old countries are constantly impelled to employ machinery, and new countries to employ labour. With every difficulty of providing for the maintenance of men, labour necessarily rises, and with every rise in the price of labour, new temptations are offered to the use of machinery. This difficulty of providing for the maintenance of men is in constant operation in old countries, in new ones a very great increase in the population may take place without the least rise in the wages of labour. (*Works*, vol. I, p. 41)

A parallel passage in the new machinery chapter reads:

> In America and many other countries, where the food of man is easily provided, there is not nearly such great temptation to employ machinery as in England, where food is high, and costs much labour for its production. The same cause that raises labour, does not raise the value of machines, and, therefore, with every augmentation of capital, a greater proportion of it is employed on machinery. (vol. I, p. 395)

With these two new passages Ricardo was home, and he fully perceived the implications of what is nowadays called 'the Ricardo effect'. As wages rise as a result of the increasing marginal cost of necessities (relative to gold and machinery produced with unchanging productivity), the ratio of total capital per worker to circulating capital per worker, F in equation (3), rises. The elasticity of F with respect to L is therefore positive, with the result that the elasticity of L with respect to K is less than 1. If, for instance, a 1 per cent increase in employment raised the wage by $\frac{1}{2}$ per cent, and this raised the ratio of total capital relative to circulating capital by $\frac{1}{2}$ per cent, the elasticity of F with respect to L would be $\frac{1}{2}$. Equation (3) shows that, if circulating capital per worker is constant (as Ricardo implicitly assumes where he analyses the influence of mechanization on employment), the elasticity of L with respect to K will then be $\frac{2}{3}$; in other words, employment will grow at a rate of just 2 per cent when the capital stock grows at 3 per cent. It would be quite wrong to graft on to Ricardo the assumption of a constant elasticity of the wage with respect to employment, or a constant tendency to mechanize as the wage rises. Where he gives numerical examples of the relationship between employment and the real cost of food, this rises at a faster proportional rate than employment.[6] The Ricardo effect therefore may be weak at first (as the first of the two above quotations implies) as population expands relative to territory, and then may become very much stronger. The elasticity of employment in relation to the total capital stock may therefore be little less than 1 for a considerable time and then become sharply less than 1.

It is of course only if employment, and therefore the demand for food (and other necessities produced with diminishing returns), rises that the effects set out in equation (3) are triggered off. Without a rise in the demand for necessities, there will be no rise in their real cost and therefore no rise in the wage relative to the cost of machinery. There will therefore be no temptation to substitute machinery for labour. That is why Ricardo believed that Barton had gone too far when he said that capital could grow and employment fall at the same time. It is only if employment is actually growing that the relative cost of labour will be pulled up to produce a lasting incentive to mechanize. If mechanization actually cut employment, the demand for food would fall back, and so reduce the wage again relative to the cost of machinery, with the result that those who had mechanized would discover that they had been mistaken. Mechanization must be associated with rising employment in this strand of Ricardo's argument, and that is why he says, in the paragraph where he goes on to quote Barton and to explain why there will be an increasing use of machinery as wages rise, 'The demand for labour will continue to increase

---

[6] The examples are in Ricardo's *Works* (vol. IV, p. 17, and vol. I, p. 81), where successive increases in capital produce increasing *proportional* reductions in marginal corn output, i.e., increasing proportional rises in the real cost of corn.

with an increase of capital, but not in proportion to its increase; the ratio will necessarily be a diminishing ratio' (vol. I, p. 395). That is precisely the relationship set out in equation (3).[7]

There is an additional aspect to the manner in which a higher wage leads to increased mechanization in Ricardo's argument, and this is seen most clearly in terms of Hicks's new analysis in *Capital and Time* (1973, pp. 97–9). Hicks distinguishes there between construction labour and operating labour, and an invention with a 'forward bias' is one that raises the labour needed to construct capital equipment relative to the labour required to operate it. That is precisely Ricardo's machinery example, an increase in construction labour and a reduction in operating labour. Ricardo has several examples involving varying time-periods between incurring costs and bringing products to market, of which the construction of machinery is an example, and he states:

> On account then of the different degrees of durability of their capitals, or, which is the same thing, on account of the time which must elapse before one set of commodities can be brought to market, they will be valuable, not exactly in proportion to the quantity of labour bestowed on them ... but something more, to compensate for the greater length of time which must elapse before the most valuable can be brought to market. (*Works*, vol. I, p. 34)

And

> Every rise of wages, therefore, or, which is the same thing, every fall of profits, would lower the relative value of those commodities which were produced with a capital of a durable nature, and would proportionally elevate those which were produced with capital more perishable. (vol. I, pp. 39–40)

Thus while Ricardo does not quite state Hicks's argument, he all but states it. Durability of machinery is the same thing as a longer time that must elapse before commodities can be brought to market, and a rise in wages is favourable to those commodities that are produced with a capital of a more durable nature. It is a very small jump from this to the proposition that a higher wage leads to the substitution of construction labour for operating labour in the terms of Hicks's argument.

---

[7] Meacci's account of Ricardo's analysis of mechanization in this volume is quite close to that presented here at this point. He agrees that there cannot be an economy-wide trend towards mechanization in the absence of accumulation, and that in Ricardo's analysis this will also generally entail growth in the absolute amount of circulating capital and therefore in the demand for labour.

That relationship is simply another that influences the elasticity of F with respect to L in equation (3). If it makes this larger, the elasticity of L with respect to K will fall that much more below 1, and total employment will grow still more slowly in relation to the capital stock. As with the previous argument that Ricardo stated, however, there must be a rising trend in wages before these incentives towards mechanization are triggered off, and this requires an increasing pressure of population on territory, so these trends will persist only if the demand for labour is on balance advancing.

There are, however, as has been shown, passages in the new machinery chapter, and in speeches in Parliament and in his correspondence, in which Ricardo certainly spoke as if machinery could produce absolute falls in employment. This can occur in the particular conditions he assumed at the start of the chapter, namely:

> To elucidate the principle, I have been supposing, that improved machinery is *suddenly* discovered, and extensively used .... (*Works*, vol. I, p. 395)

He then went on to state the argument that in practice mechanization is a process that is endogenous to the rising wage that is central to his argument:

> the truth is, that these discoveries are gradual, and rather operate in determining the employment of the capital which is saved and accumulated, than in diverting capital from its actual employment.
>
> With every increase of capital and population, food will generally rise, on account of its being more difficult to produce. The consequence of a rise of food will be a rise of wages, and every rise of wages will have a tendency to determine the saved capital in a greater proportion than before to the employment of machinery. Machinery and labour are in constant competition, and the former can frequently not be employed until labour rises. (*Works*, vol. I, p. 395)

As Hollander (1971, 1979) has pointed out, therefore, Ricardo has two distinct arguments. There is first the argument in which increasing mechanization is endogenously associated with the rising wage which is a central element of Ricardo's account of what occurs as economies develop. That process can never produce a declining trend in employment. Second, there is the case where 'improved machinery is suddenly discovered'. These exogenous discoveries of machinery can obviously take any form and have any kind of effect on employment.

It is Ricardo's argument in his machinery chapter 'That if the improved means of production, in consequence of the use of machinery, should increase the net produce of a country in a degree so great as not to diminish the gross produce, (I mean always quantity of commodities and not value), then the situation of all classes will be improved' (vol. I, p. 392). In a letter to McCulloch written on 18 June 1821, Ricardo assumes a cloth manufacturer who can produce 10,000 yards of cloth, with a labour-intensive technique, spending £18,000 on labour and selling the cloth at £2 a yard for £20,000 to yield a profit of £2,000 on his circulating capital of £18,000. He goes on to say that, if he invested the same capital in machinery and still obtained an output of 10,000 yards of cloth, society could still employ the same quantity of labour because 'you would have the same quantity of food, cloth, and all other commodities annually' (vol. VIII, p. 389). The conversion of £18,000 of circulating capital into fixed capital would involve no aggregate loss of circulating capital because the 10,000 yards of cloth the machine produced would at once make good the circulating capital used up in the year of its construction. The 10,000 yards of cloth and the proceeds from marketing it would belong to the capitalist and the income of the previously employed workmen in cloth production would cease, but the capitalist would be able to employ more menial servants, and the society's circulating capital as a whole would be in no way reduced. Therefore it is only if the *sudden* discovery of machinery involves a fall in output that there is a loss of circulating capital and therefore a fall in the demand for labour.

Here there is a temptation to suggest that Ricardo had not thought the problem through completely (as he had not thought through the case of endogenous invention prior to the third edition). He asserts in his letter of 18 June 1821 to McCulloch that the substitution of machinery for an equal circulating capital quite categorically 'will diminish the quantity of gross produce'. 'Diminish the quantity of exchangeable articles, and you diminish the demand for commodities;—you diminish the means of enjoyment of some one, or more, of the classes of the community' (vol. VIII, p. 388). He goes on to say that if, using circulating capital alone, a capitalist produces 10,000 yards of cloth, obtains 1,000 yards as profit and sells this at £2 a yard, he will be less well off than if, by using machinery but not increasing his total capital, he produces 3,000 yards of cloth, obtains 1,500 yards of this as profit and sells it for just £1.10s a yard. With a profit of 1,000 yards of cloth out of 10,000 and a price of cloth of £2 a yard, he makes £2,000 profit. With a profit of 1,500 yards out of 3,000 and a price of cloth of £1.10s a yard, he makes £2,250 profit. Mechanization is therefore profitable even if the gross output of cloth falls by 70 per cent.

But it in no way follows from this example and the argument behind it that, if inventions involving the use of machinery are *suddenly* and *spontaneously* made, employment will fall. It has been shown that spontaneous inventions are the only ones that can be associated with a falling demand for labour in the economy as a whole; but if an invention is an exogenous event there is no reason why because it would be profitable to exploit it, even if it

involved 70 per cent less output from the same capital, output should actually
fall 70 per cent. The output of cloth could equally rise 70 per cent, and that
quite probably is what happened during much of the industrial revolution,
namely a simultaneous substitution of fixed for equal circulating capitals, and
very great increases in the output of physical commodities (measured in
yards) from that capital. If inventions are spontaneous, there is no reason
why this should not occur, and it surely often did. Ricardo himself admitted
that the effects of machinery could be extremely favourable to labour if the
inventions resembled a gift from nature.

> To obtain an indestructible steam engine now, we are obliged annually
> to bestow a quantity of labour upon it, and therefore it is of great value.
> I have not said that if Almighty power would give us steam engines
> ready made, and capable of doing work for us without the assistance of
> human labour, that such a present would be injurious to any class—it
> would be far otherwise . . . . (*Works*, vol. VIII, pp. 389–90)

Newly invented machinery that simultaneously reduced the labour needed to
operate it, and raised the physical output produced with an unchanged total
capital cost, would resemble the addition of these steam engines to the capital
stock. Such inventions occurred, and according to Ricardo's analysis they in
no way reduced the demand for labour.

All of Ricardo's actual examples are in fact of inventions and machinery
that reduce the *physical* gross output obtainable from a given total capital.
The case for adopting these inventions becomes greater the higher the wage.
It is not worth adopting them at all at an extremely low wage, and there is
always a critical wage where they become more profitable than the previous
labour-intensive method of production. They are therefore all examples of
the kind of mechanization that is to be expected as a result of endogenous
invention. Spontaneous invention may take this form, but it may equally take
the 'gift of nature' form of more physical output and lower labour requirements
with a given capital investment. Ricardo's logic is therefore tight only where
he speaks of endogenous technical change associated with the rising wage
(in relation to the cost of machinery) that is central to his whole argument.
It is the influence of this on his total argument that therefore merits attention,
and given the textual evidence and his statement that he assumed the *sudden*
discovery of machinery only for expositional reasons—'to elucidate the
principle'—it is very probably endogenous invention associated with a rising
wage that he principally had in mind when he analysed the causes and effects
of mechanization.

How will continuing endogenous invention influence the growth of the
Ricardian economy? This has been analysed far more closely than before by
Hicks and Hollander and by Casarosa in their very similar restatements of

Ricardo's theory of economic growth.[8] Their models describe disequilibrium growth, in which the wage tends to be above the natural wage and the rate of profit tends to be higher than the minimum to which the rate of profit is reduced in the eventual stationary state. Both Hicks–Hollander and Casarosa assume that the labour force and the capital stock will tend to grow at similar rates in the long progression of an early nineteenth-century economy towards the eventual stationary state. In Casarosa's model,

$$\frac{1}{N}\frac{dN}{dt} = \psi\left(\frac{w-w_s}{w_s}\right) \quad 0 < \psi < 1 \tag{4}$$

where N is the population, w_s is the natural wage where population is constant and w is the market wage, both expressed in corn or, it could easily be said, necessities. That is simply the Malthusian population supply function which Ricardo adopted. The supply of capital is given by the equation

$$\frac{1}{K}\frac{dK}{dt} = \lambda\left(\frac{f'(N)-w}{w}\right) \tag{5}$$

where $f'(N)$ is the marginal product of labour in the production of corn—or preferably 'necessities'. The term $f'(N)-w$ is the surplus of output per worker at the margin over the wage, and Casarosa assumes that a fixed fraction of this surplus is invested. Casarosa then assumes that

$$\frac{1}{N}\frac{dN}{dt} = \frac{1}{K}\frac{dK}{dt}. \tag{6}$$

It was shown above that more generally:

$$\frac{1}{N}\frac{dN}{dt} = \frac{1}{K}\frac{dK}{dt}\,\frac{1}{1+\left(\begin{array}{c}\text{elasticity of }k_c\\ \text{with respect to }N\end{array}\right)+\left(\begin{array}{c}\text{elasticity of }F\\ \text{with respect to }N\end{array}\right)} \tag{7}$$

Casarosa assumes a tendency for circulating capital per worker, k_c, to fall as the economy moves towards its eventual stationary state. He therefore has a negative elasticity of k_c with respect to N which would allow employment and population (their rates of growth are not distinguished) to grow a little faster than the capital stock. He does not take this effect (which may well be slight) into account. He also, of course, ignores the tendency of total capital to grow

---

[8] Hicks and Hollander (1977) and Casarosa (1978). Their argument is developed in Eltis (1984, ch. 6).

faster than circulating capital, which makes the elasticity of F with respect to N positive. Which effect is stronger, that of the negative elasticity of k_c with respect to N, or the positive elasticity of F with respect to N?

Ricardo himself explains, in the fifth chapter of the *Principles* 'On Wages', that 'in the natural advance of society' wages will tend to fall 'as far as they are regulated by supply and demand', because the rate of growth of capital will fall which will tend to reduce the excess of the wage over the natural wage. At the same time, wages will tend to rise as a result of the continuing rise in the price of necessities. When these two effects are combined, Ricardo says, the worker would 'receive an addition in his money wages, though with that addition he would be unable to furnish himself with the same quantity of corn and other commodities, which he had before consumed in his family' (vol. I, pp. 101–2). When all the effects shown in equation (7) are allowed for by Ricardo, therefore, there is still, on balance, a rise in the cost of labour in relation to the cost of machinery which has a constant gold price, because, like gold, it is produced with unchanging technology. There is therefore a continuing tendency to substitute machinery for labour with the result that the effect of the positive elasticity of F with respect to N is decisive. The wage does rise all the time relative to the cost of machinery; machinery is substituted for labour; the ratio of total capital to circulating capital per worker rises, and employment therefore has a continuing tendency to grow less than the capital stock.

If the sole effect of a continuing tendency towards mechanization was that employment had to grow less than the capital stock, the effect on Casarosa's model would be to lower the market wage at all points of time, since the slower growth of population needed could be provided by a smaller excess of the wage over the natural wage. That is not however the sole effect of mechanization. A more extensive use of machinery could be expected to make $f'(N)$, the marginal product of labour in the production of necessities, greater than it otherwise would be at each point of time. Through equation (5) this then raises the excess of the marginal product of labour over the wage, which increases the rate of growth of capital. If continuing mechanization raises the marginal product of labour and so the rate of growth of capital because it raises the investible surplus, and at the same time increases the rate of growth of the total capital stock that is needed to provide the extra capital to equip more workers, it is not clear whether employment will, on balance, grow more or less quickly. Blaug was surely right when he wrote in 1978:

> Ricardo seems to have realized by this time [when he wrote the machinery chapter] that the rise in money wages and the fall in the rate of profit implied by his model must lead to a constantly rising ratio of machinery to labour. This contradicts his usual assumption that capital and labour grow at equal rates and creates new complications. No

wonder that this chapter seems glued on to the rest of the book as an afterthought. (Blaug, 1978, p. 138)

In Casarosa's model, which, with Hicks and Hollander's, arguably provides the clearest analysis of the long-term behaviour of the Ricardian economy, a process of continuing mechanization raises both the economy's investible surplus at the margin and the amount of surplus that is needed to provide the capital for a given increase in employment. How this influences the long-term demand for labour is therefore unclear.

Ricardo himself recognized the favourable element due to machinery in the very long run:

> I have before observed, too, that the increase of net incomes, estimated in commodities, which is always the consequence of improved machinery, will lead to new savings and accumulations. These savings, it must be remembered are annual, and must soon create a fund, much greater than the gross revenue, originally lost by the discovery of the machine, when the demand for labour will be as great as before, and the situation of the people will be still further improved by the increased savings which the increased net revenue will still enable them to make. (*Works*, vol. I, p. 396)

That recognizes the favourable effect of higher net output on the rate of capital accumulation, which must permanently raise the rate of growth of demand for labour. In the above quotation mechanization has a once-for-all negative effect on the demand for labour, which the permanent favourable effect must in due course outweigh. But what if, as the logic of Ricardo's argument demands, there is further mechanization as the wage continues to rise, and this produces a series of further once-for-all negative effects on the demand for labour, and also further permanent positive effects? There must then be uncertainty about what will happen to the demand for labour in the long run.

Ricardo himself offered his readers the immediate unfavourable effect by setting out an example where mechanization occurs haphazardly at a particular point of time. If that example were truly haphazard, it could as plausibly have raised gross physical output as reduced it, so its adverse influence on employment was no more than a fluke. Ricardo's many amendments and additional references to machinery in the third edition of the *Principles* do however make it very clear that the mechanization he had in mind in 1821 did not occur haphazardly, but was a direct consequence of rising wages. There are therefore two trends that go on continuously: (1) mechanization all the time raises the investible surplus; (2) at the same time, it raises the amount of new capital that is needed to create a job.

Ricardo nowhere resolved the question of which influence is the stronger. He resolved it favourably to employment in the above passage only by making the investment cost of extra mechanization occur just once, while the benefits of a larger investible surplus continued indefinitely. In other passages he mentioned only the unfavourable effect. He had to leave the resolution of the problem to his great successors John Stuart Mill and Karl Marx.

Mill took up the challenge, in his *Principles of Political Economy*, by repeating Ricardo's machinery example virtually without amendment; and, as was not uncommon at the time, without acknowledgement to Ricardo:

> Suppose that a person farms his own land, with a capital of two thousand quarters of corn, employed in maintaining labourers during one year (for simplicity we omit the consideration of seed and tools), whose labour produces him annually two thousand four hundred quarters, being a profit of twenty per cent. This profit we shall suppose that he annually consumes, carrying on his operations from year to year on the original capital of two thousand quarters. Let us now suppose that by the expenditure of half his capital he effects a permanent improvement of his land, which is executed by half his labourers, and occupies them for a year, after which he will only require, for the effectual cultivation of his land, half as many labourers as before. The remainder of his capital he employs as usual. In the first year there is no difference in the condition of the labourers, except that part of them have received the same pay for an operation on the land, which they previously obtained for ploughing, sowing, and reaping. At the end of the year, however, the improver has not, as before, a capital of two thousand quarters of corn. Only one thousand quarters of his capital have been reproduced in the usual way: he has now only those thousand quarters and his improvement. He will employ, in the next and in each following year, only half the number of labourers, and will divide among them only half the former quantity of subsistence. The loss will soon be made up to them if the improved land, with the diminished quantity of labour, produces two thousand four hundred quarters as before, because so enormous an accession of gain will probably induce the improver to save a part, add it to his capital, and become a larger employer of labour. But it is conceivable that this may not be the case; for (supposing, as we may do, that the improvement will last indefinitely, without any outlay worth mentioning to keep it up) the improver will have gained largely by his improvement if the land now yields, not two thousand four hundred, but one thousand five hundred quarters; since this will replace the one thousand quarters forming his present circulating capital, with a profit of twenty-five per cent (instead of twenty as before) on the whole capital, fixed and

circulating together. The improvement, therefore, may be a very profitable one to him, and yet very injurious to the labourers. (Mill, *Works*, vol. II, p. 94)

Mill's example is of an agricultural improvement while Ricardo's was of a machine, but Mill had already pointed out that

all increases of fixed capital, when taking place at the expense of circulating, must be, at least temporarily, prejudicial to the interests of the labourers. This is true, not of machinery alone, but of all improvements by which capital is sunk; that is, rendered permanently incapable of being applied to the maintenance and remuneration of labour. (Mill, *Works*, vol. II, pp. 93–4)

Mill goes on to repeat the two effects of the conversion of circulating into fixed capital on the demand for labour. As for the unfavourable effect,

All attempts to make out that the labouring classes as a collective body *cannot* suffer temporarily by the introduction of machinery, or by the sinking of capital in permanent improvements, are, I conceive, necessarily fallacious. (Mill, *Works*, vol. II, p. 96)

As for the long-term favourable effect,

even if improvements did for a time decrease the aggregate produce and the circulating capital of the community, they would not the less tend in the long run to augment both. They increase the return to capital; and of this increase the benefit must necessarily accrue either to the capitalist in greater profits, or to the customer in diminished prices; affording, in either case, an augmented fund from which accumulation may be made, while enlarged profits also hold out an increased inducement to accumulation. In the case we before selected, in which the immediate result of the improvement was to diminish the gross produce from two thousand four hundred quarters to one thousand five hundred, yet the profit of the capitalist being now five hundred quarters instead of four hundred, the extra one hundred quarters, if regularly saved, would in a few years replace the one thousand quarters subtracted from his circulating capital. (*Mill, Works*, vol. II, p. 98)

Mill has followed Ricardo up to this point with an exactitude that is a compliment to the depth of Ricardo's logic, for Mill took on board for his Victorian readers only what he firmly believed to be correct. With this foundation, Mill could at last introduce his own insights. Ricardo believed that the eventual stationary state was distant and that there was still immense potential for future investment and growth. The fourth and fifth chapters of Mill's book IV, 'Of the Tendency of Profits to a Minimum' and 'Consequences of the Tendency of Profits to a Minimum', suggest that societies can easily and rapidly approach a state of development where they have exploited all their present investment opportunities. Given this, the extra opportunities arising from newly invented methods of mechanization can only help all classes by pushing ahead the frontiers of the stationary state and permitting further growth which could otherwise not occur:

> This tendency of improvements in production to cause increased accumulation, and thereby ultimately to increase the gross produce, even if temporarily diminishing it, will assume a still more decided character if it should appear that there are assignable limits both to the accumulation of capital, and to the increase of production from the land, which limits once attained, all further increase of produce must stop; but that improvements in production, whatever may be their other effects, tend to throw one or both of these limits farther off. Now, these are truths which will appear in the clearest light in a subsequent stage of our investigation. It will be seen, that the quantity of capital which will, or even which can, be accumulated in any country, and the amount of gross produce which will, or even which can, be raised, bear a proportion to the state of the arts of production there existing; and that every improvement, even if for the time it diminish the circulating capital and the gross produce, ultimately makes room for a larger amount of both, than could possibly have existed otherwise. It is this which is the conclusive answer to the objections against machinery; and the proof thence arising of the ultimate benefit to labourers of mechanical inventions even in the existing state of society, will hereafter be seen to be conclusive. But this does not discharge governments from the obligation of alleviating, and if possible preventing, the evils of which this source of ultimate benefit is or may be productive to an existing generation. (Mill, *Works*, vol. II, pp. 98–9)

A vivid instance of the 'evil ... to an existing generation' which the substitution of fixed for circulating capital may impose is provided when he gives an instance of agricultural improvements in practice:

> The remarkable decrease which has lately attracted notice in the gross produce of Irish agriculture, is, to all appearance, partly attributable to the diversion of land from maintaining human labourers to feeding cattle; and it could not have taken place without the removal of a large part of the Irish population by emigration or death. We have thus ...

recent instances, in which what was regarded as an agricultural improvement, has diminished the power of the country to support its population. (Mill, *Works*, vol. II, p. 95)

Ricardo's argument does indeed apply to Ireland and the Irish famine, as Mill perceived. The failure of the potato crop raised the wage that capitalists had to pay for labour in Ireland. At the former wage the workers could be expected to live largely off potatoes; after the failure of the potato, they had to be able to afford dearer food. That rise in wages persuaded capitalists to prefer a more capital-intensive agriculture, which required more farm animals (which Ricardo also regarded as a part of fixed capital—see vol. I, pp. 394–5) and fewer workers. Hence the evictions and the starvation, which continued long after the potato crop failed. Mill satisfied himself that the long-term effects of inventions and continuing mechanization must be beneficial to all classes, with his new argument that capital was at most times close to its limits, which technical progress extended; but he and Ricardo also rightly emphasized the dark side of this progress. Before the welfare state, machinery often killed, and Mill remembered and reminds us that, in the nineteenth century as in the sixteenth, sheep and indeed cattle were the 'devourers of men' (More, 1516). In England in 1581, as in Ireland three centuries later, 'wheare XL persons had theire lyvinges, nowe one man and his shepard hathe all' (Lamond, 1929, p. 15). Ricardo explained why.

In Marx's argument, written between 20 and 40 years after Mill's, this darker side to mechanization became dominant. Marx praises Ricardo and Barton,[9] and develops their argument in two important ways. First, he assumes continuing mechanization, where Ricardo restricted his examples to a single substitution of fixed for circulating capital. With Ricardo, as has been shown, the demand for labour therefore falls just once, and the benefits from the extra accumulation that results from the higher profits arising from mechanization continue indefinitely. In Marx, both the displacement of labour and the increase in profits occur all the time.

Marx's wage goods are variable capital, while machinery and raw materials or means of production are constant capital; and

With the progress of accumulation, therefore, the proportion of constant to variable capital changes. If it was originally say $1:1$, it now becomes successively $2:1$, $3:1$, $4:1$, $5:1$, $7:1$, etc., so that as the capital grows, instead of $\frac{1}{2}$ its total value, only $\frac{1}{3}$, $\frac{1}{4}$, $\frac{1}{5}$, $\frac{1}{6}$, $\frac{1}{8}$, etc., is turned into labour-power, and, on the other hand, $\frac{2}{3}$, $\frac{3}{4}$, $\frac{4}{5}$, $\frac{5}{6}$, $\frac{7}{8}$, into means of production. Since the demand for labour is determined not by the extent of the total

---

[9] Marx (1969–71, vol. II, pp. 555–85; and 1867–83, vol. I, pp. 591–2) (Moscow edition for Lawrence and Wishart: missing from Penguin edition).

capital but by its variable constituent alone, that demand falls progressively with the growth of the total capital ... . With the growth of the
total capital, its variable constituent, the labour incorporated in it, does
admittedly increase, but in a constantly diminishing proportion ... .
This accelerated relative diminution of the variable component, which
accompanies the accelerated increase of the total capital and moves
more rapidly than this increase, takes the inverse form, at the other pole,
of an apparently absolute increase in the working population, an
increase which always moves more rapidly than that of the variable
capital or the means of employment. But in fact it is capitalist
accumulation itself that constantly produces, and produces indeed in
direct relation with its own energy and extent, a relatively redundant
working population, i.e. a population which is superfluous to capital's
average requirements ... . (Marx, 1867–83, vol. I, pp. 781–2)

In addition to assuming that means of production are increased all the time
in relation to wage goods, and not merely once, as Ricardo assumes, Marx
also differs in the assumptions he makes about the influence of relative factor
prices on the substitution of capital for labour. In Ricardo's argument
mechanization occurs predominantly because of the continuing rise in the
wage relative to the cost of machinery. In Marx there are no references to the
substitution of capital for labour as a result of changes in relative costs, and
mechanization occurs because advances in productivity are achievable only
if capitalists continuously increase the means of production they use relative
to the labour they employ in the manner set out in the above passage. This
continual increase in the ratio of means of production to labour can make
possible vast increases in productivity, as the following up-dating of Adam
Smith's pin factory makes clear:

According to Adam Smith, ten men in his time, using the system of the
division of labour, made 48,000 sewing-needles every day. A single
needle-making machine, however, makes 145,000 needles in a working
day of 11 hours. One woman or one girl superintends four such
machines, and so produces nearly 600,000 needles in a day, and over
3,000,000 in a week. (Marx, 1867–83, vol. I, pp. 588–9)

Hence in Marx's Victorian England, one woman or one girl produced four
times as many needles in a day as ten men in Smith's time. This advance in
productivity is attributed by Marx to the immense extensions of the division
of labour and the extra mechanization that had occurred since the last half of
the eighteenth century. According to Marx, the productivity benefits from the
further division of labour are obtainable only if capitalists mechanize to the
extent required. They must also keep expanding their firms in order to take

advantage of the scale economies which permit the increases in efficiency that they need to achieve in the competitive struggle with other firms:

> The battle of competition is fought by the cheapening of commodities. The cheapness of commodities depends, all other circumstances remaining the same, on the productivity of labour, and this depends in turn on the scale of production. Therefore the larger capitals beat the smaller. It will further be remembered that, with the development of the capitalist mode of production, there is an increase in the minimum amount of individual capital necessary to carry on a business under its normal conditions. (Marx, 1867–83, vol. I, p. 777)

It is as if output expands using the sequence of techniques linked by the dotted line in figure 1. These are drawn with little scope for substitutability between capital and labour to reflect the lack of weight that Marx places on the influence of relative factor prices on the technique of production. The achievement of the successive equilibria involves far faster increases in means of production than in labour to reflect Marx's assumption that this is one of the inevitable characteristics of technical progress. Finally, the distance between the isoquants narrows to represent the underlying assumption of increasing returns which permeates chapter after chapter in the first volume of *Capital*.[10] With these technological developments, capital has to increase more and more to provide a given rate of growth of employment. If capital fails to expand in this way, the growth of employment will fall continuously.

It is also simple to show algebraically how lethal for employment a combination of an ever-rising capital–output ratio and increasing returns is liable to be.[11]

Marx's assumptions about technology can be described with the help of two equations. Suppose, first, in order to reflect Marx's assumption that means of production have to be increased consistently faster than wage goods and employment, which will almost always entail an ever-rising capital–output ratio that:

$$\frac{1}{K}\frac{dK}{dt} = H\frac{1}{Y}\frac{dY}{dt} \quad H > 1. \tag{8}$$

Suppose, second, in order to make the simplest possible assumption, that there is a linear relationship between labour requirements and the growth of capital and output; i.e.,

[10] Marx's *Capital* (vol. I, pp. 439–639) is quite largely concerned with the influence of co-operation and the division of labour and increasing mechanization on industrial organization and efficiency.

[11] The restatement of Marx's argument which is outlined below is presented at greater length and developed more fully in Eltis (1984, ch. 8).

K

$$A\frac{1}{N}\frac{dN}{dt} = \frac{1}{Y}\frac{dY}{dt} - B\frac{1}{K}\frac{dK}{dt} \tag{9}$$

where A and B are constants. It is easy to show that, if there are increasing returns as Marx believed (in contrast to Ricardo's assumption of diminishing returns in the production of necessities), B will have to equal $(Z - A)$ in this equation, with $Z > 1$ and $A < 1$. Rewriting equation (9) with that substitution,

$$A\frac{1}{N}\frac{dN}{dt} = \frac{1}{Y}\frac{dY}{dt} - (Z - A)\frac{1}{K}\frac{dK}{dt} \quad \begin{cases} Z > 1 \\ A < 1 \end{cases}. \tag{10}$$

It is evident that increasing returns lies behind this labour requirements equation, because if both labour and capital increase at a rate of x per cent, output grows at a rate of $Z \cdot x$ per cent, and Z exceeds 1. Output therefore grows Z times as fast as labour and capital where these grow at the same rate, and, since Z exceeds 1, total factor productivity will grow at a rate of $(Z - 1)$ per cent for each 1 per cent increase in labour and capital. Total factor productivity will not grow at all in the absence of growth in labour and capital, so there is no productivity growth in the absence of investment, which reflects Marx's many statements about the interconnection between productivity growth and capital accumulation.

Equation (10) describes the many possible ways in which an economy can achieve higher productivity. There is however only one way in which an economy will in practice raise productivity, if Marx is right to believe that the ratio of constant to variable capital and the capital–output ratio must rise continually if the particular techniques of production which permit continuous productivity growth are to be achieved. The attainment of the series of optimum techniques that Marx had in mind, like those shown in figure 1, entails the continual increase in the capital–output ratio shown by equation (8) as well as the 'increasing returns' labour requirements function shown by equation (10). When equations (8) and (10) are both satisfied,

$$\frac{1}{N}\frac{dN}{dt} = \left\{1 - \frac{Z - (1/H)}{A}\right\}\frac{1}{K}\frac{dK}{dt}. \tag{11}$$

This equation shows that, when the influence of a rising capital–output ratio (i.e. an H greater than 1) and increasing returns (a Z greater than 1) are taken into account, employment always grows more slowly than the capital stock. If $Z = 1$ and $H = 1$, as on a neoclassical steady-growth path, which always entails a constant capital–output ratio and constant returns,

$$\frac{1}{N}\frac{dN}{dt} = \frac{1}{K}\frac{dK}{dt}$$

so employment grows at the same rate as the capital stock. If, in contrast, it is assumed that $Z = 1.2$, so that a 1 per cent increase in capital and labour would raise output 1.2 per cent, and $H = 1\frac{1}{3}$, so that capital grows $1\frac{1}{3}$ times as fast as output, and $A = \frac{3}{4}$, which means, from equation (10), that in the absence of capital accumulation a 1 per cent increase in employment would permit a 0.75 per cent increase in output, then

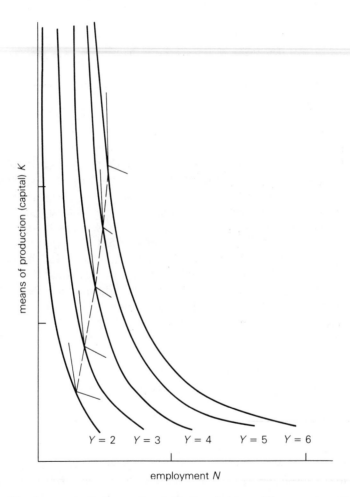

FIGURE 1 The isoquants that permit substitution between labour and capital are drawn from equation (10) with the assumption that $A = 0.75$ and $Z = 1.20$. The fixed coefficient techniques which are linked by the dotted line also satisfy the condition set out in equation (8) with $H = 1.33$, so they describe the sequence of tecnniques of production a Marx economy would follow in these conditions.

$$\frac{1}{N}\frac{dN}{dt} = \frac{2}{5}\frac{1}{K}\frac{dK}{dt}.$$

Hence, with this quite modest degree of increasing returns, and this relatively moderate tendency towards a rising capital–output ratio, employment would grow just two-fifths as fast as the capital stock. Figure 1 illustrates this example. Employment could quite easily decline as the capital stock grows. It follows from equation (11) that

$$\frac{dN}{dK} \begin{matrix} > \\ < \end{matrix} 0 \text{ depending on whether } A \begin{matrix} > \\ < \end{matrix} Z - \frac{1}{H}. \tag{12}$$

With neoclassical steady-growth assumptions where $Z = 1$ and $H = 1$, dN/dK will always be positive, but it can easily be negative if Z and H exceed 1 as Marx believed. If, for instance $A = \frac{3}{4}$, which is the kind of coefficient for the increase in output owing to extra employment alone that is generally assumed, positive accumulation will be associated with a decline in employment if $Z > 1.75$ and $H = 1$, i.e. if the capital–output ratio is constant and a 1 per cent increase in capital and labour would raise output more than 1.75 per cent. Proponents of increasing returns do not believe they are as strong as this. Alternatively, positive accumulation would be associated with declining employment if $Z = 1$ and $H > 4$, i.e. if there were constant returns and capital increased more than four times as fast as output. Most would regard that as an implausibly rapid increase in the capital–output ratio. It is however by no means implausible that $Z > 1.25$ where $H = 2$, or that $Z > 1.35$ where $H = 1\frac{2}{3}$, which would suffice to reduce employment as capital accumulates. Fairly strong but not implausibly strong increasing returns plus quite a sharp rate of increase in the capital–output ratio could therefore produce the result of a negative association between capital accumulation and employment.

Marx suggested that, as capitalism developed, a stage might conceivably be reached where the demand for labour would begin to decline:

> A development in the productive forces that would reduce the absolute number of workers, and actually enable the whole nation to accomplish its entire production in a shorter period of time, would produce a revolution, since it would put the majority of the population out of action .... The barrier to capitalist production is the surplus time of the workers. The absolute spare time that the society gains is immaterial to capitalist production. (Marx, 1867–83, vol. III, pp. 372–3)

More often, as in the passage quoted on p. 278 above, Marx stated that employment 'does admittedly increase, but in a constantly diminishing proportion' as capital accumulates. The kind of development illustrated in figure 1 may therefore come closest to giving an impression of the inter-relationship between accumulation and employment as he saw it. He believed, in other words, that the demand for labour would grow in an economy that invested massively, but still too little to keep pace with even a minimal rate of population growth.

Marx and Mill therefore provided very different answers to the fundamental questions that Ricardo's analysis of the machinery question raised. Is either answer satisfactory? The difficulty with Marx's approach to the problem has proved to be his assumption that the capital–output ratio has an inevitable upward trend. The best evidence available indicates that the capital–output ratio has been relatively stable in the century since the publication of *Capital*.[12] That would make H equal to 1 in the above equations, which removes much of the pessimism from Marx's analysis by bringing the growth of employment far closer to the growth of capital. The demand for labour has indeed risen in most of the past century, which has helped to pull up wages in a way Marx never thought possible. Marx's analysis is still, however, a valid warning of what could occur in some future period, if the capital–output ratio resumes the upward progression that he predicted.

Mill's answer to Ricardo's problem has worn better. Keynes (1936, pp. 220–1) echoed his belief that in developed economies capital accumulation would rather quickly and easily exploit available investment opportunities. When real interest rates are close to their practical floor, as they sometimes have been in recent decades, the output of efficient economies has been close to practical limits. Extra invention leading to further mechanization, which will always raise labour productivity, must extend those limits and raise a society's potential output, which modern fiscal policy can in principle redistribute so that all can benefit. That answer to Ricardo's problem has been dominant since he wrote. Marx's wholly different answer is a frightening indication of what can happen if technological progress has the capital-using bias that it may well have had in Ricardo's lifetime.

REFERENCES

Barton, John (1817). *Observations on the Circumstances which Influence the Condition of the Labouring Classes of Society*. London.

[12] The work of Matthews, Feinstein and Odling-Smee (1982) on the measurement of the growth of capital and output in Britain from 1856 to 1973 is the most professional to date, and they find that the ratio of the domestic British capital stock to the gross domestic product, measured at constant prices, averaged 4.0 in 1856–73, 4.1 in 1873–1913, 4.8 in 1924–37 (when the level of output was depressed as a result of generally weak effective demand) and 4.1 in 1951–73 (p. 133). See Klein and Kosobud (1961) for evidence on the United States capital–output ratio.

Berg, Maxine (1980). *The Machinery Question and the Making of Political Economy, 1815–1848*. Cambridge: CUP.

Blaug, Mark (1958). *Ricardian Economics: A Historical Study*. New Haven: Yale University Press.

Blaug, Mark (1978). *Economic Theory in Retrospect* (3rd edn). Cambridge: CUP.

Casarosa, Carlo (1978). 'A New Formulation of the Ricardian System'. *Oxford Economic Papers*, 30, 38–63.

Eltis, Walter (1984). *The Classical Theory of Economic Growth*. London: Macmillan.

Hicks, J. R. (1969). *A Theory of Economic History*. Oxford: OUP.

Hicks, J. R. (1972). 'Ricardo's Theory of Distribution'. In Bernard Corry and Maurice Peston (eds), *Essays in Honour of Lord Robbins*. London: Weidenfeld & Nicolson.

Hicks, J. R. (1973). *Capital and Time*. Oxford: OUP.

Hicks, J. R. and Hollander, Samuel (1977). 'Mr Ricardo and the Moderns'. *Quarterly Journal of Economics*, 91, 351–69.

Hollander, Samuel (1971). 'The Development of Ricardo's Position on Machinery'. *History of Political Economy*, 3, 105–35.

Hollander, Samuel (1979). *The Economics of David Ricardo*. Toronto: Toronto University Press.

Keynes, John Maynard (1936). *The General Theory of Employment Interest and Money. Vol. VII of the Collected Writings of John Maynard Keynes*. London: Macmillan.

Klein, L. R. and Kosobud, R. F. (1961). 'Some Econometrics of Growth: Great Ratios of Economics'. *Quarterly Journal of Economics*, 75, 173–98.

Lamond, E. (ed.) (1929). *A Discourse of the Common Weal of this Realm of England* (1581). Cambridge: CUP.

Malthus, Thomas R. (1820). *Principles of Political Economy*. Partly reprinted in Ricardo *Works* (1951–73), vol. II. Cambridge: CUP.

Marx, Karl (1867–83). *Capital* (3 vols). Harmondsworth: Penguin, 1976–81 edn.

Marx, Karl (1969–71). *Theories of Surplus Value* (3 vols). Moscow: Progress Publishers for Lawrence & Wishart.

Matthews, R. C. O., Feinstein, C. H and Odling-Smee, J. C. (1982). *British Economic Growth, 1856–1973*. Oxford: OUP.

McCulloch, J. R. (1820). 'Taxation and the Corn Laws'. *Edinburgh Review*, 33, 155–87.

McCulloch, J. R. (1821). 'The Opinions of Messrs Say, Sismondi and Malthus, on the Effects of Machinery and Accumulation Stated and Examined'. *Edinburgh Review*, 35, 102–23.

Mill, John Stuart (1963ff.). *The Collected Works of John Stuart Mill* (17 vols to date). Toronto: Toronto University Press.

More, Thomas (1516). *Utopia*.

O'Brien, D. P. (1975). *The Classical Economists*. Oxford: OUP.

Pasinetti, Luigi L. (1960). 'A Mathematical Formulation of the Ricardian System'. *Review of Economic Studies*, 27, 78–98.

Ricardo, David (1951–73). *The Works and Correspondence of David Ricardo* (11 vols), ed. P. Sraffa. Cambridge: CUP.

Sismondi, J. C. L. Sismonde, de (1819). *Nouveaux Principes d'Economie Politique* (2 vols). Paris.

12

Ricardo's Chapter on Machinery and the Theory of Capital

FERDINANDO MEACCI

1 INTRODUCTION

The thirty-first chapter, 'On Machinery', of Ricardo's *Principles* has always drawn the attention of economists whatever their school, style or generation. McCulloch (1821a), J. S. Mill (1871), Marx (1867–94), Wicksell (1901), Hayek (1941) and Hicks (1969, 1970, 1973) are only some of the scholars who have dealt with it or have been inspired by it. On various occasions and with different purposes, they have provided their own criticisms, elucidations and applications of the chapter's propositions. As yet, their various contributions cannot be reduced to a unified whole while the question of what the chapter is about seems still unsettled. On the other hand, the most recent reinterpretations of Ricardo's thought as put forth by Samuelson (1959), Pasinetti (1960), Hicks and Hollander (1977), Casarosa (1978), Caravale and Tosato (1980) and others contain no formalizations of the reasoning of chapter 31,[1] while the revival of interest in Ricardo's theory that has followed Sraffa's works (Ricardo, 1951–73; Sraffa, 1960) has shunned so far the thirty-first chapter—and the theory of capital that it is a part of—perhaps because it is not the classic theory of reproduction (wherein capital plays so crucial a role) but the theory of distribution that is coming to life again.

The aim of the present paper is threefold. It is an attempt, first, to clear up some concepts that seem to have been overlooked or misunderstood in the course of past interpretations; second, to place Ricardo's chapter in the mainstream of the theory of capital, as it runs from the classics to the neo-Austrians; in order, third, to show its implications in terms of the distinction between *individual* and *social* capital on one hand and between theory of *reproduction* and theory of *distribution* on the other.

The paper is divided into two parts. The first deals with the meaning of the

I am grateful to Giovanni Caravale for encouragement and to Ludwig M. Lachmann for criticisms.

[1] For a very early mathematical treatment see J. E. Tozer (1838). A brief exception is now provided by Eltis, in this volume.

chapter, the second with its theoretical implications. Two appendixes have been added, the first of which regards certain facts of our century which seem to realize Ricardo's proposition, while the second is a flash on what the chapter ultimately teaches us.

2 WHAT THE CHAPTER IS ABOUT

I would like to start out from Ricardo's starting-point itself: his change of opinion about the subject of machinery. As he himself says, the change was due to his realization that the statement, 'whenever the net income of a society increases its gross income would also increase', was wrong.[2] Important as this admission is, I think that this may not be the only change that occurred in Ricardo's mind before his new opinion took shape. Another, unadmitted but equally important, change can be singled out by looking closely at the words he uses—and the concepts he understands—while speaking of his change of opinion. Whereas his previous opinion was worked out in connection with the problem of, as he puts it, 'an application of machinery to any branch of production', the new opinion is concerned with the problem of a capitalist who 'employs half his men in constructing a machine'. The two words to be noticed here are 'application' in the former and 'constructing' in the latter sentence. While the word 'application' seems to refer to machinery that is *already built*, the word 'constructing' clearly refers to machinery that is still *to be built*. While in the former case machinery presents itself as something that is bought by—or is even free to—an individual capitalist, in the latter, machinery is viewed in the perspective of its production.[3] More important still, its production is considered here—though Ricardo may mislead the reader by speaking of 'a capitalist'—not within a particular business, sector or region but within the framework of the general equilibrium of a closed industrial system within the economy as a whole.[4] Within this framework the expression 'introduction of machinery' is the same thing as 'production of machinery'. On the other hand, the latter expression

[2] See Ricardo, *Works* (vol. I, ch. 31, p. 388). On Ricardo's change of opinion see Sraffa (1951, pp. lvii–lx), Hollander (1971, 1979), Blaug (1958, 1978) and Eltis's paper in this volume. For an analysis of the machinery question in an historical perspective see also Berg (1980).

[3] 'I think we must remember how the problem presented itself to him. He was becoming conscious of the Industrial Revolution; rather late, some would say, but no one, at that depth, had thought it out earlier. What, in that context, he will surely have had in mind is not "improved machinery" (though he says "improved machinery") but the introduction of machinery: the introduction of a strongly fixed-capital-using technique in place of one which, as an approximation, would be regarded as circulating-capital-using only' (Hicks, 1973, pp. 98–9).

[4] On 30 May 1823 in the House of Commons 'Mr Ricardo said, his proposition was, not that the use of machinery was prejudicial to persons employed in one particular manufacture, but to the working classes generally' (*Works*, vol. V, p. 303). In this sense see also Sylos Labini (1967, p. 186).

implies a particularization of the more general process which the classics called 'conversion of circulating into fixed capital'. It is this process—and the effects it brings about in the distribution of national income—that chapter 31 deals with.[5] For its effects to be *actually* harmful to the labouring class, Ricardo's only condition is that machinery be '*suddenly* discovered and extensively used' (see Ricardo, *Works*, vol. I, ch. 31, p. 395).

As the concepts of circulating and fixed capital are so crucial to the whole chapter, it is worthwhile dwelling on their meaning before delving into the chapter's inner truths. In his famous example, Ricardo says that a capital of £7,000 'is invested in fixed capital' while the remaining £13,000 'is employed as circulating capital in the support of labour'. The expressions 'invested in' in the former case and 'employed as' in the latter are neither casual nor alternative. Taken together, they imply rather a conception of capital whereby this is conceived within the process of its rotation and as affected by the irreversibility of the material transformations implied by it.[6]

This insight can be arrived at by carefully construing Ricardo's passages. The first step may be overcome by looking at the material substance the two kinds of capital consist of. While circulating capital is dealt with by Ricardo as consisting of 'food and necessaries', his fixed capital is said to consist of 'buildings, implements, etc., etc.'[7] From this it follows that, when a circulating capital is 'invested' in order to become a fixed capital, its material substance changes both its shape and its utility. What concerns Ricardo in chapter 31 is the relevance of this change from the standpoint of labour. For, while circulating capital enters the labour market as demand for living labour (it consists of the same things that are demanded by labourers in exchange for their labour), fixed capital, though eventually the result of that exchange, presents itself in a shape that makes it unable to command living labour to be exchanged for it: looked at from labour's standpoint, 'it is capital in the wrong form' (see Hicks and Hollander, 1977, p. 361).

A characteristic feature of this form is that, in addition to being wrong, it is also irreversible. Both the wrong form and the irreversibility of it can best be seen in Jevons's definition of fixed capital (1871, p. 242). 'I would not say,' he claims, 'that a railway is fixed capital, but that capital is fixed in the railway.' The past participle does here emphasize that capital, once fixed or

---

[5] As J. S. Mill says, 'This is true not of machinery alone, but of all improvements by which capital is sunk, that is, rendered permanently incapable of being applied to the maintenance and remuneration of labour' (Mill, 1871, vol. II, bk I, ch. 6, p. 94).

[6] On the relevance of this irreversibility in the theory of capital see Meacci (1978). On its practical relevance to different countries see Ricardo's chapter, 'Sudden Changes in the Channels of Trade' (*Works*, vol. I, pp. 265ff.).

[7] In his *Notes on Malthus* Ricardo goes further into this difference by stating that, while a circulating capital is capital 'realized in those things which are consumed by the labourer', fixed capital 'is realized in machinery', i.e. in things that are not consumed by the labourer. See *Works* (vol. II, pp. 234–6, n. 149).

invested, is lost in its 'right' form, namely as funds destined for the maintenance of labour: these funds can support labour only *once*.

Whatever insight a material definition of circulating and fixed capital may provide us with, one thing is to define what goods the two kinds of capital consist of; another, what their function is in the process of *reproduction*. After all, a distinction based on the material aspect of the two kinds of capital is not exactly what even the famous definition of chapter 1 implies. Here, Ricardo clearly places the emphasis on the process of reproduction when he states that, 'according as capital is rapidly perishable, and requires to be frequently reproduced, or is of slow consumption, it is classed under the heads of circulating, or of fixed capital' (see *Works*, vol. I, p. 31; also ch. 8, p. 150). Given the intimate connection between capital and reproduction, we should here remark that it is not because it is rapidly perishable or of slow consumption, but more precisely because it is frequently or slowly reproduced, that capital 'is classed under the heads of circulating or fixed capital'. On the other hand, though the word 'reproduced' is used by Ricardo as synonymous with 'returned' in the same passages of the *Principles*, the two words are not necessarily equivalent when referred to capital. While the former undoubtedly implies the reproduction of capital in its *productive* form (a material trans- formation), the latter may simply refer to the circulation of capital in its *money* form (a formal transformation):[8] to circulate—that is, 'to be returned to its employer' in its initial form—the former must be materially reproduced while the latter may simply 'change hands'. It is true that circulating capital may well be defined in both cases as that part of capital which—unlike the fixed part—is parted with.[9] But what is parted with is a different thing which begets different consequences in the two cases: it is wage goods, fostering the process of social reproduction, in the former case; it is money as a tool of individual enrichment in the latter. From this viewpoint, raw materials and semi-finished products appear only as a stage both in the reproduction of consumption goods and in the circulation of money: they are neither a departure nor a terminal point, both in the reproduction of social capital (which begins and ends with consumption goods) and in the circulation of money capital (which begins and ends with money). Of the two processes it is the reproduction of social capital that Ricardo—as well as other classical economists—has mostly in mind in chapter 31. This seems to be the reason why raw materials, semi-finished products and money are neglected in this

[8] On the relevance of this distinction see Marx (1867–94, bk II, section I).

[9] This definition is first given by Smith when he speaks of a farmer who makes a profit of his fixed capital 'by keeping it in his own possession' and of his circulating capital 'by parting with it' (Smith, 1776, bk II, ch. 1). The same track is followed by, among others, Storch when he brilliantly says: 'The constant and incessantly repeated path which circulating capital describes in order to take leave of the entrepreneur and in order to return to him in the first form is comparable to a circle; hence the name *circulant* given to this capital, and the use of the word circulation for its movement' (Storch, 1823, vol. I, p. 405).

chapter's definition of circulating capital: while money creeps into the chapter only as a convenient numeraire to describe the size and composition of national wealth, raw materials and semi-finished products are not taken into consideration because, in addition to being of no concern to 'those who live by the wages of labour', they neither begin nor close the cycle of social reproduction. More generally, this is also the reason why Marx is consistent when he maintains that machines are part of the circulating capital of *their* own manufacturer (1867–94, bk II, ch. 10); and, in addition, why Keynes's criticism against what he calls 'a famous confusion of the classical economists' (i.e. the confusion between Keynes's 'working capital' and their 'circulating capital') is based on his own misunderstanding of their multiform concept of circulating capital (Keynes, 1930, vol. II, p. 114); while Knight's claim that 'their crucial error' lay in the interpretation of the nature and role of capital 'as reproduced in an annual cycle starting anew from zero each year' (1935, p. 196)[10] should be interpreted in the sense that this is one of their 'crucial contributions'. For what was at stake, both in most of their writings on capital and in Ricardo's thirty-first chapter itself, was the elucidation of the principles of social reproduction (as distinguished from individual circulation), not the description of the manifold complications that affect the process of actual reproduction in an advanced stage of accumulation.[11]

To sum up, the perspective of social reproduction and the material aspect of circulating capital enable us to overcome within chapter 31 the note added to the distinction in chapter 1 between circulating and fixed capital: 'a division not essential, and in which the line of demarcation cannot be accurately drawn'.[12] The particular assumptions of chapter 31 enable us to draw it accurately instead: not only does circulating capital consist here—unlike fixed capital—of *food and necessaries*; it also differs from the other kind of capital because the period of its reproduction is here conceived—unlike that of fixed capital—as *one year*: wage goods are advanced as circulating capital at the beginning of each year; they have to be reproduced at the end of the same year in order to be advanced again to carry forth the process at the beginning of the next.

Once the different roles that circulating and fixed capital play in the aggregate demand for labour have been admitted, one should still realize that this difference may be approached along two different lines of thought. These intersect exactly where that distinction lies, but come from and lead to very different points. By moving along one line, the two kinds of capital appear as

[10] This paper is full of many controversial points and is generally unfaithful to Ricardo's thought.

[11] On the concept of an 'annual cycle' as a framework of analysis, see particularly J. Mill (1821). On the relevance of this concept in classical thought see Blaug (1958, p. 122). The concept stems, through 'the great trunk of the *Wealth of Nations*', from the Physiocrats' theory of capital (O'Brien, 1975).

[12] See *Works* (vol. I, p. 31, note). On why this is 'a division not essential' see below p. 293 ff. and particularly n. 23.

alternative transitory aspects of capital in general, i.e. of capital in the process of its material transformations. By moving along the other, they rather appear as two *complementary* portions of an individual capital at a particular moment of time, i.e. of capital invested in a particular business.[13] It is important to distinguish between these two directions because their confusion may breed a still deeper confusion between two fundamental concepts of political economy: namely, the concepts of *value* on one hand and *wealth* on the other. Each of these can be met at the beginning of either one or the other of these two lines of thought: while by moving along the line of individual capital we are led to the problem of value, by moving along the line of social capital we are led to the problem of wealth.

'Value and Riches. Their Distinctive Properties' is the title given by Ricardo to chapter 20 of his *Principles*, one of the most important chapters of the book. From the point of view we are dealing with, this chapter may be viewed as a link between two chapters as different as chapter 1, 'On Value' and chapter 31, 'On Machinery'. To be sure, Ricardo deals with machinery in both of them, but the same subject is considered in a very different perspective on the two occasions. Whereas in chapter 1 machinery 'and other fixed and durable capital' comes into consideration so long as its existence 'considerably modifies' the principle of value (i.e. the value of individual commodities in terms of other commodities produced by capitals of different size and composition), in chapter 31 machinery is approached from the point of view of the effects that its 'introduction' causes in the reproduction of the annual produce, i.e. in the reproduction of wealth. 'I mean always quantity of commodities not value', says Ricardo himself in the middle of chapter 31; which apparently means: 'Throughout this chapter I am dealing with riches not values of particular commodities—as I did in the 1st.'[14]

This is why Marx's distinction between variable and constant capital has

---

[13] This point is repeatedly raised by Marx (see for instance 1939, Notebooks VI–VII, but also 1867–94, bk II). It may be summarized in the simile whereby 'the course of human life consists of passing through different ages. But at the same time all ages exist side by side, distributed amongst different individuals' (Marx, 1939, Notebook VI, p. 639). The point throws a special light on the word 'combined' which Ricardo uses in a passage of the *Principles* in relation to 'the capital that is to support labour' and 'the capital that is invested in tools, machinery and buildings' (*Works*, vol. I, p. 30).

[14] Where Ricardo actually concludes that 'thus then is the public benefited by machinery' (*Works*, vol. I, p. 42). This passage is *not* part of his 'previous opinion': though we may have read it before, it was published by Ricardo *with* chapter 31 in the same third edition of his book. Therefore, what Hollander says in connection with Hicks's recent distinction between Fundism and Materialism in the theory of capital (see Hicks, 1974), namely that in Ricardo 'the materialist dimension tends to fade away once *time* comes to the fore' (Hollander, 1979, p. 313), may be interpreted in the sense that the materialist dimension tends to fade away when Ricardo deals (as he does in chapter 31) with the theory of reproduction (whereby it comes true that 'labour works *on* land *through* capital, not on capital nor with capital'), while it tends to become stronger and stronger when he focuses (as he does in chapter 1) on the theory of value.

little to do with the distinction in chapter 31 between circulating and fixed capital;[15] and also why Edelberg's proposition (1933, p. 52) that 'Ricardo's observations on the nature of capital are, for the most part, to be found in Sections III, IV, and V of Chapter 1 of his *Principles*' seems to be the opposite of the truth. What can be found in those sections are, for the most part, Ricardo's observations on how the principle of value is affected by the employment of 'machinery and other fixed and durable capital'. Here, machinery is considered as given: what is here investigated is not its nature but the effects its existence brings about in the exchange values of individual commodities produced through it. This is a problem that arises within the theory of *distribution*, not that of *reproduction*.[16]

As for Marx's distinction, its likeness to that of Ricardo is due to the fact that the concepts of circulating and variable capital undoubtedly refer to the same material substance (wage goods). Still, they are not conceived in the same perspective: while Marx's distinction is put forth within his theory of distribution in order to explain the origin of surplus value, the distinction in chapter 31 is put forth within the theory of reproduction to explain how changes in the shape of wealth may affect the condition of labourers with the rate of profit remaining the same. In Marx's terms, chapter 31 deals with the *Entwertungsprozess* of circulating capital, not the *Verwertungsprozess* of capital in general: it is a change in the speed of its circulation, not a change in its yield, that is dealt with here by Ricardo.[17]

If one enquires which of the two lines discussed above has been the one mostly followed in literature, this seems to be the direction of an individual capital as subdivided in two portions and employed at the same moment in

[15] On Marx's distinction see Marx (1867–94, bk I, section III, ch. 6). On the difference between Marx's and Ricardo's distinction see book II (section II, ch. 8). On the important distinction between *circulating* capital and *circulation* capital see again book II (section II, chs 8 and 9).

[16] These two perspectives are first distinguished and immediately later confused by Edelberg himself when he says: 'When he is not discussing the effects of capital on relative exchange values, Ricardo speaks not so much in terms of the time element in capital but rather in terms of the amount of capital relatively to the amount of population. The two terminologies are in their content identical' (Edelberg, 1933, p. 54). That the two terminologies are *not* identical might instead be noticed if Edelberg's sentence were worded thus: 'When he is not discussing the effects of capital on relative exchange values, Ricardo speaks not so much in terms of the time element embodied in *fixed* capital, but rather in terms of the amount of *free* capital relatively to the amount of population' (on these two other kinds of capital see below and section 2). For the distinction between a *production* period and an *exchange* period in the 'year' of the classics, see Eagly (1974, p. 44).

[17] Therefore Schumpeter's assertion that his 'wage capital is identical not only with Marx's variable capital, but also with the classic wage fund' (Schumpeter, 1954, p. 635) is valid only in terms of the material aspects of capital. The same can be said about the similarity between his own distinction between *wage* and *technological* capital and the distinction in chapter 31 between circulating and fixed capital.

a particular business: in other words, the direction of value, not of wealth. This movement has resulted in interpretations of chapter 31 by which Ricardo's 'capitalist' is turned into the owner of a particular business,[18] and the appearance of a fixed capital instead of the disappearance of a circulating capital becomes the exclusive focus of attention.[19]

By moving along this direction, one may be prevented from coming to a full understanding of the two general truths found so far on Ricardo's chapter. One is Schumpeter's statement that chapter 31 is an excellent illustration of the wages fund doctrine (Schumpeter, 1954, p. 680). The other is J. S. Mill's assertion that the inevitability of Ricardo's conclusions is based on his fourth fundamental proposition respecting capital: demand for commodities is not demand for labour.[20] Since the wages fund is social capital at the beginning of its material transformations, it is not the wages fund and the problems connected with its reproduction, but rather a particular machine and the problems connected with its technical coefficients that is taken into consideration while moving along the line of individual capital. Accordingly, a change in the technical coefficients by which fixed capital is marked is here usually misunderstood for a change in the quantity of wage goods of which circulating capital consists. While the relevance and the effects on employment (especially in particular sectors) of machinery carrying new technical coefficients cannot be denied, it is none the less clear that, according to Ricardo, 'distress and poverty' may follow the introduction of machinery not exactly because new machines are born, but because an old capital—more precisely, the 'right' form of an old capital—has at the same time and for the same reason ceased to exist.[21]

---

[18] Such a deviation can be clearly seen in Wicksell's ten-landowners example (Wicksell, 1901, Part II, section 1c).

[19] The introduction of 'already built' machinery in a particular business, sector or region seems to be the way Marx frames the 'struggle between worker and machine' in a famous chapter of his *Capital* (Marx, 1867–94, bk I, section IV, ch. 13).

[20] See J. S. Mill (1871, bk I, ch. 5, section 9). On Mill's fourth proposition as a reflection of Smith's distinction between 'work done' and 'work to be done', see Meacci (1978, ch. 3, section 7).

[21] If this conclusion were unfounded, then what Ricardo says in his 'ten men attending a corn mill' example is either contradictory or meaningless: 'If ten men turned a corn mill,' he says in chapter 20, 'and it be discovered that, by the assistance of wind, or of water, the labour of these ten men may be spared, the flour which is the produce partly of the work performed by the mill, would immediately fall in value, in proportion to the quantity of labour saved; and the society would be richer by the commodities which the labour of the ten men could produce, the funds destined for their maintenance being in no degree impaired' (*Works*, vol. I, p. 286; see also vol. VIII, pp. 389–90). The example here is clearly about a labour-saving invention: not some, but all, the labourers previously employed in the production of flour are made redundant by the invention. Yet no 'distress and poverty' is here assumed to befall the labourers, '*the funds destined for their maintenance being in no degree impaired*'. The difference between this example and that of chapter 31 is that a fall in value with a steady circulating capital is assumed in the former case while a fall in circulating capital with values (relative difficulties of production) remaining the same is what is assumed in the latter.

3 WHAT THE CHAPTER IMPLIES

By moving along the line of thought that leads to the insights of Schumpeter and J. S. Mill, we are able to place Ricardo's chapter in the mainstream of the theory of capital[22] and to read it in a somewhat new perspective. To do that we need to start out from Jevons's distinction between *free* and *invested* capital. By free capital he means 'the wages of labour either in its transitory form of money or its real form of food and other necessaries of life' (Jevons, 1871, p. 241). From this standpoint, while circulating capital is capital to be invested for only a single period of time, a fixed capital is capital invested for longer periods: the former is capital that returns free in a one-year rotation; the latter is capital that returns free in a rotation requiring more than one year.[23] This clarifies what the conversion of circulating into fixed capital really means: it is the same thing as a *lengthening* of the average period of time that must elapse before capital returns free.

This reminds us of the Austrians and their period of production.[24] Unfortunately, the Austrians have always been reluctant to ascribe to the classics any preview of their own theory, while Böhm-Bawerk's capital theory has never been regarded as fully satisfactory even within the Austrian school itself.[25] This is not the place to go into the details of the various shortcomings implied in the Austrian concept of the period of production: fortunately, it is not even needed here. For it is not Böhm-

---

[22] A mainstream in the theory of capital is clearly admitted by Hicks when he says, while speaking of the history of Austrian theory, that 'the Austrians were not a peculiar sect, out of the main stream; they were in the main stream; it was the others who were out of it' (Hicks, 1973, p. 12).

[23] This may be the reason why the distinction between circulating and fixed capital is said by Ricardo to be more a matter of degree than of kind: see his example of the 'wheat bought by a farmer to sow', which 'is comparatively a fixed capital to the wheat purchased by a baker to make it into loaves' (*Works*, vol. I, ch. I, p. 131). Here Schumpeter seems to hit the mark when he says: 'Both are nothing but immature [elements of] consumers' goods—intermediate products or "inchoate wealth", as Taussig was to call them about 80 years later (1896). Or both may be "resolved" into hoarded labour—James Mill's term, which expresses Ricardo's meaning very well and was to be used again by Wicksell, also about 80 years later (1893)—though we must not forget that the various agglomerations of hoarded labour embodied in the various goods carry different indices of time distance or indices of places in the time sequences to which they belong' (Schumpeter, 1954, p. 637). However, the sentence is ambiguously worded: both a forward-looking and a backward-looking approach to the two concepts of capital intermingle in Schumpeter's statement.

[24] The concept was developed by Böhm-Bawerk (1889).

[25] It is known that Menger, according to Schumpeter (1954, p. 847), once said that 'Böhm-Bawerk's theory is the greatest error ever committed'. His theory was never fully shared by Wicksell (1901) and Hayek (1941), his two most eminent followers. For an internal and more recent overcoming of Böhm-Bawerk's capital theory see Lachmann (1956). On Mises's footsteps (1949) see also Kirzner (1966).

Bawerk's concept of the period of production that is at stake in chapter 31. It is simply a lengthening of the *reproduction* period of free capital (a classical concept) for society as a whole. To put it in Austrian terms, it is only a forward shift in the centre of gravity of capital investment arising from a substitution of a growth of capital in *height* for its reproduction in the usual *breadth*.[26]

The same conclusion could be reached if, instead of starting out from Jevons's concept of free capital, we were to start out from a concept worked out by Marx (1867–94) with a very different purpose: the organic composition of capital (see bk I, section VII, ch. 23, and bk III, section II, ch. 8). This ratio's secular tendency to increase is assumed by Marx as the core of his 'general law of capitalistic accumulation' (bk I, chs 23 and 24). The first stage of this law is 'the formation of a relative overpopulation or industrial reserve army', the last stage, 'the poverty of ever growing strata of the workers' active army and the dead weight of pauperism'.[27]

One may think that Marx is here bringing Ricardo's chapter 31 to its ultimate conclusions. However, many a break keeps the two arguments apart and makes Marx's continuation look rather like a deviation.

Besides the important distinction between 'circulating vs. fixed' and 'variable vs. constant' capital discussed above, Marx differs from Ricardo in that, while the latter more properly deals with a process of conversion, the former argues rather in terms of a process of accumulation. Furthermore, while Ricardo views his process as an isolated one and limits himself to considering its temporary effects, Marx's process is viewed as a continuous one and is dealt with in the perspective of its final effects: pauperism is viewed in the former case as historically possible,[28] in the latter as inevitable.[29]

---

[26] See Wicksell (1901, vol. I, part II, pp. 163–4) and his famous distinction between the capitalist, 'the friend of labour', and the inventor, 'not infrequently its enemy'. See also Hayek (1941, appendix II, p. 426). As for Hayek, what he writes in this connection, namely that 'the proposition which the classical economists used has really little to do with the particular distinction between circulating and fixed capital as defined by them, but is connected with changes in the time dimension of capital in general' (1941, p. 426), seems to be valid if the word 'little' is deleted and 'but' is substituted by 'and'. On the other hand, when Hayek says that the 'reduction of the funds destined for the support of labour' implied in the conversion of circulating into fixed capital describes 'the same phenomenon which later became generally known under the name of forced saving' (1941, p. 426), he seems to neglect the fact that it was only for the sake of brevity that Ricardo used to drop the adjective 'productive' before the word 'labour' in the recurring expression 'funds destined for the support of labour'. In this sense Hayek's assertion is untenable unless he means a 'reduction of the funds destined for the support of *unproductive* labour'.

[27] For a long and detailed introduction to this 'general law' and its consequences on social life, see Marx (1867–94, bk I, section IV, ch. 13, esp. sections 5 and 6).

[28] Consider the verb 'may', often used by Ricardo in chapter 31 to mean the possibility rather than the inevitable necessity of the chapter's conclusions.

[29] It is true that Marx himself maintains, following in Ricardo's footsteps and attacking the

On the other hand, when a continuous process of accumulation is involved, growing unemployment and growing mechanization cannot last together for long in the economy as a whole. The secular tendency of the organic composition to increase is compatible with growing unemployment if the trends of both the composition and the unemployment are looked at from the standpoint of a particular business, sector or region: here, machinery appears as something that is simply introduced somewhere or is even imported from somewhere else. But, so long as constant capital is to be produced within a closed system and reproduced on an enlarged scale, the process of mechanization can continue throughout time on condition that, given the principle of the greater frequency of lengthening inventions, more and more living labour, instead of being expelled from the sphere of production, is invested into it in the form of what the Austrians would call 'indirect' or increasingly indirect labour.[30] While to an individual capitalist the problem of mechanization reduces itself to laying out a given capital in a fixed rather than a circulating shape, in *buying* machinery instead of living labour, the same problem presents itself to a growing economy as something that can be solved by substituting a particular kind of labour for another kind in the general structure of production or, more precisely, in the time profile of investment; in Hicks's terms, by substituting 'construction' for 'operation' labour or, what amounts to the same thing, construction labour time for the utilization labour time annually spent in the economy as a whole.[31] While in

---

supporters of the 'compensation theory', that the subject under discussion is here the process of *locking up* a capital, not of *liberating* it—as 'an entire set of bourgeois economists' would instead maintain (Marx, 1867–94, bk I, ch. 13, section 6). However, on the one hand, Marx's example is here based on the process of 'fixing' from the standpoint of an individual capitalist; on the other, when he turns to the social implications of such a process, he is led to neglect another important 'general law of capitalistic accumulation'. This law—later discovered though never actually labelled thus—is based on the principle of the greater frequency in a growing economy of *lengthening* relative to *shortening* inventions. This law may not apply to an isolated case of mechanization (such as the 'ten men attending a corn mill' example quoted in n. 21 above, where a shortening invention is involved), but it certainly does apply to a continuous process of accumulation as past and present experiences of capitalistic and socialist economies prove alike (see the following note).

[30] On this principle see Böhm-Bawerk's *Positive Theory of Capital* and particularly its 'Excursus' in Böhm-Bawerk (1889, vols II and III; especially 'Excursus II', pp. 24ff.).

[31] In Hicks's 'Simple Profile' there is for each technique 'a construction period, lasting *m* weeks, in which labour is applied at a constant rate but in which there is no final output. It is followed by a utilization period, lasting a further *n* weeks, in which labour is applied at a constant (but different) rate, and in which final output appears at a constant rate'. *m* and *n* are the 'time parameters', a_c and a_u the 'input coefficients' of the technique. Improvements are 'backward-biased' when the main saving in cost is on the side of a_c, 'forward-biased' when it is on the side of a_u. Both kinds of improvements are 'strong' or 'weak' depending on whether only one or both 'sectoral ratios' (the ratios between a_c and a_u of the new and the old technique) are greater than 1. The 'introduction of machinery' in chapter 31 is viewed by Hicks as a switch of techniques with a 'strong forward bias' (Hicks, 1973, chs 4 and 8).

the individual case substitution is simply made by an act of *will* on the part of an individual capitalist choosing among alternative combinations of labour and machinery, for this to occur in the whole society the availability of a *power* is needed, namely the availability of free capital to support an increasing amount of construction labour until the fruits of accumulation are reaped.[32]

To be sure, a shift of perspective from a process of (sudden) conversion to one of (continuous) accumulation is what takes place at the end of Ricardo's chapter itself (see *Works*, vol. I, p. 395). But on one hand, such a shift simply introduces what appears to be an appendix to the whole chapter; on the other, the role assigned to such an appendix seems to be to fend off any possible prejudice (something very far from Ricardo's mind, even when he is dealing with the process of conversion) against fixed capital as such.[33] Hence Ricardo's final observations on accumulation and foreign trade, plus his statement that 'it is not easy to conceive **that** under any circumstances an increase of capital should not be followed by **an increased** demand for labour; the most that can be said is that the demand for labour will increase at a diminishing ratio.'[34] This statement implies, or is consistent with, some propositions on the role of fixed capital in a growing economy which can be construed from various passages of Ricardo's works. These propositions may be summarized as follows:

(1) the introduction of machinery must not be discouraged; if only because, besides any complication due to foreign trade,

---

[32] This is why Edelberg is wrong again in supposing a lengthening where there is only a substitution of the former kind (Edelberg, 1933, p. 69).

This Austrian insight is sometime implied by Marx himself. For instance, in his *Grundrisse*'s chapter on capital he says: 'The part of production which is oriented towards the production of fixed capital does not produce direct objects of individual gratification nor direct exchange values. This requires that society be able to *wait*; that a large part of the wealth already created can be withdrawn from immediate consumption in order to employ this part for labour which is not immediately productive' (Marx, 1939, Notebook VII, p. 707). See also Marx (1905, vol. I, ch. 4, sections 3 and 17).

[33] See the sentence with which this 'appendix' begins: 'The statements which I have made will not, I hope, lead to the inference that machinery should not be encouraged'. Where I see an 'appendix', Eltis sees the 'core' of Ricardo's chapter (see his paper elsewhere in this volume).

[34] *Works*, vol. I, p. 396, note. This statement is used by Ricardo to criticize Barton (1817, p. 16; quoted by Ricardo, *Works*, vol. I, p. 396), when the latter says: 'It is easy to conceive that, under certain circumstances, the whole of the annual savings of an industrious people might be added to fixed capital, in which case they would have no effect in increasing the demand for labour.' This passage may be badly worded and is easily misunderstood: 'Fixed capital,' says Barton himself in another passage, 'when once formed ceases to affect the demand for labour, but during its formation it gives employment to just as many hands as an equal amount would employ, either of circulating capital, or of revenue' (1817, p. 56).

(2) a society's circulating capital can increase beyond a certain point only after its fixed capital has itself increased; so that

(3) a diminishing ratio between circulating and fixed capital is the only way for an industrial society to increase the aggregate demand for labour; it being however understood

(4) that a diminishing ratio between the two kinds of capital does not rule out an increase in the absolute amount of circulating capital (the demand for labour); and

(5) that it is better anyway for circulating capital to increase at a lower rate than fixed capital than for it not to increase at all.[35]

The shift of attention towards a continuous process of accumulation is also at the roots of what has been called the 'Ricardo effect'.[36] In its most authentic version, this expression recalls that famous passage where Ricardo says:

With every increase of capital and population, food will generally rise, on account of its being more difficult to produce. The consequence of a rise of food will be a rise of wages, and every rise of wages will have a tendency to determine the saved capital in a greater proportion than before to the employment of machinery. Machinery and labour are in constant competition, and the former can frequently not be employed until labour rises. (*Works*, vol. I, ch. 31, p. 395)[37]

Here Ricardo refers to accumulation as if it presented itself first as a *widening* process, whose ultimate outcome is a rise in food as the difficulty of providing

[35] Ricardo's scruples may derive from Smith's inaccuracy in that famous passage where the latter says that 'the demand for those who live by wages naturally increases with the increase of national wealth, and cannot possibly increase without it .... It is not the actual greatness of national wealth, but its continual increase, which occasions a rise in the wages of labour' (Smith, 1776, bk I, ch. 8). In Ricardo's terms, Smith would here be right if by 'national wealth' we were to intend not 'revenue and stock', as Smith himself says, but, besides revenue, only that part of stock which is circulating capital. See however Smith himself (1776, bk II, ch. 1) and, *inter alios*, J. S. Mill (1871, bk I, ch. 6, p. 98) and Marx (1939, Notebook VII, p. 734).

[36] It was Hayek who first called it so (see Hayek, 1969, p. 274, n. 2). According to Hayek's definition of the 'effect', and contrary to his opinion as stated in the footnote just quoted, one could infer that Schumpeter may have been more accurate in avoiding Ricardo's name by calling it the 'Hayek effect'. On Hayek's 'Ricardo effect' see also Hayek (1939, 1942).

[37] On 'why it is that old countries are constantly impelled to employ machinery, and new countries to employ labour', see *Works* (vol. I, ch. 1, p. 41, note). The likeness of these two passages, far from undermining the general unlikeness of chapters 1 and 31 discussed above, is only a proof that a sudden change of perspective takes place in the final passages of chapter 31. On this change see following paragraph. On why there is no contradiction between the general unlikeness of chapters 1 and 31 and the particular likeness of the two passages cited in this note, see above the distinction between value and wealth.

constant additions to it increases, and subsequently as a *deepening* process, whose outcome may be a rise in unemployment as more and more of the 'saved capital' is fixed into machinery.[38]

Two remarks should be made here to qualify Ricardo's meaning. First, the widening case is here conceived on a global scale as affecting an economy running up against the growing scarcity of land. On the contrary, the deepening case is focused on the reactions of individual capitalists to changes in the relative prices of labour and machinery. Besides, while the widening case is here conceived as being financed out of new savings, the deepening case resounds with the chapter's particular assumptions whereby both savings and the propensity to save are given.

These two qualifications should make it clear that any increase of wages is not in itself sufficient to give rise or to sustain the industrialization of a country. For, the accumulation of capital on a social scale is one thing; the mechanization of production on an individual scale, another.

APPENDIX I

If we shift our attention from Ricardo's chapter to the reality of our time, we can gain a deeper insight into some historical facts of our century and their possible consequences on our life. A similar attempt was first made by Hicks in his *A Theory of Economic History* (1969, ch. 9). In this book Hicks refers to the early phases of industrialization in nineteenth-century England (when the rise in real wages 'was so long delayed ...') as a case where Ricardo's propositions come true (Hicks, 1969, ch. 9 and appendix). No matter whether or to what extent Hicks's interpretation is well founded,[39] his attempt is worth extending. After all, just because Ricardo's chapter was written 'to elucidate the principle',[40] not to explain a given reality, any argument about its actuality is more of degree than of substance; it is more about the extent to which a specific situation approaches Ricardo's propositions than about their direct coming true.[41] In this sense three examples may still be provided to extend Hicks's 'plausible guess': (1) Soviet industrialization in the 1920s and 1930s; (2) the growth of the military industrial sector after

---

[38] 'The widening is required to equip the actual working population with capital on the basis of the existing structure of production. The deepening means an increase in the capital equipment needed for a given population.' 'Accumulation, so long as it is limited to the widening of capital, increases the demand for labour in proportion. But, in so far as there is deepening, it does not' (Hawtrey, 1952, pp. 64, 130).

[39] See for instance Beach's criticisms (1971, p. 916) and Hicks's reply (1971, p. 922).

[40] See Ricardo himself in *Works* (vol. I, ch. 31, p. 395).

[41] Hicks (1971, p. 922) calls his own argument 'a plausible guess'.

the Second World War; (3) the growth of the shelter-goods sector ever since the oil crisis of 1973–4 and the depression of 1974–5.

I shall give here some hints as to why these experiences may have had an impact on living standards not very different from what Ricardo assumed. Other scholars more versed in economic history may provide further elucidations about these complicated facts and their relation with the pure theory focused above.

(1) *Soviet industrialization* After the Bolsheviks took over in Russia in 1917, the men in charge of supervising the process of capital reproduction (Ricardo's 'capitalist') had to decide whether the economy should develop in an open or closed-system framework; whether agriculture or industry should be developed first; whether the industry to be developed should be light or heavy industry.[42] As is well known, the choice was: heavy industry first, a closed system, a rapid rate of growth. The case seems to fulfil Ricardo's condition that machinery be 'suddenly discovered and extensively used'. As a consequence, millions of peasants supported by the scanty circulating capital employed in Russian agriculture were suddenly shifted from their usual and annual reproductions into the new industrial centres to produce things to be consumed only much later—if ever—by following generations. This sudden lengthening of the reproduction period may provide a reason for the 'poverty and distress' that spread in those difficult years among the ranks of the population.

(2) *The military–industrial sector* Since the Second World War the military–industrial sector has become a permanent characteristic of the superpowers' economies, and an increasingly capital-intensive industry as well. Growing amounts of free capital are being sunk into it to produce weapons. These sums may be borrowed by governments in the form of capital but are usually expended as revenue. Since weapons, like machinery, are not things that can be exchanged for labour, it may be that sooner or later a capital invested in such a sector will return free with a profit in the hands of those who manage the investment. None the less, the same capital is destined never to return free to society as a whole. Fortunately, the process of technological fall-out has so far often acted as an outlet valve within this process: it has enabled capital to return free earlier or to be saved and invested anew in other sectors of the economy. The story of the electronics industry is some comfort to those who are used to bemoaning an otherwise inevitable conversion.

(3) *The shelter-goods sector* After the 1973 4 oil crisis and the 1974–5 depression, speculation in commodities, antiques, foreign currencies, etc., became a widespread fashion for the multi-currency money capital of the

---

[42] On this most interesting case see Carr (1950ff.; particularly vol. II: *Socialism in One Country*, book I, and vol. III: *Foundations of a Planned Economy*, books I and II).

world. In some circumstances such a fashion may be even more harmful than the sudden introduction of machinery discussed above. For, while the latter may help—at least in a distant future—to reproduce, the former is intended right from the beginning to provide a profit without reproducing any gross revenue, any 'funds destined to the maintenance of labour'. Contrary to the military–industrial sector, there is here not even the hope of some invention liable to be usefully adopted in the civilian sector. Here Storch provides a good explanation of what this kind of circulation amounts to:

> In recent years we saw examples of artificial circulation in St Petersburg, Russia. The slack state of foreign trade had led the merchants to realize their unemployed capitals in another way; no longer being able to employ them to bring in foreign commodities and to export domestic ones, they decided to take advantage of this by buying and reselling the commodities on hand. Monstrous quantities of sugar, coffee, iron, etc., rapidly passed from one hand to the other, and a commodity often changed proprietors twenty times, without leaving the warehouse. This kind of circulation offers the dealers all manner of speculative opportunities: but while it enriches some, it ruins others, and the nation's wealth gains nothing thereby. (Storch, 1823, p.410)[43]

APPENDIX II

Whatever the content of Ricardo's chapter 31 may be, and whatever implications it may disguise in terms of other theories, it still has an unquestionable lesson for us. This lesson is more about a way of thinking than the conclusions it reaches; more about a method of analysis than the analysis itself. Hicks sums it up very finely when he says: 'Ricardo had candour and courage; he followed his reasoning where it led him, not just where he (or his friends) wanted it to go' (Hicks, 1969, ch. 9, p. 151).[44]

REFERENCES

Barton, J. (1817). *Observations on the Circumstances which Influence the Condition of the Labouring Classes of Society*. In *The Economic Writings of John Barton* (2 vols), ed. G. Sotiroff. Regina, Saskatchewan.
Beach, E. F. (1971) 'Hicks on Ricardo on Machinery'. *Economic Journal*, 81, 916–22.

[43] Storch (1823) calls this kind of circulation 'circulation postiche'.
[44] See also Marx's acknowledgement of Ricardo's open-mindedness and love for truth, in Marx (1867–94, bk I, ch. 13, n. 213).

Berg, M. (1980). *The Machinery Question and the Making of Political Economy 1815–1848*. Cambridge: CUP.

Blaug, M. (1958). *Ricardian Economics*. New Haven: Yale University Press.

Blaug, M. (1978). *Economic Theory in Retrospect*. Cambridge: CUP.

Böhm-Bawerk, E. von (1889). *Positive Theory of Capital*. Vol. 2 in Huncke and Sennholz (1959).

Caravale, G. and Tosato, D. (1980). *Ricardo and the Theory of Value, Distribution and Growth*. London: Routledge & Kegan Paul.

Carr, E. H. (1950ff.). *A History of Soviet Russia*. London: Macmillan.

Casarosa, C. (1978). 'A New Formulation of the Ricardian System'. *Oxford Economic Papers*, 30, 38–63.

Eagly, R. V. (1974). *The Structure of Classical Economic Theory*. New York: Oxford University Press.

Edelberg, V. (1933). 'The Ricardian Theory of Profits'. *Economica*, 51–74.

Hawtrey, G. (1952). *Capital and Employment*. London: Longmans Green.

Hayek, F. von (1939). *Profit, Interest and Investment*. London: Routledge & Sons.

Hayek, F. von (1941). *The Pure Theory of Capital*. London: Macmillan.

Hayek, F. von (1942). 'The Ricardo Effect'. *Economica*, 9, 127–52; reprinted in F. von Hayek, *Individualism and Economic Order*. London: Routledge & Sons, 1948.

Hayek, F. von (1969). 'Three Elucidations of the Ricardo Effect'. *Journal of Political Economy*, 77, 274–85.

Hicks, J. R. (1969). *A Theory of Economic History*. Oxford: OUP.

Hicks, J. R. (1970). 'A Neo-Austrian Growth Theory'. *Economic Journal*, 80, 257–81.

Hicks, J. R. (1971). 'A Reply to Professor Beach'. *Economic Journal*, 81, 922–5.

Hicks, J. R. (1973). *Capital and Time*. Oxford: OUP.

Hicks, J. R. (1974). 'Capital Controversies: Ancient and Modern'. *American Economic Review*, 64, 307–16.

Hicks, J. R. and Hollander, S. (1977). 'Mr Ricardo and the Moderns'. *Quarterly Journal of Economics*, 91, pp. 351–69.

Hollander, S. (1971). 'The Development of Ricardo's Position on Machinery'. *History of Political Economy*, 3, 16–31.

Hollander, S. (1979). *The Economics of Ricardo*. Toronto: University of Toronto Press.

Huncke, G. D. and Sennholz, H. F. (eds) (1959). *Capital and Interest* (3 vols). South Holland, Ill.: Libertarian Press.

Jevons, S. (1871). *The Theory of Political Economy*. London: Macmillan (first published in 1888).

Keynes, J. M. (1930). *A Treatise on Money* (2 vols). In *The Collected Writings of John Maynard Keynes*, vols V and VI. London: Macmillan, 1971 edn.

Knight, F. H. (1935). 'The Ricardian Theory of Production and Distribution'. *Canadian Journal of Economics and Political Science*, 1, 3–25; 2, 171–96.

Kirzner, I. M. (1966). *An Essay on Capital*. New York: Augustus M. Kelley.

Lachmann, L. M. (1956). *Capital and Its Structure*. Kansas City: Sheed Andrews and McMeel, 1978 edn.

McCulloch, J. R. (1821a). 'The Opinions of Messrs Say, Sismondi and Malthus on the Effects of Machinery and Accumulation Stated and Examined'. *Edinburgh Review*, 35.

McCulloch, J. R. (1821b). Letters to Ricardo. In *The Works and Correspondence of David Ricardo*, vol. VIII, p. 381ff.

Marx, K. (1867–94). *Capital* (3 vols). Harmondsworth: Penguin Books, 1976 edn.

Marx, K. (1905). *Theories of Surplus Value* (3 vols). London: Lawrence & Wishart, 1968 edn.

Marx, K. (1939). *Grundrisse*. Harmondsworth: Penguin Books, 1976 edn.

Meacci, F. (1978). *La teoria del capitale e del progresso tecnico*. Padua: Cedam.

Mill, J. (1821). *Elements of Political Economy*. London: Baldwin, Cradock and Jay.

Mill, J. S. (1871). *Principles of Political Economy*, vols 2–3. Toronto: University of Toronto Press, 1977 edn.

Mises, L. von (1949). *Human Action*. New Haven: Yale University Press.

Pasinetti, L. (1960). 'A Mathematical Formulation of the Ricardian System'. *Review of Economic Studies*, 27, 78–98.

O'Brien, D. P. (1975). *The Classical Economists*. Oxford: Clarendon Press.

Ricardo, D. (1951–73). *The Works and Correspondence of David Ricardo* (11 vols), ed. P. Sraffa. Cambridge: CUP.

Samuelson, P. A. (1959). 'A Modern Treatment of the Ricardian Economy'. *Quarterly Journal of Economics*, 1, 1–35; 2, 217–31.

Schumpeter, J. A. (1954). *History of Economic Analysis*. New York: Allen and Unwin.

Smith, A. (1776). *An Inquiry into the Nature and Causes of the Wealth of Nations*, ed. R. H. Campbell and A. S. Skinner. Oxford: The Clarendon Press, 1976 edn.

Sotiroff, G. (ed.) (1962–3). *Economic Writings of John Barton* (2 vols). Regina, Saskatchewan.

Sraffa, P. (1951). Introduction to *The Works and Correspondence of David Ricardo*, vol. I. Cambridge: CUP.

Sraffa, P. (1960). *Production of Commodities by Means of Commodities*. Cambridge: CUP.

Storch, H. F. (1823). *Cours d'économie politique* (2 vols). Paris.

Sylos Labini, P. (1967). *Oligopolio e progresso tecnico*. Turin: Einaudi.

Taussig, F. W. (1896). *Wages and Capital*. London: London School Reprint, 1933 edn.

Tozer, J. E. (1838). *Mathematical Investigation of the Effect of Machinery on the Wealth of a Community in Which It is Employed and on the Fund for the Payment of Wages*, ed. D. Collard. New York, 1968 edn.

Wicksell, K. (1893). *Über Wert, Kapital und Rente*. London: London School Reprint, 1933 edn.

Wicksell, K. (1901). *Lectures on Political Economy* (2 vols). London: Routledge & Sons, 1934 edn.

PART VI

A Critical Summing up of the Issues

13

Sraffa and Ricardo: A Critical View

JOHN HICKS

Sraffa's great edition of Ricardo began to be published in 1951. It was nearly complete when he published his other book, *Production of Commodities by means of Commodities* (*PCC* I shall call it) in 1960. There could thus be no reference to *PCC* in the early volumes of the Ricardo, where one would otherwise have looked for it; and the references to Ricardo in *PCC* are confined to a few points that are made about him, and others, in the Appendix. It has nevertheless been generally held that there is a close connection; that interpretation of Ricardo by means of *PCC* is Sraffa's own. Whether or not that is so, this interpretation is one that must nowadays be taken into account; one must decide, when making up one's own mind about Ricardo, whether one is for it or against it. I am against it, not against the *PCC* model when that is considered independently (that is a separate question) but against its use for interpretation of the model of Ricardo. I believe that it differs from Ricardo's in at least two, probably three, ways; they have not received sufficient attention.[1]

I

The first of these differences can be expressed by saying that Ricardo's system is essentially 'dynamic', at least in the elementary sense that it is concerned with directions of change; Sraffa's by contrast is entirely, even deliberately,

---

[1] I have myself constructed a model which has some similarities to Sraffa's (see Hicks, 1965, chs 12–15). I cite it here as evidence that I am not wholly out of sympathy with that kind of approach; I shall be able to make a good deal of use of it in what follows.

Though *PCC* was available to me when I was working on it, I made no reference to Sraffa, except very casually; for I had come to 'input–output', not from him, but from the activity analysts, from Leontief and especially from von Neumann. (This is made evident in my 'Survey of Linear Theory' (Hicks, 1960) and must have been written before *PCC* could have come into my hands.) I am sorry, nevertheless, that I did not append to my relevant chapters some discussion of Sraffa. It would have been well to have done so, though I could not then have brought out the contrast with Ricardo, for I had not then yet done my later work on Ricardo, which I shall also be using in what follows (Hicks and Hollander, 1975; Hicks, 1979, ch. 4).

static. He tells us himself, in the preface to his *PCC*, that 'no changes in output are being considered'. That, when one first meets it, is a surprising statement; but (as we shall see) it takes a good deal of thought before one sees all that is involved.

The second is a fundamental difference in the structure of the model. Production, according to Sraffa, is *fully interlinked*. This is emphasized in the very title of his book. And consider his definition of 'basic commodities' (*PCC*, p. 8):

> The criterion is whether a commodity enters (no matter whether directly or indirectly) into the production of *all* commodities. Those that do I shall call basic, and those which do not, non-basic.

I think I can show that there is nothing of this in Ricardo. His 'industries' are not interlinked, as Sraffa's are. It is true that there are degenerate cases (in the mathematical sense) where there is hardly any room for linkage, so that they can be analysed either in Ricardo's terms, or in Sraffa's. (Such a one is the model of the *Essay on Profits*.) But when we go on from that, the contrast is marked.

I shall have much more to say under each of these headings; but before I come to that there is a third difference (I think it is a third difference) which I should like to mention.

It concerns the function, or perhaps even the meaning, of prices. Sraffa is insistent that his prices are not costs; Ricardo, one feels sure, would not have accepted that for his. Ricardo's prices are 'natural' prices, in the sense of Smith; that is to say, in more modern language, they are equilibrium prices, such as would be formed in a market, when that market had 'settled down'. It is the market which keeps his prices in line with costs. Sraffa leaves us to find out what his prices are, but I doubt if they are equilibrium prices. They seem to be prices which are set upon products, by their producers, according to some rule. Now it is perfectly true that we are nowadays familiar with that method of price-fixing, by 'mark-up'; but when that method is used, the rate of profit that is used to establish the mark-up is conventional. Now it may be that Sraffa wants us to think of his rate of profit as being conventional; and that the uniformity of the rate of profit throughout his system, of which he makes so much, is just a uniformity of convention. So when he lets the rate of profit change, he is just asking the hypothetical question, What would be the result if a different rate of profit became conventional?

If this is what Sraffa means about the formation of prices, it is miles away from Ricardo. So if one is to try to use the Sraffa model for the interpretation of Ricardo, the first thing to be done is to let prices be formed in Ricardo's manner. The uniformity of the profit rate must then be established through the market. So the system, in an appropriate sense, must be in equilibrium.

If it is to be an equilibrium in which outputs are unchanging, it must be a static equilibrium. How is that to be interpreted?

II

One may say, and I suppose that this is the interpretation which most naturally occurs to readers of Sraffa, that his model is a model of an actual economic system, as it is in a period that may be chosen at random. An actual system, in such a period, will not be in equilibrium; but it may be replaced, for purposes of analysis, by another, as similar to it as possible, which is. So if one looks at a sequence of periods, the actual sequence has been replaced by a sequence of static equilibria. They will not describe it fully; they cannot, even logically, be linked together; but they may be supposed to provide some outline of what is supposed to happen.

This is of course a device which is very familiar to economists; I fully believe that it was very commonly used by Ricardo himself. It is nevertheless an awkward device. It easily gets one into trouble. I think it did get Ricardo into trouble.[2] So it will be useful to see what happens if one refuses to stomach it—if one insists that the model is to be a consistent model over time. If one still keeps the condition that outputs are to be unchanging, there is then nothing for it. The model is a model of a stationary state.

It turns out to be quite useful, as a step in the argument, to look at the Sraffa model in this manner. We do not have to exclude the production of a 'surplus', so long as that surplus is wholly consumed. Since it is distribution, not production, in which Sraffa is interested, that would suit him quite well.

The stationary state is however itself a special case of the steady state, or growth equilibrium model, in which all *quantities* are expanding at the same growth rate (g). It is just the special case where $g = 0$. We shall need an abbreviated name for the more general model. Since SS and GE are otherwise occupied, I propose to call it UG, for uniform growth.

UG is possible only if there are constant returns to scale, if scale has no effect on productivity. Sraffa was anxious not to introduce such an assumption; but if the cost of refraining from it is confinement to stationariness, the cost is high. However we assess the importance of scale economies, the working of a model from which they are excluded is one of the things we need to understand.

There is no great difficulty in extending the Sraffa equations to make them apply to UG. Quantity equations will require some adjustment, but since in UG relative prices remain unchanged over time, the price equations of Sraffa need not be altered. I have myself written out what corresponds quite closely to the Sraffa price-equations, keeping the sense of UG (Hicks, 1965, ch. 14

[2] As has been shown by Casarosa (1978). See also Hicks (1979, p. 54; 1983, p. 39).

and appendix B).[3] My terminology was different. What he called 'basics' I called 'capital goods'; what he called 'non-basics' I called 'consumption goods'; but in formal terms there is complete correspondence. Like him, I found the prices (in my case, quite definitely equilibrium prices) of the capital goods to be determined, relatively to the wage, once the rate of profit is given. (Quite apart from what happens in the consumption goods sector.) I had a proof, which is very similar to his, which shows that with given technique (given production coefficients) the rate of profit must be less than a certain critical value, if the prices of the capital goods are to be positive.[4] Once the prices of the capital goods are determined, the prices of the consumption goods follow from them. In the version I gave myself, I allowed myself the simplification of supposing that there was just one consumption good; so I found no difficulty in taking that to be my standard of value. I could thus regard my (single) consumption price equation as determining the (real) wage in terms of that consumption good, once the rate of profit was given.

So the inverse relation between the rate of profit and the real wage may be reckoned to hold in the UG model, just as it does in Sraffa. But in the UG model there is more to be said.

In the UG model there is an extra condition of equilibrium, which in a stationary model (as we have found Sraffa's to be) is suppressed. It is necessary, for a stationary economy to continue stationary, remaining all the time in equilibrium, that the supply of labour should be constant, and that net saving should be zero. But in the UG model the supply of labour is increasing; so it is necessary, for the maintenance of equilibrium, that there should be net saving to match it. This gives the extra equation, which Sraffa leaves out.

Because he has left it out, his system is one equation short. He has determined prices, including real wages (wages in terms of the consumption good, or of some bundle of consumption goods), once the rate of profit is determined. But he has nothing to determine the rate of profit. If the rate of profit were different, the real wage would be different, as he shows. But any rate of profit (subject to its being less than the critical level), with its corresponding real wage, is equally possible. They can be what they like, so long as they are tied together, *in his stationary state*.

As soon as one admits a relation (*any* positive relation) between profits and

---

[3] In my simplest version, which most nearly corresponds to Sraffa's simplest version, I admitted fixed capital goods, but gave them constant rates of depreciation, or wear-and-tear. That can readily be removed, thus reducing the model to a pure circulating capital model, as Sraffa's simplest model is. His peculiar simplification, of supposing the 'wage' to be paid at the end of the period, while other inputs come in at the beginning I did not of course adopt.

[4] I myself put more faith in the mathematical proof, which I gave in appendix B (Hicks, 1965). It there comes out clearly, as I observed in the footnote on p. 317 (after prompting by Morishima) that the proof depends on the matrix being indecomposable, on which more below.

saving, the picture looks very different. In the stationary state, the receiver of profit is a pure parasite; but in the progressive economy, he has a function, as Ricardo would surely have thought that he has. It does look as if, on going over to UG, we are getting nearer to Ricardo.

III

The UG model, considered as an extension of Sraffa's, is certainly not in Ricardo, but there is something very like it which would seem to be implied. Ricardo does not rule out the possibility that in a process of expansion, there should be a preliminary stage in which land is not yet scarce (so that on his principle there is as yet no rent); at that stage, but not at the diminishing returns stage which is to follow it, there can be uniform growth. He must have had some idea how things would work at that stage; could it have been very different from our UG?

It could not have been very different, but I think there would have been some differences. The version that would have been given by Ricardo would in the first place have been simpler. For here we come to the second difference which, as I said at the beginning, I detect between Ricardo and Sraffa. I do not believe that the interlinkages, which are so important in Sraffa (and which in my own 1965 version of UG I maintained) were recognized by Ricardo. It may be that these input–output linkages have in our time become so important that no model should neglect them; that may be so, though I think myself that one should be able to manage without them if one's interest lies elsewhere. (Keynesian economists, very often, seem able to manage without them.) I am sure that Ricardo neglected them. Why should he have bothered about them? Remember that he died before the beginning of railways. Though horses were intermediate products in the production of corn, the production of horses could be regarded as a stage in corn production; the production of looms as a stage in the production of cotton goods; and so on. It was a fair simplification, in Ricardo's time, to think of all industries as vertically integrated.[5] It was so natural a simplification that he could make it without emphasizing it. I have no doubt that he made it.[6]

---

[5] I am not forgetting that it has been maintained by historians of technology that it was the development of machine-tools 'machines to make machines' which from their point of view was the essential feature of the Industrial Revolution. (See the passage from the *Oxford History of Technology* which is quoted in Hicks, 1969, on p. 147, and my own comment on it.) This was beginning to happen in Ricardo's time, but he was no technologist. How could he be expected to have seen it, from his City of London stance, when it was only just beginning to happen?

[6] The transition from a vertically integrated model to an input–output type model is discussed in logical terms in a recent paper of my own (Hicks, 1981).

To follow through the transition, as it appears in the work of nineteenth century economists, would be a good subject for research.

Once one makes it, final products are all on a par. There is no basic–non-basic distinction. It follows directly, without complication, that the (equilibrium) prices of all products will be higher, relatively to the wage, if the rate of profit is higher. (For the price of each product must be equal to the value of its labour content, when that is accumulated, at the profit rate, for the average period for which the labour has been invested.) So one gets to the principle that the real wage is lower the higher is the profit rate, much more simply.

Beyond that, I have one more thing to say about the UG model, that which I have suggested is implied in Ricardo's work. It concerns the 'extra equation', that which ties the growth rates of labour and capital together. A modern economist would naturally proceed, as I did myself in my 1965 version, to take as the first case to be considered that in which the growth rate of labour supply is given, while all saving is out of profits. The proportion of profits saved will have to be constant over time; it is natural to take it to be fixed. If s is this ratio, r the rate of profit, and K is the value of the whole capital stock, as it is at the beginning of a representative period, we have rK as total profits, srK as saving. This, in equilibrium, must equal gK, the increment of capital during the period. The same g must equal, again in equilibrium, the rate of growth of the labour supply. So $g = sr$; with g and s given, r is determined.[7]

That would not do for Ricardo. He would certainly not have allowed the growth rate of the supply of labour to be given. Some sort of a 'Malthusian' relation between the real wage and that growth rate is essential to his thinking. The real wage must be above some minimum (subsistence) if the growth rate of labour is to be positive; this must surely mean that it rises as the real wage rises, at least up to a point. It would then have been natural for him to look at the growth rate of capital in a similar way. There would be a minimum to the rate of profit that is consistent with positive net saving (whether that minimum is zero or above zero does not matter to the argument); a rise in the rate above that minimum would increase the rate at which capital would accumulate. Thus with the inverse relation between the rate of wages and the rate of profit already established, he would have the growth rate of capital diminishing as the real wage rose, while a rise in the real wage would increase the growth rate of labour. There would thus be two 'curves', one falling and one rising, at the intersection of which equilibrium would be determined.[8]

One could thus conclude that in the preliminary phase, when UG is possible, the real wage will be higher the more elastic is the supply of capital and the less elastic is the supply of labour. Ricardo himself could not have put

[7] It is amusing to see, in these terms, what happened to Sraffa. He had put his $g = 0$ and his $s = 0$; so his r, being $0/0$, was of course indeterminate.

[8] I have drawn out these curves in Hicks (1979, p. 49), to which reference may be made for a slightly fuller treatment.

it that way; but it nevertheless does appear to represent the substance of what, so far, he is saying.[9]

IV

Now at last we can proceed to the further stage, when diminishing returns have set it, the stage which of course really mattered to Ricardo.

He now has two sectors, but they are *not* the basic and non-basic of Sraffa. There is food production (F) which is produced under diminishing returns, and non-food production (N) which is produced under constant returns. It clearly is the case that his N is produced under constant returns; for the scale economies, of which Adam Smith had made so much, he notoriously leaves out of account.

He is here confronted with two, quite distinct, difficulties. In the first place, as he emphasizes himself, a UG growth path (with uniform expansion at constant price ratios) is no longer available. Relative prices will have to be changing from period to period. He gets over this by keeping his system in static equilibrium in each period, so that he can have a uniform rate of profit (and wage) *within* each period—the device on which I had some hard things to say at the beginning of this paper; there can be no doubt that Ricardo adopted it. He can then proceed (much as in the manner I have above described) to establish relations between prices and the rate of profit, in that period. The price of each commodity can be got from the value of the labour embodied, accumulated over the average production period of that commodity, at the rate of profit; the price of F being of course determined at the margin, at its marginal cost. But this has not determined the rate of profit, which (as in Sraffa) remains arbitrary.

But Ricardo would not accept that as a place to stop. He would still want to invoke the extra condition, which, as we saw, rounds off UG. But how is he to use it? He cannot use it, as in UG, to make the whole system determinate. His system has become a sequence of equilibria, which differ from one another. He can only use it as determining the movement from one position to the next.

So, mathematically speaking, what appeared in UG to be an ordinary equation, which could be combined with others in what we might think of as a Walrasian manner, has here been transformed into a differential equation. It is well known that a differential equation does not by itself determine

---

[9] It will be noticed that no notion of a 'wage fund' is needed to get this result. It will also be noticed that Ricardo, from his point of view, has no need to be concerned with the maximum to the rate of profit, derived from the mathematical properties of the input–output matrix, of which Sraffa makes so much. He has a maximum, derived from the subsistence requirements of labour, which is much less than that which appears in Sraffa.

motion; it only does so when initial conditions are provided. So Ricardo cannot hope to *determine* the path of his sequence; all he can do is, starting from some given initial position, to trace out where it will go.[10]

That is how his sequence will have to be taken;[11] but in describing it a difficulty remains. It is here that he encounters his problem of the standard (which, as I shall be showing, is quite different from Sraffa's). In which of the things that appear in the model should prices be reckoned?

It is important to recognize that, at least as the issue first appears, this is a pure matter of convenience. All of the models so far discussed have been concerned with *relative* prices (including wages); so it is possible for the model to be described using anything we like as a standard (or, as Walras would have said, a numéraire). It will need to be noted that the profit rate itself will have to be reckoned in terms of that standard; so it will have to be (formally) adjusted as one moves from one standard to another. But that is all.

There may nevertheless be some things which, on this principle, might permissibly be chosen as standard, but which would make the model quite hard to explain. Even if no more than this is involved, there is a question of standard.

In UG, since relative prices are constant, the question does not (directly) arise. The model could be stated the same way, whatever standard we take. But in the Ricardian version of UG, which I endeavoured to reconstruct, it was the real wage (the wage in terms of wage goods) which governed population. That in itself would be sufficient to make Ricardo want to take the wage good as standard.

Once UG is left behind, and he has his two sectors (F and N), it would still be open to him to keep the wage good as standard, provided that the lines between F and N, and between wage good and non-wage good, were the same. So long, that is, as wage-earners are supposed to consume nothing but F. One can see that Ricardo did in fact begin by allowing himself that assumption.

For this is the model of the *Essay on Profits*. Corn is the only wage good, and corn is the only product that is produced under diminishing returns. So corn production has been segregated, and corn can still be used as standard of value. The wage is reckoned in terms of corn. For any given rate of wages,

---

[10] It is true that the paths, which are generated by a differential equation, will often have a 'singular point'; all paths must proceed to that point, whatever the initial condition. This is commonly the point where the motion stops. We can recognize that point in Ricardo; it is his *ultimate* stationary state.

[11] I now think that it was our use of the Ricardian equation, to generate a growth path from given initial conditions, which was the real breakthrough in the Hicks–Hollander paper (1975). That Ricardo was working with a differential equation had already been noted by Pasinetti (1960).

and given output of corn, the rate of profit is determined; it will have to be a lower rate of profit, at the given rate of wages, the lower is the productivity of labour, in terms of corn, at the margin. This rate of profit, it must be emphasized, is also in terms of corn. The same rate of profit, and rate of wages, must hold in equilibrium in other (N) industries; they are still reckoned in terms of corn, and so are the prices of those products. It is a consistent model, so far as it goes.[12]

V

The passage from this first model to that of the *Principles* is most easily taken in two stages, interposing a stage which I admit is not in Ricardo; for it is not in accordance with his habits of thinking. Nevertheless, like my former reconstruction of his UG, it asks a question which could have been put to him, and which he would have been able to answer.

When one drops the assumption that corn (or F) is the only wage good, it ceases to be *the* wage good, so the former case for taking it as standard disappears. A modern economist would seek to replace it with some 'bundle' of commodities; but there are reasons, to which I shall be coming (see p. 318 below), why that device would not occur to Ricardo. He would look for some *particular* alternative.

The relative prices of final products are now to vary; there will be variations, both in the price of F, relatively to those of N products, and among the prices of different N products themselves. These raise different issues; it is useful to take them separately. That can be done by my intermediate step. Let there be just one N product, produced at constant cost, independent of output. F is also to be taken as homogeneous, so there are just two final products, F and N. Both classes, labour and non-labour, consume some F and some N. Having decided to reject F as standard, the only *particular* alternative that is open to Ricardo is to choose N. Because N is produced under constant returns, it looks more stable than F.

If w (the wage) is given in terms of N, the rate of profit (r), *also in terms of N*, is determined in N production. For the price of a unit of N is unity; so if a_n is the labour required to make a unit of N, and t_n is the average time required

$$1 = wa_n(1+r)^{t_n}.$$

Thus if a_n and t_n are given (as Ricardo at this stage would clearly have supposed) this r is determined by this w. The same wage, and the same r, must

---

[12] I do not think that this is inconsistent with Sraffa's (1951, p. xxxi) interpretation of the *Essay*. It is afterwards that our roads diverge.

rule (in the static equilibrium) in F production also; so there we must have

$$p_f = wa_f(1+r)^{t_f}$$

where p_f is the price of F, again in terms of N, a_f is the labour required to make a (marginal) unit of F, t_f the corresponding time required.

Diminishing returns in F production mean that a_f will increase as the output of F increases, while a_n is independent of output. This if (over a sequence) we keep w fixed in terms of N (and *therefore* r fixed in terms of N), p_f will rise in terms of N as expansion proceeds. The wage-earner will find that his constant N wage will buy less than it did, over the whole range of things that he wants. The cost of living having risen, the real wage will fall.

On Ricardo's Malthusian principle, a decline in the real wage will check the increase in population. By the extra equation (which in differential form is still operative) the growth of capital must also be checked to match, at least to some extent; so (still to maintain the static equilibrium over the sequence) the rate of profit must decline. It is reasonable to suppose that it is the rate in terms of N which mainly matters to the capitalist; so it is the rate in terms of N which must decline. But this means that the wage, in terms of N, will, over the sequence, rise. That will offset some part of the fall in real wages; but it cannot offset the whole, if the equilibrium is to be maintained. Both the rate of profit, and the level of real wages, will tend to decline as expansion proceeds. This is entirely in accordance with the interpretation of Ricardo I have given elsewhere (Hicks and Hollander, 1975; Hicks, 1979); for the textual evidence which supports it I may refer to those places.

VI

To proceed from this to the more general case where there are many N products raises no difficulty of principle. For most of the way the argument is the same whichever of those products is taken as standard. The wage would be reckoned, for purposes of computation, in terms of that chosen commodity; the prices of the other N products would then be calculated, in terms of that standard, just as happened with the price of F in our previous example. The real wage would follow, just as before, with quantities of F and various N products being included in the wage-earner's budget.

Why then did Ricardo attach so much importance to the selection of a standard commodity? The logical reason for doing so, in terms of the theory as just set out, would refer to the behaviour of capitalist savers. If there were some particular commodity, in terms of which savers may be expected to do their reckoning, it would be in terms of that commodity (the rate of profit being expressed in terms of that commodity) that saving propensities would most conveniently be expressed. If this had been the way in which the issue presented itself to Ricardo, one can see that he would have maintained that there is such a standard; people do their reckoning in terms of money. But whether or not it did present itself to him in that way, there is no doubt that he chose money to be his standard. But why should money be one of the N commodities, or products?

This, to the modern student, is a formidable stumbling block; but if we put Ricardo's argument into historical perspective, it is not hard to understand it. We have to remember his other concern, during the years when he was working at his 'growth model'; his preoccupation with monetary policy. In that field also there was a question of standard. What, from the monetary point of view, does one mean by stable prices? That is a problem which in our day is once again vexing us. There is no doubt that it vexed Ricardo, as it did his contemporaries.[13] What is the standard by which one measures inflation?

Is monetary stability stability of the wage level, or of some price level or other? Looking at this issue through the eyes of Ricardo, he will not want to say that a rise in the wage level is necessarily inflationary; for if the productivity of labour is improving, wages ought to rise. And he will not want to say that a rise in prices, which is the direct result of a rise in the real costs of production of primary products, is inflationary. Does one not agree with him? But if both labour and food are rejected as standards, what is left? It must be among the N products that he will have to find his standard.

The relative prices of N products will change, in practice, both because of changes in labour coefficients (a_n), because of changes in production periods (t_n) and because of changes in r. Within his model, it is changes in r that are

---

[13] Let me give two examples. One is the preoccupation of Henry Thornton (*Paper Credit* 1802, Bullion debates 1811), with the definition of over-issue, which is to say, of inflation. (I have discussed his apparent changes of opinion in my paper on Thornton: see Hicks, 1967, pp. 183ff.)

The other, which rams home the point, is the anonymous poem, published in 1811, that was discovered by Jacob Viner. It is worth quoting verbatim.

> What must we for a standard own,
> By which the price of things are known?
> 'Twas thought, time past, by men of sense,
> 'Twas guineas, shillings, pounds and pence:
> The Bank has said, and says so still
> 'Tis nothing but a paper bill;
> 'Tis in Sir Francis Burdett's head
> The standard is a loaf of bread,
> Whilst Adam Smith did always say,
> It was the labour of a day.

I take this from Viner's *Studies in the Theory of International Trade* (1933, p. 119). What a pity it is that Viner's book does not get classified in libraries under history of economics, so that students of that subject miss one of the best books about it that has ever been written!

important. If the rate of profit (however measured) has to change, as it will change in the course of his expansion, the relative prices of N products will change (even with the a_n and t_n unchanged) since the t_n of different products will be different. Those where t_n is large will fall in price, when r falls, relatively to those where t_n is small. So he looks for a standard that is somewhere in the middle, such that when r varies, there will be a good many Ns which will rise in price, relatively to that standard, and a good many that will fall.[14] He allows himself to guess that he has found such a standard in the money metal—presumably gold.

One is tempted to look at that guess as rather pathetic; but would he not say, if later experience had been available to him, that it had borne him out? The gold standard, which he was defending, did in fact provide a good deal of the stability for which he was looking, for quite a long time afterwards.

But whatever we think of the answer that was given by Ricardo to this monetary question, there can be no doubt that the question itself is important; but it has nothing to do with the logic of his model, which (as I have repeatedly emphasized) can be set out with *any* standard. His standard commodity is accordingly quite different from the standard commodity of Sraffa (in *PCC*) which does emerge as a purely logical property of his particular model, and this, as I have explained, is not Ricardo's.

If, as in Sraffa, there is complete interlinkage,[15] not only are all relative prices (of basics) dependent upon the rate of profit, but the relative *outputs* of basics are similarly determined. (When the Sraffa model is turned into a UG model, it emerges that there is the same dependence of the price vector on the rate of profit, and of the output vector on the rate of growth. The two are *duals*.) Since the proportions in which the outputs of basics are combined are fixed, they can be taken together and treated, in the modern manner, as if they were a single commodity. That is how Sraffa finds *his* standard commodity.

This cannot possibly find a place in Ricardo's system.[16] But in Sraffa's it has pretty properties. By using it as standard, he is enabled to find what appears to be a linear relation between the rate of profit and the share of profit in the total product; so he can replace, in his further discussion, the rate of profit (which depends on the standard) by the share of profit, which apparently does not. It is however unfortunately the case that this proposition is valid, only in the stationary state of Sraffa; in a UG version, where g is not zero, it only holds with some qualification.[17]

---

[14] This is surely how the issue is presented in the paper on 'Absolute Value and Exchangeable Value' which Sraffa dug up (*Works*, vol. 4).

[15] In mathematical terms, his matrix is indecomposable.

[16] For Ricardo does not have an indecomposable matrix.

[17] See Hicks (1965, p. 173 and thereabouts), where I show that a change in g may affect the profit share. This is much the same point as Kaldor makes (1955), when he shows that the profit share may depend on the saving rate. See also the paper by Tosato in this volume.

There are indeed other ways in which Sraffa's *standard* is a useful concept. It plays an important part in von Neumann, but the context in which it there appears is very different. von Neumann's is a UG model, but it is not only in that way that it differs from Sraffa's. von Neumann's is an optimum theory; there is a choice of techniques; the problem is to find the technique at which the rate of growth is maximized. He shows that it is on a balanced-growth path (with commodities combined in suitable, rather Sraffa-like, proportions) that the growth rate is maximized. In order to show this, he has to introduce prices, which are dual to the balanced quantities, again as in Sraffa. But these prices are not to be interpreted like Sraffa's prices, derived (as we saw) from a conventional profit rate; nor are they equilibrium prices, as in Ricardo; they are a third type, whose only role is to be used as instruments of optimization. All three varieties need to be distinguished.[18]

VII

That completes my 'traverse' from Sraffa to Ricardo, and (incidentally) to von Neumann. There remain two general points about Ricardo, which I should like to make in conclusion.

In the first place, Ricardo was no Marshallian. He maintained, consistently, that prices are determined by cost; demand has nothing to do with them. It may indeed be objected that when he lets the (marginal) cost of food production rise, under pressure of population, he is admitting demand; it is the increased demand for food which forces the extension of cultivation. I do not believe that Ricardo looked at the matter like that. His sequence, I have insisted, was a succession of equilibria. It is not a change in demand which marks the transition from one equilibrium to its successor; it is the increase in population itself. Keep firmly to the succession, without bothering about the transition (how the succession comes about) and that is how it will

---

[18] A word should perhaps be added on Sraffa's treatment of fixed capital in the final chapters of *PCC*. I am not discussing it at length, as I do not think it is relevant. It is nevertheless a remarkable part of his book, and he deserves much credit for it. He seems to have discovered, quite independently, the same device as was used by von Neumann, of treating the 'unexpended' capital goods carried over at the end of the period, as separate products. And he discovered, as von Neumann discovered, that the use of this device involves formidable problems of joint supply.   Ricardo's approach, in the little that he had to say on fixed capital, was—indeed it had to be—entirely different. Since he was thinking in terms of vertically integrated industries, the only approach that was open to him was that which we have come to think of 'Austrian', considering the effects of a change in the profit rate (or interest rate) on the average period of production (t_n); and this is what he does.

As we now know, that runs into the obstacle of joint supply, of outputs over time, which rather ruins the average period. (I have tried to show that something can still be made of an 'Austrian' approach in Hicks, 1973). On the Sraffa–von Neumann approach, the joint supply is made contemporaneous, but it remains hard to deal with.

appear. Maybe (as Marshall and many later economists would hold) this was a defect in Ricardo's treatment. A cost (not a labour) theory of value was nevertheless fundamental to Ricardo's thinking; in the interpretation I have been giving I have tried to recognize, consistently, that this is so.

Secondly (and somewhat relatedly) one must be careful, in interpreting Ricardo, to refrain from thinking in terms of those 'macro'-concepts from which a modern economist finds it hard to get away. He thought very little in terms of macro-aggregates; and there was a good reason why he should not use them. He knew, in his own world, a good deal about prices, but his knowledge of quantities was very defective. He could get some information about imports and exports; and the (inadequate) censuses of 1801 and 1811 told him something about the movement of population. Beyond that there was not much. So we find that there is little about quantities that he needs for his theory. He has to have some idea of the make-up of the wage-earner's budget in order to proceed from 'money' wages to real wages; but it is no more than he could pick up from people whom he himself employed. In his day there were no *sample surveys*.

It follows that it was not open to him to proceed on the 'macro' lines of the modern economist. If he had been able to proceed on those lines, he could have made his theory much simpler. In the model of the *Essay on Profits* he could have dispensed with the ridiculous assumption of the wage-earners living only on corn; he could have presented it as a preliminary model in which the proportions of goods in the representative consumer's budget were kept fixed. He would then have been able to treat consumption output as a single product, which (since some constituents would be produced under diminishing returns and the rest under constant returns) would as a whole be produced under diminishing returns. So, to the whole output, the argument of the *Essay* would apply.

He could then have gone to observe that he had already shown, in this first model, how distribution would change in the course of expansion; and this must mean (the different classes consuming commodities in different proportions) that the composition of the commodity 'bundle' must change accordingly. With distribution changing (according to the *Essay*) in favour of labour, at the expense of profits *and* rents, and with labour having a greater propensity than non-labour to consume the things that were produced under diminishing returns, the 'overall bundle' would change in such a way as to accentuate the tendency to diminishing returns. (A rise in real wages which was not accompanied by a rise in population would have the opposite effect.)

An approach such as this is so natural to the modern economist that it is hard to keep it out of our minds. It is indeed a perfectly good way of explaining the substance of what Ricardo was saying. I have used it that way myself (Hicks, 1972). But it is not a means of expression that was open to Ricardo.

REFERENCES

Casarosa, C. (1978). 'A New Formulation of the Ricardian System'. *Oxford Economic Papers*, 30, 38–63.

Hicks, J. R. (1960). 'Survey of Linear Theory'. *Economic Journal*, December.

Hicks, J. R. (1965). *Capital and Growth*. Oxford: OUP.

Hicks, J. R. (1967). *Critical Essays in Monetary Theory*. Oxford: OUP.

Hicks, J. R. (1969). *A Theory of Economic History*. Oxford: OUP.

Hicks, J. R. (1972). 'Ricardo's Theory of Distribution'. In *Essays in Honour of Lord Robbins*, ed. M. Peston and B. Corry. London: Weidenfeld & Nicolson. Reprinted in his *Classics and Moderns*. Oxford: Blackwell, 1983, p. 37.

Hicks, J. R. (1973). *Capital and Time*. Oxford: Clarendon Press.

Hicks, J. R. (1979). *Causality in Economics*. Oxford: Basil Blackwell.

Hicks, J. R. (1981). 'Valuation of the Social Income: The Cost Approach'. In his *Wealth and Welfare*, vol. 1 of *Collected Essays*. Oxford: Blackwell.

Hicks, J. R. (1983). *Classics and Moderns*. Oxford: Blackwell.

Hicks, J. R. and Hollander, S. (1975). 'Mr Ricardo and the Moderns'. *Quarterly Journal of Economics*, 91, 351–69.

Kaldor, N. (1955). 'Alternative Theories of Distribution'. *Review of Economic Studies*, 23, 83–100.

Pasinetti, L. (1960). 'A Mathematical Formulation of the Ricardian System'. *Review of Economic Studies*, 27, 78–98; reprinted in his *Growth and Income Distribution*. Cambridge: CUP, 1974.

Ricardo, D. (1951–73). *The Works and Correspondence of David Ricardo* (11 vols), ed. P. Sraffa. Cambridge, CUP.

Sraffa, P. (1951). Introduction to *The Works and Correspondence of David Ricardo*, vol. 1. Cambridge: CUP.

Sraffa, P. (1960). *Production of Commodities by Means of Commodities*. Cambridge: CUP.

Viner, Jacob. *Studies in the Theory of International Trade*. New York: Harper; London: Allen and Unwin.

The Contributors

MARK BLAUG is Professor Emeritus of the Economics of Education at the University of London and Consultant Professor of Economics at the University of Buckingham. His publications include *Economic Theory in Retrospect* (1985) and *The Methodology of Economics* (1980). His first book was on *Ricardian Economics* (1958).

GIOVANNI A. CARAVALE is Full Professor of Political Economy at the University of Rome. He studied at the University of Rome and at Trinity College, Cambridge, and taught for several years at the University of Perugia. He is the author of numerous publications on the theory of growth, market structures, value and distribution, including *Il Credito al Consumo, Cicli Economici e Trend* and (with D. Tosato) *Ricardo and the Theory of Value, Distribution and Growth.*

CARLO CASAROSA is Professor of Political Economy in the Faculty of Economics, University of Pisa, where he is also Director of the Institute of Economics. His main works are in macroeconomics, fiscal policy and Ricardian economics.

GIACOMO COSTA studied at the Catholic University of Milan and the University of Michigan and now teaches monetary economics at the University of Pisa. He is the author of *La legge di Say e la teoria della domanda effettiva* (1980) and various articles on Ricardian economics.

WALTER ELTIS is a Fellow of Exeter College, Oxford. He is the author of *The Classical Theory of Economic Growth*, concerning the theories of economic growth of Quesnay, Smith, Malthus, Ricardo and Marx, and co-author (with Robert Bacon) of *Britain's Economic Problem: Too Few Producers* (1976).

PIERANGELO GAREGNANI studied economics at the University of Pavia, the University of Cambridge and the Massachusetts Institute of Technology. He is presently teaching economics at the University of Rome and is the author of several publications.

SIR JOHN HICKS is a Fellow of All Souls College, Oxford, and until 1965 was Professor of Economics at the University of Oxford. He was awarded the Nobel Prize in 1972. He has written many books and articles since publication of his classic works, *The Theory of Wages* (1932) and *Value and Capital* (1939), including *The Crisis in Keynesian Economics* (1974) and *Causality in Economics* (1979).

SAMUEL HOLLANDER, Professor of Economics at the University of Toronto, was appointed to the rank of University Professor in 1984. He is a Fellow of the Royal Society of Canada, and the author of *The Economics of Adam Smith* (1973), *The Economics of David Ricardo* (1979) and *The Economics of John Stuart Mill* (2 vols, 1985).

FERDINANDO MEACCI is Professor of Growth Theory at the University of Padua. He was formerly Professor of Political Economy at the University of Trieste and Visiting Professor of Economics at New York University and City University of New York. He has written a critical overview of the theory of capital from the classics to the moderns, and several papers on the subjects of capital, technical progress, investment and growth. He is a member of the executive committee of the Atlantic Economics Society.

PIER LUIGI PORTA studied at the Bocconi University of Milan and the University of Cambridge. He is Associate Professor of Economics at the State University of Milan. He edited in Italian the first three volumes of the variorum edition of Ricardo's *Works and Correspondence*.

ALESSANDRO RONCAGLIA is Professor of Political Economy at the University of Rome, and Deputy Editor of the *Banca Nazionale Lavoro Quarterly Review*. His main publications include *Sraffa and the Theory of Prices* (1978), *The International Oil Market* (1985) and *William Petty and the Origins of Political Economy* (forthcoming).

ANNALISA ROSSELLI, a graduate in mathematics of the University of Florence, teaches political economy at the University of Rome. She is the author of publications on general equilibrium and a book on the theory of gold standard in Ricardo.

DOMENICO A. TOSATO studied at the Bocconi University of Milan and Yale University, and now teaches at the University of Rome. He has written essays on the Walrasian theory of capitalization and on Wicksell's theory of the cumulative process. He is co-author (with Giovanni A. Caravale) of *Ricardo and the Theory of Value, Distribution and Growth.*

Author Index